On Saramago

Portuguese Literary & Cultural Studies
6 Spring 2001

On Saramago

Portuguese Literary & Cultural Studies is a multilingual interdisciplinary peer-reviewed journal published semi-annually by the Center for Portuguese Studies and Culture at the University of Massachusetts Dartmouth. The journal addresses the literatures and cultures of the diverse communities of the Portuguese-speaking world in terms of critical and theoretical approaches.

Manuscript Policy

Portuguese Literary & Cultural Studies welcomes submission of original and unpublished manuscripts in English, Portuguese, or Spanish appropriate to the goals of the journal. The first page of the submission must include the following: (*i*), name, mailing address, e-mail address, and appropriate phone and fax numbers; (*ii*), a brief biography, not exceeding a quarter of a page, with reference to institutional affiliation, no more than three publications, and current research; (*iii*), a half-page abstract of the content of the article or review. The article itself may not exceed 20 pages and should be submitted along with the above information in a single digital file. All of the information must be in the same language. PLCS encourages electronic submission in the form of an attached document addressed to greis@umassd.edu. Submission in hard copy and 3.5" diskette (in a protected envelope) may also be sent by regular mail to *Portuguese Literary & Cultural Studies*, Center for Portuguese Studies and Culture, University of Massachusetts Dartmouth, Dartmouth, MA 02747 USA.

Manuscripts should be in accordance with the MLA Style Manual and Guide to Scholarly Publishing (latest version) with parenthetical documentation and list of works cited. The author is responsible for the accuracy of all quotations, titles, names, and dates. Notes must be manually typed out at the end of the article (before the list of works cited), regardless of whether they were entered as footnotes or endnotes into the word processor.

The preferred digital format for submissions is, in order, (*i*) the latest version of MS Word (Windows), (*ii*) the latest version of MS Word (Macintosh), or (*iii*) any previous version of MS Word (Windows or Macintosh). The first page mentioned above should have a reference to the format and version in which the article was saved. Font and sizes as close as possible to the style of the previous issue of PLCS should be used throughout the text.

Subscription Information

The annual subscription (2 issues) for institutions is $80.00 and $40.00 for individuals. Single issues may also be purchased for $25.00. From outside the United States add $12.00 for shipping and handling.

Inquiries should be sent to *Portuguese Literary & Cultural Studies* Subscription, Center for Portuguese Studies and Culture, University of Massachusetts Dartmouth, Dartmouth, MA 02747 USA, or by e-mail to: greis@umassd.edu.

Advertising

Portuguese Literary & Cultural Studies accepts advertising that is of interest to scholars in the field of Portuguese, Brazilian, and Luso-African Studies and Critical Theory. Further information is available by contacting the Center for Portuguese Studies and Culture, University of Massachusetts Dartmouth.

Cover

Design: Spencer Ladd. "Esta es mi tierra, José Saramago." Photograph courtesy TVE S.A.

ISSN 1521-804X

Printed by RPI Printing, Fall River, MA

Table of Contents

Other Reviews and Articles

Introduction: Saramago's World

Anna Klobucka

> ... we would understand much more about life's complexities if we applied ourselves to an assiduous study of its contradictions, instead of wasting time on identities and coherences, seeing as these have a duty to provide their own explanations.
>
> José Saramago, *A Caverna*

For many decades, José Saramago has been a staunch defender of the role of literature to both serve and be perceived as public discourse. When, in October 1998, he became the first Portuguese-language author to be awarded the Nobel Prize for Literature, his conviction was supported by the assurance that, at any rate, this particular writer's literary discourse was guaranteed to be widely (and globally) publicized. If, as Wlad Godzich has claimed, the severely limited possibility of *public discourse* in the contemporary world is compensated by the ever-multiplying variety of ways to *publicize discourses* ("Workshop"), Saramago has taken full advantage of the opportunities offered in this respect by the Nobel prize as probably the most effective institutionalized instrument of publicity that high literary discourse which is produced worldwide has at its annual disposal. His international visibility greatly amplified, Saramago could be seen in the last two years shuttling the globe and making globally publicized statements on behalf of the many political causes that have attracted his attention and support. One of the most recent instances of his internationalist engagement is the foreword he wrote for *Our Word is Our Weapon*, a volume of selected writings by

Subcomandante Marcos of the Zapatista National Liberation Army (EZLN), one of a series of statements Saramago has issued in recent years—before and after the Nobel Prize—on behalf of the Chiapas rebels. In that text, he described the international dimension of the Mexican tragedy in the following terms: "No matter how much of an attempt has been made to reduce the question of Chiapas to merely a local conflict… what is being played out in the Chiapas mountains and the Lacandon Jungle reaches beyond the borders of Mexico to the heart of that portion of humanity that has not renounced and will never renounce dreams and hopes, the simple imperative of equal justice for all" (xxi). This statement may be seen as an encapsulated expression of Saramago's characteristic viewpoint, both as a writer and as a public intellectual: it conjugates a local and a global perspective (an aspect to which I will return); it projects an image of humankind (or, at any rate, of its progressive "portion") as a morally responsible and forward-thinking community; and it strikes the high utopian note in its insistence on the "simple imperative of equal justice for all," in an emblematic illustration of what Orlando Grossegesse, in the article included in this issue, describes as Saramago's "materialist Messianism."

In his summary outline of some key methodological issues concerning the process of globalization, Godzich refers to the radical restructuring of the social imaginary taking place in the world today in topographic terms: as a loss of collective *stakes*, understood in the figurative sense of the expression as "shared interests," but also, and above all, in the precise sense of boundary markers defining and protecting a territorial domain shared by a stable, settled community ("Workshop"). The current progressive weakening and dissolution of such boundaries, objectively verifiable in technological, economic and political terms, manifests itself, at the same time, in a profoundly subjective manner, as a disappearance of multiple, uniquely differentiated horizons that various communities might claim as their own and theirs alone: "When the whole planet is your frame of reference, then there is no horizon, this supremely subjective notion of boundary" (Godzich, "What Happened to My Horizon?" 2). Against this destabilizing background, it has become perhaps more vitally important than ever for social and cultural collectives (be they territorially rooted or, as is increasingly common, deterritorialized as diasporic or virtual aggregations) to engage in what Arjun Appadurai has described as the new social practice of imagination: no longer ideologically suspect entertainment for the masses or an elite pastime of little general consequence, "the imagination has become an organized field of social practices, a form of work (in the sense of both labor and culturally organized practice), and a form of negotiation between sites of agency (individuals) and globally defined fields of possibility" (31).

Modern Portuguese society has had powerful, historically and politically determined, reasons of its own to engage, over the past two and a half decades, in what can be described as a complex renegotiation of identity, whose motivation and expression have tended to be articulated in predominantly spatial terms. Two key events of that period have been the country's loss of its African colonies following the 1974 Revolution of Carnations and, twelve years later, its incorporation, along with Spain, into the administrative fabric of the European Community. In a very short course, Portugal has traversed a route leading from international ostracism and isolation (as the world's only surviving colonial empire) to full absorption in a closely knit transnational organism, and from a historical destiny that consisted, according to Salazar's propagandists, in being Europe's enterprising threshold and protective bulwark to a contemporary reality as one of Europe's underdeveloped, peripheral dead ends.[1] It is no wonder therefore that grappling with imaginative implications of such a violent unsettling of the national space has taken place on many levels, from ongoing political and philosophical polemics all the way to popular culture, with Portuguese literature, in particular the novel, playing a prominent role in the process of "restaking," so to speak, the newly constituted territory of the national imagination.

Saramago's career as a successful novelist—to be distinguished from his career as a writer—has coincided almost precisely with the post 25 de Abril reformulation of collective Portuguese identity. Having debuted in 1947, at the age of twenty-five, with the novel *Terra do Pecado* (briefly but insightfully discussed in this issue by Horácio Costa), he then abandoned for thirty years the genre that was to bring him later such remarkable achievement, publishing, in the meantime, several volumes of *crónicas* and columns originally written for the newspapers *A Capital*, *Jornal do Fundão*, *Diário de Lisboa* and *Diário de Notícias*. Between 1966 and 1975 he also produced three volumes of poetry (*Os Poemas Possíveis*, *Provavelmente Alegria*, and *O Ano de 1993*); and in 1978 his short stories were collected and published under the title *Objecto Quase* (for a complete listing of Saramago's literary works see the Bibliography). Saramago's return to the novel—the genre he now practices almost exclusively, albeit with significant exceptions, such as the novella *The Tale of an Unknown Island* (1997) and the successive volumes of his diary, *Cadernos de Lanzarote*—had thus been slow but by no means idle. When in 1976 Saramago published his second novel, *Manual of Painting and Calligraphy*, it was tellingly subtitled "Ensaio de Romance," a label translatable into English as both a "novel-essay" and a "rehearsal for a novel." This designation points to Saramago's often repeated assertion that he is not really a novelist, but rather an essayist who writes novels because he does not know how to write essays (Reis 46); however, at the same time it also emphasizes the notion of writing as an apprenticeship, a laborious process that must be faced with patience and humility if it is to fructify in a mature, accomplished product.[2]

The chronological coincidence between the period of post 25 de Abril "restaking" of the territory of Portuguese collective imagination and the golden age of the writer José Saramago's literary creativity is a complex notion; several of the essays gathered in this issue address Saramago's engagement with the history and contemporary reality of his country in terms that question and clarify, without simplifying, the ideological charge of his fictional interventions. Unsurprisingly, the novel most often evoked by the critics interested in addressing Saramago's literary politics and his attitude with regard to the transformations undergone by his country and his region turns out to be *The Stone Raft* (1986), a magic-realist utopian fable published in the year of Portugal's and Spain's accession to the European Community, in which the Iberian Peninsula, by a freak and incomprehensible accident of nature, becomes detached from Europe and, having progressed along a somewhat idiosyncratic trajectory (it takes a detour to avoid crashing into the Azores), ends up stationary in the middle of the southern Atlantic Ocean, half way between Africa and South America. As Ellen Sapega has noted, many contemporary Portuguese novels rely on spatial metaphors, thus indicating "a common desire to comment on the abrupt changes and discontinuities that have characterized recent Portuguese national experience" (181). Among Saramago's novels, *The Stone Raft* is certainly the most explicit and insistent in its reliance on topographic tropes, as well as in its referential framing in a contextually specific, contemporary reality. The improbable, centrifugal voyage of the Peninsula, which results in a global reorganization of geopolitical space, is paralleled by multiple centripetal dislocations of its inhabitants: as the novel unfolds, these migrating masses of

Iberians coalesce into new, experimental "ethnoscapes," central building blocks of what Appadurai (extending Benedict Anderson) calls "*imagined worlds* ... the multiple worlds that are constituted by the historically situated imaginations of persons and groups spread around the globe" (33; original emphasis). *The Stone Raft* may therefore be read as, first and foremost, an ethnographic parable dedicated to exploring (in a historically and culturally situated context) "the nature of locality as a lived experience in a globalized, deterritorialized world" (Appadurai 52).

For more on *The Stone Raft* and its complexities and contradictions, which to a considerable extent reflect the complexities and contradictions that may be said to inform the political and aesthetic attitudes espoused by its author, I direct the reader to the essays by, particularly, Orlando Grossegesse, Mark J. Sabine, and Maria Alzira Seixo. My reason for singling out this particular novel for discussion in the limited space of the editor's introduction is that what I have described above as its primary project finds a continuation of sorts in Saramago's latest work of fiction, published in November 2000 (and therefore too recently to have been addressed by any of the articles gathered here): the much anticipated *A Caverna* [The Cave].

The first novel by Saramago published since his 1998 Nobel Prize, *A Caverna,* completes what the writer himself has described as a trilogy of narratives, with its first two installments represented by the novels *Blindness* (1995) and *All the Names* (1997); these three works form (in the words of Teresa Cristina Cerdeira da Silva's essay included in this issue) "a triptych reflecting humanity's quest for meaning in the midst of its end-of-millennium crisis." Following Saramago's grand cycle of historical novels published in the 1980s (which extends to the 1991 *Gospel According to Jesus Christ*), these three works mark a different course and occupy a distinct place in the Portuguese writer's *oeuvre* (see, in particular, David Frier's essay for a comprehensive commentary on *Blindness* and *All the Names*). Nevertheless, as Seixo's provocative take on *The Stone Raft* and *Blindness* demonstrates, they can be shown to relate on many levels to Saramago's earlier works; from my perspective, it is in particular between *The Stone Raft* and *A Caverna* that the web of correspondences thickens to the point where their comparative and contrastive reading becomes something of an imperative.

A Caverna tells the story of Cipriano Algor, a sixty-four year old, village-dwelling potter, who sells the bulk of his earthenware products to the otherwise nameless Center, an enormous shopping and residential compound located in the nearby, likewise nameless metropolis. The apparent location of the Center *within* the surrounding urban fabric is at several points challenged by the narrative discourse, where the Center is implied to absorb and contain, and even to replace, the city itself, as it constantly expands its voracious and far-reaching periphery. Cipriano's daughter Marta is married to Marçal Gacho who commutes from the village to the Center, where he works as a security guard, for ten-day shifts; the young couple long for Marçal to become a resident guard and be allowed to live at the Center, thus ending the tiresome cycle of their periodic separations. As the narrative unfolds, the relocation of the entire family (including Cipriano) to the Center is contemplated and, for a period of three weeks, actually carried out. This implies the abandonment of the old man's traditional way of life and manufacture; the pressure to abandon them has been, indeed, exercised by the Center itself, since its commercial representatives have cancelled Cipriano's contract: they prefer to stock mass-produced plastic imitations of his earthenware vessels instead of the genuine articles.

A Caverna preserves many elements of the scenarios of urban dystopia painted by Saramago in *Blindness* and *All the Names* (and prefigured in the much earlier *O Ano de 1993*, which Kenneth Krabbenhoft considers in this issue). However, it no longer gives them exclusive rein over the destinies of the novel's protagonists: here, the dystopia represented by the sinister, Big Brotherish Center is contrasted with the utopian space of Cipriano's homestead, which is organically fused with his potter's workplace. If I call the novel's representation of Cipriano's living and working space "utopian" rather than "realist" (after all, households like his still do exist here and there in rural Portugal), it is because the narrative discourse itself insists on its almost impossibly anachronistic nature:

> We have already seen how the clay is mixed here in the most old-fashioned manner, we have seen how rustic and even primitive are these potter's wheels, how the kiln outside preserves signs of an antiquity inadmissible in the modern times, which, in spite of the reprehensible deficiencies and intransigence that characterize them, have proven benevolent enough to admit, until now, the existence of a pottery such as this one side by side with a Center such as that one. (147; my translation)

As an unapologetic leftist of the old school (and to this day a card-carrying Communist) who came into his own as a writer at the ripe age of sixty-something, and by plunging into the ambivalent waters of postmodern metafictional poetics, Saramago is, not unlike his country and his region, a complicated hybrid, and both *The Stone Raft* and *A Caverna* reflect this hybridity at many levels.

In *The Stone Raft*, it may be detected in the narrative's contrapuntal treatment of events on the macro level (predominantly dystopian), where references to mass media, satellite images and computer-generated models of the wayward Iberia abound, and on the micro scale (predominantly utopian), where the novel's five protagonists evolve, in their travels, toward a distinctly premodern *modus vivendi*, the most telling symbol of which is perhaps the exchange of their original mode of transportation, a Citroën Deux Chevaux, for a covered wagon pulled by two actual horses. This is less a sign of a nostalgic escape from modernity than an acknowledgment of the heterogeneous makeup of contemporary Iberian societies (which is perhaps particularly true in the case of Portugal) as semiperipheral, intermediate formations, whose distinguishing characteristics may be summarily qualified as "pre-post-modern" (Santos 89), containing elements of asynchronic stages of development and a corresponding variety of relationships between their social agents.

In *A Caverna*, the "pre-post-modern" counterpoint is updated for the new millennium, as its author paints, with narrative brush strokes that are alternatively (and sometimes simultaneously) broad and fine, an allegorical satire of the totalitarian assumptions of global consumer capitalism. In the end, however, it remains as unresolved as the conclusion of *The Stone Raft*, where the reinvention of (Iberian) locality in its new global (postcolonial) context is left open-ended, albeit, at the same time, pregnant (literally) with hope and opportunity. Like the women of the Iberian Peninsula in *The Stone Raft*, Cipriano's daughter Marta is also expecting a child as the novel comes to a close, and it is her refusal to let it be born in the sterile and suffocating atmosphere of the Center that propels the family to abandon their new residence. They recognize, however, that Cipriano's pottery has no future either; as Marta comments, "we're finished with the Center, the pottery had already met its end, from one day to another we have become like strangers in this world" (347). Therefore, *A Caverna*'s last paragraph finds the novel's protagonists (who, in a trademark Saramago move, include the long-widowed Cipriano's new love, Isaura) piled together with their belongings into the old man's delivery truck, about to hit the road in search of a new life "far away from here" (347). If, on the basis of *The Stone Raft*, Saramago could still be suspected of clinging to what Bruce Robbins diagnoses as "the romantic localism of a certain portion of the left, which feels it must counter capitalist globalization with a strongly rooted and exclusive sort of belonging" (3), the darker, more disillusioned closure of *A Caverna* leaves little room for such alternatives. It does, nevertheless, allow for a preservation—however tentative and vulnerable to critical scrutiny—of the dialectical concept of "rooted cosmopolitanism," which also appears to be guiding Saramago's recently magnified career as an international public figure. As Mitchell Cohen describes it, rooted cosmopolitanism "accepts a multiplicity of roots and branches and … rests on the legitimacy of plural loyalties, of standing in many circles, but with common ground" (483). The rickety panel truck of an old, unemployed potter, advancing toward a new life in an unknown, faraway location thus supplants the impossible, floating "stone raft" of Saramago's utopian Iberian homeland in providing a fictional blueprint for such a rootedly cosmopolitan world whose horizons, if any, have yet to be imagined.

This sixth issue of *Portuguese Literary & Cultural Studies*, dedicated to José Saramago, was conceived with several interrelated objectives in mind. Given the scarcity of published Saramago criticism in English, however, the issue's primary goal is to provide the growing audience of non-Portuguese speaking readers and students of Saramago with a wide selection of in-depth analytic approaches to his major works, adding up to a comprehensive and theoretically informed overall perspective on the writer's work, with particular emphasis on his novels. Therefore, all articles were either originally written in or translated into English, and the references to Saramago's works also follow the English translations of his novels by Giovanni Pontiero and, more recently, following Pontiero's untimely death in 1996, by Margaret Jull Costa.[3] At the same time, however, the editors' intention was that this volume should account for, reflect, and enter into a critical dialogue with the spectacularly flourishing field of Saramago criticism published in Portuguese. The international cast of contributors includes thus many, if not most, prominent and widely recognized critics of Saramago's work, whose pioneering research has already become an indispensable reference to the many who have followed in their steps (and who are also well represented in this issue).

Following George Monteiro's eloquent presentation of José Saramago during the *honoris causa* ceremony at the University of Massachusetts Dartmouth in

October 1999, and Saramago's address at the same ceremony, the first four articles offer synthetic and panoramic approaches to the study of the Portuguese author's novels; the progression of their subject matter is also roughly chronological, spanning half a century from *Terra do Pecado* (1947) to *All the Names* (1997). In "Saramago's Construction of Fictional Characters: From *Terra do Pecado* to *Baltasar and Blimunda*," Horácio Costa relies on his comprehensive understanding of Saramago's *período formativo* in tracing a complex evolutionary trajectory within the writer's work. Adriana Alves de Paula Martins dedicates her essay on "José Saramago's Historical Fiction" to one of the central issues in Saramago scholarship, assessing the writer's literary representation of the Portuguese national past in terms of an original typology that comprises the main trends of postmodern historical fiction. Teresa Cristina Cerdeira da Silva's critical meditation "On the Labyrinth of Text, or, Writing as the Site of Memory" considers another key aspect of Saramago's novels published in the 1980s: their intertextual engagement with the Portuguese, Iberian, and generally Western cultural tradition. Finally, David Frier's essay, "Righting Wrongs, Re-Writing Meaning and Reclaiming the City in Saramago's *Blindness* and *All the Names*," discusses the allegorical turn that Saramago's fiction has taken in the more recent years and analyzes the two novels' insistence on the individual moral responsibility for the construction of a better society.

Further contributions focus on selected crucial aspects of the Portuguese writer's multifaceted literary identity. It is Saramago the moralist who emerges, above all, from Kenneth Krabbenhoft's "Saramago, Cognitive Estrangement, and Original Sin?" and from Harold Bloom's "The One With the Beard Is God, the Other Is the Devil." Saramago the Iberian is the object of Orlando Grossegesse's discussion in "Journey to the Iberian God: Antonio Machado Revisited by Saramago" and, from a different angle, of Mark J. Sabine's "'Once But No Longer the Prow of Europe': National Identity and Portuguese Destiny in José Saramago's *The Stone Raft*." And it is Saramago the writer, who has always surreptitiously challenged the solidity and coherence of personal and political identity postulated by his celebrated public superego, Saramago the Author, that emerges from the two concluding essays, with their, respectively, postcolonial and feminist focus on difference and displacement at work in Saramago's texts: Maria Alzira Seixo's "The Edge of Darkness, or, Why Saramago Never Wrote about the Colonial War in Africa" and Ana Paula Ferreira's "Cruising Gender in the Eighties (from *Levantado do Chão* to *The History of the Siege of Lisbon*)."

Following George Monteiro's translation of a short story by Saramago, the four publications discussed in the Reviews section offer collectively both a representative and superlative sampling of the latest in Saramago criticism in Portugal and Brazil: the monumental tribute to the Nobel Prize winner presented by the journal *Colóquio/Letras* in its special double issue (reviewed by Onésimo T. Almeida); *Diálogos com José Saramago* by Carlos Reis, perhaps the most inspired and inspiring among the several volumes of Saramago interviews already available (reviewed by Mark J. Sabine); Maria Alzira Seixo's prize-winning collection of her essays on Saramago, *Lugares da ficção em José Saramago* (reviewed by Ana Sofia Ganho); and Beatriz Berrini's *Ler Saramago: o romance* (reviewed by José Ornelas), a book that testifies to an unflagging interest in Saramago among literary critics in Brazil, where for many years already he has been the bestselling Portuguese author.

Notes

[1]. In more recent years, of course, Portugal's political and economic standing in Europe has greatly improved. Already in the second half of the 1980s, the country's economy grew faster than that of any other of its fellow European Community members for several consecutive years; to quote but one assessment, in 1992 *The Wall Street* Journal would praise Portugal's exemplary transition from "dirt-poor dictatorship to stable and increasingly prosperous democracy" (Gumbel A11).

[2]. It is interesting to note (as many have done) that the second edition of *Manual*, released by Caminho in 1983, and therefore after Saramago had been catapulted into the literary spotlight with the 1980 *Levantado do Chão* and, particularly, the 1982 *Memorial do Convento* (later to be translated into English as *Baltasar and Blimunda*), did not carry the subtitle "Ensaio de Romance." It is almost as if Saramago had performed an act of anachronistic historical intervention—a device on which his novels (particularly *The History of the Siege of Lisbon*) frequently rely—upon his own work: by 1983, this novelist was no longer "rehearsing" anything, he was performing with great confidence, center stage and facing a crowded, increasingly enthusiastic audience.

[3]. The editors gratefully acknowledge the permission granted by the journal *Colóquio/Letras* to reproduce, in English translation, two of the essays originally published in its 1999 issue dedicated to Saramago: Horácio Costa's "Saramago's Construction of Fictional Characters: From *Terra do Pecado* to *Baltasar and Blimunda*" and Teresa Cristina Cerdeira da Silva's "On the Labyrinth of Text, or, Writing as the Site of Memory."

Works Cited

Appadurai, Arjun. *Modernity at Large: Cultural Dimensions of Globalization.* Minneapolis: U of Minnesota P, 1996.

Cohen, Mitchell. "Rooted Cosmopolitanism. Thoughts on the Left, Nationalism, and Multiculturalism." *Dissent* 39.4 (Fall 1992): 478-83.

Godzich, Wlad. "What Happened to My Horizon? Or, How to Cope With Global Culture." Unpublished manuscript, distributed at the International School of Theory in the Humanities in Santiago de Compostela, 1998.

———. Workshop presentation. International School of Theory in the Humanities. Santiago de Compostela. 30 July 1998.

Gumbel, Peter. "Portugal: A Recovery that East Europe Can Emulate." *Wall Street Journal.* 1 May 1992.

Reis, Carlos. *Diálogos com José Saramago.* Lisboa: Caminho, 1998.

Robbins, Bruce. "Introduction Part I: Actually Existing Cosmopolitanism." *Cosmopolitics: Thinking and Feeling Beyond the Nation.* Eds. Pheng Cheah and Bruce Robbins. Minneapolis: U of Minnesota P, 1998. 1-19.

Santos, Boaventura de Sousa. *Pela Mão de Alice. O Social e Político na Pós-Modernidade.* Porto: Afrontamento, 1994.

Sapega, Ellen. "No Longer Alone and Proud: Notes on the Rediscovery of the Nation in Contemporary Portuguese Fiction." *After the Revolution: Twenty Years of Portuguese Literature 1974-1994.* Eds. Helena Kaufman and Anna Klobucka. Lewisburg: Bucknell UP, 1997. 168-86.

Saramago, José. *A Jangada de Pedra.* Lisboa: Caminho, 1986. [English translation by Giovanni Pontiero, *The Stone Raft*, New York: Harcourt Brace, 1995.]

———. *A Caverna.* Lisboa: Caminho, 2000.

Subcomandante Marcos. *Our Word Is Our Weapon. Selected Writings.* Ed. Juana Ponce de León. New York: Seven Stories Press, 2000.

Presentation of José Saramago, Ceremony to Confer Doctor of Humane Letters, *Honoris Causa* Upon José Saramago, October 22, 1999, University of Massachusetts Dartmouth

George Monteiro

The wisest man he ever knew could neither read nor write, José Saramago has said. His grandfather Jerónimo was a man who lived gracefully with his animals and who, when he sensed that his death was imminent, "went out to say good-bye to the trees in his orchard, embracing each of them in turn and weeping because he knew he would never see them again." In 1998 the Swedish Academy awarded the grandson of that illiterate but profoundly cultured man the Nobel Prize for Literature.

The prize had been so long in coming, the seventy-six year old Portuguese writer indicated at the time, that he had long since given up hope that the award would be his. He was well aware, moreover, that the Nobel was an even longer time in coming for his country and for all the Portuguese-language writers throughout the world who had preceded him over the long years. Yet, for José Saramago, the Prize had come only sixteen years after he achieved his first success with the novel known in English as *Baltasar and Blimunda* and less than a quarter of a century since he resumed the writing of fiction. (He had abandoned it after a first novel, the modest success of which landed him a job in journalism.)

Since the overthrow of the Salazar-Caetano dictatorship on the 25th of April in 1974, he has produced fiction, novels and short stories, plays and poetry, most of which have been translated into most of the major languages of the world. Until recently, he has been served especially well by his English-language translator, the late Giovanni Pontiero. Among his most trenchant narratives, all of them available in English translation, are *The Tale of the Unknown Island, The Year of the Death of Ricardo Reis, The Gospel According to Jesus Christ, The Stone Raft, The History of the Siege of Lisbon, Blindness*, and, recently, *All the Names.* Each of them seems to have begun, invariably, one thinks, with the question "what if?" What if blindness was perceived to be a dangerously contagious disease? What if Saint Joseph was wracked by guilt for not having warned his neighbors that the innocents were to be killed? What if, during the fictional poet Ricardo Reis's return to Portugal, he was visited by the spirit of the recently dead poet Fernando Pessoa, his creator? What if a clerk or lowly scribe or proof-reader had the temerity to intervene ever so slightly in the historical account he was checking by inserting before everything the single word "not," thereby changing the course of the written record of history? What if the entire Iberian peninsula were to break off from the rest of Europe, much as a northern or southern hemisphere iceberg might, becoming a huge clod floating freely in the Atlantic, with a population that carries with it its culture, history, and social truths?

Described rightly by the *New York Times* as "a writer with an ear for the melody of human speech," José Saramago is also a master of the wondrous and awe-inspiring narrative. While insisting that the true narrator in each book is always himself, José Saramago nevertheless brings off the near-illusionist's trick of narrating richly and wonderfully through various voices. It is the achieved phenomenon of his prose that his characters always strike us as being in motion (an achievement that owes nothing to easy psychologizing or the surrender to the sirens of paradigmatic rationalizing), an accomplishment that accounts for the strong flow of narrative that carries one along with it. In *The Gospel According to Jesus Christ*, for example, he reimagines as a narrative the life of the historical Jesus, not as the Son of God, but as a human being. He follows closely the outline of the story everyone knows, but inferentially working out the details of the dust and dirt of his everyday life. He searches in what must have been the human dimension of the life of Joseph the father, with its oppressive sense of moral responsibilities fulfilled or evaded. What José Saramago always does is to provide, in its fullest sense, what the writer Henry James called the true fictional effects of "felt life," that is, the very feel of life as lived. Everyone knows what happened mythically and emblematically, but he reverses the usual process of the magic realist by humanizing—that is, by making ordinary—that still, and now somehow, enhanced extraordinary life. He provides thus the missing narrative, the unwritten narrative that might have preceded those of Matthew, Mark, Luke, and John.

In *Blindness* José Saramago turns everyday actuality into an extraordinary reality in which a breakout of a batch of sudden, unexplainable, mysterious blindness triggers widespread fear and terror, leading immediately to the exercise of the institutional power to coerce, segregate, round-up, intern, and punish. Here he allegorizes the sins of the victims of the Holocaust, reimagining thereby all holocausts—including those, still unimagined, that yet await us.

José Saramago is a moralist, a rather broadly political moralist, to be exact. But this longtime champion of the people, champion of the cultural and spiritual values of nations, chooses to show more than he will tell, inspiring his readers to trust the truth of the tale while efficiently deflecting all focus away from its inspired teller. It is with humility and pride that one can welcome to the University of Massachusetts, this honored but also honoring place, José Saramago, this native of Portugal, this honorable and honest citizen of the realm we know as humankind.

Address at the *Honoris Causa* Ceremony, University of Massachusetts Dartmouth

José Saramago
Translated by
Robert Moser

Honorable Chancellor of the University of Massachusetts Dartmouth
Illustrious Professors
Esteemed Students
Ladies and Gentlemen
My Friends

In recent months I have had, frequently, the privilege of rising to similar university podiums, on more or less solemn occasions, to express my gratitude and to expound upon some broad ideas related to both my activity as a writer as well as my concerns as a citizen. Presumably these invitations stem from personal merits which, I fear, do not always rise to the distinctions awarded them. Nevertheless, like any other human being entitled to my modicum of vanity, I will not venture to question your judgement, even though I am predisposed, either by virtue of a natural tendency or perhaps an acquired one, to render coolly those merits all relative, to view them as contingent, variable, accidental, the mere fruit of whimsical tastes, and, therefore, dependent on the conditions of time and place. I have already received the degree of Doctor *Honoris Causa* from universities in Spain, Italy, France, Brazil, and the United Kingdom, as well as Portugal. From this moment on, thanks to what is perhaps best understood as a particularly generous show of charity in your academic evaluation of me, I am similarly honored by the University of Massachusetts Dartmouth.

My reference to those countries and universities, which have previously opened their doors to me, was by no means gratuitous, nor did it stem from some irresistible temptation for self-indulgence. If I have allowed myself the liberty to ponder such a wide trajectory, indeed one that covers almost half the planet, it is only to underscore the importance, and reflect upon, with as much rigor as I can muster, the relevance of my stepping before you today in Dartmouth. In truth, I sense or recognize in this ceremony, at least as I am experiencing it now, a singularity, a unique quality, which, I confess, moves me in a way that is both intimate and profound. It is not due, as some of you, who are able to recall the list of my academic distinctions, might imagine, to the fact that this is the first time that an honorary doctorate has been bestowed upon me by a North American university. Presumably this would serve as a sufficient and justifiable motive for the emotion that envelops me now, and yet I recognize that the roots of my sentiment go much deeper. I stand as witness as they break down the walls that surround us, and extend beyond the limits of the university campus, to finally unite with those people who, although I have not met them, are fully recognizable to me (if you will pardon this apparent contradiction). Their roots, both close and distant, from abroad and from here, pulled less by their sense of adventure and more by their response to necessity, thousands of Portuguese immigrants at one point in time came to this State, in many cases for two or three generations, to live and to work. Theirs is an unremitting human chain and, as such, has always been and will continue to be an example of living history, one that inevitably carries within itself the recollection of a distinct past and the memory of a distant country, of a continent, an island. A place invoked by desire, at times pain, but always nostalgia, even when it seemed to us forgotten, sometimes forgotten, sometimes remembered, remembered and forgotten, forgotten, remembered. Here, in this place, as I speak to you, I would like to be seen, above all, as a Portuguese who came to be with other Portuguese, as someone born and raised on the Other Side of the Ocean, and as one whom life's circumstances taught to cultivate with love and respect the full harvest of the Portuguese language. I would like to be seen as someone who in time developed into a writer, one who, in turn, with the help of both the knowledge and the will he had acquired, ended up by returning to the earth itself the handful of kernels that he had collected from life, with the idea that the renewal of the harvest can take place only through the rejuvenation of different generations and their experiences, as well as the lively clash between the works of yesterday and the works of today. It is from the same tree that dropped its leaves that the new buds grow.

Presumably for reasons of political convenience, excessive optimism or, perhaps, a propensity for round figures, it has been said countless times that there are two hundred million speakers of Portuguese on this planet. In actuality, there are not so many of us, but some day undoubtedly there will be. That day will come when the African nations with Portuguese as their official language are able to free themselves once and for all from the ravages of war and the equally devastating misfortune of economic and cultural underdevelopment, and assume, at least according to the usual rhetoric, their own destinies. It is not by chance that I invoke here that part of Africa that decided to adopt Portuguese as their basis, as an instrumental link in national unity, and as a privileged medium for literary and artistic expression. Following the historical precedent of an independent Brazil, and free from their colonial yoke after sustained fighting, immeasurable human sacrifice and devastating structural wreckage, these countries repaid the injury we inflicted upon them, with their offering to choose forever Portuguese as their language. (And I truly believe it will be forever.) Surrounded, constrained, and one might even say oppressed economically and culturally by an extensive chain of countries who use English as their official language, Lusophone Africa has elected to continue living with the minority language of yesteryear, and in so doing has entrusted it to their teachers, their writers, their people, as the key to unlock the door to the world. By choosing this route they were unaware, in all likelihood, that the Portuguese would also ultimately benefit from their decision. Even as the courageous and martyred people of East Timor have done, albeit for different reasons, when they have articulated their grievances on international television in fluent and correct Portuguese, much to the surprise, probably, of many people. Allow me then to pose a loaded question: Would we be happier, would we communicate any better or look forward to a brighter future if we had chosen to speak and write in a language that was more widespread, predominant, and universal? There are undoubtedly reasons why someone would answer yes to this question, and yet this is not the position defended by the Angolan and Mozambican writers who just a few weeks ago, in Luanda and Maputo, called my attention to something that I had never considered. They explained to me, in all seriousness, that if, for example, they had written in English, they would find themselves now submersed in an immense ocean of Anglophone authors from around the world; whereas, writing in Portuguese, they at least enjoy the advantages afforded them by the *difference* they represent. They are therefore *others*, who can benefit from the curiosity that seeks out that which is qualitatively *distinct*. As this example clearly demonstrates, there are not merely disadvantages to speaking and writing in the language of the minority... which, as we have seen, is not such a small group after all, when we consider that we are on the road to 200 hundred million people and are unlikely to stop at this number.

We may be compelled, then, to speak and write in different languages spread across this vast world, either out of a unilateral necessity for communication or when the simple pleasure to extend our knowledge possesses us. And yet, we must always be prepared to defend, through its practice and study, the common tree of the Portuguese language with its diverse national expressions, a tree whose branches spread out over the Earth, casting a shadow that we recognize as no less than the projection of our mutual heritage. There are those who contend that languages have no need for a savior, that a language is an extremely adaptable, living organism and that this capacity for continuous adaptation is the very stuff of life. All of this is indeed true. In this day and age, however, a language that does not defend itself will die. It suffers not a sudden death, but rather one of gradual disintegration through consumption that may take centuries to complete, thus creating the illusion of a language that is long-lived, and which, in turn, cultivates the indolence and masks the complicity, consciously or subconsciously, of its suicidal speakers. Clearly we would have our language avoid this fate. Fortunately, we are at this moment at a university in which Portuguese Studies have prospered and where our hope for its future development will undoubtedly solidify its achievements. It is my ardent desire, as a writer and a Portuguese, that your endeavors be fully realized. I am confident that I share this sentiment with the Portuguese immigrants in the State of Massachusetts, whom I cordially address as well.

To conclude, Honorable Chancellor, I would like to express my gratitude to the University of Massachusetts Dartmouth for bestowing upon me the honor of including me among its own. I shall strive always to be worthy of this honor and to live up to the thoughtfulness with which you welcomed me to your house, a place that, henceforward, I shall also consider my own. Thank you very much.

Articles

Saramago's Construction of Fictional Characters: From *Terra do Pecado* to *Baltasar and Blimunda*

Horácio Costa
Translated by
Kimberly DaCosta Holton

At a particular moment in *Terra do Pecado* (*Land of Sin*, 1947) Maria Leonor, the widow-protagonist in José Saramago's first novel, says to Dr. Viegas, her doctor and confidant,

> I wish I did not feel ashamed at this moment, but I do… I need something that would give me certainty of my wretchedness. Look, doctor, I am asking you, go to the office and bring... bring *First Principles* by Spencer… I want to feel that, fundamentally, this means nothing, as long as I maintain the calm necessary to continue thinking about the overwhelming greatness of the Universe. I want to feel small, identical to the irrational female who betrays her mate for the first time just after his death. (207-08)

Besides the melodramatic tone that imbues Maria Leonor's speech with the stale flavor of a nineteenth-century novel, the mention of Herbert Spencer (1820-1903), who together with Charles Darwin was one of the Victorian masters of evolutionary theory, aligns the belief systems in *Terra do Pecado* with an earlier historical period than the one in which the book was composed. In fact, upon reading this book, a strange sense of anachronism assaults us: written fifty years ago, the novel recalls a culture that is over a hundred years old, one dominated by sexual taboos of various types, and by an agrarian or urban bourgeoisie characteristic of the work of Camilo Castelo Branco or Eça de Queirós, not of the universe of modern urban and rural life. *Terra do Pecado* features, in sum, a society less marked by the habits of the twentieth century than by the mores of a world whose time still obeyed the rhythms of village bells.

This point applies not only to the novel's plot, but also to its prose and structure. If *Terra do Pecado*'s plot typifies a late nineteenth-century story—a widow suffers from sexual incontinence, becomes involved with her brother-in-law and, driven by her guilty conscience, seeks out the family doctor, all of this giving rise to a foreseeable conclusion of calculated pathos—the novel's language and structure also clearly demonstrate the distance between Saramago and other novelists writing in Portugal and the rest of the world at the time of the book's publication. Considering this asynchronism, few of Saramago's 1947 readers could have anticipated that, fifty years later, the author of *Terra do Pecado* would receive international acclaim as one of the most powerful and original writers of the late twentieth century, becoming the first Nobel Laureate in Portuguese, a language that had waited a considerable time for this recognition.

So as not to focus solely on *Terra do Pecado*'s plot, let us also consider the nature and design of the novel's characters. If in critical terms little is gained by asserting that Maria Leonor, Benedita and Dr. Viegas would be better off in a Portuguese novel of the nineteenth century rather than of the mid-twentieth, even less is gained by a reader's comparing these characters to those of Alves Redol or Carlos de Oliveira in *Gaibéus* and *Casa na Duna*—books that influenced the development of Portuguese prose fiction immediately following their publication, seven and four years before *Terra do Pecado*, respectively. To mark the distance between Saramago's formal vocabulary and that of his contemporaries, let us recall also that much of the innovative fiction produced in Northeastern Brazil by novelists such as Jorge Amado and Graciliano Ramos, who exerted a tremendous influence on young Portuguese writers of the time, was written in the 1930s.

It was, therefore, not from his foreign and domestic contemporaries that the young Saramago drew inspiration for his first characters. We would have to look back to Abel Botelho's "Social Pathology" series and its typology of human stereotypes, not to mention Júlio Ribeiro's heroine in *A Carne*, to find figures that were similarly shaped by an aesthetic, ethical and even ideological model artificially tailored to the preconceived trends of a literary current. If exhibited in a gallery of characters, the hysterical Maria Leonor, the paternal Dr. Viegas, and Benedita, an example of servile generosity and dedication, would not be out of place beside the Barão de Lavos and Próspero Fortuna, or the protagonists of Júlio Ribeiro's novel, the young Lenita and her similarly paternal and respectable Dr. Lopes Matoso.

Terra do Pecado's lineage resides much more in the Portuguese version of Zola's naturalism—which, today, is clearly identifiable as the book's antecedent—rather than in the twentieth-century novel, be it the developing prose of early Neo-Realism or the fiction indebted to the literary experiments of international modernism. If all of this turns young Saramago's anachronism transparent, it also demonstrates in and of itself the independence of the writer within the Portuguese literary context. We will later return to the consideration of this distance between Saramago and the trends and dominant literary discourses at the time his first book was published. In fact, we can see how—through the employment of an evolutionary perspective in order to compare the construction of fictional characters from *Terra do Pecado* to *Manual of Painting and Calligraphy* (1976), to the short stories of *Objecto Quase* (*Almost an Object*, 1978), to *Levantado do Chão* (*Raised from the Ground*, 1980) and to *Baltasar and Blimunda* (1982), as is the purpose of this essay—dating from his original asynchronism, Saramago gradually charted his own course, arriving eventually at the center of the most advanced literary production in the world of Lusophone writing today.

Following *Terra do Pecado*, nineteen years would pass before Saramago published a new book. Twenty-nine years would pass before he conceived of a significant cast of characters driven by an extensive fictional plot. Saramago's return to prose fiction was slow and steady. It is surely not in the two books of poetry (*Os Poemas Possíveis* [*Possible Poems*] of 1966, and *Provavelmente Alegria* [*Probably Joy*] of 1970), with which Saramago reinaugurated his literary activity, nor in the two books of *crónicas*[1] (*Deste Mundo e do Outro* [*From This World and From the Other*] of 1971 and *A Bagagem do Viajante* [*The Traveler's Baggage*] of 1973), that we may be able to discern the first drafts of a return to the construction of fictional characters. Nevertheless, it is also important to note, particularly in some *crónicas*, traces of a revival of the creative impulse. I would underscore, to cite one of many possible examples, "Travessa de André Valente," a *crónica* published in *Deste Mundo e do Outro*, in which the narrator encounters and maintains a dialogue with the ghost of Bocage; this constitutes a certain anticipation of the situation that, a decade and a half later, would be developed in *The Year of the Death of Ricardo Reis*.

For obvious reasons, it is not useful to search the compilations of political writing published at the time (*As Opiniões que o DL Teve* of 1974 and *Os*

Apontamentos of 1976) for prefigurations of Saramago's fictional characters. Nor is it useful to search the two texts, *O Ano de 1993* (*The Year 1993*, 1975) and "O Ouvido" ("Hearing"), the latter published in the volume *Poética dos Cinco Sentidos* [*Poetics of the Five Senses*, 1979]), which I have called "experimental" in my study, *José Saramago: O Período Formativo*, for reasons elaborated in that work. We will not encounter in *O Ano de 1993* and "O Ouvido," neither *in nuce* nor in full bloom, so to speak, characters whose fictional status is comparable to those in *Terra do Pecado*. Meanwhile, however, in order to underscore an important point, let us dwell a bit on these two texts.

O Ano de 1993, a fragmentary account written in short verses that narrates the emancipation of an occupied city, is a text composed in a futuristic-dystopic convention that since the time of its publication has come to play a very important role in Saramago's writing. In both *O Ano de 1993* and "Ouvido," a text inspired by a suggestive medieval tapestry belonging to the series *La Dame à la Licorne* in the Parisian Cluny Museum, Saramago creates narration without constructing fictional characters. In both texts, the writer privileges collective processes: in the first, it is the insurrection of a terrorized population and the consequent expulsion of the invaders from the liberated city. In the second text, even though the principal female figure in the tapestry (who also possesses a historical name and identity: Claude Le Viste, a young maiden of petty nobility in medieval France, whose betrothals the "Licorne" cycle commemorates) might suggest a narrative development in which she is "encapsulated," Saramago's discourse concentrates on the manufacture of the tapestry itself, from the combing of the wool to the designing of the image by an unknown artist; only then is mention made of the maiden there represented. The process of narration in both texts privileges the hero or the anonymous laborer who is not marked by identifying signs, or better yet, "subjectifying" marks, through which, as we know, fictional characters are construed.

In *Manual of Painting and Calligraphy* (1976), Saramago constructs complete fictional characters, if not for the first time, given the antecedence of *Terra do Pecado*, then at least in the sense that their conception reveals an identifiable margin of authorial conscience, this time attuned to contemporary fiction writing. Accordingly, *Manual of Painting and Calligraphy* can be viewed as the first demonstration of a dialogue on an equal footing between the not-so-young José Saramago and his political and particularly literary environment. Unlike *Terra do Pecado*, this second novel remains open to the Portuguese and European literary horizons. On the one hand, *Manual* recuperates a narrative tone and digressiveness in the tradition of Almeida Garrett; on the other, Saramago's debt to the contemporary European novel, and the French novel in particular, becomes evident.[2]

Let us emphasize that due to the abovementioned factors, *Manual* can be considered the first demonstration, in reach and scope, of a mature work of fiction by Saramago. In addition, the hero of *Manual of Painting and Calligraphy* inaugurates a series of middle-aged male characters that will multiply throughout the fictional human universe of the "adult" Saramago. The painter, a "portraitist," designated by the initial "H," characterizes himself as a mediocre artist. Certain of his limitations and of his somewhat pathetic role as the painter of portraits in the gallery of Portuguese society, lethargic and stratified before the revolution of 25 de Abril, H decides to conduct a profound self-examination, throwing himself into an enterprise with which, until then, he has had little familiarity: writing. Calligraphy is for him like Ariadne's string: it reproduces itself incessantly, unlike the world of images in which H feels more comfortable. This man in crisis reflects upon his life and his interest in art, while executing a self-cleansing operation (or really an eugenic operation, as the process brings about the perfecting of life-conditions). Gripped by doubt, a prisoner of his labyrinth, H seems to suffer from an affliction to which the medieval world gave a precise designation: *acedia*, the "midday demon" that especially affected monks and men of letters insecure about the efficacy of their intellectual contribution to a world of concrete labor.[3] Be that as it may, this sometimes cruel scrutiny sparks the execution of a singular "Manual of Self-Surpassing," perhaps the source of the suggestive and original title of the novel. In this writing, stylistically marked by digression—the importance of which, we might say in passing, is fundamental to the structure of Saramago's prose—H gradually reveals himself as the first complete and complex character written by Saramago: an anonymous hero, but about to become identified with himself and with history. After having felt himself evaporate in the ease of a life without horizons, as if he had become his own analysand—although, to be sure, his self-examination is far removed from psychoanalytic technique—the portrait painter witnesses a change in his relationship to art and turns into an artist, into a painter *lato sensu*, defined as such in view of himself and of the world.

In this process of change and individual reaffirmation before reality and art, the decisive intervention in H's life by a new romantic companion, also designated by an initial (M), and who provides a substitute within the life of the protagonist for a previous relationship characterized by mutual indifference, is fundamental; M makes H more sensitive and motivates a new interest in his country's situation, driving him to become involved in the emergent political and social forces of the days before the fall of the Salazarist regime. M functions as a catalyzing agent in H's change: her overwhelmingly positive intervention in the recuperation of the frustrated artist-narrator's self-esteem helps H reach the highest point on the psychological ground prepared by his calligraphic, millimetric self-exam. Without M, H's analytic efforts would never have been crowned; the fact that he arrives at this propitious point in synchrony with the emergence of 25 de Abril merely underscores the positive nature of the entire journey.

Moving from apathy to participation, from insensitivity to love, and from lethargy to activity, the character of H inaugurates a lineage of heroes who are distributed in a regular fashion throughout Saramago's novels: H is echoed—to cite only two examples from the writer's more recent work—in the figure of Raimundo Benvindo Silva, the proofreader in *The History of the Siege of Lisbon*, and in the obscure Sr. José, the clerk in *All the Names*. In terms of feminine characters, *mutatis mutandis*, we see M reflected in the publisher Maria Sara in *The History of the Siege of Lisbon* and in the lost woman who takes her own life in *All the Names*. If the appearance of Maria Sara in the life of Raimundo Benvindo da Silva precipitates his authorial capacity—it is then that the proofreader, who rebels against the official version of history, becomes capable of writing his own "History of the Siege of Lisbon," in a first effort at producing an authorized fiction—the female figure in *All the Names*, even though she is merely a name undisclosed to the reader, becomes a leading light in a quest that obsesses the timid clerk, sparking a true revolution in his life. This elusive figure becomes the Ariadne who, *in absentia*, guides Sr. José when he resolves to confront as an individual and an equal his hierarchical superiors and the authority that emanates from the massive archives at the General Conservatory.

We can thus observe the importance of the conception and configuration of the characters in *Manual of Painting and Calligraphy* in the development of Saramago's novels. Concerning this topic, I'll offer some concluding observations. In the case of H, his anonymity is contrasted with the described process of individuation, the novel becoming in fact a peculiar kind of Bildungsroman, in which the "Bildung" relates more to the uncommon transformations of the middle-aged than to the more typically occurring changes in youth, as opposed to what happened in Goethe's exemplary narrative. On the other hand, perhaps it would not be excessive to establish a link between the portrait-painter turned artist, who purifies himself through the act of writing, and José Saramago himself, who at fifty-four years of age, after having experimented with various literary genres and having performed various activities connected to creative writing such as journalism, translation and literary criticism, finally decides to establish himself as a novelist. There is no other character in Saramago's work, either before or after this second novel, who—bearing in mind differences that arise from the fact that H is not a mask for a veiled exercise of autobiography, and is indeed a fictional character *tout court*—approximates his creator so precisely and from so many different vantage points.

On the other hand, the configuration of Saramago's characters in a tension between the pole of anonymity and greater individual density versus that of nomination and lesser subjective density seems to constitute a vector in a good part of Saramago's recent novels. It is sufficient to recall, with regard to *Blindness*, that the doctor's wife, whose vision, let us say in passing, is like an impalpable Ariadne's string that orients and liberates the prisoners from the city turned into a deconstructed urban labyrinth and a backdrop for the epidemic of "white blindness." She is a character who is not only progressively individualized throughout the narrative, but who in fact facilitates the subjective development of those she leads.

This "individualizing anonymity" becomes one of the qualities that distinguish Saramago's characters. Nevertheless, there are texts in which anonymous characters are described according to their exteriority, excluding any other process of individuation. Both *O Ano de 1993* and the short stories in *Objecto Quase* privilege collective processes. In the majority of these works, the author employs an omniscient point of view, less concerned with accompanying a character in a determined time period—whether at the level of the narrated events or in his or her subjective life—as he is with articulating an external state of things through events related to the character. This point of view also favors an aesthetic and ideological affinity with the literary subgenre of dystopic futuristics established by Wells, Huxley, and Bradbury (and also manifested in some of Saramago's *crónicas* that I have studied elsewhere).[4]

Let us consider, for example, the anonymous character in the short story "Coisas" ("Things"). A clerk without any importance in a society subjected to total bureaucratic control, he is as thinly individualized as Raimundo Benvindo da Silva or Sr. José. However, as opposed to these characters, the "hero" of the story "Coisas" does not "grow," does not transform, we might say, from a larva into a dragonfly; rather, he ends up becoming one of the victims of the rebellion of the objects that, suddenly anthropomorphized, rise and subvert the dominant order. In this "rebellion of the things," the character is not given space to attempt a transformation that would afford him subjectivity; in this soulless world it is easier for objects to gain consciousness and animation than it is for members of the degraded human society. A dynamic similarly lacking in dimension, although equal in metaphoric wisdom, shapes the character in "Embargo," another of the stories in *Objecto Quase* that are couched in an aesthetic and ethical framework of dystopic futurism. Imprisoned in a car seat, in a position that demeans him and reminds the reader of the servitude to which the mechanisms of consumer capitalism reduce the citizen, a man dies, literally, before knowing how to evaluate what has happened to him. Nor do we encounter characters in "Centauro" or "Refluxo" that are comparable to those in *Manual of Painting and Calligraphy.* In each story, the characters—the last centaur on earth in the former, and a capricious King who is fascinated with the construction of cemeteries and mausoleums in the latter—are undoubtedly related to the lineage of protagonists in mythological fables and narratives. However, two of the stories in *Objecto Quase* present characters that are differentiated, as much from one another as with regard to other stories included in the collection.

In the story "The Chair," which from a literary point of view may perhaps be considered the boldest in *Objecto Quase,* Saramago masterfully engages recent history in order to tell, through the prism of cinematographic language and popular culture, the tale of Salazar's fall from a common, everyday summer chair in 1968 in the Forte de Santo António in São João do Estoril, an accident that resulted in the dictator's death. Displaying with notable results the *parti pris* of irony, the writer transforms the *anobideo* insect—which had eaten away at the leg of the chair, an object-turned-instrument used to terminate a dictatorship—into a generic pop-culture protagonist (typical of those in comic book stories): Anobium, a termite species of Tom Mix who, without firing a single shot, yet certain of the efficacy of his *démarche*, is elevated by the author into one of the most deserving heroes in Portuguese history. Under the guise of parody, Anobium's *sui generis* conception is a crucible of information and aesthetics, not to mention the deconstruction of the grandiloquence of redemptive political discourse that such a conception makes possible. Saramago undoubtedly creates one of the narratives in contemporary Portuguese literatures that most directly inculcate the satirical spirit of the *Farpas* of Eça de Queirós and Ramalho Ortigão.

Written in frank language stripped of any extra-literary references, "Desforra" ("Revenge"), the last short story in *Objecto Quase*, narrates the sexual initiation of an adolescent couple in a bucolic, summer setting. In a type of modern *fabliau*, composed not in verse but in clear prose that features a lyrical tone absent from the other stories in the collection (with the exception of "Centauro"), the frog that observes everything and the pig that chews his own testicles after being castrated hold as much importance in the development of the action as the adolescent who avenges the animal, advancing toward the water to enjoy his first sexual experience with a girl hiding in the grove across the brook. In tone, form and content, this story clashes unabashedly with the others in the same collection, taking up what in the context of Saramago's work at large is a recurring theme of probable autobiographical extraction related to life in the rural world, which can also be observed in various *crónicas*.

Curiously, it is the trajectory represented by "Desforra" that comes to bear fruit in Saramago's prose fiction immediately after the publication of *Objecto Quase*. But before we consider *Levantado do Chão*, a novel that takes up once again some key elements in "Desforra," it is convenient to remember the "shadow," or better yet, the progeny that this singular volume of short stories projects upon the subsequent work of Saramago.

While the aesthetics and ethics of dystopic futurism present in "Coisas" and "Embargo" were manifested for the first time in some of the *crónicas* in *Deste Mundo e do Outro* and in *A Bagagem do Viajante*, and encountered their earliest development in *O Ano de 1993*, the successive recuperations of this framework in Saramago's more recent work are notorious. The reading of *Blindness*, for example, is greatly enriched upon returning to the short stories; they deal with the same chaotic, deconstructed city that subjects its inhabitants to a kind of totalizing servitude, as I have had the opportunity to consider at greater length in another essay (Costa 1999). The short story "Refluxo," on the other hand, reappears in *All the Names*: the cemetery in which Sr. José gets lost while searching for his anonymous beloved who has taken her own life reproduces in detail the one that the King in "Refluxo" orders to be built.

These individual examples of auto-intertextuality alert us to the internal cohesion of Saramago's work—at least at the level of the imaginary, to say nothing of the linguistic or stylistic formulation per se—and thus of the importance of the first works produced during his so-called "formative period." In light of these examples, it is possible to discern a means to understand the path followed by Saramago in his writing before and after 1980, the year in which *Levantado do Chão* was published. An important aspect of his narrative from 1980 on has to do with fictional situations that recreate, amplify, and develop preexisting constructs, as if his work consisted of fragments in constant internal evolution. The writer himself appears to refer to this dynamic in an indirect way during the 1980s in a reedition of his poetry collection *Os Poemas Possíveis*, when he comments in the prologue that the contemporary reader will encounter in them "connections, themes and obsessions" which reemerge in his later work.[5]

Correspondingly, the same can be said in relation to the creation of Saramago's characters. At the same time, in *Levantado do Chão*, this panorama—perhaps more ideal than real, given the intrinsic complexity of the writer's use of fictional discourse, employed in different ways in each of his novels—this panorama of successive auto-intertextualities, carefully and conscientiously reworked, is interrupted. In fact, *Levantado do Chão* can be viewed as a book of rupture, of self-rupture, if you will.

On the one hand, everything functions as if the author's concern in conceiving various generations of Mau-Tempos, the heroes of the story, owed more to a dialogue with the Portuguese Neo-Realist tradition of novel writing than to the assemblage of important characters generated in the first part of his work and reclaimed in Saramago's more recent novels, particularly in the cases discussed above. On the other hand, one cannot forget that *Levantado do Chão* emerged out of Saramago's direct contact with rural workers during his 1975 sojourn in Alentejo, as the writer has had occasion to confirm more than once.[6] This quality of "empiricism," so to speak, in the narrative's genesis differentiates this novel from the others. I will return to this point later in the essay.

Thus, in spite of the importance of the Mau-Tempos within the sum total of Saramago's work, these characters seem to remain, at the level of narrative plotting, relatively isolated from the rest. This fact, debatable as it may be, corroborates the precarious assertion that this book seems to establish its most significant dialogue not with recent novelistic production but rather with key novels of Portuguese Neo-Realism, such as Alves Redol's *Barranco de Cegos* (1961), to name just one example, in spite of many notable differences between the two works.

I will pursue a parenthetical thought in order to clarify this problematic assertion. The relationship between *Levantado do Chão* and Portuguese Neo-Realism can be, *en passant*, compared to that of *Grande Sertão: Veredas* in the context of Brazilian literature. Both books are terminal apexes of vigorous literary currents that have predated them. The nineteenth-century regionalist fiction of Brazil, taken up and elaborated by the so-called "Northeastern cycle" of novels by Jorge Amado, Lins de Rego, and Graciliano Ramos, arrives at its (glorious) end and concomitant surpassing in Guimarães Rosa's work. So too the Neo-Realist currents that had predominated in the prose of Portuguese fiction for decades, with profound roots in Portuguese realism and naturalism, must recognize, in Saramago's *Levantado do Chão*, their ultimate and fundamental crystallization, as well as their subsequent literary overcoming.

Obviously, there are great differences at the level of writing between *Levantado do Chão* and *Barranco de Cegos*—that is, between the work in which Saramago breaks with his own narrative tradition and what is perhaps the most significant, if not paradigmatic, Portuguese Neo-Realist novel. As opposed to the still conventional literary discourse employed by Redol (with the exception of the novel's third part, "O Livro das Horas Absurdas"), José Saramago for the first time in his fiction seems to yearn to give his characters speech. In summary, the discourse—served by a much greater lexicalization, following the use of orality (or of "aurality," as the writer terms this very important seasoning in the chemistry of his texts)—is injected as it were into the characters, generating the definitive appearance of a distinct narrative voice, underscored by an original form of diacritical marking that from this novel forward will characterize the rhythm of Saramago's prose. Clearly, unlike H, who writes his diary/manual/deposition, the Mau Tempos speak through the narrator.

As in *O Ano de 1993*, the theme of authoritarianism and its overthrow flourishes with undeniable originality in *Levantado do Chão*. Thus, as we have already observed, if in that fragmentary text there are no characters in the usual sense of the word, and if the few human figures that appear in it are distinguished by the anonymous "functionality" of "agents of historical transformation," in this novel, although the characters are defined by their historical placement since narration is marked by precise temporal delineation, they come imbued with personality of their own. In the story, which condenses the peasant saga of the Mau-Tempos—a clan that from a markedly sociological point of view could be considered as a multi-faceted, collective "macro-character"—Saramago scrutinizes the generational and temperamental differences between the characters. In addition to obvious distinctions—e.g., parents who differ from their children, wives from granddaughters, employers from employees, the young from the old—every opportunity of establishing an individualizing economy is explored by the writer in an effort to capture through literature the human plurality masked by the classist, homogenizing notion of the rural worker.

Perhaps the most complex character in the novel, who boldly illustrates the above point, is Domingos Mau-Tempo, "a sad, disgraced man" (59) as the narrator defines him, a peasant shoemaker driven to suicide by the double circumstance of his social condition and volatile temperament, and whom the narrative resuscitates sixty years later in order to make him participate in a final workers' march toward political affirmation as a defined social class during the revolutionary period. The narrator's game of unveiling these characters' internal dimension is described in the following way by Teresa Cristina Cerdeira da Silva, with specific reference to Domingos Mau-Tempo:

> Following one of his unwise decisions, after he runs away to Ladeira with his entire family, the narrator analyzes his attitude as someone who sees inside the character, anxious for a freedom he did not possess. Because of this very dynamic, acting in a way that sets him apart from the others, the narrator gives him speech so that he may analyze himself. (233-34)

Silva continues with a revealing quotation from the novel:

> but Domingos Mau-Tempo could stand neither speech nor silence, and dragging himself too late to Ladeira, in the extreme west of the county, like a bird that throws itself against iron bars, what prison is this, my soul with thirty demons. (*Levantado do Chão* 29)

As opposed to H or M, and in perfect opposition to the characters in *Objecto Quase*, these peasants, who move toward redemption, toward a positive socio-historical transformation, and whose avatars are accompanied by a narrator profoundly identified with them in solidarity, reveal to the reader, in the spaces in which speech has been given to them through the use of free indirect discourse, a consistent capacity for fantasy mixed with an objective and often critical apprehension of the surrounding reality.

In this sense, the place of the Mau-Tempos in Saramago's fiction is similar to that of the protagonists of *Manual of Painting and Calligraphy* (principally H). Thus, assuming just for a moment that the clan of rural workers in *Levantado do Chão* constitutes a type of collective character, we encounter here the two arch-characters of the writer's later work.

After the experience of writing *Levantado do Chão*, Saramago was in a position to profit completely from the creation of his fictional characters. Within the magnificent textual mass of *Baltasar and Blimunda*, the clairvoyant Blimunda and the soldier Baltasar Sete-Sóis can be viewed as extensions of the characters in *Levantado do Chão*, yet even more fictionalized, if possible, and with the following proviso: between the lived experience at the basis of *Levantado do Chão*, owing to which narrative invention blends with what the writer presumably heard with his own ears, and the conception of fictional characters in *Baltasar and Blimunda*, there is a *plongée* in the literalizing imaginary. If the Mau-Tempos emerged from or were inspired by real sources, if at the origin of the oralization-auralization of *Levantado do Chão* there is a confrontation between the author-narrator and verifiable reality (in which, to draw a parallel, Saramago assumes an authorial stance privileged, for instance, by the "regionalist literature" of the nineteenth and early twentieth centuries), in *Baltasar and Blimunda* the author relies on literary-historical information, as can be deduced from the relationship between the character of Blimunda and the data pertaining to the history of Portugal in the Baroque period.

As I have outlined in a previous essay, the conception of Blimunda draws on historical information, in the form of a travel account of Baroque Portugal by a Frenchman with the suggestive name of Chevalier Charles Frédéric de Merveilleux. The text was published in Amsterdam in 1732 and translated into Portuguese (after the publication of Saramago's novel) by Castelo Branco Neves in *O Portugal de D. Jõao V Visto por Três Forasteiros* (1983). Merveilleux refers to the wife of a Gascon resident in Portugal, a certain Madame

Pedegache, who "possessed the ability to see into the interior of the human body since her youth," adding that "she only enjoyed this marvelous gift when fasting" (160-62). It is not important to know for certain if this eighteenth-century medium was the exact source of Blimunda's character, or if Saramago had encountered related information in documents at the Torre do Tombo or other historical archives. What is important in any case, however, is to emphasize the distinct authorial attitude that informs the conception and development of the plot, and, particularly, of some of the novel's characters—an attitude absent from both *Levantado do Chão* and *Manual of Painting and Calligraphy*, to say nothing of Saramago's *crónicas* and poems. In *Baltasar and Blimunda*, there exists a new authorial method and a new writerly horizon, clearly related to the articulation of history and fiction and the novel's imbrication within a certain lineage of contemporary narrative. In this sense, it would be particularly profitable to analyze the convergence of Saramago's new authorial attitude with a large number of twentieth-century Spanish-American novels, particularly those of Alejo Carpentier.

If we add to the above the "shadow" cast over the novel by the stylistics of the Portuguese literary Baroque—especially the model of Padre António Vieira's prose—we can confirm that in *Baltasar and Blimunda* José Saramago brings to full fruition a precise and well-founded literary trajectory.

From Maria Leonor to Blimunda, Saramago's unique trajectory demonstrates the obvious importance of binding the conception of the fictional character to the production of fully realized, and therefore literarized, novelistic language. The fact that the reiteration of this link (an interesting topic in and of itself) may be demonstrated with regard to the most important body of prose writing in Portuguese in the second half of the twentieth century calls our attention to yet another intrinsic asset of Saramago's work, which in its extraordinary quality allows and solicits the reader to establish multiple vectors of reading. I have attempted to explore one of these vectors throughout my essay; if the exploratory effort has invited and incited others to share in this endeavor, then my intention has been fully realized.

Notes

[1] [Translator's note] I have retained the term "crónica" in its original Portuguese throughout the text because I believe there to be no equivalent genre in the Anglophone tradition.

[2] In fact, it would be interesting to establish a correspondence between *Manual* and the French *nouveau roman.* Let us only recall the supplanting of the subjectively imagined character by the character objectively considered, whose status has been much discussed. This surpassing was extolled by Alain Robbe-Grillet in some of his most important and programmatic books vigorously debated at the time of Manual's publication. The essay "Pour un nouveau roman," published in 1963, for example, was at the time virtually required reading. But a study of the relationship between Saramago's novel and modern French literature would warrant development beyond the scope of the present essay.

[3] See, in this regard, Giorgio Agamben's *Stanze.*

[4] I refer the interested reader to my study *José Saramago: O Período Formativo*, in which I develop the points elaborated here, principally in chapter 3, "Da Poesia à Prosa: Saramago Cronista—*Deste Mundo e do Outro* e *A Bagagem do Viajante*" (85-116), and in chapters 6 and 7, "Produção Textual e Experimentação em O Ano de 1993 e 'O Ouvido'" and "A Reconquista da Prosa: *Manual de Pintura* e *Objecto Quase*" (211-349).

[5] "There was a poetic constant in the work... that legitimated the resuscitation of this book, because in it one can begin to define connections, themes, and obsessions that have become the structurally invariable backbone of a metamorphosing body of writing" ("Nota da 2a Edição," *Os Poemas Possíveis* 13).

[6] Saramago made this assertion during an interview I conducted with him at the Mexican Institute in Madrid in February 1998, later published in São Paulo ("José Saramago: o Despertar da Palavra"). In this interview, Saramago speaks explicitly of *Levantado do Chão*'s genesis, concomitant with the genesis of a particular form of narrating that from then on takes root in his writing: "I think that this happened because without knowing it, in the act of writing, I suddenly found myself in their place [the rural workers from the Alentejo who inspired the conception of Mau-Tempo], only now I narrate to them what they had narrated to me" (23).

Works Cited

Agamben, Giorgio. *Stanze. La parola e il fantasma nella cultura occidentale.* Milan: Einaudi, 1977.

Chaves, Castelo Branco, ed. *O Portugal de D. João Visto por Três Forasteiros.* Lisboa: Biblioteca Nacional, 1983.

Costa, Horácio. "Alegorias da Desconstrução Urbana: *The Memoirs of a Survivor*, de Doris Lessing, e *Ensaio sobre a Cegueira*, de José Saramago." *José Saramago. Uma Homenagem.* Org. Beartiz Berrini. São Paulo: EDUC (PUC-SP), 1999, 127-48.

———. *José Saramago: O Período Formativo.* Lisboa: Caminho, 1997.

Saramago, José. Interview with Horácio Costa. "José Saramago: o Despertar da Palavra." *Cult* 17 (Dez.1998): 16-24.

———. *Levantado do Chão.* Lisboa: Caminho,1980.

———. *Manual de Pintura e Caligrafia.* Lisboa: Moraes, 1976. English translation by Giovanni Pontiero, *Manual of Painting and Calligraphy*, Manchester: Carcanet, 1993.

———. *Memorial do Convento.* Lisboa: Caminho, 1982. English translation by Giovanni Pontiero, *Baltasar and Blimunda*, San Diego: Harcourt, 1987.

———. *Objecto Quase.* Lisbon: Moraes, 1978.

———. *Os Poemas Possíveis.* Lisboa: Caminho, 1982.

———. *Terra do Pecado.* Lisboa: Minerva, 1947.

Silva, Teresa Cristina Cerdeira da. *José Saramago. Entre a História e a Ficção: Uma Saga de Portugueses*. Lisboa: Dom Quixote, 1989.

José Saramago's Historical Fiction

Adriana Alves de Paula Martins
Translated by
Elena Zagar Galvão

It is best to be wary of what we see or think we see.
Saramago, *Deste Mundo e do Outro*

The past is filled with voices which cannot keep quiet and alongside my shadow there is an endless multitude of people justifying it.
Saramago, *A Bagagem do Viajante*

Everything in the world is giving us answers, what has not yet arrived is the time to ask questions.
Saramago, *Baltasar and Blimunda*

José Saramago's mastery of different literary genres is widely recognized; it is the novel, however, that undoubtedly constitutes his favorite genre.[1] My aim in this article is precisely to concentrate on Saramago's novels. Taking into account the development of the author's literary project, I will devote my attention particularly to his historical fiction, that is, to the novels in which Saramago explicitly uses history as his narrative subject. These novels are *Levantado do Chão* (*Raised from the Ground*, 1980), *Baltasar and Blimunda* (1982), *The Year of the Death of Ricardo Reis* (1984), and *The History of the Siege of Lisbon* (1989). All these works reflect, in different ways, on the past of the Portuguese nation, seen from a present perspective while a process of revision of the history of Portugal unfolds within the fictional text. This process translates into the adoption of an attitude that seeks to rewrite and to correct history, and is made possible by conjecturing about the supposed objectivity of historical discourse and the representation of events it gives. This reappreciation of Portuguese history gives rise not only to an analysis of the intimate relations between the writing of history and political power, but also to an epistemological and ideological examination of the historical, human, linguistic, literary, ethical and political heritage of the Portuguese nation.

On the basis of the above-mentioned *corpus*, and considering Saramago's special attraction to history, I will attempt to demonstrate that his historical fiction reflects the writer's politics of representation, which are characteristic of postmodern fiction in general. It is a literary production that seeks to understand a complex and constantly evolving present by turning to the past, to the writing of history, and to the ways in which our knowledge about the past is processed and transmitted. Thus, I will propose a typology of postmodern historical fiction, through which I will show how the different fictional representations of historical events and characters in Saramago's novels, while promoting the dialogue between fiction and historical discourse, suggest the notion that literary and historical representation are both political constructions whose logic is challenged by the fictional text itself.[2]

Focusing our attention on postmodern fiction, we identify two great trends resulting from the same need, namely, the need to investigate empirical reality and the ways in which it is interpreted and represented. Ever since the end of World War Two, human beings have struggled to come to terms with a profound sense of anguish caused, on the one hand, by the many attempts to annihilate the human subject in the various conflicts happening throughout the world, and, on the other, by the uncertainty about the truthfulness of our representations of the empirical world. More specifically I am referring, first, to the great interest in the past that literary fiction has taken, which manifests itself especially in the rejection of a clear distinction between truth and fiction and between past and present (Fokkema), and, second, to the attention that literary works dedicate, in a process of self-reflection, to fiction itself, i.e., to the linguistic and literary conventions underlying its construction. The former literary trend is connected with the production of different types of historical fiction where the dialogue between fiction and history predominates; the latter has to do with the experimental character of literature, revealed through the great interest in the aesthetic use of language to create literary texts, as well as through the predominance granted to metafiction.

Though recognizing the important role played by experimental fiction, the objectives of this essay clearly restrict my analysis to the former literary trend. The degree of interest in the past that literature has taken has helped pave the way to granting the same degree of credibility to the different representations of reality provided by historical and fictional discourse.[3] It is important to note that fiction and history were regarded for a long time as completely separate domains, on the premise that fictional discourse dealt with so-called imaginary referents whereas historical discourse had to do with supposedly real referents. This conferred a status of truth on the latter type of discourse alone, even when the former made explicit reference to chronologically precise historical periods reconstructed with the utmost accuracy.[4] In other words, it was as if only history could be deemed certain in relation to empirical reality, while fiction was relegated to the domain of fortune, that is, to the realm of the merely possible. This situation was mostly the result of the belief in historiography as based on documentary record, without questioning, however, either its validity or the criteria that guided the selection of the documents, or the way in which the historiographer used them.[5]

The dialogue between fiction and history takes on special significance when narrative discourse starts working as a sort of a "seam" (Bessière), that is, as a link between fictional and historical representation, destroying the status of certainty that had, until then, characterized historical discourse. The "seam" becomes visible when historians distinguish the presence of a verbal structure, in the form of a narrative discourse, in the historical task of explaining the structures and processes of the past (White, *Metahistory* 2). As Hayden White aptly summarizes, a narrative "is not merely a neutral discursive form that may or may not be used to represent real events in their aspect as developmental processes, but rather entails ontological and epistemic choices with distinct ideological and even political implications" (*Content* ix), an observation that calls our attention to the partial and fragmented character of history as well as to the interrelations between history, fiction, and politics.[6] The notion of historical truth is thus irremediably compromised, and it becomes possible to regard history as a space for the configuration of different possibilities, that is, to accept the fact that history does not proceed in one single direction and that a given event "happens within a range of possibilities and, as a realization or a translation of a given possibility, is not entirely contained in its determinations"

(Gusmão 89). This statement reminds us of the distinction between *facts* and *events* that Linda Hutcheon makes in relation to postmodern literature, highlighting both history and fiction as human mental constructions, systems of signification through which we can understand the past (*Poetics* 89). According to Hutcheon, the meaning of the past does not lie in the events, but rather in the meaning(s)-producing systems that transform these past events into historical facts.[7]

Considering that novelists' interest in the past is not an exclusive prerogative of postmodern writers and that such interest underlies the mimetic process itself—if *mimesis* is what Barbara Foley suggests, i.e., a "*mode of cognition*, enacted through a generic contract of which the purpose is to interpret and evaluate past or present historical actuality" (64; original emphasis)—we have to question ourselves as to the innovative character of postmodern historical fiction. This innovation is closely linked with the way in which we regard the old relation of opposition between fact and fiction.[8] In fact, historians and novelists alike have come to understand historical facts as the result of human mental constructions arising from the different possible representations of a certain event. This position leads to a significant blurring of the line separating fact from fiction and allows for a dialogue between historical and fictional discourse as representations of the empirical world that draw our attention to the unstable nature of these representations. Within this dialogue, it is important to consider the potentiality and the viability of some fictional techniques, described by Maria Alzira Seixo (*Lugares* 84), in the modification of the symbolic and ideological scope of both historical and fictional representation. The most significant of these techniques are: introducing unexpected, imaginary, or fantastic events into the narrative; elaborating certain fictional characters; and using heritage in its multiple forms as a parodic tool to reconstruct the past, correct history and (re)write it. In view of the above, let us consider the following proposal for a typology of the main trends of postmodern historical fiction.

Starting from the assumption that quite a large range of historical fictions appeared in the second half of the twentieth century, I propose the following typology, composed of four main types of novels that incorporate historical matter and transform the past and written history into their subject. What interests me above all is to observe the different meanings created by the transformation of history into narrative matter, especially with regard to Saramago's works. It is important to note that this proposal is simply an attempt to approach and classify postmodern historical fictions and, therefore, it needs to be seen as a starting rather than a finishing point within a still ongoing research project. Thus, it neither excludes different readings and approaches nor denies the possibility of discovering other historical fictions likely to introduce changes in this typology and to lead to its rearrangement.

The first type is the historical novel. This denomination arises for the following reasons: first, the novel is modeled after historiography and focuses on history's process of change; second, it follows events, respecting the canonical version of history; and, finally, it projects external reality in a detailed and rigorous way through its characters (both fictional and historical). The denomination was chosen because this type of novel represents, as it were, a development of two models: the nineteenth-century historical novel, which followed the pattern set by Walter Scott, and modernist historical fiction. In other words, I believe that postmodern historical novels inherited a concern with reconstructing the past with rigor and detail from nineteenth-century historical fiction, taking on a role that seeks to complement historiography while affirming their character as fictional works with a potential to depict history in a creative and attractive way. On the other hand, postmodern historical novels show similarities with modernist narratives that focused on the past. Indeed, the postmodern model performs not only the didactic function of disseminating knowledge about history through fiction, but also the eminently critical function of making frequent and explicit comments of a metahistorical and metafictional nature. These comments are used above all to draw attention to the relativity of historiography and to the verbal translation of empirical data. However, whereas modernist historical fiction stressed the subjective process of shaping the experience and consciousness of history, what I have termed postmodern historical fiction highlights not so much the writing of history as, rather, the process of construction and affirmation of one specific version of history, with its consequent political and ideological implications. In other words, this type of novel is more interested in investigating the motives that led, *a posteriori*, to the historical record of a certain event than in the event *per se*. This interest draws our attention to two factors: the partial and subjective nature of historical knowledge and explanation, and the likelihood of there being diverging views on the same event, which in its turn calls into question the legitimacy of historical sources. An example illustrating this first type of postmodern historical fiction is Gore Vidal's series *American Chronicle*, which is composed of six novels tracing the history of the United States from its foundation as an independent nation until the mid-twentieth century.[9]

The second type of postmodern historical fiction corresponds to novels combining historical data with elements that are characteristic of the fantastic genre, as interpreted by Seixo (*Lugares* 51-52). For this Portuguese critic, the use of fantastic elements in contemporary fiction allows

> first, **the interference of two worlds** *or* **two orders**—the natural and the supernatural, the rational and the irrational—where it is unclear which of the two converts into the other; second, the category of **alterity** that results from this interference (and which takes on various configurations such as ghost, spirit, double personality, etc.), with special emphasis on the *proximity* of this *otherness* which would be expressed, in logical terms, as a *non-disjunction*, giving rise to a second level of double entities functioning in the opposite way; third, the inclusion of elements of the **unusual**, which upsets the system previously organized by the *doxa*, and provokes specific reading reactions (of the characters in relation to the facts, of the readers towards the fictional work) ranging from curiosity to fear, from perplexity to terror, and from bewilderment to the mesmerizing attraction that Duarte Faria calls "*assombro*" ["awe, dread"], a simultaneously physical and mental attitude of awe and wonder. (*Lugares* 52)[10]

In this type of historical fiction, there are no deviations from official history, and the common strategies used to highlight empirical reality and the instability of its representation are the comparison between different orders and the circulation of certain characters through various worlds and time periods.

Although Seixo (*Lugares* 52) distinguishes between the fantastic genre and other contiguous genres (such as, for instance, fantasy, science fiction and horror fiction), in the second category of my typology I include elements that historical fiction typically borrows from science fiction. The reason for this inclusion is that the degree of alterity needed to deconstruct possible mythifications of historical discourse is often introduced into works of historical fiction by referring to worlds and ways of living that are completely different from those experienced in everyday life.[11]

It is interesting to note that literary criticism generally finds it difficult to classify the novels that belong to this second category of postmodern historical fiction, or rather, given their generic permeability, to choose a fitting label for them. On the one hand, it is not pertinent to regard them as historical novels, if we bear in mind the abovementioned characteristics of this category. On the other, it would be hasty to classify them as fantastic novels *tout court*, because, although they invite a flight into alternative worlds, they respect the canonical version of history by referring, directly or indirectly, to the real world. Thus, it is more functional to give them the more encompassing denomination of supra-real historical fiction, which alludes both to the incorporation of historical material and to the reference to the possible existence of one (or more) world(s) organized according to rules that are different from those governing the empirical world.[12] It is this very sense of estrangement caused by alternative ways of life that sheds light on the complexity of human existence and its relations. Typical examples of this type of historical fiction are José Saramago's *Baltasar and Blimunda* and *The Year of the Death of Ricardo Reis*, which will be discussed below. An illustration of supra-real fiction incorporating elements characteristic of science fiction is Kurt Vonnegut's *Slaughterhouse-Five or The Children's Crusade* (1969).

The third type of novel in the typology proposed here corresponds to what Elisabeth Wesseling has called "uchronian fiction," that is, those works that, while using history as their narrative subject, propose alternative histories on the basis of a series of events that did not take place, but which could have. Uchronian novels have a counterfactual character, as they are based on the notion that any historical situation could have developed within a framework of possibilities different from those that are socially and historically accepted. This type of novel resembles the other two. On the one hand, just like historical novels, it uses canonical history as its source; on the other, it finds inspiration in elements and discursive modes that are typical of the fantastic genre and of science fiction. In other words, in conceiving a uchronian novel, the writer resorts to the creation of possible alternative worlds that, when they intersect with the literary model of the real, draw attention to the need to establish a new relation with history.

This type of fiction places special emphasis on the process of constructing history, on its writing, and on the transformation of events into facts, attributing great importance to the sources and archives of official history. These are parodied and subverted in the projection of a different course of events, which is consequently represented by a character who often plays a role equivalent to that of a historian. Underlying this process is the need to call the reader's attention to the fact that historiography, being a verbal representation of reality, can be corrected, which, in its turn, stresses the uncertain and provisional character of history and of the notion of historical truth. An example of this category is José Saramago's novel *The History of the Siege of Lisbon* (1989), to which we will return below.

It seems appropriate to include another novel by Saramago in this category: *The Gospel According to Jesus Christ* (1991). Indeed, in this text, the importance of rewriting and correcting history derives from a rereading of the Bible and from the presentation of a different version of Jesus Christ's life. The literary text reveals a Christ who is, above all, human, as are all the other members of his family. It is a Christ who loves his companion as any other man loves a woman whom he has chosen to share his life; a Christ who does not hesitate to question God's love for his Son and for human beings in general; a Christ able to question the possible reasons underlying his mission, a mission that he supposedly has to fulfil through a sacrifice that he did not choose, but for which he was chosen. These are but a few examples of the changes that this work of fiction introduces in Christ's life on the basis of its rereading of the Bible, which is seen here, above all, as a historical document. This interpretation of the biblical text, on the other hand, does not prevent the novel from establishing a new dynamic in the relation between the sacred and the fictional, through the suggestion that God is, as stated by Wladimir Krysinski in his analysis of this work by Saramago, "a structure of power, a superstructure of manipulation, a construction of inequality" (403).[13]

The fourth type of historical fiction in my typology is historiographic metafiction, a denomination made popular by Linda Hutcheon, who has regarded it as the representative model of the postmodern novel. However, here I will use this concept in a more limited sense, largely because I consider Hutcheon's proposal to be too inclusive. In my opinion, what this author regards as the representative model of the postmodern novel comprises only the novels belonging to the first category of postmodern fiction I identified at the beginning of this discussion, that is to say fiction that is interested in the past and in the rewriting of history. Novels like *If on a Winter's Night a Traveler* (1979) by Italo Calvino and *Duluth* (1983) by Gore Vidal, which are postmodern texts and undoubtedly self-reflexive, but which do not evoke history, clearly call into question Hutcheon's theoretical premise. These two novels, although making use of different fictional techniques (the discussion of which goes beyond the scope of this article), are a good illustration of the reflection on the (im)possibility of escaping from the prison of language in representing the empirical world. Moreover, they challenge not only the limits imposed by literary and linguistic conventions, but also the established reading protocols, including, in the case of Vidal's novel, the conventions and protocols characteristic of postmodernism.

Therefore, the term "historiographic metafiction" is used here to consider a type of novel that, combining elements of self-reflection and historical evocation based on the belief that both history and fiction are human constructions, reassesses and rewrites past forms and contents always from a present perspective (Hutcheon, *Poetics* 5). In other words, in adopting Hutcheon's concept, I refer only to those fictional narratives that, without resorting to elements and discursive modes of the fantastic genre or science fiction and without deviating from historical facts (as do uchronian novels), promote a dialogue with historical and/or literary intertexts and draw attention to their own internal structure. Examples of this category are John Fowles's *The French Lieutenant's Woman* (1969) and José Saramago's *Levantado do Chão.*

Levantado do Chão is an interesting case of historiographic metafiction.[14] The predominant historical intertext corresponds to the events that marked the twentieth century in the world and, more specifically, in Portugal: the foundation of the Republic, World War I, Salazar's Estado Novo, the Spanish Civil War, World War II, the Portuguese Colonial War, and the April Revolution of 1974. All these events are seen through the eyes of various generations of a poor peasant family from Alentejo and are filtered through a narrator who critically analyses historical facts from a present viewpoint. The narrator maintains that "all this can be told in a different way" (14), thus summarizing one of the main themes of the novel: the recording of the stories of the people whom official history has chosen not to hear, or even to silence. Fiction can thus vindicate a new way of writing history and—why not—a new way of making history.[15] The metafictional component is not, however, as explicit as in Fowles's novel. This component takes on an increasing significance within *Levantado do Chão* through the narrator's voice, which compares the official and unofficial versions of history; the former corresponds to the discourses of the clergy, the landowners and the state, and the latter to the peasants' discourse.

Levantado do Chão discusses the ideological writing of official history by playing with two intertexts that are well known to its potential Portuguese readership: the literary and the biblical. Teresa Cristina Cerdeira da Silva identifies the novel's heroes, the Alentejan farmhands, with the "heirs of the old epic," seeing them as the "distinguished barons" of the "inland sea" epic, that is, of Alentejo, a clear allusion to Camões's *The Lusiads* (*José Saramago* 193-94 and 230). Silva also shows how biblical language (which appears in the novel, especially in the sermons of Father Agamedes and the other priests, all of whom share the same name, an indication of the uniformity of the clergy's discourse) served the interests of both the State and the landowners by helping them preserve their privileges and oppress the peasants economically and politically (Silva, "O Quinto Evangelho" and "Do Labirinto"). The novel's innovation consists in enriching the historical intertext with the oral version of facts presented by the farmers, given that there are no written historical documents laid down by those whom the novel wishes to "raise from the ground." The oral testimony of those who have been silenced by official historiography thus acquires the status of historical testimony within the literary text. It is precisely by confronting the voices of power (represented by the landowners, the church and the state) with the voices stifled by the dominant classes that the novel uncovers both the project of the perpetuation of injustice and social inequality and that of the battle against it through a progressive raising of political and social awareness in those who have the courage to fight to make themselves heard. In sum, *Levantado do Chão* is a fictional text that rereads and rewrites Portuguese history in a politically and socially committed way (Seixo, *Lugares* 125-27), thereby drawing attention to the need for a more humanized history. It is a history that demands the presence of those who go through this world without leaving any mark, a constant claim in Saramago's fictional production.

Considering my proposal for a typology of the main trends of postmodern historical fiction in more general terms, it is important to note the problematic underlying the four great types of novel that make up the typology, i.e., *error, deformation* and *correction*, or, in other words, the consciousness that any representation of the past, being a linguistic construction, can be manipulated ideologically. Hence the necessity to tell what has already been told in a different way. These different ways of telling and writing are exactly what my typology seeks to encompass, emphasizing in all of them the importance of the consciousness of alterity, manifested through the adoption of the Other's point of view in the narrative (the Other who has been forsaken by history, the Other who has been offended by official historiography, the Other who presents a version that history tries to destroy at all costs).[16] Each type of novel proposes different discursive formulations, which correspond to different ways of representing the empirical world symbolically. Presiding over these modalities is a common concern based on three components: the pedagogical, epistemological, and politico-ideological, which correspond, respectively, to the fictional text's teaching about the past as seen from multiple viewpoints; discussing problems related to how the past is learned and represented; and promoting a reflection on the ways in which various versions of history function as power mechanisms (in the past and in the present). In short, and to paraphrase the quotation from *Baltasar and Blimunda* that appears in the epigraph to this article, there are different ways of formulating questions to the answers that the world gives us.[17]

It is important to return now to the category that I have termed the postmodern historical novel, since in the other categories it is usually the narrator who dictates the rules of the "game" that combines the present (of the enunciation) with the past. It is the narrator who frequently tells about past events long after their occurrence, and who knows better than all the other characters the course of historical events and the impact they will have on the narrative and on the empirical reality. Thus it is most commonly the narrator who ingeniously regulates the mechanisms of analepsis and prolepsis, the introduction of anachronisms, and the announcing of prophecies, which act within the limits of the expectations of the potential readers of literary texts, prefiguring, to a great extent, the symbolic dimension of literary representation. Given all the above, it is pertinent to ask the reasons for the inclusion of a category called "historical novel" in our proposal for a typology of postmodern historical fiction. Seixo's observation with regard to Saramago's novels provides an answer to that question. Reflecting on the great significance of history in Saramago's works, the critic maintains that his historical fiction is constructed "thinking about the present much more than about the past that constitutes its object" (*Lugares* 55). Nonetheless, we cannot forget the existence of historical fictions such as the abovementioned works of Gore Vidal. In these novels, the narrators (usually fictional characters whose existence is not historically documented) do not inscribe the author's present perspective in the plane of enunciation (here it would be interesting to analyze in detail how each narrator in the novels that illustrate the different categories of our typology introduces a present perspective to be compared with the past). In sum, it is on the basis of the novels composing Vidal's representative *American Chronicle* that I identify three key features that lead me to propose the category I have called the postmodern historical novel: one, respect for the canonized version of History (even though underlying this series is the postmodern concern for unveiling and interpreting the ideological meanings that inform the distortions in the representation of, for instance, North American political history); two, exclusion of the present from the plane of enunciation (the present is here understood as the period in which the author writes each novel in the series); and, three, the use of introductions, prefaces, postscripts and notes, in which the author marks out the boundaries of what is fictional and what is historically documented in his novels.

From now on, I will focus my attention exclusively on the part of Saramago's literary production that uses the history of Portugal as its subject. This will enable me to consider the specificity of the novels belonging to the categories of supra-real historical fiction and uchronian fiction. What interests me above all is to see how the boundary is drawn between *this* world (the real world which is modeled by historical discourse) and the *other* world, which incorporates elements from the fantastic genre and creates alternative fictional worlds.[18] I will examine to what extent this boundary allows a glimpse into the epistemological and ideological analysis of the heritage of the Portuguese nation, considered here in its various components: historical (relevant historical events recorded in the novels); human (historical figures transformed into fictional characters, and the people who achieve the status of equality as regards their place in history); linguistic (the retrieval of a popular voice neglected by official historiography and the metalinguistic observations that frequently appear in the novels); literary (intertextuality with representative Portuguese authors and texts, such as Camões, Almeida Garrett, Eça de Queirós, a process that reaches its zenith with Fernando Pessoa and his heteronyms); and ethico-political (the frailties and contradictions of political power caused by personal vanity and power-hungry alliances). Thus, I propose to consider, on the one hand, where and how fantastic elements enter *Baltasar and Blimunda* and *The Year of the Death of Ricardo Reis* (that is, where and how historical fiction becomes supra-real) and, on the other hand, where and how *The History of the Siege of Lisbon* becomes a uchronian novel. To this effect, I have selected the following passages on which to comment: chapter five of *Baltasar and*

Blimunda; chapter one of *The Year of the Death of Ricardo Reis*; and chapters two and three of *The History of the Siege of Lisbon.*

Chapter five of *Baltasar and Blimunda* contains a detailed description of the first auto-da-fé in the novel, when Blimunda, Baltasar, and Bartolomeu Lourenço meet for the first time. These three characters will be responsible for building Father Bartolomeu's airship, a realistic project within the historical context of eighteenth-century Portugal (although there is no historical evidence that the actual airship did fly), which, in the overall framework of the novel, will run parallel to the construction of the Mafra Convent as the fulfillment of a pledge made by the king, Dom João V, in return for the queen giving him an heir. However, no mention is made of the airship in chapter five of the novel, which deals with a special encounter between a crippled soldier, Baltasar Mateus, and Blimunda, simple people who apparently are brought together while watching the procession of those accused by the Inquisition. Their meeting is somehow contrived by a gagged woman in the procession. She is Sebastiana de Jesus, who has visions and revelations, and who feels her heart jump when she is about to locate her daughter Blimunda in the middle of the crowd. The supernatural is introduced in the novel through this character, while the potential present in Blimunda's eyes is suggested in the following passage:

> At last my heart has given me a sign—my heart has given a deep sigh. I am about to see Blimunda, I am about to see her. Ah, there she is. Blimunda, Blimunda, Blimunda, my child. She has seen me but cannot speak, she must pretend that she does not recognize me, or even pretend to despise me, a mother who is bewitched and excommunicated, although no more than a quarter Jewess and converted. She sees me, and at her side is Padre Bartolomeu Lourenço. Do not speak, Blimunda. Just look at me with those eyes of yours, which have the power to see everything. Who can that tall stranger be who stands beside Blimunda? She does not know—alas, she does not know who he can be or where he comes from. Whatever will become of them? Why do my powers fail me? Judging from his tattered clothes, that harrowed expression, that missing hand, he must be a soldier. Farewell, Blimunda, for I shall see you no more. Blimunda said to the priest: That's my mother. Then, turning to the tall man standing beside her, she asked: What is your name? And the man immediately told her, thus acknowledging that this woman had a right to ask him. He told her: Baltasar Mateus, called Sete-Sóis. (39)

It is in this same chapter that Blimunda and Baltasar are united through a marriage ritual that is directed by the young woman and violates the laws of Catholicism. I am referring to Blimunda's use of the blood of her lost virginity to cross herself and to draw a cross on the soldier's chest, thus sealing a union that will come to an end many years later, during another auto-da-fé, in which Baltasar is burned alive. It is significant that this supernatural framework appears in a chapter centered around an auto-da-fé, an instrument of the Church's political power. The wealth of detail in the scene reveals not only the ponderous workings of the Inquisition, but also the hierarchy prevailing in the relations among the various religious orders that fought over the king's endowments. The monarch honors the ceremony of the auto-da-fé with his presence, emphasizing the support given to the clergy. Most curious of all is the irony used by the narrator in describing the procession, his mingling with the condemned, and his characterization of the event as a moment of general cheerfulness, an entertaining show for the people. The auto-da-fé therefore loses part of its religious character to reveal a recreational component that, in its turn, deconstructs the authority of the Church. This process is then reinforced by the importance given to the marriage ritual between Blimunda and Baltasar, undoubtedly heretical and deserving punishment, according to the religious laws of that age. The introduction of supernatural elements only in the fifth chapter confirms what the first four chapters had already announced, that is, the criticism of the power structure of D. João V's reign, based on a dependent and passive court that exploited the riches from Brazil and contented itself with the Church's forgiveness for its excessive self-indulgence. In fact, the introduction of another world in the novel does not surprise the reader, since the preceding chapters have prepared him or her for a narrative that privileges subversion. This is made clear by the narrator's sharp irony, whose favorite targets are the king and the queen (witness the minute and comic description of their sexual intercourse), as well as the all-powerful clergy represented, in addition to the critical description of the auto-da-fé, in the episode of the theft of the lamps from the Franciscan church, on which occasion the narrator draws a map of a large part of Lisbon using the city's countless churches.

By emphasizing the heretical side of the political and religious ceremony of the auto-da-fé, by describing the union of a specific couple among the many that have come together to celebrate the event, and by associating Blimunda, from the very beginning, with the supernatural, Saramago hints at the important role that will be played by Blimunda and Baltasar in the political and ideological criticism leveled by the novel in its retelling of the history of the building of the Mafra Convent.

The Year of the Death of Ricardo Reis is the novel by Saramago in which the inclusion of fantastic elements is taken to an extreme. Its main character is Ricardo Reis, one of the heteronyms of Fernando Pessoa, who is transformed into a fictional character. Saramago takes advantage of the fact that Fernando Pessoa died in 1935 to (re)create Ricardo Reis, who in the narrative returns to Portugal after many years in Brazil. Moreover, Saramago wakes Pessoa from the deep slumber of death and brings him back to the world of the living as a critical and attentive observer of the year 1936 in Portugal and the world, converting the dead poet into Ricardo Reis's privileged interlocutor. Reis is an alter ego of Pessoa, who, deep in the maze of his multifaceted mind, debates over the anguished questions: "who?," "where?" and "what for?"[19] In *The Year of the Death of Ricardo Reis*, Reis's questioning somehow extends to José Saramago himself. Indeed, by resorting to a paper character, the fruit of Pessoa's creative feigning, Saramago does not limit himself to recovering and problematizing Pessoa's and Reis's writing. He reflects on his own literary work when, apart from Pessoa and Reis, he converses with other guiding figures of Portuguese literature, such as Camões and Eça, whose works are recaptured in the narrative, especially through Reis's and/or Pessoa's passing through certain areas of 1930s Lisbon.[20] The novel focuses on the complex period of the mid-1930s in Europe and, above all, in Portugal; this historical context is described in detail through the newspapers that Reis eagerly reads and which introduce into the narrative another aspect of the reflection on the representation of the empirical world: the role of the press. It is important to note that Portuguese newspapers of the time, haunted by the ghosts of the political police and the blue pencil of censorship, wrote about what interested the regime of Salazar's Estado Novo.

The fantastic component enters the narrative surreptitiously in the very first chapter, through the gloomy atmosphere of a rainy winter day surrounding the *Highland Brigade*'s arrival in Lisbon. The ship's sluggish approach, the view of the "silent city ... the somber city, enclosed by facades and walls" (3) and the routine procedures in the customhouse, disquietingly characterized as an "antechamber, a limbo ... to what awaits outside" (4), precede the presentation of the novel's protagonist, whose identity is revealed little by little. He is an apparently middle-aged man with a Brazilian accent who, despite being Portuguese, does not know where to go. The presence of the fantastic is "formalized" (given that a somber atmosphere has pervaded the narrative from the very beginning with phantasmagoric tones) when the character fills out the hotel registration form. It is then that Ricardo Reis's intimate quest for an identity is alluded to; in a broader perspective, it is a quest that can be read to a certain extent as Saramago's own, since he has to come to terms in his own literary production with the inevitable reference represented by Pessoa's work:

> Meanwhile the guest returns to the reception desk, somewhat out of breath after all that effort. He takes the pen and enters the essential details about himself in the register of arrivals, so that it might be known who he claims to be, in the appropriate box on the lined page. Name, Ricardo Reis, age, forty-eight, place of birth, Oporto, marital status, bachelor, profession, doctor, last place of residence, Rio de Janeiro, Brazil, whence he has arrived aboard the Highland Brigade. It reads like the beginning of a confession, an intimate autobiography, all that is hidden is contained in these handwritten lines, the only problem is to discover the rest. (10)[21]

The "rest," besides Reis's identity, is, on the one hand, the cultural and literary heritage represented by the legacy of Pessoa's poetry and, on the other, the year 1936 (the time reference of "this" empirical world), which represents the year of the death of Ricardo Reis (the time reference of the "other" world, the world of Saramago's fictional text).

The incorporation of another world—which is, in reality, the world of poetic work, a world that exists only on paper—is reinforced by references to the books brought along by Ricardo Reis. One of them in particular acquires special significance because it belonged to the ship but was kept by the passenger upon leaving the vessel. It is *The God of the Labyrinth*, an imaginary book that appears in one of Borges's *Fictions* (1944). The work, apart from alluding to the importance of the image of the labyrinth (and the literary references it evokes), suggests the character's search for an identity through the similarity between the pronunciation of the name of the book's author (Quain) and the Portuguese pronoun "*Quem*" ("Who"), a personal search highlighted by Saramago's use of Ricardo Reis's verses in the prose text. These verses remind us of the first of Ricardo Reis's odes, which is dated as the final one and which points to the difficulty in finding an answer to the question "Quem?," since Pessoa's heteronym describes himself as inhabited by countless entities. The assimilation of Reis's poetry within narrative prose is an ingenious device used by Saramago to signal the characters' (and also the potential readers') passage through different worlds, revealing in the process an extremely elaborate fictional technique, which comprises not only Saramago's own creative inventiveness, but also Pessoa's and Reis's.

Also emerging in the first chapter is another element that will acquire particular significance in the course of the novel: the mirror. The large mirror in the living room of the Hotel Bragança suggests the importance of the process of duplication as well as the theme of the double within both Pessoa's poetry and the organization of the narrative (Seixo, *Lugares* 40-41).[22] This mirror enables us to reaffirm the importance of newspapers in the novel. Newspapers can, indeed, be interpreted as a sort of mirror of the actuality of 1936, a mirror reflecting the somber image of Fascism, which was gaining ground in Portugal and in Europe, an image of the world distorted by censorship and power interests. The novel's first chapter not only appears to be the frame that delineates the boundaries of supra-real historical fiction, but also introduces the main themes of the narrative, which will then be developed in the second chapter, when Reis goes to Pessoa's tomb in the Cemitério dos Prazeres.

Among Saramago's novels, *The History of the Siege of Lisbon* is the one that explicitly focuses on the construction of historical and fictional discourse. This is achieved through the narration of a version of the siege of Lisbon that contradicts official historiography, starting from the assumption that the Crusaders did *not* help Dom Afonso Henriques fight the Moors in 1147. The first chapter functions as a sort of prologue, in which the proofreader Raimundo Silva introduces his opinions regarding the relative character of historical discourse and the importance of correction, referring to the epigraph of the novel, taken from an imaginary *Book of Exhortations*. The second chapter functions as a gateway to an alternative world. It is in this chapter that we learn about Raimundo's propensity to fabulate on the basis of the texts he has corrected, a characteristic that is revealed in the description of the muezzin's waking Lisbon at dawn and which prepares the potential reader for possible intrusions by the proofreader into the historian's text:

> The proofreader has this remarkable flair for splitting his personality, he inserts a *deleatur* or introduces a comma where required, and at the same time, if you'll pardon the neologism, heteronomises himself, he is capable of pursuing the path

> suggested by an image, a simile, or metaphor, often the simple sound of a word repeated in low voice leads him, by association, to organize polyphonic verbal edifices capable of transforming his tiny study into a space multiplied by itself, although it is difficult to explain in plain language what that means. (14)

The passage into an alternative world occurs, in effect, in the third chapter, when Raimundo introduces, in the historian's text, the "not" that modifies the historical truth concerning the Crusaders' support of Dom Afonso Henriques's siege of Moor-occupied Lisbon. Before introducing the "not" the narrator carefully identifies the proofreader, gives him a name, and describes him as a single, solitary man, who lives in old lodgings on the castle hill, from where he can see the river. Underlying this painstaking care in identifying the proofreader is the narrator's attempt to explain Raimundo's unexpected action, almost as if he were trying to protect Raimundo from the mistake he is about to commit. In this chapter, the notion of error becomes relevant again, going back to the reflection begun at the outset of the book in the conversation between the proofreader and the historian. This time, we are confronted with Raimundo's greatest mistake, his impertinent "not," the seriousness of which is played down to some extent by the discussion of the errors consecrated by the authority of history (the reference to the number of legs of a fly is a perfect example). Thus, the proofreader's impulse for correction (which went beyond his duty) is, to a certain extent, justified.

The passage into the world of historical deception is not direct. It happens in the midst of many doubts resulting from the mistakes and inaccuracies found in the historian's book, which led Raimundo to conjecture, for instance, about the correct name of the weapons used in the siege and about the origin and nature of the political speech delivered by Afonso Henriques to the Crusaders in order to try to convince them to fight against the Moors. The passage into another world is, in effect, surrounded by an enchanted atmosphere, characterized by a thick fog and by the sounding of a siren that alerted vessels to the perils of the sea, recalling the "low bleating" (31) of a seductive mermaid. It is interesting to note that the fog and the sound disappear after the introduction of the rebellious "not," as if the old order went back to normal, or rather, as if it were now easier to go from one world to the other, as well as because the proofreader's house was coincidentally located on the site of the siege. It does not matter; the "not" was already there in the historian's text, which was asking to become something else,[23] that is, to become that which was in turn to become the novel *The History of the Siege of Lisbon* by the proofreader Raimundo Silva, a perfect *mise en abîme* through which Saramago recovers, rewrites and corrects history as writing subject to possible changes, to the fictional text (the novel that makes history into its narrative subject), and the proverb (as a minimal narrative condensation that translates popular wisdom throughout time) (Seixo, *Lugares* 73-82). After all, as Raimundo Silva recalled in his conversation with the historian, "platitudes, clichés, repetitions, affectations, maxims from some almanac, refrains and proverbs, *all of these can sound new*, it's merely a question of knowing how to handle properly the words that precede and follow them..." (5; my emphasis). At the time, Raimundo did not know that the impertinent "not" he was introducing into the historian's text would become the motor for endowing history with the newness of a novel.

Considering postmodern fiction's great attraction towards the past and the writing of history, along with the fact that a significant number of Saramago's novels contain a rereading of important episodes and periods in the history of Portugal, I have tried to show that Saramago's historical works reflect the main trends of postmodern historical fiction. To this effect, I have analyzed some of the reasons for the interest that postmodern literature has taken in the past and in the weaknesses of historical discourse, so as to present a proposal for a typology which can account for some of the regularities characterizing historical fiction produced in the second half of the twentieth century.

José Saramago's novels that explicitly use Portuguese history as their narrative subject can be included in the categories of supra-real historical fiction, the uchronian novel, and historiographic metafiction; all of them reveal the writer's deep concern for the destiny of contemporary Portugal. For this reason, these novels should not be apprehended simply as rereadings of the past, but also, and especially, as investigations into the present seen from a social, cultural, and political perspective. Saramago's narratives are thus privileged ways of gaining knowledge about the past; furthermore, it is particularly those that contain fantastic or supernatural elements, or that construe possible alternative worlds contradicting the official historiographic version of facts, that highlight the ruling classes' political and ideological investment in the writing of history. In all the narratives, this investment is laid bare by privileging the point of view of the Other, without which the correction and the critical rewriting of the past would not be possible. In sum, Saramago's literary works that deal with the past reflect the writer's politics of representation, capable of transforming the literary text not so much into an aesthetic artifact, as, rather, into an ethical model revealing the novel's potential for intervention and historical transformation. Thus, Saramago's novels about Portugal's past posit themselves as socially and politically committed, ultimately engraving, in the memory of literature and history, the role of the people in the building of the Portuguese nation.

Notes

1 On the novel as Saramago's favorite genre, see also Seixo *Lugares* and Martins "A Crónica."

2 On the relations between postmodernism and politics, see Bertens and Best and Kellner, who report on the main trends and give specific bibliographic indications in this area. On the political dimension of postmodern literary representation, see Foley, Hutcheon *Poetics* and *Politics*, and Wesseling.

3 On the representation of reality in western literature see also Auerbach, Foley, Foucault, Hutcheon, Jameson, and Wesseling.

4 On this see White *Content*. On the problem of historical representation and its relation with the narrative discourse, besides the aforementioned volume, see also White *Metahistory*.

5 For a discussion of the possible relations between history and fiction based on the opposition between certainty and accident, and particularly in José Saramago's fictional work, see the interesting essay by Jean Bessière.

6 The expression "partial and fragmented character of history" was used by Saramago in a conversation with Carlos Reis (Reis 79).

7 On this, see also Hutcheon, *Politics* 57.

8 Although an analysis of historical fiction before postmodernism is clearly beyond the scope of the present article, I would like to draw attention to three models based on different interpretations of the relationship between fact and fiction: the narratives Barbara Foley has called "pseudofactual novels," which became popular in the eighteenth century; the nineteenth-century historical novel, with Walter Scott as its canonical author; and modernist historical fiction from the first half of the twentieth century. For a discussion of novels that use authentic materials and which Foley calls "documentary novels," see Foley, as well as Hutcheon *Poetics* and Wesseling. On postmodern historical novels in Portugal, see Marinho "Pós-moderno" and *O Romance*. For a study of the "pseudofactual novel," see especially chapter five of Foley's study. For an explanation on how the first novelists viewed the relation between fact and fiction, see David Lodge's comments in the volume edited by Currie (152). On the model of the historical novel created by Walter Scott, besides Georg Lukács's famous study, see Foley, Wesseling and Hutcheon *Poetics*. On modernist historical fiction, see Wesseling and Hutcheon *Poetics*.

9 These are the titles of the novels making up the series *American Chronicle* in the order in which they were published: *Washington* D.C. (1967), *Burr* (1973), 1876 (1976), *Lincoln* (1984), *Empire* (1987) and *Hollywood* (1990). At the end of 2000, Vidal published *The Golden Age*, which is also part of this series of novels.

10 Seixo's italics; my boldface.

[11] On science fiction from the middle of the 1920s to the 1970s, see McCaffery and Clareson. On the main trends in scientific fiction produced from the 1950s onwards, see Ebert. For a concise history of scientific fiction, see chapter two in José Manuel Mota's PhD thesis.

[12] I rely here on Seixo who, as regards *The Year of the Death of Ricardo Reis*, stresses that while the novel respects historical truth completely, "nothing about the central characters corresponds to reality" (*Lugares 42*), the reason why this fiction is said to be supra-real. I also find it pertinent to include in the category of "supra-real" fiction those literary texts in which the main characters sometimes behave in ways that do not follow the rules of empirical reality.

[13] Although I include *The Gospel According to Jesus Christ* in my proposal for a typology of postmodern historical fiction, I will not discuss this work in more detail here, since it is not one of Saramago's novels that evoke important events in the history of Portugal. For more on *The Gospel According to Jesus Christ*, see, apart from Krysinski, Saramago "Interview," Viegas, Costa, Seixo "Narrativa" and *Lugares*, Silva "O Quinto Evangelho" and "Do Labirinto."

[14] On *Levantado do Chão*, see, among others, Seixo *Lugares* and Silva *José Saramago*, "O Quinto Evangelho" and "Do Labirinto."

[15] This vindication of a new history is corroborated by the principles of the French *Nouvelle Histoire*, with Georges Duby as one of its main proponents; Saramago was very familiar with these principles. See Silva 1989 and 1999, as well as Lourenço.

[16] On the adoption of the point of view of the Other in Saramago's fiction, see Seixo, *Lugares* 126 and Bessière 463-64.

[17] My position here is clearly different from McHale's, who maintains that postmodern fictional production is characterized by a predominance of ontology, in radical opposition to the dominant feature of modernism, which is, in his opinion, epistemologic. For a discussion about the pertinence of the ontological dominance in postmodernism, see, among others, Hutcheon, *Poetics*, and Wesseling.

[18] On the possible worlds in Saramago's novels and, especially, in *The History of the Siege of Lisbon*, see Martins História.

[19] See the ode written on 13 November 1935, whose first line is "Vivem em nós inúmeros" (Pessoa 291) and which Saramago includes in his novel (13).

[20] See the following passage from the first chapter of the novel, when Reis chooses his hotel room and the narrator evokes Eça de Queirós's literary legacy:

> What I wanted was a room with a view of the river. Ah, in that case you will like room two hundred and one, it was vacated only this morning, I'll show it to you right away. The door at the end of the hallway had a little enameled plate, black numerals on a white background. If this were not a humble hotel room without any luxuries, and the room number were two hundred and two, and if the guest were called Jacinto and like Eça de Queirós's hero owned an estate in Tormes, then this episode would not be set in the Rua do Alecrim but on the Champs Elysées, on the right as one goes up, just like the Hotel Bragança, but that is the only detail they have in common. (9)

[21] [Editor's note] Giovanni Pontiero's translation of the last sentence of this passage has been slightly modified here.

[22] The importance of the mirror and of the projection of the same image seen from different perspectives in Ricardo Reis's search for an identity is clearly shown in the following passage:

> Perhaps the guest wishes to slip out quietly in search of Lisbon by night and its secret pleasures ... although the wintry night makes the cozy atmosphere of the lounge seem more enticing, here at hand, the deep highbacked armchairs in leather, the chandelier in the center of the room so rich in crystal pendants, and that big mirror that encompasses the

> entire room and duplicates in it another dimension. This is no simple reflection of the common and familiar proportions the mirror is confronted with, length, width, height, they are not reproduced in it one by one and readily identifiable. Instead they are fused into a simple intangible apparition on a plane that is at once remote and near, unless there is some paradox in this explanation which the mind avoids out of laziness. Here is Ricardo Reis contemplating himself in the depths of the mirror, one of the countless persons that he is, all of them weary. (16)

23 In the same chapter and before the introduction of the "not," the historian's text is characterized as follows: "In those four hundred and thirty-seven pages [Raimundo Silva] did not find a single new fact, controversial interpretation, unpublished document, even as much as a fresh reading. Nothing more than yet another regurgitation of those interminable, played-out accounts of the siege, the description of places, the speeches and deeds of the royal personage…" (30).

Works Cited

Auerbach, Erich. *Mimesis. The Representation of Reality in Western Literature.* Trans. Willard R. Trask. Princeton: Princeton UP, 1991.

Bertens, Hans. *The Idea of the Postmodern. A History.* London: Routledge, 1995.

Bessière, Jean. "Certitude et hasard, ordinaire et enigme du roman." *Colóquio/Letras* 151/152 (Jan.-Jun. 1999): 463-72.

Best, Steven, and Douglas Kellner. *Postmodern Theory: Critical Interrogations.* New York: Guilford, 1991.

Clareson, Thomas D. *Understanding Contemporary American Science Fiction.* Columbia, SC: U of South Carolina P, 1990.

Costa, Horácio. "The Fundamental Re-Writing: Religious Texts and Contemporary Narrative (Gore Vidal's *Live from Golgotha*; Salman Rushdie's *The Satanic Verses*; José Saramago's *O Evangelho Segundo Jesus Cristo*)." *Dedalus* 6 (1996): 245-53.

Currie, Marc, ed. *Metafiction.* Essex: Longman, 1995.

Ebert, Teresa L. "The Convergence of Postmodern Innovative Fiction and Science Fiction." *Poetics Today* 1.4 (1980): 91-104.

Elliott, Emory, ed. *Columbia Literary History of the United States.* New York: Columbia UP, 1988.

Fokkema, Douwe W. *História Literária, Modernismo e Pós-Modernismo.* Trad. Abel Barros Baptista. Lisboa: Vega, 1984.

Foley, Barbara. *Telling the Truth. The Theory and Practice of Documentary Fiction.* Ithaca: Cornell UP, 1986.

Foucault, Michel. *As Palavras e As Coisas.* Trad. António Ramos Rosa. Lisboa: Edições 70, 1991.

Gusmão, Manuel. "Da Literatura como Transporte e Travessia dos Tempos. Algumas Notas sobre a Historicidade da Literatura." *Vértice* 87 (Nov.-Dez. 1998): 72-85.

Hutcheon, Linda. *A Poetics of Postmodernism: History, Theory,Fiction.* New York: Routledge, 1995.

Hutcheon, Linda. *The Politics of Postmodernism.* New York: Routledge, 1995.

Jameson, Fredric. *The Political Unconscious. Narrative as a Socially Symbolic Act.* London: Routledge, 1996.

Krysinski, Wladimir. "Le romanesque et le sacré: observations sur *L'Évangile selon Jésus-Christ.*" *Colóquio/Letras* 151/152 (Jan.-Jun. 1999): 403-11.

Lodge, David. "The Novel Now." Currie 145-59.

Lourenço, António Apolinário. "José Saramago, A Falácia do Romance Histórico." *Jornal de Letras* IX.399 (26 Fev. 1990): 9.

Lukács, Georg. *The Historical Novel.* Trans. Hannah and Stanley Mitchell. Lincoln: U of Nebraska P, 1983.

Marinho, Maria de Fátima. *O Romance Histórico em Portugal.* Porto: Campo das Letras, 1999.

———. "O Romance Histórico Pós-Moderno em Portugal." *Actas do Quinto Congresso da Associação Internacional de Lusitanistas.* 3 vols. Org. e coord. T. F. Earle. Oxford and Coimbra: Associação Internacional de Lusitanistas, 1998. II.1011-21.

Martins, Adriana Alves de Paula. "A Crónica de José Saramago ou uma Viagem pela Oficina do Romance." *Colóquio/Letras* 151/152 (Jan.-Jun. 1999): 95-107.

———. *História e Ficção: Um Diálogo.* Lisboa: Fim de Século, 1994.

McCaffery, Larry. "The Fictions of the Present." Elliott 1161-77.

McHale, Brian. *Postmodernist Fiction.* London: Routledge, 1991.

Mota, José Manuel. "O Efeito de Irreal. A Fantasia Científica de Philip K. Dick." Diss. Univ. de Coimbra, 1995.

Pessoa, Fernando. *Obra Poética.* Org. e introd. Maria Aliete Galhoz. Rio de Janeiro: Nova Aguilar, 1986.

Reis, Carlos. *Diálogos com José Saramago.* Lisboa: Caminho, 1998.

Saramago, José. *A Bagagem do Viajante.* Lisboa: Caminho, 1986.

———. *Baltasar and Blimunda.* Trans. Giovanni Pontiero. San Diego: Harcourt Brace Jovanovich, 1987. Trans. of *Memorial do Convento.* Rio de Janeiro: Bertrand do Brasil, 1987.

———. *Deste Mundo e do Outro.* Lisboa: Caminho, 1986.

———. *The Gospel According to Jesus Christ.* Trans. Giovanni Pontiero. New York: Harcourt Brace, 1994. Trans. of *O Evangelho Segundo Jesus Cristo.* Lisboa: Caminho, 1991.

———. *The History of the Siege of Lisbon.* Trans. Giovanni Pontiero. London: Harvill, 1996. Trans. of *História do Cerco de Lisboa.* São Paulo: Cia. das Letras, 1989.

———. Interview with Clara Ferreira Alves on *O Evangelho Segundo Jesus Cristo.* "'No meu caso, o alvo é Deus.'" *Expresso* 2 Nov. 1991: R82-87.

———. *Levantado do Chão.* Lisboa: Caminho, 1988.

———. *The Year of the Death of Ricardo Reis.* Trans. Giovanni Pontiero. San Diego: Harcourt Brace Jovanovich, 1991. Trans. of *O Ano da Morte de Ricardo Reis.* Lisboa: Caminho, 1986.

Seixo, Maria Alzira. *Lugares da Ficção em José Saramago. O Essencial e Outros Ensaios.* Lisboa: Imprensa Nacional-Casa da Moeda, 1999.

———. "Narrativa e Ficção—Problemas de Tempo e Espaço na Literatura Europeia do Pós-Modernismo." *Colóquio/Letras* 134 (Out.-Dez. 1984): 101-21.

Silva, Teresa Cristina Cerdeira da. "Do Labirinto Textual ou da Escrita como Lugar de Memória." *Colóquio/Letras* 151/152 (Jan.-Jun. 1999): 249-66.

———. *José Saramago—Entre a História e a Ficção: Uma Saga de Portugueses.* Lisboa: Dom Quixote, 1989.

———. "José Saramago—A Ficção Reinventa a História." *Colóquio/Letras* 120 (Abr.-Jun. 1991): 174-78.

———. "O Quinto Evangelista ou da Tigela ao Graal." *Vértice* 52 (Janeiro-Fevereiro 1993): 17-21.

Viegas, Francisco José. "Uma biografia de Jesus, segundo José Saramago." *Ler* 16 (Outono 1991): 24-36.

Waugh, Patricia. *Metafiction. The Theory and Practice of Self-Conscious Fiction.* London: Routledge, 1996.

Wesseling, Elisabeth. *Writing History as a Prophet. Postmodernist Innovations of the Historical Novel.* Amsterdam: John Benjamins, 1991.

White, Hayden. *Metahistory: The Historical Imagination in Nineteeth-Century Europe.* Baltimore: Johns Hopkins UP, 1985.

———. *The Content of the Form. Narrative Discourse and Historical Representation.* Baltimore: Johns Hopkins UP, 1987.

On the Labyrinth of Text, or, Writing as the Site of Memory

Teresa Cristina Cerdeira da Silva
Translated by
Anna Klobucka

> And Françoise, when transmitting to us the Marquise's message: "She said to me, 'You'll be sure and bid them good day,' she said," would counterfeit the voice of Mme de Villeparisis, whose exact words she imagined herself to be quoting textually, whereas in fact she was distorting them no less than Plato distorts the words of Socrates or St. John the words of Jesus.
>
> Marcel Proust, *Remembrance of Things Past*

Although it is rescued from banality only by its conclusion, the above passage from Proust appears to suit perfectly my proposed reading of the novels forming José Saramago's first major narrative cycle, from *Levantado do Chão* (*Raised from the Ground*, 1980) to *The Gospel According to Jesus Christ* (1991), such a grouping being of necessity somewhat arbitrary, but, as I hope to demonstrate, not devoid of coherence. The question that interests me—captured in an ironic synthesis by the Proustian quote—is the representation of the other's speech in a literary discourse, which, through its reference to the other, establishes with him or her a double-faced relationship composed in equal parts of respect and betrayal. In other words, writing is understood here as a labyrinthine agglomeration of discourses belonging to different times, places and genres and whose fragmentary irruptions break up the allegedly smooth continuity of the text. At the same time respected and betrayed, those singular utterances, when brought into the discursive present, place in check the historical linearity that had situated them in a given chronological context, henceforward rendered inoperative. Respect and treachery: such is the fate of the words pronounced by Proust's Mme. de Villeparisis, literally repeated by Françoise and, on a second level, transcribed by the narrator within rigorously displayed single quotation marks, but then followed by a reference to the "distortion" produced by the speaker's tone of voice. In a more general sense (and here the passage assumes its exemplary meaning), any citation or reference to an earlier enunciation is likely to retain the same ambiguity, as indicated by the Proustian narrator's surprising evocation of acts of infidelity committed by the generally unsuspected discourses of philosophy and religion when they resolve to quote a preexisting source: thus Plato betrays Socrates and John is unfaithful to Jesus. This final allusion, as we shall see, proves to be especially expedient with regard to José Saramago's novels and in particular to *The Gospel According to Jesus Christ.*

The enterprise of writing under the weight of the remembered past is not limited to any given author or historical period. Even in those times when the act of quotation lacked an ethical or aesthetic justification (for instance in antiquity, with its Platonic disapproval of poetic imitation), writers were incapable of producing texts resplendent with an inaugural purity of origin. Remnants and ruins have always been treasured material, zealously preserved by time in order to be preyed upon by our memory in a conscious exercise of cultural pillage. It should be noted, however, that such a plunder is a generous undertaking, since it brings up to date our interpretation of tradition, whether it proceeds in a reverential mode or is carried forth by a countercurrent of anti-canonical defiance. The new text subjects the past to a regenerative action, making it leave its own bounds and thus acquire unexpected shapes and angles.

On the other hand, it is also undeniable that different ways of dealing with the intertext do not always share the same motivations nor lead invariably to the same results. Modernity has exacerbated the consciousness of the text's dialogic nature; it has discovered that readers are not merely receptive or ironic accomplices of the text, but rather negotiate its meanings while armed with their own cultural assumptions. It has also challenged the absolute authority of authors and their property rights with regard to the truth of the text, and it has understood that the recovery of traditions is not tantamount to endorsing them or placing oneself in their debt. As Foucault concluded, in his reading of Flaubert's *La Tentation de Saint Antoine,* "in order to dream it is not necessary to close one's eyes, it is necessary to read" (106).

Already Montaigne had said, in a most modern fashion, that writing has always been a kind of gloss or comment on other writing. But books that read books do not cease to function as well as readers of the world: the intertextual commitment cultivated by the contemporary age, far from trapping the texts in a web of self-referentiality, historicizes instead these acts of reading, privileging, albeit in an unorthodox manner, the viewpoint of the present in its reappraisal of the past. The act of quotation is thus transformed into an ongoing process of recognition and provocation, which accomplishes much more than mere repetition, in conformity with the Latin etymology of the term "citation" evoked by Antoine Compagnon: the past is set in motion and the present text allows it an opportunity to participate actively in the renewal of its meanings.[1]

One possible way of reading the novels of José Saramago takes as its point of departure the author's role as a reader of the Portuguese, Iberian and generally Western cultural traditions, and whose writing is fundamentally a site of memory, as his entire body of work ceaselessly reiterates. It suffices to recall in this context his recent novel *All the Names* (1997), where Sr. José's search is nothing if not a demonstration of the necessity to disturb the traditional image of the present as life and of the past as death. To refuse to separate the dead from the living is to maintain them all present, since, after all, the freedom associated with the present does not consist in its autonomy in relation to the past, but rather in the possibility of the two engaging in a fruitful dialogue, capable of responding in a different manner to those echoes from the past that have remained unanswered.

The role of Saramago as a writer/reader of culture becomes manifest in some recurring facets of his work. For the purposes of this article, I will focus on his recovery of the texts that compose the foundations of Portuguese and Western imagination, with particular emphasis on Camões, the Bible, and the narratives of history. Along these lines I will consider the novels of Saramago's first great narrative cycle, distinguished by certain ideological postulates (namely, the revisiting of history or of cultural formations) and by a distinct narrative voice, that has been described by some as Baroque: the long musical sentence, a discourse more *conceptista* than *cultista*, the vastly spreading scope of the narrative. These characteristics have become less pronounced—which represents neither a loss nor a gain—in the most recent novels, *Blindness*, *All the Names* and *A Caverna*, a triptych reflecting humanity's quest for meaning in the midst of its end-of-millennium crisis. While the selection of the works for discussion could have been different, other texts would have required a distinct analytic perspective; the choice I have made possesses one clear advantage: an unambiguously identifiable presence of the textual characteristics outlined above.

The Camões Intertext

It is hardly by accident that the author most commonly quoted, referred to or parodied in the Portuguese literary tradition should be Camões, particularly Camões the author of *The Lusíads*. Saramago's narrator in *The Year of the Death of Ricardo Reis* (1984) affirms, in a proverbial tone, that "all the Portuguese roads lead to Camões," presenting his fiction, in a Borgesian manner, as a sort of theory of the text. Using the roads that lead to Rome as the source for his pastiche, Saramago creates his own version of the expression, which designates Camões as the meeting point of all Portuguese utterances. If, at the level of the narrative, the Lisbon square with the statue of the poet becomes a basic reference guiding the traveler through the streets of the capital, the reach of Saramago's proverb-like quip is clearly much broader, especially if we consider that the traveler in question is another Portuguese poet experiencing a personal and political identity crisis; here, the geographic layout gains the significance of a cultural confluence. In such an emblematic manner, the third novel of the cycle gives concrete shape to the rhetoric of Camonian evocation that has always been present in the cultural imaginary informing Saramago's writing. As Eduardo Lourenço expressed it (and as I repeat here, following the medieval practice of citation as a guarantee of critical *auctoritas*), "It is impossible to commemorate *The Lusíads* innocently" (158). When these words were written, just a few years distant from the fourth centenary of Camões's death, any form of tribute might have appeared dated; Lourenço's postulate, however, reached much further, pointing to the meaning of commemoration as an exercise of *co-memory*. This is tantamount to saying that when our collective memory evokes Camões, it never does so innocently.

Saramago's novel *Levantado do Chão* (*Raised from the Ground*, 1980) exemplifies this process by treating the phantasmagoric presence of *The Lusíads* as a structural device. The citation is not necessarily made manifest by explicit quotation or by direct reference to Camões's emblematic characters; instead, the book's more ambitious project is to produce a peasant epic drawn, in a willful distortion of the original source, around men and women "raised" from the ground (the soil of Alentejo and, by extension, of Portugal), just as Camões's intrepid sailors once "rose" from the sea. It is not the "matchless heroes" ("*barões assinalados*") but rather peasants of no distinction who cross the "interior sea" of the latifundium, their desired land no longer situated in the remote Calecut, but in the villages of the agrarian revolution: "Mantas and Pedra Grande, Vale da Canseira, Monte da Areia, Fonte Pouca, great hunger, Serralha, worth nothing, over the hills and valleys" (365). It is a story whose stated objective is to sing the "little people who came with the soil" (14), to bring into writing the subjects without history, and, finally, to carry out a victorious crusade against the new, emblematically named "infidels": the Latifundium, the State, and the Church, three powers dramatically shaken up by the agrarian revolution of 1975, which took away their power, authority and public voice.[2] Leaving their estate unoccupied, the landowners Bertos escape, after the Revolution of 25 de Abril has prompted the collapse of the authoritarian state. The priest Agamedes falls silent, since he does not know what to say, and only "speaks in parables," because "the prudence of the church is infinite" (354). Similarly, "the guard does not leave the barracks" (364), because the corporal Tacabo, the sergeant Armamento or the lieutenant Contente—redundant even in their own names, which mark but do not identify them—have "their hands tied": they no longer have the old orders to turn against the villagers who invade the abandoned lands. There is the symbolic substitution of the robust name "Espada" ("Sword") for the fatal "Mau-Tempo" ("Bad Time/Weather"), which suffices to curb the authority and brilliance of the "Bertos" (etymologically: "luminous," "famous," "noble"). A reflex of another generation that managed to turn fatalism into action, this revolutionary generation includes women as well, metonymically represented by Maria Adelaide Espada, whose blue eyes are a legacy of her grandfather and whose name boasts a most singular etymology, as Germanic in origin as the names of the former masters: *ade, adde, adal, adel*, meaning "noble," a new nobility that is neither of the blood nor "of the cloak," but of the struggle. This is why, at the end of the novel, "waves never cease to make circles in the interior sea of the latifundium" (363), the "sun is just" (364), and all the men and women, the dead and the alive, experience the apocalypse of the revolution in a day that is "elevated and essential" (366). These are ideal ingredients of an epic discourse that claims the right to come to a standstill in the moment of conquered glory. When *Levantado do Chão* was published, the victory of the Alentejan peasants, who had built their first rural cooperatives based on communal principles, was no longer quite so complete. However, in spite of the fact that this historical conquest was being threatened by the inevitable crises that affect any inaugural experience, Saramago allowed himself the right to celebrate a fully realized utopia: in his version of the epic, the explorers' ships triumphantly return to Lisbon with no counterbalancing equivalent of Camões's "heartlessness and degrading pessimism" ("*austera, apagada e vil tristeza*") (226).

Returning now to the question of intertextuality and to the dialogic concept of the text as a mosaic of citations, I will forgo here the task of compiling an inventory of Saramago's sources, inasmuch as my objective is not to uncover influences, but rather to capture formal constructs that structure the not always orderly dialogue between the quoted discursive voices and the monuments of the past or the echoes of their own historical setting. If we continue, for instance, to follow the thread of Camonian references in *Baltasar and Blimunda*, it becomes especially crucial to note the various ways in which Saramago's text evokes *The Lusíads* in two exemplary episodes: the flight of Father Bartolomeu's Passarola and the recruitment of the workers who will built the convent in Mafra.

In each of these narrative moments, discursive affinity with epic loftiness is given a particular textual shape. When Bartolomeu, Baltasar and Blimunda are about to take off in the Passarola, the narrator, aware that the project is precarious, its chances of success fragile, and its participants face great obstacles, comes to their aid and invokes—as in the epic—divine assistance: the Guardian Angel takes here the place of the goddess Venus, protectress of the Portuguese in Camões's poem:

> And now, Guardian Angel, what will you do? For your presence has never been so necessary since you were first entrusted with this role. Here you have three people who will shortly go up into the sky, where man has never ventured, and they need your protection. They have done as much as they can on their own... Unless you are prepared to give a little help, Guardian Angel, you are neither an angel nor anything else... She is that woman who is holding the glass phial. Protect her, Guardian Angel, for if the phial should break, there will be no journey, and that priest who is behaving so strangely, will not be able to make his escape. Also protect the man working on the roof. His left hand is missing, and you are to blame, for you were inattentive out there on the battlefield when he was wounded. (176-77)

In structural terms, what the narrator performs here is the epic invocation, customarily followed by the description of imminent dangers. He had already referred to the Passarola as an "aeronave," a ship of the air, thus linking the aerial adventure to the maritime epic, and further commented on the departure as a form of abandoning "the port and its moorings in order to go off in pursuit of secret routes" (182), or, in other words, of "oceans where none had ventured" ("*nunca dantes navegados*") (Camões 3). Through an extended metaphor, the narrator goes on to evoke in a consistent manner the archetypal elements of *The Lusíads*: "Who knows what dangers await them, what Adamastors they will encounter, what Saint Elmo's fires they will see rise from the sea, what columns of water will suck in the air only to expel it once it has been salted?" (182). And later, when the Passarola is about to crash, "A shadowy form looms up before them—the Adamastor, perhaps, of their voyage—and mountainous curves rise from the ground crested with streaks of crimson light" (184). What happens here is that the classic text, consecrated by tradition, is made to bestow on the present adventure a measure of heroic bravery and an epic dimension that it is deemed to deserve.

Not always, however, is Camões's epic evoked to support the heroic dimension of Saramago's text. In the episode in which the workers are brought to Mafra against their will, in order to expedite the construction of the basilica, the intertext is deployed with bitter irony, as a model of a rebellious diatribe against the arbitrary implementation of royal power. The scene of the workers' painful departure from their land recreates masterfully the episode of the Old Man of Restelo from *The Lusíads*, with its lamenting women, despairing men and the vociferating patriarch. Here however the similarities end, since the narrated story lacks the epic scope of the glorious past venture and the expectation of a victory over the unknown that justified, in principle, the departure of the sailors. Although they are criticized by the Old Man, whose speech reveals the mendacity of ideological discourse, the deceptiveness of language that conceals truth instead of uncovering it, and the masking of vanity as fame and of bestial cruelty as bravery, in the end Camões's sailors escape the wrath of the "old man of venerable appearance" (95) and the forces of the destiny that he has summoned against them (97):

> The devil take the man who first put
> Dry wood on the waves with a sail!
> [...]

And may no solemn chronicler,
No sweet harpist nor eloquent poet
Commend your deeds or celebrate your fame,
But let your folly vanish with your name! (97)

Notwithstanding all the moral reservations voiced by the narrator of *The Lusíads* in the famous stanza 145 of the tenth Canto, the sailors complete their voyage and return victorious to Portugal. But their salvation is most of all due to the fact that the "sweet harp" destined to celebrate them—Camões's epic—did not fall silent, as the old man had wished, but instead spread widely their memory and fame.

The workers' departure for Mafra, on the other hand, appears not to have any meaning for the community that finds itself involved in a project of purely individual grandeur. Its actors are no longer the "matchless heroes" of Camões's epic, but rather poor men, "tied like sheep" (270), who witness the suffering of their women—tearful, humiliated, violated—and whose voices echo the Old Man's curses, couched in a language that substitutes colloquial profanity for erudite allusion: "May you be damned unto five generations… may you be impaled from ass to mouth, thrice-cursed villain" (270).

If, up to this point, the Camonian intertext could be taken to function merely as a sort of rhetorical background, further development of the scene makes the allusive commitment definitive by reprising literally a number of verses from *The Lusíads*. With no concern for verisimilitude, these mothers and wives also say farewell to their sons and husbands in classic decasyllables, expressly quoted by Saramago as a textual ready-made that produces an inescapable semantic estrangement. The text is woven from shreds of Camões's verse (here rendered in italics), connected by phrases that serve to recreate the rhythmic feel of the heroic decasyllable (the segments in bold type):[3]

> que vão clamando, *qual em cabelo, Ó doce e amado esposo*, e outra protestando, *Ó filho a quem eu tinha só para refrigério e doce amparo desta cansada já velhice minha*, **não se acabavam as lamentações**, *tanto que os montes de mais perto respondiam, quase movidos de alta piedade*, **enfim já os levados se afastam, vão sumir-se na volta do caminho**, rasos de lágrimas os olhos, **em bagadas caindo aos mais sensíveis, e então uma grande voz se levanta**, é um labrego **de tanta idade já que o não quiseram, e grita subido a um valado**, que é pulpito de rústicos, *Ó glória de mandar, ó vã cobiça*, ó rei infame, **ó pátria sem justiça**… (293).

[weeping as they go, heads uncovered: Oh, sweet and beloved husband; while another wails: Ah, my beloved boy, who gave me comfort and protection in my weary old age. The lamentations went on and on until the nearby mountains echoed those cries, moved by pity for these poor creatures. The men are already at some distance and finally disappear from sight where the road curves, their eyes filled with tears—large teardrops in the case of the most sensitive among them—and then a voice rends the air. It is that of a farmer so advanced in years that the magistrate's men were reluctant to take him. Having mounted an embankment, a natural pulpit for countryfolk, he calls out: Ah, empty ambition, senseless cupidity, infamous King, nation without justice... (270)]

Saramago's discourse becomes here a kind of resonant fabric that incorporates quotations from Camões with great skill, but without diminishing their visibility. The writer's intertextual strategy does not seek to cover up difference; on the contrary, it is emphasized, precisely owing to the effort involved in the co-optation of the old text by the new. As the proofreader in *The History of the Siege of Lisbon* puts it, "the interesting thing about life has always been in the differences" (3).

In *The Year of the Death of Ricardo Reis*, the privileged group of intertextual references derives, naturally, from the writings of Fernando Pessoa—from the texts themselves and, in particular, from the heteronymic play of masks[4]—but Camões's epic also makes a prominent appearance through an inverted quotation of the famous line from the third Canto: "Where the continent ends and the sea begins" (52). In its original form, this line is a splendid emblem of the view of Portugal as a pier of departures and of the expansionist project that continued to sustain the phantom of Portuguese glory long after its persistence had been recognized as fallacious. The catastrophic defeat at Alcácer-Kebir appears, in this version, as merely a stage, yet another calamity, which, in any case, becomes translated into the Sebastianist myth and as such nourishes for centuries, in the words of Eduardo Lourenço, "the prodigious unreality of the Portuguese society's own self-image" (19). Saramago's project, formed at a time when the country struggled to awaken from its delusion of greatness, situated itself of necessity on the antipodes of that image. The two versions of the emblematic sentence, placed, respectively, at the novel's opening—"Here the sea ends and the earth begins"(1)—and at its closure—"Here, where the sea ends and the earth awaits" (358)—signal instantly a change of perspective. Symptomatically, the novel begins with Ricardo Reis's return trip to Portugal, made over what are now much-traveled seas—"between London and Buenos Aires like a weaving shuttle on the highways of the sea, backward and forward, always calling at the same ports" (1)—and on board the *Highland Brigade*, an English steamer of the Royal Mail Line, a choice that cancels irrevocably any recollection of the glorious ships of yesteryear. In addition to this voyage devoid of epic qualities that brings Dr. Reis home from Brazil, and with him, albeit in third-class cabins, the usual proportion of failed emigrants, the novel avails itself as well of the already mentioned roads leading to Camões—to Lisbon's Largo Luís de Camões—and of the statue of Adamastor in Alto de Santa Catarina, likewise symbolically charged.

Another epic reference may be found in Saramago's "stone raft," which, unmindful of the laws of nature, navigates whenever necessary. It would be reductive to see in the novel a simplistic allegory of a refusal to join the European Union, in spite of the author's frank disclosure of his convictions in this regard. When the novel was published in 1986, the year of both Spain's and Portugal's accession to the EU, the connection was surely too obvious to satisfy a writer who had already proven his skill in plotting narratives that blend fantastic adventure with historical realism. In its vision of a separatist utopia, *The Stone Raft* reaches beyond a strategic intervention in the history of the present. Having repeated, by means of the breach in the Pyrenees, the original ritual of separation of earth and sea in the Genesis, the novel invites the reader to embark on a different voyage, which retraces a geographic trajectory comparable to that inscribed in Camões's epic, even while placing the old project under erasure. As the Iberian Peninsula is rotated upside down, its seafaring tradition receives a metaphorical guarantee of preservation through a simultaneous depiction of two voyages—by land and by sea—toward the final resting point in the southern Atlantic Ocean, a location perceived by Saramago as Iberia's cultural destiny and justification. No longer a colonialist epic, the novel represents this expedition as both an encounter between equals and a recovery of historical roots, just as the protagonists' travels across their land culminate in its explosive renewal—contrasted with the sterility of the old European continent—when all the women of Iberia become simultaneously pregnant and the dry elm branch stuck into the ground turns green again. Such is Saramago's reconstruction of

Camões's argument in *The Stone Raft*: it has no need for the scene of laments at the Restelo pier, since it does not send off sailors in search of the unknown. Instead, it is the land itself, the raft-peninsula, that embarks on a voyage, reorienting its bearings in order to find its own direction. And, given that the novel recycles the scenario of Camões's maritime epic, its discourse does not shy away from explicit quotation. This is how the narrator comments on the separation of the Iberian landmass (my emphasis to mark the quotation from *The Lusíads*, first stanza of Canto One): "*Human strength could do nothing* [*Não podia a força humana nada*] on behalf of the cordillera that was opening up as a pomegranate, with no apparent suffering, and simply, who are we to know, because it had matured and its time had come" (24). If human strength had once been surpassed by the sailors who assumed the task of conquering the unknown, it was now helpless in face of an irreversible geological spectacle, which overlaid the tragedy with a suggestion of an erotic charge produced by the collusion of natural forces and history: the peninsula is like a fruit that opens because its time has come. This is why Camões's text resurfaces in the novel after the breach between the Pyrenees and Europe has become definite. The Peninsula's just-beginning adventure is new, inaugural and epic, so new that it frightens, and epic because truly, in this case, unprecedented:

> a series of satellite pictures [showed] the progressive widening of the canal between the peninsula and France, *flesh froze and hair bristled* [*arrepiavam-se a carne e o cabelo*] at the sight of this great catastrophe, *beyond human powers* [*maior que a força humana*], for this was no longer a canal but open sea, where ships sailed at will, *over water that had truly never been sailed before* [*em mares*, estes sim, *nunca dantes navegados*]. (77)

Finally, when this peculiar raft threatens to crash its Cabo da Roca into the Azores archipelago and speculations with regard to its destiny are again overtaken by fear, the giant Adamastor makes an implicit appearance: "*one shudders just to think* [*arrepiam-se as carnes e o cabelo*] of that horrendous moment" (177). To speak of one cape and to evoke another (Adamastor's "Cape of Storms"), to evoke a new fear and to recall an old one, these are Saramago's suggestive ways of reawakening his Portuguese readers' culturally conditioned responses to the novel experience of his text.

The Historical Intertext

In this section, I do not intend to return to the question of Saramago's approach to the historical novel, a much discussed topic that I also have addressed on some earlier occasions, and one to which the author himself has dedicated a great deal of ongoing reflection.[5] I will instead consider the intersections of historical texts within his novels, with an understanding that the "historical texts" explored by Saramago are not necessarily of an academic nature; the writer has also utilized, to great advantage, journalistic sources, whose fictionalized integration in his novels does not prevent the author from submitting their real-world referents to a careful and ingenious consideration.

Not surprisingly, a good illustration of this approach may be found in *The Year of the Death of Ricardo Reis*, since for the more recent historical record, such as that explored in the novel, the press has been a rich source of documentation. It does not matter, in reality, that the documents in question are monuments to the political power of Salazar's dictatorship and that, as a consequence, they tend to disguise rather than expose the historical "truth." As Jacques le Goff has rightly argued, no document is truly innocent and, in one way or another, every document has a monumental dimension, since it exists as a result of the society's conscious or unconscious effort to pass on to the future generations a certain image of itself. Therefore, when faced with newspaper sources, a writer who is aware of the traps they contain learns to question them in such a way as to make them disclose their submerged meanings.

Along with the manuscript of *The Year of the Death of Ricardo Reis*, Saramago deposited in the National Library in Lisbon an authentic calendar from the year 1936, into which he had entered information that he had obtained from Portuguese newspapers published that year in order to reconstitute its time and space in his fiction: news of the Spanish crisis, which absorbed a large proportion of the published material and transposed onto the neighboring country the Portuguese readers' own anxieties, leading them to interpret the events in the way intended by the authorities; Italy's invasion of Ethiopia; the growing power of the German model in shaping the militarization of the Portuguese life (as exemplified by the Mocidade Portuguesa, a version of the Hitler Jugend); as well as some apparently anodyne bits of information, such as weather forecasts and commercial advertisements. These elements reappear in the novel not as a merely specular registry of events; instead, they become endowed with a symbolic meaning by the narrative context into which they are integrated. Such is, for instance, the case of the weather. Nineteen thirty-six was, in fact, a grey and rainy year, as daily newspaper reports consistently confirm. Nevertheless, Saramago's processing of this bit of information colors it with a qualitative tinge. In the following examples, all taken from the first pages of the novel, references to rain carry an incriminating charge:

> It is raining over the colorless city. The waters of the river are polluted with mud, the riverbanks flooded. A dark vessel, the *Highland Brigade*, ascends the somber river… (1)
> Behind windowpanes ingrained with salt the children peer out at the grey city… (2)
> But it is the silent city that frightens them, perhaps all its inhabitants have perished and the rain is only falling to dissolve into mud what has remained standing. (3)
> Beyond the docksheds lies the somber city, enclosed by façades and walls… (3)
> The first passengers disembark. Their shoulders bent under the monotonous rain… (3)
> It is growing dark although it is only four o'clock… (4)
> The rain had died away, only a few scattered drops continued to fall, but in the sky there was not a trace of blue, the clouds had not dispersed and they formed one vast roof the color of lead. Has there been much rain, the passenger inquired. For the last two months it has been bucketing down like the great flood, the driver replied as he switched off his windshield wipers. (7)

The association of the rain with expressions such as "the somber city," "a dark vessel," "the silent city," "bent shoulders," and "roof the color of lead" helps construe a scenario in which the cold darkness and the intimations of death and silence point to a reality characterized by fear, oppression, secrecy, weakness of spirit, censorship, political persecution and curtailment of freedom. The narrative transforms a fortuitous, circumstantial piece of data into a symbolically charged, motivated and necessary fictional construct.

Another form of appropriation of newspaper data can be illustrated by the narrative episode in which the writer's virtuosity of composition reaches its highest point: the report on the invasion of Addis-Abeba. Saramago mixes together authentic newspaper headlines, fragments of radio news broadcasts, excerpts from political speeches, and a short story by Borges ("A Survey of the Works of Herbert Quain"). There is also an ode by Ricardo Reis and a variation on it produced by the narrator who displaces the poet's ancient Persia to Addis-Abeba and the poem's past tense ("they burned," "they were") into the narrative present ("they burn," "they are"), even as he preserves, in a compliant echo, the same syntactic rhythm and the same scenes, with raped women, burning houses, looted possessions and children bleeding in the streets. The coming together of all these apparently disparate elements produces a text of many voices and varied rhythms, in which tragedy and irony go hand-in-hand and the patchwork of borrowings from different narrative registers never disguises its composite nature. The episode creates a sort of rhythmic vortex, sweeping up the reader into a state where the constant jumping between discourses of diverse nature and orientation generates a contradictory multiplicity of responses and emotional reactions. In this skillfully orchestrated confusion, the startled reader is not allowed to ignore the process of narrative construction, as he or she follows attentively the narrator's mood swings, from anger to compassion, and from irony to astonishment, in the face of that rehearsal of the violent destiny that fascism was preparing to wreak upon the world.

Historical discourses are also present in *Baltasar and Blimunda*, the novel whose writing required extensive research into the documents of the Inquisition, Portuguese convents, the court of Dom João V and, of course, the construction works at Mafra. The author was able to reconstitute these realities while at the same time subverting and parodying the perspective of the official record by celebrating the oppressed workers instead of the king who had been the intended beneficiary of the architectural tribute. But it is surely in *The History of the Siege of Lisbon* that we can perceive most clearly Saramago's strategy in composing his narrative discourse with or from preexisting discourses, namely, a radical irreverence with regard to institutionalized knowledge and a reliance on the paradox as a leading device in the author's critical rereading of the *doxa*. Saramago's appreciation of the paradox may be verified at the very beginning of the novel: its epigraph, taken from an imaginary *Book of Exhortations*, explains that amending the truth is the only way of attaining it. What *The History of the Siege of Lisbon* postulates is precisely this: if, according to the traditional logic, it is necessary to reach the truth in order to be able to correct it, the novel makes this affirmation fold in on itself by proposing correction as the primary act. This play on words, instead of immobilizing the novel's action through its apparent impossibility, is vindicated by the doubly troublesome attitude of a proofreader who extrapolates ("voluptuously," the narrator notes) the function of an attentive reader of historical truth in order to remake himself into the writer of a history that did not take place. Far from engaging in gratuitous playfulness, Saramago asks here some very serious questions with regard to a new concept of history.

It is, therefore, less important to detect in the novel traces of historical accounts of the siege of Lisbon (undoubtedly researched by Saramago) than to uncover its engagement with the theoretical premises of a new historiography founded on the principles supplied by the French *Nouvelle Histoire*, with which Saramago had already shown himself to be familiar. *The History of the Siege of Lisbon* conjugates a narrative project with a theoretical one, a strategy that has gained ground in Saramago's more recent works, where the seductive pleasure of a well-told story seems to become subordinated to a greater substantive economy determined by a central idea; although the narrative never loses its zest, it clearly gains an almost essay-like functionality.

This is not yet the case in *The History of the Siege of Lisbon*, where, in fact, what we perceive in the novel's discourse is the opposite: a narrative delight in the excess produced by the tripled version of historical data. The first level is situated outside the novel: it consists of the siege, the event itself, obviously inaccessible to us today, except through historical record. The second level, referred to in the narrative, is a history of the siege of Lisbon written by an academic historian, whose galleys are being "corrected" by the proofreader Raimundo Silva. The reader of Saramago's novel has no access to the text of that book, with the exception of a single sentence. That is the sentence bound to arouse the humble proofreader to a state of unexpected voluptuousness, as he modifies it with a "not" and thus generates a contrary version, not only of the specific historical fact in question, but quite possibly of Portuguese history in its entirety. The third level is the alternative history of the siege whose point of departure is the "not" added by the proofreader. But before this history can materialize, a new narrative line has to unfold, situated in the present: the love affair between the proofreader and his editor, Maria Sara. It is therefore a woman—as often happens in Saramago's novels—who, noticing the error, perceives its great transformative potential and who impels the writing of the new history. The proofreader's boldness is reinterpreted from a more progressive and generous perspective. Once the error is discovered, the integrity of the edition is restored by the insertion of an erratum; but there remains one "copy without any erratum, a book which preserves the deception, that makes no attempt to remove this error or falsehood" (92), a book that is returned to its author by the woman's hand. (This book of pure fiction, of which only one copy exists, may be compared with the reference to Borges' book of Herbert Quain in *The Year of the Death of Ricardo Reis.*)

> This book belongs to you… Let me rephrase that, This is your book… Mine, he asked, Yes, it's the only remaining copy… that does not carry an erratum, the only copy which still claims that the crusaders refused to help the Portuguese… (92)

What is left unsaid, but what will be made clear immediately afterwards, is that the book is not a gift, but property restored to its owner—an embryonic, barely established property, still in need of a fresh and irreversible qualitative jump that would transform it into a homonymous work of fiction: *The History of the Siege of Lisbon.*

> Don't ask me to explain, it's something I can sense rather than explain, and this is what made me decide to make a proposal, And what is it, That you yourself should write a history of the siege of Lisbon in which the crusaders do not help the Portuguese, therefore taking your deviation literally, the word I heard you use a moment ago… (96)

It is not for the first time that we see love create a world: Maria Sara and Raimundo Silva will have the right to their own story, ingeniously mirrored by a love story from the past, which is boldly brought into relief by the proofreader turned writer in the text he sets out to compose, and which resonates also with echoes of another ancient narrative, the medieval romance *Amadis de Gaula.* This specular love, born of the comings and goings of the love experienced in the present, is lived by a new Oriana (of the *Amadis* fame), now named Ouroana, who in her own way becomes a teacher of the ways of passion. The multiple levels of these overlapping stories, with their images reproduced in duplicate or triplicate, are all contained in what is, in the end, the only narrative that we read from the beginning to the end: *The History of the Siege of Lisbon,* a novel by José Saramago.

But what the reading also yields, beside the narrative itself, is the author's conscious proposal for a new way of writing history. The first chapter, which serves as a sort of a theoretical prologue of the novel, determines the text's coordinates as it presents two characters in a face-to-face dialogue: one, a traditional historian, secure in his positivist convictions and firmly aware of his obligation to uncover absolute, objective truth; the other, a simple proofreader, who will later become a writer, and who already throws a shade of doubt that disturbs and perplexes his interlocutor's seriousness and certainty. It is the proofreader who declares "in my modest opinion, Sir, everything that is not literature is life," prompting the historian's retort—"History as well[?]"—an expression of such fatal innocence that it can only lead to a more radical restatement of the concept: "Especially history, without wishing to give offence" (6). This brings me to reiterate, in other words, what I have suggested earlier, that this novel is a sort of deductive parable, an exemplification of an idea expressed in the initial chapter. *The History of the Siege of Lisbon* does not tell a story in order to intuit a principle; on the contrary, its narrative serves to illustrate the novel's foundational notions: the fallibility of any reconstruction of the real and the bankruptcy of specular writing. Neither one of these concepts, however, is aimed at discrediting the historical project as such; indeed, they have the opposite effect, as they serve to empower the truth-generating potential of the historical fiction.

The Biblical Intertext

Saramago has stated, on a number of occasions (particularly when asked about his novel *The Gospel According to Jesus Christ*), that it is not necessary to be a believer in order to see oneself as immersed in Christian culture. An unexceptionable affirmation, as the writer is well aware, considering to what extent the formation of Western ethical discourse has been indebted to the Judeo-Christian imaginary, as have been Western aesthetic models in the areas of literature, visual arts, architecture or music: from the Gregorian chant to Moissac's *Christ*, from the stained-glass windows at Chartres to Chagall's grand Biblical paintings, and from Gil Vicente's religious *autos* to Chateaubriand's *Génie du Christianisme*.

The Christian imaginary recurs frequently in Saramago's work, and while the author certainly rereads it from an unorthodox perspective, the consequences are not necessarily sacrilegious. Although desecration tends to be the end result when Saramago writes in a predominantly ironic or parodic mode, often enough religious references crop up in his work without losing their numinous aura, albeit dislocated from the divine to the human level. It is not even necessary to refer to the notorious *Gospel* in order to identify such instances of revisionist reiteration of the biblical text in Saramago's novels, beginning with *Levantado do Chão*.

In that novel, religious references employed by the discourses of the Latifundium, the Church and the State in order to legitimize their violent and authoritarian actions are ironically desecrated when denounced as instruments of political power. In a number of episodes, the narrator's ironic discourse exposes the ideological underpinnings of the religious project or reveals the absurdity of its claims by simple juxtaposition of the ideal Christian model and the actual human behavior: the scene of the rally in Évora (94), the distribution of alms to the children by the grotesque D. Clemência (187), Father Agamedes's speech on behalf of the secret police (120), and, in the novel's extraordinary first chapter, the evocation of the impersonal and abstract voice of authority, which relies on a mythical narrative to justify the history of the land's occupation by the latifundia (14).

On the other hand, Saramago often avails himself of a strategy of narrative displacement in producing heretical versions of religious models. A more radical procedure than the deconstruction of sacred truths by means of irony, this form of usurpation does not negate the value of the model, but rather denies its uniqueness and exemplary character, insofar as it multiplies the original pattern or discovers its recurrences in places and people that have no relation to divinity. An example may be found in the references to the Way of the Cross, the birth of Jesus Christ and the resurrection of the dead that occur in three central episodes of the novel. The motive of the *via crucis* is rewritten twice, in the respective episodes of João Mau-Tempo's carrying an exceptionally heavy wooden log and Germano Vidigal being taken in for torture by the police. Thus doubled, the suffering of Christ loses the singularity that has given it its exemplary force: Golgota and the Cyrenian, Veronica with her handkerchief, the Last Supper and the centurions are reiterated by the narrative in what is not a repetition, but an enactment of a new, greater drama (if of lesser value to the official history) by a different group of actors.

> There's been much sermonizing over the last two thousand years about how Christ carried the cross to the top of Golgota, assisted by the Cyrenian no less, and of this crucified man coming along here no one says a word, he who ate little for supper last night and almost nothing today, still half a way to go, eyes growing bleary, it's agony, gentlemen, as everyone can see. (76)

> They found him. Two guards are taking him... and now this really seems intentional, it's all uphill, as if we were watching a film on the life of Christ, there on top is the Calvary, these are centurions in heavy boots and sweating as befits warriors... and the procession has only a hundred meters left to go, high up above the wall we see a woman hanging a bedsheet out to dry, wouldn't it be something if her name were Veronica, but no, she's just a Cesaltina and not much of a religious type. She sees the man led by the guards, follows him with her eyes, she doesn't know him but has a sense of foreboding, she rests her face against the wet sheet as if it were a sweat cloth and says to her little boy who wants to play in the sun, Let's go inside. (167)

Saramago redeploys this sacrilegious method with reference to the birth of Christ. The newborn child turns out to be, in this time of new "miracles" (295), a girl, the daughter of Gracinda and Manuel Espada, who also merits a luminous aura ("a reflected luminosity is falling over the bedsheet, let us not speculate where it is coming from") and her own three wise men: grandfather, uncle and father. The gifts she receives instead of gold, myrrh and frankincense are geraniums, daisies and hands open to form a huge flower, and her star of Bethlehem metamorphoses into fireflies that illuminate the road Manuel Espada takes to see his newborn daughter; they come to rest over the door frame, waiting and signaling an homage to the "glory of man on earth" who takes precedence over God in the heavens. Furthermore, to complete the traditional association of Christ with light, the narrative discourse invents a deceptive falsehood: "The two waiting fireflies started to fly again, close to the ground, shining so brightly that the ants who were keeping guard over their anthills gave a shout to announce the sunrise" (301). The falsehood is deceptive because although the ants confuse the radiance of the fireflies with sunlight, metaphorically they are not mistaken in their announcement of another sunrise, represented by the birth of Maria Adelaide: the bright day of the revolution, introduced in the novel with the words "This is the sun of justice" (364).

As if to complete a narrative cycle begun with the Genesis, the novel ends with an epic-Biblical scene of the resurrection of the dead, which does not occur in a transcendental space and time, but in the time where human victories are achieved and in the earthly space of the Portuguese Alentejo, where the agrarian revolution is taking place. That which the example of Christ promises for an afterlife is realized in the present, as a utopia made concrete within history.

Some might call these heretical appropriations, and they would be right, at more than one level of reading. In the first place, we may understand "heresy" in its etymological sense, with no religious reference yet attached to the term, as "choice" (from the Greek "*airesis*"); in this sense, Saramago "chooses" to displace sacred attributes or stories from the plane of transcendence to that of human experience. At a second level, heresy is perpetuated through the voluntary inversion of dogmas or of supposedly divine truths in such a way as to subject them, if not to an outright denial, then at least to a questioning, which has a naturally disconcerting effect with regard to situations that traditional consensus, established religion and morality have considered unquestionable. To agitate, stir up, set into motion: these actions are only possible from within religious discourse, as is the case, in fact, of all heretical processes. Whether labeled as heresy or as sacrilege, it is a form of audacity that opts to work with fragments of referential texts, remnants or castaways of a culture, and to reuse them in a manner different from their original purpose.

The most ample material for this kind of reflection may of course be found in Saramago's *The Gospel According to Jesus Christ*, which presents in the guise of a fictional construct the discourse transmitted by the tradition as an expression of absolute truth. This is a text that not only avails itself of the Christian repertoire of cultural references, but also articulates its own writing formula on the basis of sacred texts. Its sacrilegious character consists ultimately in its close approach to the model in order to absorb it skillfully within a conscious exercise of pastiche.

In truth, however, let it be said that Saramago's audacious dialogue with the Christian tradition does not obliterate it, but, on the contrary, offers it an opportunity to learn to speak for itself not in eternal but in present time. Is not this the meaning of the artful somersault performed in the novel's second epigraph, which quotes Pontius Pilate's words, *Quod scripsi, scripsi*? "What I have written, I have written" signifies here not only an authoritarian gesture of the man in power who refuses to go back on his actions, but also an ironic indictment—on the narrator's part—of the speaking subject's ignorance with respect to the fatality of the written language itself that is unable, once written down, to elude the many readings it is bound to unwittingly generate. Once written, the Holy Gospels became liable to engender apocryphal, parodic and even heretical versions, since their words are not stamped with the seal of copyright and, on the contrary, have grown richer with the liberty of their diverse interpretations.

Saramago's writing, taking the sacred as its point of departure in order to endow it with unexpected meanings, invests in a revolution that, like all revolutions, consecrates the sacrilege.[6] In choosing its sacrilegious strategy, it rests on etymological roots that suggest as much a theft of the sacred as its possession or reading (*lego*: "to bring together, gather," but also "to read," and, by way of litotes, "to take, appropriate or steal"). The result is a contradictory game played against the other (text), which seduces and invites parodic reconsideration: it requires the courage to touch what must not be touched (the sacred) so that it does not become soiled (sacrilege), marked or branded. In this sense, the revolution to which fiction subjects the holy document is not just sacrilege directed against it, but also, paradoxically, its consecration. The narrative does not place itself in opposition to holiness: its goal is merely recontextualization.

To recontextualize the sacred means, for example, to displace the scene of the Last Supper from the eve of the crucifixion to the celebration of Jesus' lovemaking with Mary Magdalen. Their love affair begins after the woman applies healing ointments to Jesus' foot: thus Saramago rewrites the episode in which Jesus washes his disciples' feet before the feast, replacing, in the process, an expression of the Master's humility before his followers with a prelude to physical passion that consists in educating the senses and learning the body: "Discover my body," says Mary Magdalen, and then "Discover your body" (213).

To recontextualize the sacred also means to create Jesus as a disciple and not as a master, a disciple who needs masters and will have them: in Pastor, whom he does not understand, and in Mary Magdalen, who finally makes Jesus apprehend what he had earlier perceived but dimly, until he himself discovers the impending tragedy and is driven ineluctably towards the sacrifice. God's design is thus revealed as an enormous betrayal and an immoderate exercise of power, which cannot be countered for reasons of historical verisimilitude and internal coherence of the narrative. To invert God's plan, making Jesus die on the cross without having realized his own divinity, would be tantamount to inaugurating a history that did not take place. This strategy, therefore, has no future, and God's words, which identify Jesus—"This is My beloved Son" (341)—are moved from the scene of baptism to that of crucifixion, during which, according to the Biblical text, the skies in reality fell silent. An immense irony, nevertheless, attends the fact that God chooses to impose his presence even though the dying Jesus desires to remain unrecognized and has not asked the question: "Father, why hast Thou forsaken me?". The disclosure of Jesus as the Son of God amounts to a denial of a possible reversal of history and is a gesture that effectively sanctions the bloody horrors to be brought about by the Christian dominance of Western culture. This authoritarian gesture of the Father can only be countered by the last generous action of the Son, who perverts the discourse of paternalistic charity aimed at saving from damnation the inconsistent, sinful humans who have crucified him—"Father, forgive them, for they know not what they do"—by choosing (*airesis*) a formula that identifies him conclusively with those very humans: "Men, forgive Him, for he knows not what He has done" (341).

I like to think, with Compagnon, that an author recreates in the process of writing the primordial gestures of playing with paper: cutting and pasting. All literary texts are construed through the superposition of successive layers of knowledge, showing marks of incisions and corrections, traces of dialogues and borrowings, voices of the present and shadows of the past. José Saramago negotiates in a manner both critical and generous his ample baggage as an attentive cultural traveler: he is well aware that in the constructs of the present a thousand living beings exist side-by-side with a hundred thousand dead, and that the sighs of the dead rising from the ground are the remains of the works bequeathed by the past. To know how to deal with these remains is to reproduce in writing a passion for reading, since reading and writing are similar, complementary and supplementary practices: they allow the transmission of the echoes of human knowledge—beyond mere repetition—by new utterances that are added daily to the immense universal library of humankind.

Notes

[1]. "Que la substance de la citation, par-delà les accidents du sens et du phénomène, soit une *dynamis*, une puissance, l'étymologie le confirme. *Citare*, en latin, c'est mettre en mouvement, faire passer du repos à l'action. Les sens du verbe s'ordonnent ainsi: d'abord faire venir à soi, appeler (d'où l'acception juridique d'une sommation à comparaître), puis exciter, provoquer, enfin, dans le vocabulaire militaire, délivrer une mention. En tout cas, une puissance est en jeu, celle qui met en branle" (Compagnon 44).

[2]. I have discussed in greater detail these structural similarities between *Levantado do Chão* and Camões's poem in "No Paraíso da Memória....".

[3]. [Translator's note] I have retained here the Portuguese original along with the translation, in order to better illustrate Saramago's intricate reworking and absorption of Camões's verse.

[4]. All these references and strategies of appropriation are comprehensively described in my *José Saramago. Entre a História e a Ficção.*

[5]. See, in addition to my book, Silva 1991 and 1998.

[6]. As Octavio Paz put it, "Every revolution is at the same time a profanation and a consecration. The revolutionary movement is a profanation, because it overthrows old images, but this debasement is always accompanied by a consecration of what up to that point had been considered profane: the revolution consecrates the sacrilege" (269).

Works Cited

Camões, Luís de. *The Lusíads.* Trans. Landeg White. Oxford: Oxford UP, 1997.

Compagnon, Antoine. *La Seconde Main ou le travail de la citation.* Paris: Seuil, 1979.

Foucault, Michel. "La Bibliothèque fantastique." In *Travail de Flaubert,* Ed. R. Debray-Genette et al. Paris: Editions du Seuil, 1983.

Le Goff, Jacques. "Documento/Monumento." *História-Memória. Enciclopédia Einaudi.* Vol. 1 Lisboa: Imprensa Nacional-Casa da Moeda, 1984. 95-106.

Lourenço, Eduardo. *O Labirinto da Saudade.* 1978. Lisboa: Dom Quixote, 1992.

Paz, Octavio. *O Arco e a Lira.* Rio de Janeiro: Nova Fronteira, 1952.

Proust, Marcel. *Remembrance of Things Past.* Vol. I. Trans. C. K. Scott Moncrieff and Terence Kilmartin. New York: Vintage Books, 1982.

Saramago, José. *O Ano da Morte de Ricardo Reis.* Lisbon: Caminho, 1984. English translation by Giovanni Pontiero, *The Year of the Death of Ricardo Reis.* San Diego: Harcourt, 1991.

———. *O Evangelho Segundo Jesus Cristo.* Lisboa: Caminho, 1991. English translation by Giovanni Pontiero, *The Gospel According to Jesus Christ.* New York: Harcourt Brace, 1994.

———. *História do Cerco de Lisboa.* Lisboa: Caminho, 1989. English translation by Giovanni Pontiero, *The History of the Siege of Lisbon.* New York: Harcourt Brace, 1996.

———. *A Jangada de Pedra.* Lisboa: Caminho, 1986. English translation by Giovanni Pontiero, *The Stone Raft.* New York: Harcourt Brace, 1995.

———. *Levantado do Chão.* Lisboa: Caminho, 1980.

———. *Memorial do Convento.* Lisboa: Caminho, 1982. English translation by Giovanni Pontiero, *Baltasar and Blimundaa.,* San Diego: Harcourt, 1987.

Silva, Teresa Cristina Cerdeira da. "The Aura of History in Historical Fiction." *Portuguese Studies* 14 (1998): 205-14.

———. "José Saramago: a Ficção Reinventa a História." *Colóquio/Letras* 120 (Abril-Junho de 1991): 174-78.

———. *José Saramago. Entre a História e a Ficção: Uma Saga de Portugueses.* Lisboa: Dom Quixote, 1989.

———. "No Paraíso da Memória, Um Outro Valor da Terra Se Alevanta." *Actas do XIII Encontro de Professores Universitários Brasileiros de Literatura Portuguesa.* Rio de Janeiro: 1992. 297-302.

Righting Wrongs, Re-Writing Meaning and Reclaiming the City in Saramago's *Blindness* and *All the Names**

David Frier

The two most recent novels by José Saramago to have appeared in English, *Blindness* (1995) and *All the Names* (1997), constitute the first two parts of a trilogy that was completed by *A Caverna* (*The Cave*, untranslated), published in November 2000. The author has gone on record as acknowledging the Platonic echoes of the title of this latest work, declaring at a conference in Spain in February of last year that in his opinion humanity has never found itself more firmly entrenched inside the Greek philosopher's cave than it is today.[1] Such declarations clearly place these more recent novels in a different context from the earlier works that established the novelist's success at home and abroad. Works such as *Levantado do Chão* (*Raised from the Soil*, untranslated, 1980), *Baltasar and Blimunda* (1982) and *The Year of the Death of Ricardo Reis* (1984) are all firmly rooted in Portuguese history, whereas the two more recent novels are set in a vaguely defined present, in nameless cities,[2] and with characters who remain unnamed throughout, with the sole exception of the main protagonist of *All the Names*, Senhor José; even in his case, however, the text manages to avoid giving him a surname to accompany this most unremarkable of Portuguese given names.

This should not, however, be understood as a radical change in the author's essential vision of the world: the "radical break" that he mentions in an interview immediately after the publication of *Blindness* refers to the harrowing nature of the subject-matter of this novel and not necessarily, therefore, to the mentality that produced it.[3] Hence, I would argue that the change that the author's works have undergone during recent years should be seen as occurring more in style and emphasis than in underlying direction. A common thread running through all of Saramago's major novels has been the need for a reappraisal of where humanity finds itself today, as well as of where Portugal has been in the past.[4] The value of the specific events recounted in a work such as *Baltasar and Blimunda* lies in the reflections that they prompt in the present-day reader (often stimulated by anachronistic allusions in the text to events subsequent to the period in which the novel is set). The novelist himself has recognized this, quoting Fernand Braudel: "History is merely a constant examination of the past, carried out in terms of the problems and the points of interest, as well as the fears and concerns surrounding and afflicting us in the present."[5] This allegorical tendency to write about something more than the immediate subject-matter in hand is therefore one that is not totally new to the author, even if it appears now in a purer form.[6]

Nonetheless, the key difference between the earlier and the more recent novels in this respect is that, with the elimination of specific references to time, place and name, the reader's attention is drawn explicitly and immediately to considerations that are more universal in character than those prompted by works set in specific historical moments. More particularly, the Platonic context should lead us to see these texts as reflecting the imperfections of the world in which we live by comparison with a more ideal model (even if the author's pronouncements outside the literary arena on political and social issues make it clear that his ideal society would bear little resemblance to the hierarchical one proposed in *The Republic* and, in fact, no specific solutions for a better society are advanced in either of the novels under consideration here).

Setting this allegorical tendency to one side, it is not easy to see many other features in common between *Blindness* and *All the Names*; in the earlier of these two texts social order breaks down completely, while the world of Senhor José is one marked by a rigid and hierarchical respect for order. In terms of the reception given to the two works, Craig Nova wrote of *Blindness* that "by the way it is written, in the details that Saramago uses to such good effect, almost all of the horrors of the twentieth century are addressed,"[7] while *All the Names* prompted one reviewer (José Leon Machado) to criticise it for its blandness. Finally, whereas *Blindness* eventually sees the recreation of community from the bleak circumstances that bring its protagonists together, Senhor José remains an essentially solitary creature throughout *All the Names*. However, an analysis of the narrative structure of these two novels will reveal that they share as their defining narrative event a symbolic descent into the underworld that brings profound changes in the lives of their protagonists and permits them to find the prospect of life where previously there was only death and a lack of real meaning. As part of the process of affirmation of the dynamic potential of human life that arises from this realisation, both novels stress the importance of a creative and imaginative response to the world as a mark of true civilisation, and in both novels the act of remembering and recording human experience acquires importance as their respective protagonists struggle to assert some control over the circumstances in which they must live their lives.

In the case of *Blindness*, the motif of the descent into the underworld exists in two separate forms: in general terms, all of the major characters of the novel might be said (to use a colloquialism) to go through Hell and back before emerging as stronger human beings with a greater bond to their fellows at the end of the text. More specifically, however, it is the doctor's wife (the one figure who retains her sight throughout the text while all others lose theirs) who has to endure most, in that she sees the misery that others can only imagine: "I am simply the one who was born to see this horror" (247). She is also the only character to willingly sacrifice her sight (when she descends into the unlit basement storeroom of a supermarket to find food for her comrades [204-08] and, again, when she goes, "Blind in the darkness" [248], to fetch water from the toilet in her home for the boy with the squint). It is her insistence on retaining contact with the notion of humanity as a civilised species that helps to bring the others through their period of greatest difficulty, as she insists on burying the dead body of the old woman (268), bringing her friends into her clean home in spite of the dirt on their bodies and clothes (243) and then washing (250-51) and dressing them in fresh garments (246). The concepts of Heaven and Hell recur in this episode, as her apartment—which has surprisingly remained unoccupied during the period of crisis—is compared to Paradise (242), so that the other members of the group (described here as "pilgrims") fear that their dirt will transform it from this Edenic state into a Hell similar to the one from which they have emerged (242-43). The real mark of civilisation on the part of the doctor's wife, however, is surely that she is willing to accept this contamination of her own space for the sake of the others.

The obvious specific problem in understanding this novel is that of the interpretation to be placed on a sudden and devastating epidemic of blindness that strikes an entire country. There are a variety of straightforward explanations that it would be tempting to put forward, yet none of them proves adequate to account for the events recounted. There is an obvious temptation to see the mass blindness as a process of contagion, for some link can be traced amongst all of the early victims, who have either been present in the doctor's surgery during the first blind man's visit or who have had other direct dealings with the early victims before their incarceration. Yet this would not account for the fact that the doctor's wife remains unaffected by the condition throughout the novel, nor would it explain the sudden blindness of the first man at the beginning of the novel, an event that occurs in the most prosaic of circumstances.

Equally some readers might be tempted to place a moral judgment on the characters, and, once again, there is textual evidence that could be used to support such a view: the second person to go blind is the man who steals the first victim's car and he does so before he has moved thirty paces away from the vehicle (17), a fact that has been seen as an echo of Judas Iscariot's thirty pieces of silver in the Bible.[8] Secondly, on at least two occasions the narrator (21 and 219) brings into discussion the sexual behaviour of another of the first victims, the girl with the dark glasses, who is a prostitute and who loses her sight during an encounter with a client (23). Yet, as will become apparent on a closer examination of the passages that recount these events, it surely becomes unsustainable to argue that the novel seeks to impose any kind of exemplary judgment on these two characters; rather, I intend to argue that any such treatment of these two characters merely reveals that the figure of the narrator is as bewildered by the sequence of events that he narrates as are we, the readers, and that explanations for events based on notions of superhuman moral retribution can exist only in the eye of the beholder and not in any objective reality.

Firstly, as regards the girl with the dark glasses, it is only narratorial insistence that brings the woman's profession into our consciousness at all (21), and, even then, the comments made about her are by no means filled with moral indignation; instead, the over-elaborate tone of the discourse adopted by the narrator here should remind us that this is merely a subjective perspective imposed upon events by one particular observer.[9] In fact, as the novel unfolds, it becomes evident that any such hasty judgment of this woman's sexual practices not only accords them an unjustified level of significance (certainly by comparison with some of the events that take place later in the text). Any such judgment would also mean ignoring all other aspects of her character: her subsequent actions demonstrate that, in spite of her profession, she is no easy conquest (45-46), while she also possesses many traditional virtues, displayed most prominently in her repeated kindness to the young boy with the squint, in her voluntary act of washing the back of the old man with the eye patch (255), and in her remorse for having wounded the car thief (56 and 71).

Similarly, the thirty steps taken by the car thief can be related to the betrayal of Christ only if we care to read that interpretation into the words used by the narrator. It should be noted that the blindness strikes when the thief "had gone not even thirty paces" (17).[10] One wonders therefore how many paces he had taken: perhaps twenty-eight or twenty-nine? If the number of steps taken were counted more precisely here, or measured in metres rather than in paces, then there would be no significance readily visible in this event at all. There is a temptation to apportion blame here, then, but in fact this leads us as readers no further than it does the hotel maid who blames her blindness on seeing the girl with the dark glasses lying naked in bed, only in the end to find herself quarantined in the same ward as her (58-59). Both in regard to this character and to the girl with the dark glasses, therefore, any reader who might be tempted to leap to hasty morally based judgments of their affliction is, ironically, succumbing to the same kind of blindness as the chambermaid does in seeking a simplistic scapegoat for a much more deeply rooted problem; in fact, these incidents demonstrate no evidence of any real connection based on cause and effect and function rather as an ironically alluring invitation to the reader to perceive such a causal relationship while then subsequently revealing its essential irrelevance and over-simplicity when confronted with the complexities of modern life.

This type of portrayal of events has its precedents in earlier works such as *The Stone Raft* (1986), where the reader closes the text without becoming any wiser as to the causes of the strange events recounted in its pages.[11] In fact, both in that novel and in this one, it could be argued that it is the changing relationships amongst the various characters that give the text its real significance, rather than the events taking place around them. The real explanation for the epidemic in *Blindness*, therefore, is surely that we should not waste our time looking for rational explanations for it, as we would do if this were a real-world event; this is a literary work and the greatest importance of the outbreak of blindness may lie as easily in the plane of significance as in that of science. The key point is that the epidemic happens and that certain consequences flow from it; any attempts that we may make to offer a logical explanation for the blindness indicate that we ourselves have failed to follow the lesson of the epigraph to the work (taken from Saramago's invented *Book of Exhortations*): "If you can see, look. If you can look, observe." As Maria Alzira Seixo writes, "What Saramago does not do is to tell an allegorical story where he implicitly suggests what is wrong and how that wrong can be put right; rather, Saramago *warns* us of a danger, the danger of not seeing, of not noticing" ("Os espelhos virados para dentro" 196; original emphasis).

Previous critics have seen precedents for *Blindness* in some of the author's own writing of the 1970s, notably in *O Ano de 1993* (*The Year 1993*, untranslated, 1975) and in the short stories "Embargo" and "Things," in *Objecto Quase* (*Almost an Object*, untranslated, 1978).[12] In the case of "Embargo," the story arises from a similar situation to that of this novel: an unnamed man, driving his car in an unnamed city, suddenly finds that he has lost all control over his own life as he effectively becomes a prisoner of his vehicle. This story (written at the height of the international oil crisis of the early 1970s) could be read as a satirical fancy based around our modern over-reliance on technology (as, indeed, could also be said of *Blindness* itself at times). What makes this story particularly interesting in the current context, however, is that the desperate conclusion, where the man is thrown out into the wilderness by the car once it runs out of fuel, is completely avoidable, for at one point the driver is able to stop outside his own house and summon his wife down to the street and explain the problem to her. He then becomes embarrassed at the situation in which the emergency services would find him and chooses to give himself up to whatever fate the car may have in store for him rather than wait to be saved and lose face in the process (16-17). Ultimately, therefore, it is a lack of faith in others and excessive concern with his own image that condemns him and not his situation itself, however unpleasant that may be.[13]

In the case of *Blindness*, Maria Alzira Seixo has pointed to this issue of trust, specifically discussing the hesitancy in the relationship between the first victim and the car-thief, which she sees as the commencement of the essential plot of the novel ("Os espelhos" 193),[14] and in general terms it seems appropriate to say that it is a lack of trust in others and generosity of spirit towards others that magnifies the impact of the epidemic here. This is true at two different levels. Firstly, in terms of the relationships between those who have not been struck blind and those who have (and who are quarantined in a disused mental asylum), the victims are effectively treated by the authorities as undesirable aliens rather than as fellow human beings in distress. One of the most striking instances is the execution of the car thief, who approaches the edge of the compound to seek medical assistance, only to be executed instantly by a panicking soldier (69), an incident that recalls the summary elimination of the solitary sailor during a similar state of national emergency in *The Stone Raft* (184). However, the same principle also applies to relationships within the asylum itself, where smaller quarrels over food supplies and hygiene eventually escalate into bullying and exploitation of the whole community by the residents of one ward.

One of the key aspects of the presentation of the worst side of human nature in this novel, however, is the fact that this is no simplistic opposition of cruel oppressors and innocent victims. The lack of faith in others runs throughout this society, with the blind themselves calculatedly oppressing the blind, never more clearly than when those who have stockpiled the food supplies demand women in return for releasing rations to the other wards (150). What is equally alarming, however, is the response to this problem amongst the small group of characters on whom the text focuses, for one can see by their reactions that they, too, are in danger of ceasing to treat their fellow humans with the full respect that is due to them: some of the men callously expect that the women should do their duty towards the community as a whole by simply accepting their own rape as the price that must be paid for the survival of all (150). However, even the superficially honourable reaction of the first blind man, who wishes to forbid his wife to prostitute herself for food (152), proves, on closer examination, to be equally possessive in its implications for gender relations, as it implies not only that women other than his wife must accept their own degradation in order that they may eat (153), but also that he has not, as yet, succeeded in recognising and respecting his wife's ability to make her own judgments in a moral dilemma such as this one. This incident also briefly raises the question of homophobic intimidation, when one of the women raises the awkward question of what would have happened if the demand had been for men rather than for women, producing the reply "There are no pansies here" (151), a declaration impossible to confirm or to refute as a statement of fact and which merely indicates another potential path of suffering, one which is not, however, followed up later in the novel.

Essentially, the picture of humanity in *Blindness* is an abject one, with little left towards the end of the text to distinguish the human beings from the scavenging dogs around them in the streets of the city. It is therefore tenable to suggest that the author's decision not to name his characters is not only a choice intended to make this a novel of any city in any country but also a realistic reflection of the loss of humanity in a society that has lost its sense of compassion and solidarity. For not only are the characters themselves unnamed, but even other references remain anonymous: the artists whose paintings are mentioned as one character recalls going blind in a museum of art are identified only by nationality, even though the works referred to include such famous paintings as Botticelli's *The Birth of Venus*, Leonardo da Vinci's *The Last Supper*, Constable's *Haywain* and Picasso's *Guernica* (116). Similarly, in the scene in the church in the final chapter of the novel, the references to all of the religious figures (including both Jesus and Our Lady, as well as various saints) are also reduced merely to physical descriptions, as if the narrator had lost his memory, as certainly appears to have happened to the characters themselves (284).[15]

More striking still in this scene is the fact that all of these images have had their eyes covered over (284). When the doctor's wife reveals this fact, all of the blind people who have been seeking shelter in the building abandon it in panic, surely an indication that they have been waiting for a miracle (286).[16] It is only after this incident (when hope for externally imposed solutions has been exhausted) that sight begins to be restored to the population, as mysteriously and as suddenly as it had been lost, and it is also this incident that prompts the doctor's wife to raise the issue of reciprocity in vision, commenting that the saints see through the eyes that see them (284). When taken together with her suggestion that her vision will eventually lose its worth in a world where nobody else can see ("I'll see less and less all the time, even though I may not lose my eyesight I shall become more and more blind because I shall have no one to see me" [284-85]), this implies that her solitary role as the custodian of values cannot be borne indefinitely: civilisation is a precious inheritance that we all have a responsibility to preserve.

This incident is reminiscent of the scene towards the end of *Baltasar and Blimunda*, where Baltasar and Blimunda go to see the statues of the saints that are to be placed on top of the Convent at Mafra (316-18). In that dialogue, Blimunda (said by the novelist himself to be the twin sister of the doctor's wife, a woman with greater powers of eyesight than the others around her)[17] reaches the conclusion that the saints have been silenced and rendered meaningless as statues (317), and then goes on to stress the dynamic nature of human existence, with all people continually growing and changing, even Francisco Marques, who was killed earlier in the text (318). These puzzling remarks raise issues that are more prominent in *All the Names* than in *Blindness*, but before discussing these more fully it will be necessary to consider the former novel in more general terms.

In *All the Names* there is no breakdown of order as happens in the earlier work: the nightmare in this text lies rather in the all-consuming nature of the order that does exist. The archaic and hierarchical organisation of the Registry where Senhor José works effectively reduces his life to a function rather than an existence, and it appears that he has no friends, only colleagues with whom he maintains distant relationships of no real substance. He has no existence autonomous from his job; his home is part of the property of the Registry and can be accessed from it at any time (something that he does not dare to question when the deputy enters his home without invitation [104]). Senhor José himself appears to have no outside interests, other than collecting information about the lives of celebrities, a pastime that may add some taste of vicarious glamour to his existence but which in effect is merely an extension of his professional life. Furthermore, his sense of awe and intimidation in the face of the Registrar indicates a person who could not imagine himself either possessing or even wishing to possess any personal qualities other than those required strictly for his limited professional obligations. Significantly, in his first conversation with the old woman who lived downstairs from the unknown woman whom he seeks, he declares that by comparison with the Registrar he himself is not worth anything (49), a chilling reminder of the words repeatedly used by the willing servants of fascism in *The Year of the Death of Ricardo Reis* "We are nobody" (313, 314, 323 and 325). During the course of the narrative, however, he grows in stature, developing talents for deception and burglary and qualities of courage and endurance that make him unrecognisable as the meek functionary who is introduced to us at the beginning of the text, so that later on he is able to see an alarming vision of his own former self in the person of the clerk who serves him at the Cemetery with "the absorbed air of one who no longer expects anything more from life" (221).

As has also been seen in *Blindness*, the hierarchy here is not one of simple opposition, for Senhor José himself relishes even the limited powers that he possesses as an employee of the Registry, threatening police action against the old woman if she does not cooperate with him in his investigation (47) and refusing to let her ask him any questions in return (48). Yet his use of authority can work only to a limited degree: the Registrar may be said to know all of the names ever used (49), but the knowledge possessed by his Registry does not pass beyond the level of the sketchiest biographical information, and when the old woman tells Senhor José some facts about her own past, she reminds him that this now makes his knowledge superior to that of the Registrar himself (49). The Registrar is therefore seen to be merely like a human version of the telephone book, which he seems to regard as a rival when Senhor José looks at it instead of him during one of their conversations (64-65). These gaps in the apparently encyclopaedic knowledge of the Registry, which are comparable to the failings of Borges' "Funes, the Memorious," the person who has a perfect memory for facts but who is unable to link them in a meaningful way, may also be related to Saramago's representation of historiography in some of his earlier novels, notably *The History of the Siege of Lisbon* (1989). There the conscious alteration made by the proofreader Raimundo Silva, who inserts the word "not" into a vital passage of an academic work of history, is seen to be no worse than the (presumably) unconscious incongruencies and anachronisms imposed on the text by its original author.[18] The telephone directory, the Registry and historical accounts of the past all contain a huge mass of potentially useful information, but these data need to be made meaningful in order to be of any use. Thus, Senhor José's search for the unknown woman whose details he unintentionally removes from the Registry becomes a search not for a handful of bare biographical details, but for the real human being who lies behind them, a search that, as has been suggested by Adrián Huici, is really a search for himself as much as for the other ("Perdidos en el laberinto" 457).

The fact that Senhor José's search ends in apparent failure (with the discovery that the woman whom he seeks is already dead) is not as important as the lessons that he learns in the course of his investigations. The most important of these is in his second conversation with the woman on the ground floor of the building where the unknown woman spent her childhood (162-73). Having used his professional role (both in this conversation with the older woman and in their previous one [48]) to elicit information useful to his own purposes (as well as to obtaining unsolicited personal information about her past sexual history [48]), Senhor José withholds until late in their conversation the most important knowledge that he has about the woman whom he seeks and whom the old woman knew as a child: namely the unexpected fact of her death (167). The fact that in their first conversation he had reprimanded her for withholding information useful to him (52) indicates that up to this moment Senhor José has not been interested in building a reciprocal relationship with this woman (or with any other person), but only in gratifying his own desires. While his sin here is a relatively small one in degree, it should be clear that this is exactly the same assumption about others in kind as that made by the rapists in the asylum in *Blindness.*

In this novel, when the old woman reproaches Senhor José for having lied to her throughout their dealings with one another (168-69), he finally begins to build a genuine relationship with another person, admitting the whole story of his unusual preoccupation with an unknown woman, which has led him to tell lies, falsify documents, and break into the school that she attended as a child in order to satisfy his curiosity about her (170). In doing so, quite unexpectedly, he has stumbled upon something closer to the real sense of his quest, which cannot be to find out the simple biographical facts of the unknown woman (for it is clear from relatively early on in the text that any member of the public, including Senhor José, would be entitled to use the facilities of the Registry to seek information on any other person [7]). The fact that he chooses to go about his search by illegitimate means (as he cannot think of a logical reason to justify his interest in the unknown woman) demonstrates that he at least, if not this society as a whole, views the wish for genuinely human contact to be something suspicious. The Registry thus acquires a vaguely Orwellian aura that is also reminiscent of the large eyes made of mercury that keep the population under surveillance in Saramago's own *O Ano de 1993* (XI: 11-13).[19]

Senhor José makes a total of four expeditions that could be viewed as descents into the underworld: the night and day that he spends in the unknown woman's school (72-95); his nocturnal exploration of the section of the dead in the Registry (141-53);[20] the visit to the cemetery to seek out the grave of the unknown woman (184-211); and, finally, his visit to the woman's apartment in search of clues as to the reasons for her death, reasons that, in the final analysis, he comes to realise are as irrelevant to him as the physical causes of the blindness should be to the reader of the earlier novel (234-39).

Not all of the traditional elements associated with a visit to the underworld are present in all of these episodes, but the key component, that of the incursion into forbidden territory, is recurrent in all of them, and, as Huici demonstrates, many of the other formal features of the journey into the underworld are reflected in the details of these episodes ("Perdidos en el laberinto" 458-59).

The most interesting of these incidents in the current context is that of the visit to the cemetery. The design of the cemetery itself is reminiscent of the one outlined in the story "Reflux" ("Refluxo") in *Objecto Quase*, where a king tries to banish the prospect of death from his awareness by creating a hermetically sealed-off zone of the kingdom that will house all of the graves needed. As time passes, however, nature overcomes order and the force of death, represented by the graves themselves, creeps beyond the boundaries that have been artificially imposed on it and back into the life of the country. Similarly, in *All the Names*, what started out as a neat, geometrically organised and strictly delimited area of the city has slowly stretched out its tentacles into every available space of clear ground, so that, paradoxically, from the air the city of the dead is said to resemble what is normally a symbol of life, the shape of a tree (186). This description reminds the reader of the potential for renewed growth in the stick placed over Pedro Orce's grave at the end of *The Stone Raft* (263), and thus asserts that death is as much a part of the continually self-renewing cycle of life as the process of living itself, thus justifying Isabel Pires de Lima's identification of the cemetery as an allegory of life itself: "ever-changing, chaotic, uncertain, meaningless" (424).

Here Senhor José meets the enigmatic figure of a shepherd, whom cultural tradition might lead us to associate with the figure of Jesus if it were not for the existence of a character called Pastor playing the part of the Devil in the author's earlier novel *The Gospel According to Jesus Christ* (1991). In view of this fact it is hardly surprising that this shepherd turns out to be anything but a reassuring figure, as he informs Senhor José that, far from having succeeded in locating the grave of the unknown woman, he has only found one of many graves that might be hers, for he rearranges at random the numbers given to each grave by the cemetery personnel so as to make identification of their places of burial virtually impossible (208-09). He is therefore a spirit who replaces order with chaos, just as his namesake in the earlier novel is less a personification of evil and more an emblem of the inevitability of change and human growth, the same spirit that inspires

Raimundo Silva's minor but far-reaching act of rebellion in *The History of the Siege of Lisbon.*

What is also striking in this episode is not only that the cemetery as a whole was originally designed on highly artificial lines but that the woman's grave is to be found in a section specifically reserved for suicides. This is not merely a reflection of the Roman Catholic tradition according to which suicides cannot be buried on consecrated ground, but also a reflection of sections of two previous literary visits to the world of the dead, in Book VI of Virgil's *Aeneid* (185) and in the thirteenth Canto of Dante's *Inferno* (129-37). In both of these works suicide is presented negatively: in Virgil the souls of those who killed themselves suffer far greater torments in the afterlife than they did on earth, while in Dante they are punished by being reduced to the status of plants. In both of these cases, however, the souls of the dead can still give an example to those whom they have left behind in this life; by contrast, in Saramago's novel there is no suggestion of any existence beyond the grave; the only thing that bears witness to the past life of the unknown woman is a silent gravestone marked only with an anonymous number. Worse even than the suffering of the souls seen in Dante and Virgil, then, is the total non-being that awaits the dead in Saramago: this woman is simply no more, and the title of the novel, *All the Names*, which previously signified a pretension to omniscience, now takes on a new sense, since it no longer matters which one of all the names is given to any particular body.[21]

Senhor José decides to spend the night in the cemetery, sheltering in the body of a hollow tree, which may be seen to represent both the hollowness of his own life up until this point and also the coffin that will await him some day in the future (205-06).[22] When he returns to the land of the living, Senhor José, who earlier used his status as an employee of the Registry to declare the unknown woman to be still alive in ignorance of the fact that she had just committed suicide,[23] now returns to the house of the old woman to find that she has been taken away in an ambulance, and neither he nor we have any further sight of her (240-41). This is therefore a final reminder to him of both the fragility of life and yet also of its importance, as he is told by the mysterious shepherd: "It's life that's sacred, Mr Clerk" (209). Like Orpheus, Senhor José returns from the underworld having glimpsed the woman whom he has pursued into the kingdom of death but unable to bring her back with him. Unlike Orpheus, however, he does not succumb to despair over her loss but sets out to participate more actively in the world than before, just as Francis of Assisi ultimately learns to do in his second life in Saramago's drama, *A Segunda Vida de Francisco de Assis* (*The Second Life of Francis of Assisi*, untranslated, 1987, 131).

The particular point of interest in the play's conclusion as regards a comparison with *All the Names* and *Blindness* is that its final words refer to Francisco's attempts to eradicate poverty from the world in terms of writing a book, for his mother declares "I'm going to help João write his first page" (132).[24] This metaphor is a recurrent one in the author's fiction (one might think, for example, of the renewed sense of purpose in life found by H. in *Manual of Painting and Calligraphy* [1977] or by Raimundo Silva in *The History of the Siege of Lisbon*), and it also reappears in the two novels under consideration here, in the form of Senhor José's diary in *All the Names* and in the figure of the blind writer in *Blindness*, who has continued to work in spite of his own condition and the chaos all around him.

This question is intimately related to the author's treatment of the realisation of the potential of the individual as an active participant in the world. One of the most frightening aspects of *Blindness* lies not in the brutal crimes that the reader sees perpetrated within the asylum, nor in the total degradation into which the city has fallen when the inmates escape from it, but in the passivity of their response to these horrors. This is highlighted at least twice in the narrative, firstly at the moment of escape from the asylum, when the inmates are reluctant to leave the familiar environment in which they have been held, however unpleasant that experience may have been: "Say to a blind man, you're free, open the door that was separating him from the world, Go, you are free, we tell him once more, and he does not go, he has remained motionless there in the middle of the road, he and the others, they are terrified, they do not know where to go" (195). The second instance occurs when the doctor's wife returns from her expedition to find food, only to discover her companions "dreaming they were stones, and we all know how deeply stones sleep, a simple stroll in the countryside shows it to be so, there they lie sleeping, half buried" (211). This section of the novel sees the sense of humanity of the main characters at its lowest ebb, for here not only do we see that people do not treat one another with the courtesy due to other human beings, but it is evident that the protagonists appear even to have accepted the loss of their own former status as self-sufficient creatures.

The mission of the doctor's wife from this point onwards lies not only in securing the short-term needs of herself and her companions but also in reminding them of their own and others' humanity, in other words, in restoring meaning to human life, as emerges from the discussion in the home of the girl with dark glasses:

> Then there is no future, said the old man with the black eyepatch, I cannot say whether there will be a future, what matters for the moment is to see how we can live in the present. Without a future, the present serves no purpose, it's as if it did not exist, Perhaps humanity will manage to live without eyes, but then it will cease to be humanity, the result is obvious, which of us think of ourselves as being as human as we believed ourselves to be before, I, for example, killed a man… (228-29)

These remarks follow speculation as to whether or not there can be a government in the land of the blind, a prospect that the doctor's wife dismisses as "a government of the blind trying to rule the blind, that is to say, nothingness trying to organise nothingness" (228), or, to use a linguistic metaphor, a signifier that has become vacuous because there is no longer a signified for it to represent. Indeed, even during the short time in which she explores the city, the doctor's wife finds that language is already losing all content of any real significance, as her fellow citizens are so bored that they can break their silence only to make cheap sexual innuendo (203). Equally, in the asylum, the only inmate other than her who has managed to preserve literacy is the blind accountant (who was already blind before the epidemic and who therefore has a system to keep records). He forms part of the group of hoodlums who hold the other wards to ransom over the food supplies; his function is therefore effectively similar to that of the Registry in *All the Names*, that is, to record bald facts of little or no real human content. With time, the doctor's wife knows that literacy will be lost and, along with it, language itself, which separates humans from the animal world; already, in her movements around the city, she has seen how others have been reduced to silent functioning, like ants, because they have nothing left to say to one another as they go about their aimless existences:

> they were constantly bumping into each other like ants on the trail, but when this happened no one protested, nor did they have to say anything, one of the families moved away from the wall, advanced along the wall opposite in the other direction, and thus they proceeded and carried on until the next encounter. (202-03)

She therefore seeks to restore meaning to the slightest gesture, turning a simple matter such as drinking clean water into a ceremony akin to a banquet or a eucharist (249) and insisting on giving a decent burial to the old woman whose dead body they find in the street (268). As they bury her, the doctor's wife exclaims "She will rise again" (270), which leads the narrator to offer the puzzling remark: "note that she did not say She will live again, the matter was not quite that important, although the dictionary is there to confirm, reassure or suggest that we are dealing with complete and absolute synonyms" (270). Giovanni Pontiero's choice of words in translating this passage suggests that he at least understood it as referring to a symbolic resurrection of the dead, comparable to that of the workers who have helped to bring about the Revolution at the end of *Levantado do Chão* (364-66).[25] In other words, when a better society has been reconstructed from the ruins of what we see in this novel, it will be possible to say that her death was not in vain.

In order for this to happen, however, the survivors of this nightmare have to relearn the values that should never have been lost, and this is where we may find the significance in the encounter with the blind writer, who has been living in the home of the first victim and writing words (which he himself cannot read) by touch and guesswork in order to record the experiences endured by this society (259-63). The two significant points to note in this encounter are, firstly, that it leads the doctor's wife to reawaken the minds and the memories of her comrades by reading to them that evening (263), and, secondly, in that, by contrast with the predatory and opportunistic mentality that dominates the city, the writer and the normal inhabitant of the apartment come to a civilised arrangement over the occupancy of the property (261). In other words, this writer has succeeded in preserving not only the signifiers (the words that he writes) but also the values of communication with others and respect for others, which lie behind the use of language and which have been all but lost during the time of crisis. His experience represents therefore the recognition of the other as a subject of discourse, as a person of equal value to oneself.

Equally important, however, is what happens in *All the Names*, where it is the main character, Senhor José himself, who turns to writing, and, significantly, he does so as his sense of independence grows from the apparently iron discipline of the Registry. There can also be little doubt that it is his actions that lead to the change in practice in this institution, when the quasi-divine figure of the

Registrar announces that henceforth the section of the dead will be reunited with that of the living (181): unknown to Senhor José, his actions have been observed throughout, and, when he returns to his home for the last time during in the novel, it is to find the Registrar himself reading the journal that he has kept of his adventures (242). Senhor José's writing, therefore, becomes valuable in that it represents the legitimate expression of the *self* as a subject of discourse, as a person of equal value with others, so that by the end of the text he abandons his previously subservient attitude towards authority and challenges the Registrar's unexpected entry into his home (242).

Throughout the novel, in fact, Senhor José's behaviour has been dominated by signifiers devoid of their signifieds (for example, the biographical facts that he collects about famous people without knowing anything of substance about their lives or characters) or by meanings that are not of his own creation (the near-sanctity of the Registry and its hierarchical functions; the repeated references to decisions or ideas taking possession of him rather than him taking decisions or formulating ideas [30-31, 55-56, and 174-75]; and the revelations about his own behaviour made to him by the ceiling of his room as he contemplates it [135 and 214-15]). Even the pursuit of the unknown woman, the turning point in his life, comes upon him unexpectedly when he finds that he has accidentally removed her documents from the Registry along with those for one of the famous people in his collection (26). The important point here is that, having been presented with this opportunity to invest her file with meaning by finding out more about the real woman (the signified) lying behind the file (the signifier), he then pursues the matter doggedly, even after he is aware of her death, thus not giving in to the temptation of passive acceptance of the world, a possibility that crosses his mind during his time in the unknown woman's school:

> And if, in order to get into each of those schools, he had to suffer as much as he had suffered breaking into this one, then it would be better to remain in the peace and quiet of his home, resigned to knowing of the world only what the hands can grasp without actually leaving the house, words, images, illusions. (89)

This refusal to submit to received truths then leads him to the discovery of a more satisfactory "truth" than that contained in the static and musty archives of the Registry, in that the school's records are progressive and dynamic, containing files for each pupil for each year spent in the school, along with photographs, which record the pupils' physical development. Not only does Senhor José recognise the superiority of these records to those in his own place of work (95), but this leads also to an immediate change in the self that he sees in a mirror: "It doesn't even look like me, he thought, and yet he had probably never looked more like himself" (95). He will no longer be deceived by appearances, so that when he collects his trousers from the dry-cleaners after the damage done to them in the burglary on the school, he cannot help but see beyond the excellent repair job done on them ("you wouldn't even know there was anything there," he is told by the shop-assistant, prompting the narrator's ironic comment "that is how people who content themselves with mere appearances speak" [157]).[26]

Senhor José comes to realise that the only signified whose meaning is absolute is that of the dead; it is for this reason that it does not matter whose body lies under which gravestone. In terms of the living, however, all the names in the world cannot sum up the inexhaustible variety of any individual, who is constantly prone to change. As the unknown woman's former downstairs neighbour reminds him, knowing another person is not an absolute; it is a constantly self-renewing process:

> And did it occur to you that, at the moment when she was actually there before you, you would know as much about her as you did on the day you first decided to look for her, that is, nothing, and that if you wanted to know who she was, you would have to begin looking again. (170-71)

This is essentially the same thought as Saramago expresses in writing about the value of travel in his own country at the end of his *Viagem a Portugal* (*Journey to Portugal*, 1980):

> The end of one journey is merely the beginning of another. It is necessary to see what has not been seen, to see again what has been seen before, to see in the spring what was seen in the summer, to see in daylight what was seen at night, to see in sunlight what was viewed before in rainfall, to see the harvest when it is still green, to see fruit once it has ripened, to see the stone that has moved and the shadow that was not there before. It is necessary to retrace the steps already taken, to repeat them, and to make new tracks by their side. It is necessary to begin the journey all over again. Always. The traveller is going back already. (387)

Signifiers, then, do not have unchanging meanings assigned to them by some objective authority of the type of Olympian superiority that appears to surround the Registrar in this novel: their meaning exists only in terms of the needs of those who require them and is prone to constant change. This lesson is brought home to Senhor José by the disruptive actions of the shepherd in the cemetery, which lead him to dream of numbered sheep swapping their numbers in a way so bewildering that he is no longer able to tell whether it is the signifiers (the numbers) which are losing their signified (the sheep) or vice versa (212). In practice, of course, it does not matter which of these possibilities is true, since the effect in either event is the same, but the really frightening implication of Senhor José's dream is the reduction of the living creatures to indistinguishable sheep, which can be led to wherever their leader chooses.

The realisation that he can never even be sure of identifying the unknown woman's grave entails a definitive loss of the security that appears to surround Senhor José's life at the beginning of the novel: "Suddenly, the ground began to shake beneath Senhor José's feet, the one remaining piece on the board, his final certainty, the unknown woman who had at last been found, had just disappeared" (208). Yet it should be remembered that this movement of the earth beneath his feet recalls the experiences of Pedro Orce and José Anaiço in *The Stone Raft*: the former as he senses the movement of the Iberian Peninsula, which initially seems to be a catastrophe in the making but which later takes on more promising aspects, and the latter when he first meets Joana Carda (92), the woman who is to become his lover but whom he approaches with some suspicion before allowing the positive force of love to enter his life (113-14).[27] Put in this context, therefore, this loss also permits a greater freedom: the liberation from a monolithic certainty dictated from above, allowing the individual to move into a world where old constraints have been removed and one may make use of the past in whatever way is most fruitful for the present, as Orlando Grossegesse acknowledges:

> Saramago sees the past as a range of possible courses of the development of history, which can be sought out anew in memorials or in creative works, thus making them productive and meaningful... in terms of the present and in terms of actions directed towards the future. (*Saramago Lesen* 31)

This is why, at the end of the novel, Senhor José returns to the section of the dead in the Registry, with the "Ariadne's thread" tied firmly around his ankle, to seek out the death certificate of the unknown woman: he is set on a course to retrieve something of value from the past, but with a commitment to using it for the benefit of the living, as the Registrar recognises in announcing that the records of the dead should be kept amongst the living to prevent their being forgotten altogether (181). This idea was already present in Saramago's first major novel, *Manual of Painting and Calligraphy*, where H. refuses to forget the dead because "To forget them… would be the first sign of death" (160).[28] In this way the death of the unknown woman, like that of the old woman in *Blindness*, may prove not to have been in vain: she has contributed productively to Senhor José's life and may continue to do so, provided that he himself is willing to live instead of merely existing. Senhor José is now capable of taking his own decisions—"After that time had passed, he realised that he had made a decision, and it wasn't just his usual decision to follow up an obsession, it really was a decision, although he couldn't have explained how he came to make it" (220-21)—and of facing the turning points and choices that need to be addressed in any meaningful existence.

After the inmates leave the asylum in *Blindness*, one of the first people whom they meet on the outside asks the doctor's wife who she is. Her reply ("I'm not from here" [199]) may at first seem a puzzling one, since she is within walking distance of her own home, until we realise that, with the events that have taken place since she was last there, this city can no longer be the place that she once called home, just as also happens to Romeiro in Almeida Garrett's nineteenth-century drama *Frei Luís de Sousa* (1843). Nevertheless the woman's reply is different from the one given by D. João de Portugal when he is challenged as to his identity in the play, for to give his reply—"No-one" (67)—would turn her into what Senhor José is before the adventure that transforms his life: a nobody. Instead, at the end of the novel, when she fears that she will go blind as others recover their sight, she discovers with relief that "The city was still there" (293). The city itself has, of course, been there throughout the novel; what has been lacking has been the "civitas," the Latin word from which the modern Portuguese and English terms "cidade" and "city" derive, but which primarily meant "society" rather than "city" and which has allowed us to develop the notion of "civilisation," of being able to live with one another in peace and mutual respect. This city (which could perhaps be considered a secular version of St. Augustine's City of God) is out there, but, like the unknown woman in *All the Names*, it cannot be found only once: the struggle for democracy and the exercise of moral values in public life must be a continual one, and one in which we all have our parts to play, as the author himself has suggested in other contexts: "It seems indecent to talk about [democracy] in the abstract, without the stimulus given by the presence, the participation and the involvement of citizens in community life" (*Cadernos de Lanzarote—V, Lanzarote Journals—V*, untranslated, 1998, 219). Only when we all contribute positively to determining our own futures can a "utopia" (literally, a "non-place," such as that of these two novels) become a "eutopia" in the sense of a "good place," and only then will the doctor's wife be able once again to identify with the city where she lives.[29]

Notes

* This article was written during a period of research leave funded by the British Arts and Humanities Research Board, whose support for my work I gratefully acknowledge.

1 Comments made at the Congreso Internacional "Literatura en Portugués: José Saramago," held at the University of Murcia, 8-11 February 2000.

2 Saramago has conceded that the city in which *Blindness* is set is based on a vaguely transformed version of Lisbon, with the opening scene occurring "in the Largo do Rato, at those traffic-lights on the Rua de Alexandre Herculano" ("O escritor vidente" 17; in this passage and all others that were originally written in languages other than English, except those taken from works with a readily available published translation, the translation is mine). There are a number of other minor details of the text that place it in a recognisably Iberian context (e.g. the *chouriço* that the doctor's wife eats in the supermarket storeroom [208]), while the church described in the final chapter of the novel is clearly a Roman Catholic one. In the case of *All the Names*, Senhor José is said to live in a "small country," which could be identified with Portugal (17). Nonetheless, these relatively minor details, when placed alongside the total absence of toponyms and references to city landmarks, do not detract from the essential anonymity of the setting in either novel.

3 "That is, I can observe myself continually and naturally adapting the manner in which I narrate my subject-matter. In this case, that is more noticeable because in terms of the content there has been an abrupt and radical break with everything that I have written previously" ("O escritor vidente" 17).

4 "That new situation will have led us (and not only me)… to consider what we are and what we have been. I believe that that is what has characterised my books up to now and what I think will continue to characterise them in the future" (Interview with Molina 257).

5 Saramago attributes this quotation to Braudel's *Le Mediterranée*; he does not offer any more specific bibliographical information than the author and title of the work ("História e Ficção" 20).

6 Pires de Lima reminds us that the Greek etymology of the word "allegory" is "made up of *alloz* ('other') and of *agoreuw* ('I speak'); or, in other words, when I speak about one thing, I am really speaking about another" (417).

7 The reference here to the horrors of the twentieth century is not an inappropriate one; in an interview given shortly after the novel was published Saramago himself uses the phrase "final

solution," with its clear echoes of Nazism, to refer to the enclosure of the blind people in the asylum ("O escritor vidente" 16).

[8] This connection was made by Adsuar Fernández in her paper given at the conference devoted to Saramago held at the University of Murcia, 8-11 February 2000.

[9] Joanna Courteau, tracing a link to Padre Antônio Vieira's sermons on blindness, argues that there is an exemplary quality in the blindness of the girl with the dark glasses, but that this relates not to the act of prostitution as such but to the hedonistic, self-involved nature of the character's sexual self-expression (10). This line of argument would, at first sight, appear to contradict my suggestion that the blindness does not strike its victims as an exemplary punishment for their sins; however, the nature of Vieira's argument, as adduced by Courteau (8), is based not on specific sinful actions but on the internal motivation for them. I believe that in this sense my own conclusions are consistent with Courteau's and that the sexual behaviour of the character could therefore be viewed negatively, not in terms of prohibitive sexual morality, but as being empty of meaning, as using the act of love as an empty signifier without its corresponding signified (the feeling of love, which she does discover later in the work in her relationship with the old man with the eyepatch [274 and 291]). The question of the distinction between signifier and signified will be discussed more fully below.

[10] The translation here is mine. Pontiero renders this phrase as "He had gone no more than thirty paces," but I have preferred to offer my own more literal version of the original Portuguese ("Ainda não tinha dado trinta passos") in order to reinforce the point that I am making here.

[11] For a discussion of causality in *The Stone Raft*, see Daniel 539-40.

[12] Although there is no translation of *Objecto Quase* in a book form, all six stories in this work have been published individually in English; the bibliographic details of the stories discussed in the present article are listed in the Works Cited. For discussion of the aspects of *Blindness* derived from "Things," see Costa ("Alegorias da desconstrução urbana" 140-41). For a fuller discussion of the importance of *Objecto Quase* and *O Ano de 1993* in the development of the author's writing in general, see Costa (*O Período Formativo*) 319-49 and 214-53 respectively.

[13] The same could also be said of Saramago's Joseph and Jesus in *The Gospel According to Jesus Christ*, where both characters give themselves up to what they perceive to be the inevitability of their own deaths rather than struggling to avert them. For further discussion of this point, see Frier ("Outline of a Newer Testament"), Grossegesse ("José Saramago, *O Evangelho Segundo Jesus Cristo*" 129-32), and Kaufman (457).

[14] Note that the driver in "Embargo" may be seen specifically to be a forerunner of the car-thief in *Blindness*, in that both of them end up driving outside the city to a deserted place (that is, both of them symbolically turn their backs on the community) before leaving the vehicles in which they are travelling.

[15] Agripina Carriço Vieira makes what is essentially the same point about the characters of *Blindness* in different terms: "In order to 'give them a name' what the narrator chooses and selects is not an inherent quality but a characteristic that is external, ephemeral and casual" (387), that is, by reducing the characters to how they function in terms of perception by others rather than in their own rights as conscious subjects and actors in the world.

[16] Courteau also sees in this incident an allusion to Vieira's reflection that the greatest virtue lies in a good act that is performed for its own sake "as if God could not see it" (Courteau 11). Her reference to Vieira is to his "Sermon for the Fifth Tuesday of Lent" ("Sermão da Quinta Terça-Feira da Quaresma" [Vieira 82]).

[17] See "José Saramago: todos os pecados do mundo" 82.

18 For further discussion of this point in relation to *The History of the Siege of Lisbon*, see Huici ("Historia y ficción") 145-46.

19 As *O Ano de 1993* does not have numbered pagination, I have followed the scheme of chapters and verses proposed by Costa to discuss this text (a scheme that he compares to that used in the Bible). See Costa (*O Período Formativo*) 234n.20 and 218.

20 In this case the association with journeys into the underworld is made explicit in the text: "Senhor José will instead use an ordinary, rustic ball of string... and that string will lead back to the world of the living the person who, at this very moment, is preparing to enter the kingdom of the dead" (141).

21 This is essentially the same point as is made by Ana Monner Sans, who writes: "What is to be gained by singling out the mortal remains of this person or that person? In the end all people ("hombres") are the same, and thus names ("nombres")—even *all* the names—are not enough to give any distinctiveness to our individual circumstances" (449; original emphasis). The words "homens" and "nomes" do not, of course, form a minimal pair in Portuguese as the words "hombres" and "nombres" (used by Monner Sans) do in Spanish, but this fact does not seem to me to weaken the essential point made here. It also finds an echo in the incident in *Blindness*, where the occupants of one ward, unable to determine which of various dead bodies came from their own group, decide that they will be doing their duty to the memory of their former friends by burying the correct number of corpses, regardless of their identities (82-83).

22 Leyla Perrone-Moisés suggests that Senhor José's decision to seek shelter inside this tree might be seen instead as a symbolic return to the womb, but she is careful to remind the reader of the multiplicity of significances that could be read into apparently straightforward symbols in this novel: "For example, viewing the night spent in the bulging trunk of an olive tree, in the foetal position, as a process of rebirth... would be tantamount to reducing to a one-to-one correspondence something that is said in such a way as to highlight the gap between signifier and signified" (436). Although Saramago does use the word "berço" ("cradle") to describe this tree trunk, he does not, in fact, specify the posture that Senhor José adopts inside it (although it must be conceded that the foetal position would be the most likely one).

23 Senhor José realises that the woman's death occurred while he was ill in bed after breaking into the school (154-55); it is only when he is given time off from work to recuperate after this illness that he tells a shop assistant that he has reason to believe that the woman whom he seeks is still alive (132).

24 Note that in the closing stages of this drama Francisco changes his name to João to indicate the change in his outlook on the world. For further discussion of this aspect of *A Segunda Vida de Francisco de Assis*, see Frier ("'In the Beginning'") 222-23.

25 In confirmation of Pontiero's translation, the dictionary Morais treats the two verbs as being near synonyms (and not exact synonyms, as declared by Saramago's narrator), but makes the sense of "restoring something to life from death" ("fazer voltar da morte à vida") a primary meaning in the case of "ressuscitar" (which Pontiero renders as "she will live again") and merely a secondary meaning (after that of "reappearing") in the case of "ressurgir," for which the translator uses "she will rise again" (Silva V., 9).

26 Note the critical perspective implicit in this remark on the famous maxim of Ricardo Reis, "Wise is the man who contents himself with the spectacle of the world," which lies at the heart of the conception of *The Year of the Death of Ricardo Reis*.

27 For further discussion of this aspect of *The Stone Raft*, see Frier, "Agouros e Oportunidades."

28 The original Portuguese places a greater emphasis on the effects of forgetfulness on H. himself than is conveyed here by Pontiero's translation, which renders "morte minha" ("my death") merely as "death." The idea of the continued exchange between the dead and their

survivors is also what Blimunda refers to in *Baltasar and Blimunda* when she declares that even the dead Francisco Marques is being reborn constantly (318). In describing *Manual of Painting and Calligraphy* as the author's first major novel, I am, of course, acknowledging the existence of *Terra do Pecado* (*Land of Sin*, untranslated, 1947), while respecting Saramago's own distancing of this very early work from his mature production.

[29] I derive the distinction between "utopia" and "eutopia" from Ceccucci (211).

Works Cited

Adsuar Fernández, María Dolores. "*Ensayo sobre la ceguera*: a propósito de la utopía." *Actas del Congreso Internacional "Literatura en Portugués: José Saramago (8 a 11 de Febrero de 2000)*." Ed. Víctor Polo García. Murcia: Universidad de Murcia, forthcoming.

Berrini, Beatriz, ed. *José Saramago: Uma Homenagem*. São Paulo: EDUC, 1999.

———. *Ler Saramago: O Romance*. Lisboa: Caminho, 1998.

Ceccucci, Piero. "L'utopia saramaghiana como progetto della storia umana." *El Girador: Studi di letterature iberiche e ibero-americane offerti a Giuseppe Bellini*. Ed. Giovanni Battista de Cesare and Silvana Serafin. 2 vols. Rome: Consiglio Nazionale delle Ricerche and Bulzoni, 1993: I. 209-15.

Costa, Horácio. "Alegorias da desconstrução urbana: *The Memoirs of a Survivor*, de Doris Lessing, e *Ensaio sobre a Cegueira*, de José Saramago." Berrini 127-48.

———. *José Saramago: O Período Formativo*. Lisboa: Caminho, 1997.

Courteau, Joanna. "*Ensaio sobre a Cegueira*: José Saramago ou Padre Antônio Vieira." *Letras de Hoje* 34.4 (Dec. 1999): 7-13.

Daniel, Mary Lou. "Symbolism and synchronicity: José Saramago's Jangada de Pedra." *Hispania* 74 (Sept. 1991): 536-41.

Dante Alighieri. *The "Inferno" of Dante: a new verse translation*. Trans. Robert Pinsky. New York: FSG, 1994.

Frier, David G. "Agouros e Oportunidades: *A Jangada de Pedra* de José Saramago e o País Desconhecido." *Actas do Quinto Congresso da Associação Internacional de Lusitanistas*. Ed. T. F. Earle. 3 vols. Oxford and Coimbra: Associação Internacional de Lusitanistas, 1998: Vol. 2. 713-20.

———. "'In the Beginning Was the Word': Text and Meaning in Two Dramas by José Saramago." *Portuguese Studies* XIV (1998): 215-26.

———. "José Saramago's *Evangelho Segundo Jesus Cristo*: Outline of a Newer Testament." Annual Meeting of the American Association of Teachers of Spanish and Portuguese. Caribe Hilton Hotel, San Juan, Puerto Rico. 5 Aug. 2000.

Garrett, Almeida. *Frei Luís de Sousa*. 1843. Selecção, Prefácio e Notas de Rodrigues Lapa. 8th ed. Lisboa: Seara Nova, 1965.

Grossegesse, Orlando. "José Saramago, *O Evangelho Segundo Jesus Cristo*." *Portugiesische Romane der Gegenwart: Neue Interpretationen*. Ed. Rainer Hess. Frankfurt am Main: Vervuert, 1993: 123-39.

———. *Saramago Lesen: Werk, Leben, Bibliographie*. Berlin: Tranvía, 1999.

Huici, Adrián. "Historia y ficción en *Historia del Cerco de Lisboa*." Lanciani 137-61.

———. "Perdidos en el laberinto: el camino del héroe en *Todos los nombres*." Seixo 453-62.

Kaufman, Helena. "Evangelical truths: José Saramago on the life of Christ." *Revista Hispánica Moderna* XLVII (1994): 449-58.

Lanciani, Giulia, ed. *José Saramago: Il Bagaglio dello Scrittore.* Roma: Bulzoni, 1996.

Lima, Isabel Pires de. "Dos 'anjos da História' em dois romances de Saramago (*Ensaio sobre a Cegueira e Todos os Nomes*)." Seixo 415-26.

Machado, José Leon. "*Todos os Nomes* de José Saramago." http://alfarrabio.um.geira.pt/vercial/letras/crit017.htm.

Monner Sans, Ana. "De aventuras, azares, amores y taumaturgias; la subversión genérica como estrategia narrativa en *Todos los nombres.*" Seixo 441-52.

Nova, Craig. "Now you see, now you don't." Rev. of *Blindness* by José Saramago. *The Washington Post* 9 Oct. 1998: D2.

Perrone-Moisés, Leyla. "A ficção como desafio ao Registo Civil." Seixo 429-39.

Saramago, José. *All the Names.* Trans. Margaret Jull Costa. London: Harvill, 1999.

———. *O Ano de 1993.* 2nd ed. Lisboa: Caminho, 1987.

———. *Baltasar and Blimunda.* Trans. Giovanni Pontiero. London: Harvill, 1998.

———. *Blindness.* Trans. Giovanni Pontiero. New York: Harcourt, Brace & Company, 1998.

———. *Cadernos de Lanzarote: Diário – V.* 3rd ed. Lisboa: Caminho, 1998.

———. "Embargo." Trans. Giovanni Pontiero. *Cimarron Review* 110 (Jan. 1995): 10-18.

———. *Ensaio sobre a Cegueira.* 1st ed. Lisboa: Caminho, 1995.

———. *The Gospel According to Jesus Christ.* Trans. Giovanni Pontiero. London: Harvill, 1996.

———. "História e Ficção." *Jornal de Letras, Artes e Ideias.* 6 Mar. 1990: 17-20.

———. *The History of the Siege of Lisbon.* Trans. Giovanni Pontiero. London: Harvill, 1996.

———. Interview with César Antonio Molina. *Sobre el iberismo y otros escritos de literatura portuguesa.* By César Antonio Molina. Madrid: Akal, 1990: 247-75.

———. "José Saramago. O escritor vidente." Interview with Maria Leonor Nunes. *Jornal de Letras, Artes e Ideias.* 25 Oct. 1995: 15-17.

———. "José Saramago: Todos os Pecados do Mundo." Interview with Clara Ferreira Alves. *Expresso* 28 Oct. 1995: 81-85.

———. *Levantado do Chão.* 8th ed. Lisboa: Editorial Caminho, 1988.

———. *Manual of Painting and Calligraphy.* Trans. Giovanni Pontiero. Manchester: Carcanet, 1994.

———. *Objecto Quase.* 2nd ed. Lisboa: Editorial Caminho, 1984.

———. "Reflux." Trans. Giovanni Pontiero. *Frontiers* (*Leopard III*). London: Harvill, 1994. 293-304.

———. *A Segunda Vida de Francisco de Assis.* 1st ed. Lisboa: Caminho, 1987.

———. *The Stone Raft.* Trans. Giovanni Pontiero. London: Harvill, 1994.

———. "Things." Trans. Giovanni Pontiero. *The Translator's Dialogue: Giovanni Pontiero.* Eds. Pilar Orero and Juan C. Sager. Amsterdam and Philadelphia: John Benjamins, 1997. 187-243.

———. *Terra do Pecado.* 2nd ed. Lisboa: Caminho, 1997.

———. *Todos os Nomes.* 1st ed. Lisboa: Caminho, 1997.

———. *Viagem a Portugal.* 10th ed. Lisboa: Caminho, 1995.

———. *The Year of the Death of Ricardo Reis.* Trans. Giovanni Pontiero. London: Harvill, 1992.

Seixo, Maria Alzira. "Os espelhos virados para dentro: configurações narrativas do espaço e do imaginário em *Ensaio sobre a Cegueira.*" Lanciani 191-210.

———. ed. *José Saramago: O Ano de 1998.* Special number issue of *Colóquio/Letras* 151-152 (Jan.-June 1999).

Silva, António de Morais. *Novo Dicionário Compacto da Língua Portuguesa.* 5 vols. Cacém: Confluência/ Livros Horizonte, 1980.

Vieira, Agripina Carriço. "Da História ao indivíduo ou da excepção ao banal na escrita de Saramago: d'*O Evangelho Segundo Jesus Cristo a Todos os Nomes.*" Seixo 379-93.

Vieira, Padre António. "Sermão da Quinta Terça-Feira da Quaresma" ["Sermon for the Fifth Tuesday of Lent"]. *Sermões.* Vol. II. Oporto: Lello e Irmãos, 1959. 82.

Virgil. The *Aeneid.* Trans. C. Day Lewis. *Great Books of the Western World.* Ed. Mortimer J. Adler. 2nd ed. 60 vols. Chicago: Encyclopaedia Brittanica, 1990. Vol. 12 (Virgil).

Saramago, Cognitive Estrangement, and Original Sin?

Kenneth Krabbenhoft

For Carlos Veloso

Introduction

José Saramago's questioning about the possibility of justice in the world often works through reduction: his view of society and human nature strips away relations and values, the better to see what lies at the core of experience. In this sense his novels are like experiments: they pose the question "what if…" In *Baltasar and Blimunda* (1982), Saramago asks what would happen if a man and a woman were to step out of their social roles and connect on a level unmediated by laws and institutions; in *The Year of the Death of Ricardo Reis* (1984) he resuscitates one of Fernando Pessoa's heteronyms, brings him back from Brazil, and sets him loose in Lisbon to "see what happens"; in *The History of the Siege of Lisbon* (1989), he asks what would happen if a tiny change in the historical record were to alter radically our understanding of the past; in *The Stone Raft* (1986), the entire Iberian peninsula becomes a laboratory to test the question of what would happen if Portugal and Spain were to disconnect from Europe and float off into the Atlantic; and in *All the Names* (1997), he imagines the impact of a startling discovery on the otherwise profoundly banal and routine life of a government functionary.

In a typical Saramago experiment, historical time is folded to create unexpected juxtapositions. The narrator retreats to a vantage point of timeless omniscience—a hallmark of Saramago's style—and speaks with a kind of distanced concern. Saramago writes with the impatient irony of the observer who knows better than the observed (and the reader, for that matter). This explains why his novels can be simultaneously lyrical and terrifying—lyrical to the extent that they point out the paradoxical wonders that the human spirit is capable of experiencing, and terrifying when they turn the observational lens on the cruelty and despair that make victims even of the victimizers. This is something that Saramago has in common with at least two previous winners of the Nobel Prize in Literature, Samuel Beckett and William Golding. Like Saramago, Beckett and Golding take an unflinching look at what lurks beneath the surface of accepted meanings. Beckett does this by viewing the world through the eyes of his charming philosopher-bums, while Golding does it by removing the social strictures that hold the lust for power in check. Is it any coincidence that the works that won both of these writers the Nobel Prize are from the stressed and paranoid 1950s? (Beckett's trilogy *Molloy*, *Malone Dies* and *The Unnameable* is from 1951-1953, *Waiting for Godot* is from 1952, *Endgame* from 1957 and *Krapp's Last Tape* from 1958; Golding's *Lord of the Flies* and *The Inheritors* are from 1954 and 1955 respectively). The characters in these novels and plays are often in flight from someone or something—we might say in flight from the abyss of self-consciousness that prevents them from integrating easily in the social and historical "now." Like Beckett and Golding, in the two works discussed below Saramago creates characters that are set adrift in shadowy landscapes illuminated only by the occasional spark of human solidarity.

I will take two approaches in examining the way in which Saramago achieves this: the first is Darko Suvin's notion of cognitive estrangement, and the second is the Augustinian notion of original sin. I have chosen the 1975 prose poem *O Ano de 1993* (*The Year 1993*) and the 1995 novel *Blindness* to make my point because in my view they most completely embody this aspect of Saramago's work, creating a nightmarish vision of humanity under stress in a readily recognizable near future when society takes a step backward into anarchy, violence, and death.[1]

Cognitive Estrangement in *O Ano de 1993*

In his 1979 book, *Metamorphoses of Science Fiction*, Darko Suvin defines science fiction as the literary genre that embodies "not only a reflecting *of*, but also *on* reality," a process that he calls "cognitive estrangement" (10).[2] Suvin supposes that the literary experience that links the author's and the reader's imaginations rests on a representational *adequatio rei ad intellectu*, in which elements common to the reality of both parties are distorted to make the familiar seem unfamiliar, thus introducing an observational distance that makes possible fresh insights into the present. It is an important distinction to make with respect to a genre like science fiction, which often creates places and periods that have not literally existed and may never exist. In this, of course, science fiction sets itself apart from mainstream realism of the nineteenth-century variety, which presents us with the world in which we live, or a world close enough to us in space and time that we can reasonably be expected to recognize it as our own.

This is where, as noted above, Suvin makes his crucial distinction, for whereas "standard" realism stresses representation, science fiction gives equal importance to evaluation in the form of implicit social criticism or overt satire. Suvin's idea is that, in order to achieve the critical distance necessary to bind evaluation to realist representation, science fiction writers transform the cognitively familiar into something unfamiliar or estranged from present-day experience. Suvin adapts this notion of estrangement from the Russian Formalist Viktor Shklovsky, who used the term "ostranenie" to designate art in general, as those forms of non-historical or non-documentary representation that produce "defamiliarization, a making strange ... of objects, a renewal of perception" (Jameson 51), "a forcing us to notice" (Jauss 85), or "a cleansing and renewal of our perceptions, brought about by the distancing properties of poetic language" (Parrinder 73). Cognitive estrangement thus defined bears a close resemblance to Bertolt Brecht's "estrangement effect" (*Verfremdungseffekt*), the purpose of which, to quote Fredric Jameson again, is "to make you aware that the objects and institutions you thought to be natural were really historical" (58): we might say that Suvin transforms what for Brecht is a tool of social realism generally into the hermeneutical principle of a specific literary genre.

It might seem incongruous to associate a writer like Saramago, heir to the rich novelistic tradition that extends from classical antiquity through Cervantes to James Joyce and Marcel Proust, with a genre like science fiction: although it, too, has roots in ancient Greece and Rome, sci-fi has blossomed relatively late in the history of the novel. The association has nevertheless been made from early on in Saramago's career, beginning with Ana Hatherly's 1976 review of *O Ano de 1993* in *Colóquio/Letras* where she compares the poem to *1984*, George Orwell's similarly named 1949 novel. Horácio Costa's pioneering study of Saramago's early work also points in the direction of science fiction: he locates the same work in the "futurist-dystopian tradition" ["linhagem futurante-distópica"] pioneered by H.G. Wells's *The War Between the Worlds* (1897) and carried on in Aldous Huxley's *Brave New World* (1932), Orwell's *1984*, and Doris Lessing's *The Memoirs of a Survivor* (1977).[3] Costa's description sounds very much like Suvin's notion of cognitive estrangement when he specifies that *O Ano de 1993*'s "specific link with Huxley and Orwell's works occurs more on the broad level of the literary subject matter and the author's moral or ethical perspective on the world he lives in *through a mirroring of this world in a future one defined by the vicissitudes of the present*, than on the level of [literary] form" (215; my emphasis). In *O Ano de 1993*, which Saramago says is a direct outgrowth of his experience of the April 25, 1974 Revolution, he creates the estrangement effect by looking forward chronologically 18 years from the time of its writing.[4] An unnamed city has been invaded and destroyed by nameless forces: we see only the aftermath—"the city sick with the plague" with its squares "piled high with ruins" (fragment 2). Even the light has been infected, "like some kind of poisonous, phosphorescent rot" (fragment 3). The forces occupying the city construct mechanical wolves and eagles to hunt people down. The few surviving pets and zoo animals are turned into robots controlled by a central computer that programs them with hatred and turns them loose on their former owners. The occupiers torture people in an attempt to understand what has happened. They build a prison that is completely transparent except at night, when the inmates are asleep and there is nothing to see. All thermometers are confiscated and the mercury in them used to make roving spy-eyes. The local commandant works with a witch doctor to reduce the city to the size of a human body so that when he whips it, all of the inhabitants get welts on their backs. Outside the city, people return to a tribal existence and hide from the mechanized beasts.

The reader experiences cognitive estrangement because, although the majority of these elements are not literally a part of the 1975 world (or the world of 2000 for that matter), they are recognizable extrapolations of technologies and social realities that are in fact known to us. Although Saramago does not specify the nature of the conflict that destroys the anonymous city of *O Ano de 1993* and of what Américo António Lindeza Diogo has called the consequent "fall back into pre-history" (68), the scenario evokes the aftermath of nuclear war, an image common in post-World War II film and television and notably explored in science fiction novels like Walter Miller's *A Canticle for Leibowitz* (1960) and Russell Hoban's *Riddley Walker* (1980). The mechanical wolves and eagles are conceptual extrapolations of the attack dogs that many American readers undoubtedly associate with both the Nazis and the enemies of the Civil Rights Movement in the Alabama or Mississippi of the 1960s, while the computer-controlled pets and zoo animals recall photographs of laboratory monkeys and cats with radio transmitters protruding from their brains. The roving spy-eyes bring us to the Cold War and the Space Race, to the U2 and peeping satellites, while the transparent prison was in effect envisioned as early as the seventeenth century, in the panopticon that Michel Foucault has studied in *Discipline and Punish.* The cognitive closeness of these elements sets off the estrangement effect much more effectively, I think, than purely fantastic, far more metaphorical details like the shrunken city; they also ally Saramago with contemporary science fiction writers like Philip K. Dick, who populate their not-too-distant futures with mechanical animals and androids (as in Dick's 1968 novel *Do Androids Dream of Electric Sheep?,* the source for Ridley Scott's 1982 film *Blade Runner*).

All is not unrelieved hopelessness and suffering in *O Ano de 1993,* however: eventually there are signs of change for the better. A real bird defeats one of the machines—an event that one tribe records in wall paintings. There is a reference to happier times that will come one hundred years in the future, which means that the narrator is speaking from a vantage point after the year 2093 (this is the science-fiction technique of the double jump forward: from now to a future time viewed from an even farther future, placing the reader in a present that is also a distant past). Saramago suggests that sex is one of the keys to repairing society: the tribes' fertility rites coincide with the retaking of the wrecked city and the execution of the former occupiers. The ending indicates that this is an inevitable circular process of destruction and recreation: "Once more then the world the world a few things accomplished just a few so many not and to know it" (fragment 30). In this we are reminded again of Saramago's proximity to the principally British tradition that goes back to the artificial incubators of Aldous Huxley's *Brave New World* (1932), the loveless and sexless society of Orwell's *1984,* and the dialectic of fertility and infertility in Anthony Burgess's *The Wanting Seed* (1962), to which I will return below.[5] In all of these, sexual love and reproduction are a powerful symbol of what is most indomitably human, as if to say that no amount of technological meddling or social engineering can long succeed in suppressing the instinct for preservation and the affirmation of life that manifests itself in human love. Because the future scenarios of these novels involve human beings that are still identifiable as such, sex and reproduction provide a backdrop against which both elements of cognitive estrangement stand out in sharp relief.

Namelessness as Estrangement

Cognitive estrangement works much the same way in *Blindness*. The year is not specified, but it is a not very distant future: all of the details are present in today's Lisbon. As in *O Ano de 1993*, the city is in the grips of a primeval affliction, a plague that is as elemental as it is inexplicable: very simply, people start going blind. The affliction does not discriminate between male and female, young and old, sick and healthy, rich and poor. There is no apparent cause for it, though it seems to be contagious; there is no cure: certainly no treatment explains the fact that at the end of the novel people regain their sight as suddenly and mysteriously as they had lost it.

This lack of specificity covers every aspect of the story. Not only do we not know exactly where or when the action takes place, we never learn the names of any of the people involved; they remain for us the doctor, the car thief, the woman in dark glasses, or the ophthalmologist—familiar labels that become as arbitrary as given names in a context where blindness renders everyone's profession obsolete and where the characters, as Maria Alzira Seixo has observed, suffer from a "degradation ... imposed by the position of socially determined isolated marginalization in which they find themselves ("Os espelhos" 200). Their anonymity or namelessness marks a new stage in Saramago's writing, as a number of critics have noted. Agripina Carriço Vieira writes:

> Indefinite or unnameable spaces take over from the recognizable, named places of the previous novels. Instead of place names, which are entirely missing from the two texts, we find generic descriptions… Proper names are also entirely missing … having been substituted by descriptive labels: the old man with the eye patch, the doctor, the doctor's wife, the young woman in the dark glasses, the evil blind men, the dog with teary eyes.... (386)

Similarly Isabel Pires de Lima states:

> This is the first of Saramago's novels that provides no information whatsoever about the place and the time of the action. We find ourselves in the midst of a nowhere and a no-when … along with the fact that the characters do not have proper names: they are merely the doctor, the doctor's wife, [et alia]. (416)

Seixo has called this phenomenon "the incompleteness of names" and identified *O Ano de 1993* as the precursor of *Blindness* because in it "the question of the *unnameable* is raised, on the level of a concept that is both verbal and ontological" (*Lugares* 165 and 100; original emphasis). She points out that "the names of Saramago's characters are either strange, from Blimunda to the characters in *The Stone Raft*, or on the contrary have an ambiguous, insipid nature (Senhor José [the only named character in *All the Names*]), although they can also be simply descriptive, as in *Blindness*" (166). By reducing all of the characters to the same status, namelessness universalizes the human condition while depersonalizing each individual's life: since what happens here could happen to anyone, anywhere, at any time, there is no guarantee that what we are reading could not apply to us tomorrow or the day after. As Carriço Vieira points out: "To name is always somehow to limit, and to limit is to exclude" (391). Significantly, Saramago makes it impossible to explain the plague of blindness scientifically. Since we know nothing of the culture, history or material conditions of this country, we can neither rationalize nor assign responsibility or blame—in other words, we cannot hold it at arm's length by persuading ourselves that although this horror makes sense for a country with (say) a history of political tyranny or scientific backwardness, it is inconceivable where *we* live. One is reminded of Sinclair Lewis's 1935 novel, *It Can't Happen Here*—what "can't happen" being the takeover of the United States by a fascist insurgency.

For Saramago, this reduction of individuals to irrelevant labels means that, when the day-to-day fabric of the social order rips apart, the person we assume ourselves to be—our identity as defined by relationships, job and possessions—ceases to have any importance. In *Blindness*, everyone becomes literally faceless: the semiotics of individuality are metamorphosed. Universal blindness makes the nuances of gesture, dress, and style obsolete; the individuals who make up the nucleus of characters that we follow through the eyes of the one person who retains her sight in effect cease being the doctor and the car thief and the woman in dark glasses and the ophthalmologist: the old categories are as unimportant as these people's unspoken names. What previously made them unique has disappeared, as Carriço Vieira has remarked: "Once sight has been lost, the other intrinsically human qualities are also lost: love, solidarity, brotherhood, and reason; and existence becomes entirely focused on the need to survive" (388). For the first time in Saramago's fiction (as later in *All the Names* "what is special gives way to the banal, the insipid. We plunge into a world of the everyday, the trivial, populated by ordinary people ... whose lives are completely dissolved in the magma of anonymity" (385).

Eventually the characters are rounded up and put under armed guard in a kind of asylum, where they are joined by additional generic types: the policeman, the cabbie, the salesman, the office worker, the cleaning lady, the married couple, parents and children. They begin to relate to each other on a level that we can't help considering more primitive (a survival of the ancient idea that sight is superior to the other senses because less dependent upon physical immediacy). They rely on hearing, smell and touch, and this means that they are often disgusted with each other, with the weeping and moaning of despair, pain and sex, the smell of unwashed bodies, and the shock of unexpected physical contact. This human "animality" is epitomized by the criminal gangs that set up an extortion racket in the asylum; their ruthlessness enables them to control the food supply even though they, too, are blind, and to exact whatever they want—usually women—in exchange for food.

The flip side of the blind people's self-revulsion is the fear they inspire in those who have yet to lose their sight—which means, from the novel's viewpoint, the soldiers who have been assigned to guard them. For their jailers, the faces of the blind become terrifying symbols of helplessness and need. Even though they cannot possibly represent a threat to the sighted and heavily armed soldiers, they are kept at a distance, all the more so after a nervous young guard machine-guns one of the inmates, and the captain declares that the best solution would be to kill all the blind, like stemming gangrene through amputation. Saramago himself has drawn attention to the obvious similarity between his novel and the present day: "All of the horrible things that I am describing and which will surely upset the reader ... are happening right now in the building next door, on the next street over, somewhere."[6] The difference between the historical record and a work of fiction is that the latter can use cognitive estrangement to create that critical distance that is fundamental to the novel's success. An effective means of achieving this is to reduce the plot elements to a minimum, by which Saramago insures that every detail stands out in sharp relief. If it is true that the blind develop an especially acute sense of hearing and touch to compensate for the loss of sight, then this vividness of description would seem to be a kind of heightened sensory expression that puts us, the readers, in somewhat the same position as the blind in the novel. This is the great irony: that through using our eyes (reading) we share the experience of those characters whose eyes are useless. At the same time, as readers, we stand above the mutual hostility of the two groups of characters: our sight gives us the power to protect us from too intimate involvement.

Why the relationship between the blind and the sighted should be one of hostility is a question that Saramago does not answer per se: he takes it as a given that, in this particular experiment, sight translates into power and blindness into weakness—sight not so much as a physical characteristic, much less a spiritual one, but rather a commodity whose possession is the key to humanity itself. Yet even this duality breaks down in the end. There is a paradox in the fact that the relationship of oppressors and oppressed provides at least some structure in a violently stressed situation: it provides identity through the knowledge of belonging to one group or the other. But as the oppressors also begin to lose their sight and the gates of the asylum-turned-concentration camp are flung open, the characters realize that the end really *is* near. When the soldiers could see, there was still the hope that they would change their mind and use their sight for charity; with everyone blind, we acknowledge the truth that there is no difference between victim and victimizer, because we are our own oppressors. As Lindeza Diogo notes, in *O Ano de 1993*, "the 'occupied' and the 'unoccupied' are bodies equally converted into a 'despotic signifier'" (69).

In a 1998 interview with Alan Riding of the *New York Times*, Saramago said that the idea for *Blindness* came to him when he was sitting in a restaurant. "The question suddenly came into my head," he said: "'And if we were all blind?' And then immediately, as if answering myself, 'But we *are* all blind'" (5). These words are echoed at the very end of the novel by the doctor's wife, the one who never lost her sight: "I don't think we did go blind, I think we are blind, Blind but seeing, Blind people who can see, but do not see" (310).

Original Sin?

What happened to reason in all of this? What is it about the humanity that Saramago portrays for us in these works that seems to turn first, in moments of social catastrophe, to the brutalization and oppression of its own members?

For all of Saramago's belief in class solidarity and social justice as the ultimate ideal, he has no illusions about humankind's capacity for inflicting injustice and suffering on itself irregardless of social context. Underlying his deeply disturbing portraits of mankind at its worst is an assumption about human nature that bears a close resemblance to views associated historically with Saint Augustine, who in the early fifth century AD first used the term original sin to describe the fundamentally fallen nature of the human race.[7] It was Augustine, too, who defended this central feature of Christian orthodoxy from the opposing view of the British monk Pelagius, who denied that all mankind inherited Adam and Eve's transgression of divine law and held, on the contrary, that all people were inherently disposed to sanctity, which could be achieved by the exercise of free will with minimal assistance of divine grace. Pelagius was condemned in 418 at the Council of Carthage and again at Ephesus in 431, but his notion of the essential inclination of human beings toward virtue can be said to underlie any number of secular ethical philosophies and political ideologies.

Anthony Burgess exploits this connection in *The Wanting Seed* when he has a schoolteacher explain the role of Pelagianism in a future social order based on the assumption of human perfectibility: "Pelagianism was thus seen [by the founders of this future state] to be at the heart of liberalism and its derived doctrines, especially Socialism and Communism... in the Pelagian phase or Pelphase, the great liberal dream seems capable of fulfillment" (10 and 18). In Burgess's future scenario, the Pelagian view exists in perpetual dialectic with the Augustinian or Gusphase, with a transitional period (the Interphase) connecting the two. The Interphase begins when the citizens awake to a realization of the essential fallenness of themselves and their fellows, and the state's response, as the schoolteacher says, is to "try and force the citizens into goodness." This is when reason gives way to brutality:

> Beatings-up. Secret police. Torture in brightly lighted cellars. Condemnation without trial. Finger-nails pulled out with pincers. The rack. The cold-water treatment. The gouging-out of eyes. The firing-squad in the cold dawn. (19)

Interphase ends when a politics of state-sanctioned homosexuality gives way to a random indulgence in heterosexuality, when the repression of reproduction and everything associated with it yields to an anarchic surrender to the forces of procreation. The wheel turns again when, as the teacher points out, people realize that "human social behavior is rather better than any Augustinian pessimist has a right to expect, and so a sort of optimism begins to emerge [and] Pelagianism is reinstated" (23).

Whether or not Burgess intends us to accept the schoolteacher's characterization of the Pelagian heresy literally, his notion of Interphase can be applied to *O Ano de 1993* and *Blindness* insofar as they portray the tension between social control doomed to failure despite its best intentions and social anarchy from which a new order necessarily emerges as the affirmation of the creative (or procreative) impulse. This in turn suggests a more general movement in Saramago's thinking: whereas in novels written prior to *Blindness* he seems to express a basically Pelagian view of society in which intolerance and violence can be dealt with through corrections to a hierarchical class structure (at least in theory), the 1995 novel seems to place the blame in Augustinian fashion squarely on human nature itself. Although described differently, this change has been observed by a number of critics. Costa, for instance, notes "the break with the canon of realistic representation in *O Ano de 1993*" that "marks for us the moment in Saramago's career in which he conclusively abandons the patterns that up to that point had characterized his writing *grosso modo*" (223 and 248). Seixo sees the beginning of this change in *The Stone Raft*, although she notes that a more purely negative and dystopian view takes over beginning with *Blindness*. She writes: "With its simultaneously fantastic and fairy-tale orientation (which is by virtue of the latter also partly utopian), and set in an uncertain future of confusing fears and attractions, *The Stone Raft* initiates the series of timeless dystopias in which *Blindness* and *All the Names* also figure, with the same uncertainty and with a markedly negative—and consequently dystopian—bias" (*Lugares* 159-60). Piero Ceccucci also identifies the source of this negativism in a negative appraisal of human nature. In *Blindness*, he writes, "an unmistakable message about the origin of evil is given free expression ...: evil is no longer thought to be solely the consequence of an unjust or cruel social order but is also related to human nature itself, imperfect and corrupt in its tendencies" (178-79).

Saramago's statements to interviewers provide further evidence of this shift towards disillusionment with reason as a means of human improvement, both ethical and social. He has spoken openly about his understanding of human nature, often in the context of a mistrust of the ability of reason to curb the tendency to abuse power. Speaking with Maria Leonor Neves, for example, Saramago states categorically: "Our reason is not used rationally" (Ceccucci 179). He makes the same point to Baptista-Bastos, speaking of *Blindness*:

> In this book I intend to question myself and the reader about our rationality, if we are in effect rational. And if this thing we call "reason" in fact deserves the

> name. And if it does deserve it, whether we use reason rationally, in the proper sense of the word, as a defense of life. And the defense of life is everything. We do not use reason as a defense of life. (64-65)

Commenting on violence in modern urban culture, Saramago says to Juan Arias: "We are much weaker that we think and reason is not much good to us, it only props us up in the non-conflictive situations of life" (Arias 49). Saramago's viewpoint often seems to stem from the disillusionment of a rationalist disabused by the reality of human history, as when he says: "I will never understand why we human beings are the ones who invented cruelty: this I cannot understand" (Arias 49-50) or "I think there is no solution for the human race" (Ceccucci 185). Other comments (e.g., "I, who am as pessimistic as it is possible to be, am nevertheless trying to create a better kind of person" [Arias 63]) support the idea that the "better" people to be found in his novels are not the products of natural creation or historical evolution but of the literary imagination, the results perhaps of a moral wishful thinking that makes sense only if the assumption of basic human fallenness is granted.

Conclusion

Saramago's moral vision derives its power from the unvarnished depiction of humanity in its most fallen and as yet unredeemed state, what Richard Zenith calls "our all too dupable and corruptible human nature." In the two texts analyzed above, he uses cognitive estrangement to remind us that the danger to the future of humanity is not external but internal: a technique fundamental to science fiction becomes an instrument of what I have described as an increasingly Augustinian view of human nature.[8] The humanity of *O Ano de 1993* and *Blindness* does seem clearly to be fallen and Saramago's message to be that the future will be a nightmare if we don't take our fallenness seriously into account. Fiction may not be a plan of action to change human nature, but it can call our attention to the destructiveness that lies within us.

Notes

[1] Similar themes are found in the short fiction of *Objecto quase* (1978), especially "Embargo" and "Coisas." For more on these stories, see Horácio Costa's analysis in *José Saramago: o período formativo*, 319-49, especially pp. 328-39. See also Margarida Braga Neves's

remarks on the "effect of estrangement" created by "the almost minimalist sobriety of each of the story titles" (124).

[2] I have adapted the following summary of Suvin's theory from my article, "Ignácio de Loyola Brandão and the Fiction of Cognitive Estrangement."

[3] Costa discusses the influence of these novels as well as Ray Bradbury's *Martian Chronicles* (214-15). See also Neves 123.

[4] In *Cadernos de Lanzarote–Diário V*: "I situated in the future this society of an unnamed country, an image of many such communities that have lived oppressed and humiliated by a greater power" (29-30; qtd. in Neves 123).

[5] Mention should also be made of the planet imagined by Isaac Asimov in his 1957 novel *The Naked Sun*, where human beings live a utopian existence at the cost of a morbid fear of physical contact.

[6] Ceccucci 179, citing an interview with Clara Ferreira Alves, "José Saramago: todos os pecados do mundo," in *Expresso* (October 28, 1995), 84.

[7] *Confessiones* Book V, ix (16): "et ibam iam ad inferos portans omnia mala, quae conmiseram et in te et in me et in alios, multa et gravia super originalis peccati vinculum, quo omnes in Adam morimur" (89).

[8] Although I have not gone into the allegorical nature of the works in question, a matter that Saramago's criticism has looked at closely, the connection between allegory and cognitive estrangement has received a good deal of attention from theorists of science fiction. See, for example, Damien Broderick, especially p. 80.

Works Cited

Arias, Juan. *José Saramago: el amor posible.* Barcelona: Planeta, 1998.

Augustine, Saint. *S. Aureli Augustini Confessionum.* Stuttgart and Leipzig: Teubner, 1996.

Baptista-Bastos. *José Saramago: Aproximação a um retrato.* Lisboa: Dom Quixote, 1996.

Broderick, Damien. *Reading By Starlight: Postmodern Science Fiction.* London: Routledge, 1995.

Burgess, Anthony. *The Wanting Seed.* 1962. New York: Norton, 1976.

Ceccucci, Piero. "La città ritrovata. Una 'frincha de esperança' in *Ensaio sobre a cegueira.*" *José Saramago: il bagaglio dello scrittore.* Ed. Giulia Lanciani. Roma: Bulzoni, 1996. 177-89.

Costa, Horácio. *José Saramago: o período formativo.* Lisboa: Caminho, 1997.

Diogo, Américo António Lindeza. "*O ano de 1993*: representação e poder." *Colóquio/Letras* 151/152 (Jan.-June 1999): 65-76.

Hatherly, Ana. Review of *O Ano de 1993. Colóquio/Letras* 31 (May 1976): 87-88.

Jameson, Fredrick. *The Prison-House of Language.* Princeton: Princeton UP, 1972.

Jauss, Hans Robert. *Aesthetic Experience and Literary Hermeneutics.* Minneapolis: U of Minnesota P, 1982.

Krabbenhoft, Kenneth. "Ignácio de Loyola Brandão and the Fiction of Cognitive Estrangement." *Luso-Brazilian Review* XXIV.1 (1987): 35-45.

Lanciani, Giulia, ed. *José Saramago: il bagaglio dello scrittore.* Roma: Bulzoni, 1996.

Lima, Isabel Pires de. "Dos 'anjos da história' em dois romances de Saramago." *Colóquio/Letras* 151/152 (Jan.-June 1999): 415-26.

Neves, Margarida Braga. "Nexos, temas e obsessões na ficção breve de José Saramago." *Colóquio/Letras* 151/152 (Jan.-June 1999): 117-41.

Parrinder, Patrick. *Science Fiction, Its Criticism and Teaching.* London: Methuen, 1980.

Saramago, José. *A história do cerco de Lisboa.* Lisboa: Caminho, 1989.

———. *A jangada de pedra* (Lisbon: Caminho, 1986). English translation by Giovanni Pontiero, *The Stone Raft.* New York: Harcourt Brace, 1995.

———. *Ensaio sobre a cegueira.* Lisboa: Caminho, 1995. English translation by Giovanni Pontiero, *Blindness.* San Diego: Harcourt Brace, 1999.

———. Interview with Alan Riding. "A Writer With an Ear for the Melody of Peasant Speech." *New York Times* Dec. 3, 1998: Arts Section, 5.

———. *Memorial do convento.* Lisboa: Caminho, 1982. English translation by Giovanni Pontiero, *Baltasar and Blimunda.* San Diego: Harcourt, 1987.

———. *O ano da morte de Ricardo Reis.* Lisboa: Caminho, 1984. English translation by Giovanni Pontiero, *The Year of the Death of Ricardo Reis.* San Diego: Harcourt, 1991.

———. *O ano de 1993.* 1975 [Lisboa: Futura]. Lisboa: Caminho, 1987.

———. *Objecto quase.* Lisboa: Moraes, 1978.

Seixo, Maria Alzira. *Lugares da ficção em José Saramago.* Lisboa: Imprensa Nacional-Casa da Moeda, 1999.

———. "Os espelhos virados para dentro. Configurações narrativas do espaço e do imaginário em *Ensaio sobre a cegueira.*" Lanciani 191-210.

Suvin, Darko. *Metamorphoses of Science Fiction.* New Haven: Yale UP, 1979.

Vieira, Agripina Carriço. "Da história ao indivíduo ou da exepção ao banal na escrita de Saramago." *Colóquio/Letras* 151/152 (Jan.-June 1999): 379-93.

Zenith, Richard. "José Saramago and the Art of Seeing." *Times Literary Supplement* Oct. 23, 1998.

Saramago, at 8 years

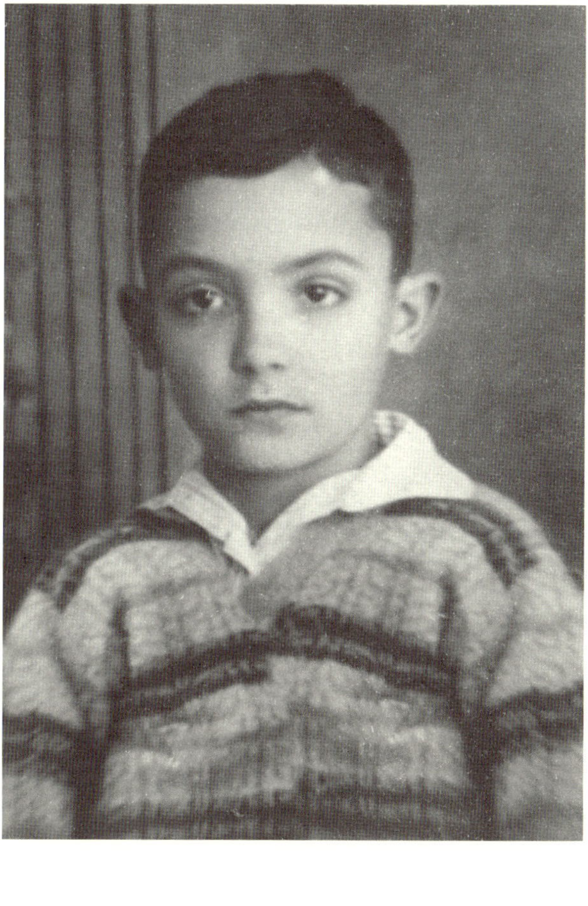

Saramago as a young man

Saramago in Firmangaya, Lanzarote

Saramago at work

Saramago with Jorge Amado and Salman Rushdie in Santiago de Compostela

Saramago with Susan Sontag in Lanzarote

Saramago in Central Park, New York

Saramago as recipient of the Nobel Prize, with the King and Queen of Sweden and Pilar. December, 1998.

"The One With the Beard Is God, the Other is the Devil"

Harold Bloom

I

José Saramago published *The Gospel According to Jesus Christ* in 1991, when he approached his seventieth year. As Saramago's fierce critical admirer, I am reluctant to choose it over all his other novels, but it is an awesome work, imaginatively superior to any other life of Jesus, including the four canonical Gospels. It loses some aspects of irony in Giovanni Pontiero's fine translation, but more than enough survives to overcome the aware reader.

Saramago's audacity is triumphant in his *Gospel* (the short title that I will employ). God, in Saramago's *Gospel*, has some affinities to the J Writer's Yahweh and some to Blake's Nobodaddy, but it is important to see that Saramago resists giving us the Gnostics' Ialdaboth. Kierkegaard in his *Concluding Unscientific Postscript* ironically observed that "to give thinking supremacy over everything else is gnosticism" (341). Yet Saramago's God scandalizes us in ways that transcend the intellect, since a God who is both truth and time is the worst possible bad news. Saramago's devil, delightfully named Pastor, is mildness itself compared to Saramago's God, who refuses Pastor's attempt to be reconciled, and who manifests neither love nor compassion for Jesus or for any other human being.

That must make the book seem sublimely outrageous, yet it is not, and I think that only a bigot or a fool would judge Saramago's *Gospel* to be blasphemous. Saramago's God can be both wily and bland, and he has a capacity for savage humor. No one is going to love this god, but then he doesn't ask or expect love. Worship and obedience are his requirements, and sacred violence is his endless resource. Baruch Spinoza insisted that it was necessary for us to love God without ever expecting that God would love us in return. No one could love Saramago's God, unless the lover were so deep in sado-masochism as to be helpless before its drive.

God tells us in the *Gospel* that he is dissatisfied with the small constituency provided him by his chosen people, the Jews:

> For the last four thousand and four years I have been the God of the Jews, a quarrelsome and difficult race by nature, but on the whole I have got along fairly well with them, they now take Me seriously and are likely to go on doing so for the foreseeable future. So, You are satisfied, said Jesus. I am and I am not, or rather, I would be were it not for this restless heart of Mine, which is forever telling Me, Well now, a fine destiny you've arranged after four thousand years of trial and tribulation that no amount of sacrifice on altars will ever be able to repay, for You continue to be the god of a tiny population that occupies a minute part of this world You created with everything that's on it, so tell Me, My son, if I should be satisfied with this depressing situation. Never having created a world, I'm in no position to judge, replied Jesus. True, you cannot judge, but you could help. Help in what way. To spread My word, to help Me become the god of more people. I don't understand. If you play your part, that is to say, the part I have reserved for you in My plan, I have every confidence that within the next six centuries or so, despite all the struggles and obstacles ahead of us, I will pass from being God of the Jews to being God of those whom we will call Catholics, from the Greek. And what is this part You have reserved for me in Your plan. That of martyr, My son, that of victim, which is the best role of all for propagating any faith and stirring up fervor. God made the words martyr and victim seem like milk and honey on his tongue, but Jesus felt a sudden chill in his limbs, as if the mist had closed over him, while the devil regarded him with an enigmatic expression which combined scientific curiosity with grudging compassion. (311-12)

God is restless and does not wish to be depressed; those are his motives for victimizing Jesus, and subsequently for torturing to death the millions who will die as sacrifices to Jesus, whether they affirm him or deny him. That God is the greatest of comedians we learn from his chant of the martyrs: "a litany, in alphabetical order so as not to hurt any feelings about precedence and importance" (321). The litany is quite marvelous, from Adalbert of Prague, executed with a seven-pronged pikestaff, on to "Wolgefortis or Livrade or Eutropia the bearded virgin crucified" (325). Four long pages in length, the catalogue of sacred violence has such delights as Blandina of

Lyons, gored by a savage bull, and the unfortunate Januaris of Naples, first thrown to wild beasts, then into a furnace, and finally decapitated. The gusto of Saramago's God recalls Edward Gibbon's in Chapter XVI of *The History of the Decline and Fall of the Roman Empire,* except that Gibbon, maintaining decorum, avoids detailing the many varieties of martyrdom by torture. But Gibbon again anticipates Saramago by observing that Christians "have inflicted far greater severities on each other than they had experienced from the zeal of infidels" (452-53). Saramago's God, his voice a little tired, speaks of the Inquisition as a necessary evil, and defends the burning of thousands because the cause of Jesus demands it. One blinks at the dustjacket of the American edition of Saramago's *Gospel,* where we are assured that defying the authority of God the Father "is still not denial of Him."

Though necessarily a secondary character in comparison to Saramago's Jesus, God demands scrutiny beyond his menacingly comic aspects. Primarily, the *Gospel*'s God is time, and not truth, the other attribute he asserts. Saramago, a Marxist (an eccentric one), and not a Christian, subverts St. Augustine on the theodicy of time. If time is God, then God can be forgiven nothing, and who would desire to forgive him anyway? But then, the *Gospel*'s God is not the least interested in forgiveness: he forgives no one, not even Jesus, and he declines to forgive Pastor, when the devil makes an honest offer of obedience. Power is God's only interest, and the sacrifice of Jesus employs the prospect of forgiveness of our sins only as an advertisement. God makes clear that all of us are guilty, and that he prefers to keep it that way. Jesus is no atonement: his crucifixion is merely a device by which God ceases to be Jewish, and becomes Catholic, a *converso* rather than a *marrano.* That is superb irony, and Saramago makes it high art, though to thus reduce it critically is to invite a Catholic onslaught. Of all fictive representations of God since the Yahwist's, I vote for Saramago's: he is at once the funniest and the most chilling, in the mode of the Shakespearean hero-villains: Richard III, Iago, Edmund in *King Lear.*

II

Pastor, or the devil, has his own charm, as befits a very original representation of Satan. A giant of a man, with a huge head, Pastor allows Jesus to become his assistant shepherd for a large flock of sheep and goats. In response to Jesus' pious exclamation—"The Lord alone is God"—the non-Jewish Pastor replies with grand pungency:

> Certainly if God exists, He must be only one, but it would be better if He were two, then there would be a god for the wolf and one for the sheep, a god for the victim and one for the assassin, a god for the condemned man and one for the executioner. (192-93)

This sensible dualism is not exactly Satanic, and Pastor remains considerably more likeable than God throughout the novel. In the dialogues between the devil and the younger Jesus, the devil's part clearly prevails, though honorably, unlike God's dominance of Jesus when father and son first meet in the desert. God demands a sheep dear to Jesus as a sacrifice, and Jesus reluctantly assents. Pastor, on hearing of this, gives up on Jesus: "You've learned nothing, begone with you" (222). And Pastor, so far, is right: Jesus' education as to God's nature will be completed only upon the cross.

What then are we to make of Pastor? Saramago's devil is humane yet scarcely a skeptic: he knows too much about God. If Saramago's God is a Portuguese *converso*, then Saramago's devil was never Jewish, and seems curiously unrelated both to God and to Jesus Christ. Why is Pastor in the book? Evidently, only as a witness, I think one has to conclude. Saramago seems to take us back to the unfallen Satan of the Book of Job, who goes to-and-fro on the earth, and walks up and down on it. And yet Job's Satan was an Accuser; Pastor is not. Why does Jesus sojourn four years with Pastor, as an apprentice shepherd? The angel, who comes belatedly to tell Mary that Jesus is God's son tells us that "the devil only denies himself" (263), which is extravagantly ambiguous, and could mean that Pastor resists playing the role that God has assigned him. Mary's angel, after telling us that Pastor was his schoolfellow, says that Pastor prospers because "the harmony of the universe requires it" (264). There is then a secret relationship between Pastor and God, a truth that dismays Jesus' disciples (302).

When God, dressed like a wealthy Jew, appears to Jesus in the boat, Saramago imagines a magnificent re-entry for Pastor:

> The boat swayed, the swimmer's head emerged from the water, then his torso, splashing water everywhere, then his legs, a leviathan rising from the depths, and it turned out to be Pastor, reappearing after all these years. I've come to join you, he said, settling himself on the side of the boat, equidistant between Jesus and God, and yet oddly enough this time the boat did not tip to his side, as if Pastor had no weight or he was levitating and not really sitting, I've come to join you, he

> repeated, and hope I'm in time to take part in the conversation. We've been talking but still haven't got to the heart of the matter, replied God, and turning to Jesus, He told him, This is the devil whom we have just been discussing. Jesus looked from one to the other, and saw that without God's beard they could have passed for twins, although the devil was younger and less wrinkled. Jesus said, I know very well who he is, I lived with him for four years when he was known as Pastor, and God replied, You had to live with someone, it couldn't be with Me, and you didn't wish to be with your family, so that left only the devil. Did he come looking for me or did You send him. Neither one nor the other, let's say we agreed that this was the best solution. So that's why, when he spoke through the possessed man from Gadara, he called me Your son. Precisely. Which means that both of you kept me in the dark. As happens to all humans. But You said I was not human. And that is true, but you have been what might technically be called incarnated. And now what do you two want of me. I'm the one who wants something, not he. But both of you are here, I noticed that Pastor's appearance came as no surprise, You must have been expecting him. Not exactly, although in principle one should always expect the devil. But if the matter You and I have to resolve affects only us, what is he doing here and why don't You send him away. One can dismiss the rabble in the devil's service if they become troublesome in word or deed, but not Satan himself. Then he's here because this conversation concerns him too. My son, never forget what I'm about to tell you, everything that concerns God also concerns the devil. (309-10)

As God and the devil are twins (we have suspected this), it is a delight to be told that we cannot live with God, and so must choose between our families and the devil. God speaks of his desire to be God of the Catholics, but this ambition I have glanced at already, and wish here only to ask: why is Pastor in the boat? His expression combines "scientific curiosity with grudging compassion" (312), but he is there because, as Jesus accurately surmises, extending God's domain also extends the devil's. And yet poor Pastor has his perplexities:

> I'm staying, said Pastor, and these were the first words he spoke since revealing his identity. I'm staying, he said a second time, and added, I myself can see things in the future, but I'm not always certain if what I see there is true or false, in other words, I can see my lies for what they are, that is, my truths, but I don't know to what extent the truths of others are their lies. (318)

Saramago dryly calls this a "torturous statement," but he means that it clearly indicts God, whose truths indeed are his lies. God's account of the Catholic Church that will be founded upon Jesus is true only insofar as it is historically horrible, and the zest God manifests as he itemizes martyrs and sums up the Inquisition has unmistakable sadistic overtones. Most alarmingly, God (a good Augustinian, before Augustine) deprecates all human joys as being false, since all of them emanate from original sin: "lust and fear are weapons the demon uses to torment wretched mankind" (325). When Jesus asks Pastor whether this is true, the devil's reply is eloquently illuminating:

> More or less, I simply took what God didn't want, the flesh with all its joys and sorrows, youth and senility, bloom and decay, but it isn't true that fear is one of my weapons, I don't recall having invented sin and punishment or the terror they inspire. (325-26)

We tend to believe this when God snaps in response: "Be quiet ... sin and the devil are one and the same thing." Does it need God to say that? Wouldn't the Cardinal-Archbishop of Lisbon do as well? Saramago's reply is uncanny. God describes the Crusades, to be waged against the unnamed Allah, whom Pastor disowns creating:

> Who, then, will create this hostile god, asked Pastor. Jesus was at a loss for an answer, and God, who had been silent, remained silent, but a voice came down from the mist and said, Perhaps this god and the one to come are the same god. Jesus, God, and the devil pretended not to hear but could not help looking at one another in alarm, mutual fear is like that, it readily unites enemies. (328-29)

Only here, in Saramago's *Gospel*, do we hear a voice beyond God's. Whose is it? Who could proclaim what God does not wish to say, which is that he and Allah are one? With a God as sly and unlovable as Saramago's, both we and Saramago long for a God beyond God, perhaps the Alien or Stranger God of the Gnostics. But whoever that God is, he does not speak again in this novel. Very deftly, Saramago has just told us explicitly what he tells us implicitly throughout: God and Jesus pragmatically are enemies, even as Pastor is the unwilling enemy of both. Yet in what does that enmity consist? Reacting to God's account of the Inquisition, Pastor remarks: "One has to be God to countenance so much blood" (330).

Pastor's great moment—and it is one of the handful of key passages in the book—comes in his vain attempt at reconciliation with God:

> Pastor searched for the right words before explaining, I've been listening to all that has been said here in this boat, and although I myself have caught glimpses of the light and darkness ahead, I never realized the light came from the burning stakes and the darkness from great piles of bodies. Does this trouble you. It shouldn't trouble me, for I am the devil, and the devil profits from death even more than You do, it goes without saying that hell is more crowded than heaven. Then why do you complain. I'm not complaining, I'm making a proposal. Go ahead, but be quick, I cannot loiter here for all eternity. No one knows better than You that the devil too has a heart. Yes, but you make poor use of it. Today I use it by acknowledging Your power and wishing that it spread to the ends of the earth without the need of so much death, and since You insist that whatever thwarts and denies You comes from the evil I represent and govern in this world, I propose that You receive me into Your heavenly kingdom, my past offenses redeemed by those I will not commit in future, that You accept my obedience as in those happy days when I was one of Your chosen angels, Lucifer You called me, bearer of light, before my ambition to become Your equal consumed my soul and made me rebel against You. And would you care to tell Me why I should pardon you and receive you into My Kingdom. Because if You grant me that same pardon You will one day promise left and right, then evil will cease, Your son will not have to die, and Your kingdom will extend beyond the land of the Hebrews to embrace the whole globe, good will prevail everywhere, and I shall stand among the lowliest of the angels who have remained faithful, more faithful than all of them now that I have repented, and I shall sing Your praises, everything will end as if it had never been, everything will become what it should always have been. (330-31)

The irony of the humane Pastor and the inhumane God could not be better juxtaposed. God makes clear that he would prefer an even worse devil, if that were possible, and that without the devil, God cannot be God. Pastor, who has been persuasively sincere, shrugs and goes off, after collecting from Jesus the old black bowl from Nazareth into which the blood of Jesus will drip in the novel's closing words.

It is not sufficient to praise Saramago's originality in limning his wholly undiabolic devil. One must go further. The enigmatic Pastor is the only devil who could be aesthetically and intellectually appropriate as we conclude the

Second Millennium. Except that he cannot be crucified, this fallen angel has far more in common with Saramago's Jesus than with Saramago's God. They both are God's victims, suffering the tyranny of time, which God calls truth. Pastor is resigned, and less rebellious than Jesus, yet that is because Pastor knows all there is to know. As readers, we remain more akin to Saramago's uncanny devil than we are to his malevolent ironist of a God.

III

The glory of Saramago's *Gospel* is Saramago's Jesus, who seems to me humanly and aesthetically more admirable than any other version of Jesus in the literature of the century now ending. Perhaps D.H. Lawrence's *The Man Who Died* is a near-rival, but Lawrence's Jesus is a grand Lawrencian vitalist, rather than a possible human being. Saramago's Jesus paradoxically is the novelist's warmest and most memorable character of any of his books. W. H. Auden, Christian poet-critic, oddly found in Shakespeare's Falstaff a type of Christ. I cite a paragraph of Auden to emphasize how far both Saramago's God and Saramago's Jesus are from even a generous, undogmatic Christian view:

> The Christian God is not a self-sufficient being like Aristotle's First Cause, but a God who creates a world which he continues to love although it refuses to love him in return. He appears in this world, not as Apollo or Aphrodite might appear, disguised as man so that no mortal should recognize his divinity, but as a real man who openly claims to be God. And the consequence is inevitable. The highest religious and temporal authorities condemn Him as a blasphemer and a Lord of Misrule, as a bad Companion for mankind. Inevitable because, as Richelieu said, "The salvation of State is in this world," and history has not as yet provided us with any evidence that the Prince of this world has changed his character. (207-08)

Saramago's God, as I have said, neither loves the world nor does he expect it to love him in return. He wishes power, as widely extended as possible. And Saramago's Jesus is anything but an appearance of God "disguised as man"; rather his Jesus has been shanghaied by God, for God's own purposes of power. As for Satan, "the Prince of this world," we know that Saramago *has* changed his character.

The title of the novel is *The Gospel According to Jesus Christ*, where "according" matters most. Saramago's Jesus is an ironist, an amazingly mild one considering his victimization by God. Before meeting John the Baptist, Jesus is told that John is taller, heavier, more bearded, is hardly clothed, and subsists on locust and wild honey. "He sounds more like the Messiah than I do, Jesus said, rising from the circle" (354).

Saramago's novel begins and ends with the Crucifixion, presented at the start with considerable irony, but at the close with a terrible pathos:

> Jesus is dying slowly, life ebbing from him, ebbing, when suddenly the heavens overhead open wide and God appears in the same attire He wore in the boat, and His words resound throughout the earth, This is My beloved son, in whom I am well pleased. Jesus realized then that he had been tricked, as the lamb led to sacrifice is tricked, and that his life had been planned for death from the very beginning. Remembering the river of blood and suffering that would flow from his side and flood the globe, he called out to the open sky, where God could be seen smiling, Men, forgive Him, for He knows not what He has done. Then he began expiring in the midst of a dream. He found himself back in Nazareth and saw his father shrugging his shoulders and smiling as he told him, Just as I cannot ask you all the questions, neither can you give me all the answers. There was still some life in him when he felt a sponge soaked in water and vinegar moisten his lips, and looking down, he saw a man walking away with a bucket, a staff over his shoulder. But what Jesus did not see, on the ground, was the black bowl into which his blood was dripping. (376-77)

"Men, forgive Him, for He knows not what He has done" testifies both to Jesus' sweetness and to Saramago's aesthetically controlled fury. No disinterested reader, free of ideology and of creed, is going to forgive Saramago's God for the murder of Jesus and the subsequent torrents of human blood that will result. Joyce's Stephen speaks of the "hangman God," as some Italians still call him, and that precisely is Saramago's God. This would be appalling enough in itself but is augmented by the long and loving portrait that Saramago gives of his Jesus.

The story of this Jesus begins and ends with an earthenware bowl, first presented to Mary the mother of Jesus by a beggar, an apparent angel. That bowl overflows with luminous earth, presumably unfallen; at the close it catches the blood of the dying Jesus. The beggar is God, rather than Pastor, and appears again to Mary in a dream-vision that is also a tryst. When Jesus is born, God manifests again as the third of three passing shepherds, bringing bread of an occult kind. One supposes that this is subtly akin to God's seed resulting in the flesh of Jesus, but so nuanced is Saramago that supposition sometimes needs to be evaded, in this mysterious book.

The thirteen-year-old Jesus leaves home because the Romans have crucified his father Joseph, an invention entirely Saramago's own, just as Joseph's partial complicity in Herod's massacre of the innocents is also Saramago's rather startling suggestion, and is another trouble for Jesus that sends him forth on his road. But why does Saramago so alter the story? Perhaps this most humane of all versions of Jesus has to suffer the darkness of two fathers, the loving, unlucky, and guilty Joseph, and the unloving, fortunate, and even guiltier God.

When the boy Jesus disputes with the doctors of the Law in the Temple, I am reminded again of how Augustinian Saramago has made both God and the Law. One doesn't quarrel with this anachronism, because Saramago's God is himself so anxious to forsake Judahism (to call it that) for Catholicism. And besides, one grants Saramago his anachronisms in this marvelous book just as one grants them endlessly to Shakespeare. Still, guilt is not a concern of the only traditional Jesus who moves me, the Gnostic Jesus of the Gospel of Thomas. Yet I am a Jewish Gnostic explicating a beautiful book by a Portuguese who is no Catholic, anymore than Fernando Pessoa was. At just this point in his narrative, Saramago brings Jesus and Pastor together, and that curious sojourn I have examined already.

And yet Jesus' principal relationship in his life, as Saramago sees it and tells it, is to neither of his fathers, nor to the devil, nor to Mary his mother, but to the whore Mary Magdalene. Of all the splendors of Saramago's *Gospel*, the love between Jesus and the Magdalene is the grandest, and their meeting and union (231-43) is for me the summit of Saramago's achievement, up to the present time. Echoing the Song of Songs, Saramago is most the artist when he intertwines a reply to Pastor with Jesus' awakening to sexual life:

> Jesus breathed so fast, for one moment he thought he would faint when her hands, the left hand on his forehead, the right hand on his ankles, began caressing him, slowly coming together, meeting in the middle, then starting all over again. You've learned nothing, begone with you, Pastor had told him, and who knows, perhaps he meant to say that Jesus had not learned to cherish life. Now Mary Magdalene instructed him.... (236)

We can void the "perhaps," and Mary Magdalene is Jesus' best teacher, eclipsing Joseph, God, Pastor, and Mary the mother. In what may be the book's greatest irony she teaches him freedom, which God will not permit any man, but in particular not to God's only son.

I myself have just turned seventy, and ask more urgently than before: where shall wisdom be found? The wisdom of Saramago's *Gospel* is very harsh: we can emulate Jesus only by forgiving God, but we do not believe, with Jesus, that God does not know what God has done.

I find the epilogue to Saramago's *Gospel* not in *Blindness*, a parable as dark as any could be, but in the charming *The Tale of the Unknown Island*, a brief fable composed in 1998, the year of his Nobel Prize, and translated a year later by Margaret Jull Costa. In the wonderful comic vein of *The Siege of Lisbon*, Saramago's tale begins with a man asking a king for a boat which can sail in quest of the unknown island. The boat granted, the man goes off to the harbor, followed by the king's cleaning woman, who will constitute the rest of the crew.

The cleaning woman, with superb resolution, vows that she and the man will be sufficient to sail the caravel to the unknown island, thus heartening the man, whose will cannot match hers. They go to bed in separate bunks, port and starboard, and he dreams bad dreams, until he finds her shadow beside his shadow:

> He woke up with his arms about the cleaning woman, and her arms about him, their bodies and their bunks fused into one, so that no one can tell any more if this is port or starboard. Then, as soon as the sun had risen, the man and the woman went to paint in white letters on both sides of the prow the name that the caravel still lacked. Around midday, with the tide, The Unknown Island finally set to sea, in search of itself. (51)

Saramago names no one: I am critically outrageous enough to venture upon some experimental namings, as an antithesis to Saramago's *Gospel*. Let us call the man Jesus Christ, try the cleaning woman as Mary Magdalene, and the king, who exists to receive favors, will do for God. Doubtless, Saramago would shake his head, but so audacious a narrative genius inspires audacity in his critic. No one will be crucified upon the masts of the Unknown Island, and the bad dreams of *this* Jesus will not be realized. Saramago's happy tale is a momentary antidote to the most tragic of his works. Beware a God who is at once truth and time, Saramago warns us, and abandon such a God to sail out in search of yourself.

Works Cited

Auden, W. H. "The Prince's Dog." *The Dyer's Hand and Other Essays.* New York: Random House, 1962. 182-208.

Gibbon, Edward. *The History of the Decline and Fall of the Roman Empire.* Vol. I. New York: Heritage Press, 1946.

Kierkegaard, Søren. *Concluding Unscientific Postscript to Philosophical Fragments.* Vol. I. Ed. and trans. Howard V. Hong and Edna H. Hong. Princeton: Princeton UP, 1992.

Saramago, José. *The Gospel According to Jesus Christ.* Trans.Giovanni Pontiero. New York: Harcourt Brace, 1994.

———. *The Tale of the Unknown Island.* Trans.Margaret Jull Costa. New York: Harcourt Brace, 1999.

Journey to the Iberian God: Antonio Machado Revisited by Saramago*

Orlando Grossegesse

In 1998, when José Saramago became the first author of the Portuguese-speaking world to receive the long awaited Nobel Prize for Literature, the outburst of joy in his home country could not conceal a touch of bitterness. National pride was injured by the Spanish media talking about "nuestro Nobel" and by the Spanish public claiming the Portuguese writer for their own. This happened from the very first moment of the international press conference in Madrid, which took advantage of Saramago's stopover as he returned home to Lanzarote from the Frankfurt book fair. Only a few days later, an aircraft of the Portuguese state with President Jorge Sampaio himself on board "reclaimed" the author from the Spanish island, transporting him back to Lisbon and conferring on him the highest national decoration, the *Grande Colar da Ordem de Santiago*, normally reserved for foreign heads of state.

This event reflects the many efforts to minimize the writer's alienation from Portuguese society.[1] According to his essay "O (meu) Iberismo" (1988), an early interest in Spanish culture, especially literature and painting, made him adopt a different view of the Peninsula and his home country. This became a geographic separation in 1993 when Saramago decided to move to Lanzarote after suffering the hostility of the Church and the Catholic public who condemned *The Gospel According to Jesus Christ* (1991), and after the "censorship" exercised by the Portuguese government when it excluded his novel from its list of candidates for the European Book Award.

Besides being a stubborn Communist and atheist, Saramago maintains an Iberian vision that injures patriotic feelings and the traditional discourse of

Portuguese identity as set against Spain, deeply rooted even among intellectuals. Large parts of the Portuguese public consider Saramago something of a seduced renegade, alluding to his marriage with the much younger Sevillan journalist Pilar del Río in 1988. The author himself denies being monopolized by Spanish public life, which indeed has naturalized him as "uno de los nuestros," and praises instead the huge generosity of Spain while stressing his indelible Portuguese nature.[2]

Saramago's acquaintance with Spanish culture started much earlier than this recent series of events. It started even before his overt claiming of an Iberian identity in the novel *The Stone Raft*, published in 1986, the same year that Portugal and Spain together joined the European Community. The author reclaims a common peninsular identity that has been buried by the anti-Hispanic definition of Portugal since the 17th century, a split that enabled both Portugal and Spain to be turned into mere playthings in the power politics of France and Great Britain. Saramago's reclamation stems from the *Iberismo* tradition cultivated by intellectuals and educated upper-class circles of the 19th century (Molina), which the author transforms into a new cultural, social and political concept of "trans-ibericidade" (Saramago "O [meu] iberismo"): the peninsula must regain its position as the European center of mediation with Africa and Latin America (Saramago "Descobrir"). But this wishful thinking remains unspecified, blurred into a general solidarity of the South, which runs counter to the existing economic force of the North.

When speaking of reclamation, Hispanists immediately think of Juan Goytisolo's *Reivindicación del Conde Don Julián* (1970). In this famous novel, pure Spanish identity is betrayed by recovering the Arabic nature of Spain. Without any allusion to Goytisolo, Saramago commits a similar betrayal by mingling Portuguese and Spanish identity.[3] He looks upon the Peninsula as one cultural space with a common history and a common future, turning it from its peripheral status into a new center of a less centralized Europe (Saramago "Europa"). But the comparison with Goytisolo is faulty. The huge difference between reclaiming Arabic and Iberian nature is obvious: in the first case there is a radical transgression in terms of civilization that is absent in *The Stone Raft*. The comparison nevertheless helps to understand the different condition of Portugal: whereas Spanish identity is defined against "los moros," Portuguese identity is defined first against "los españoles" and only secondly by the context of the *Reconquista*. This clear opposition dissolves from the moment we recognize "Spanish" identity as Castillian identity, admitting thereby other peninsular identities such as the Catalans who define themselves against "los castellanos." This explains, on the other hand, the minor scale, restricted to a few intellectuals, on which the Arabic legacy is reclaimed in Portugal. Certainly Saramago's *The History of the Siege of Lisbon* is aware of this lack, and compensates for it by introducing a double focalization from within the Moorish Lisbon and from outside the city walls, thus questioning the national and religious identities of both sides, the besieged inhabitants and the "multinational force" under the command of Afonso Henriques. But this partial, mingling perspective never achieves the vehemence of the Goytisolian *reivindicación* of Arabic nature (Grossegesse "Rückforderung").

Saramago's interest centers on the common Iberian heritage. His overall view of the Peninsula, which draws comparisons and looks for common ground, is still an unusual attitude in Portugal, bearing in mind the scarcity of Spanish history, culture and literature in traditional education. Knowledge about Spain is limited to a few negative commonplaces that match the anti-Hispanic discourse of national identity present since the battle of Aljubarrota in 1385, still idealized as the affirmation of the country's eternal independence from Spain. This situation is counterbalanced by the general ignorance of Portuguese affairs in Spain, except among intellectuals and a restricted public in Galicia.

Saramago's vision of a common Peninsular destiny does not emerge at once with *The Stone Raft*, but grows steadily in the course of his whole literary evolution, and is influenced by the author's autodidactic incursions into Spanish culture and history, which have been understandably overlooked by Portuguese scholars.[4] Ever since Saramago's first volume of poetry, *Os poemas possíveis* (*Possible Poems*, 1966), Antonio Machado has been revealed as a main reference for the Portuguese author's own poetics. The epigraph of the book, borrowed from Machado's "Proverbios y cantares" of 1919 and dedicated to José Ortega y Gasset, will be repeated throughout Saramago's whole work and can be understood as his general motto: "Demos tiempo al tiempo: / para que el vaso rebose / hay que llenarlo primero" (in Alan S. Trueblood's English translation, "Don't try to rush things: / for the cup to run over, / it must first be filled" [189]).

This plea for slowness, for the space of time to be filled entirely instead of existing in a state of rapid and often amnesiac advance from present to future, finds continuation and larger exposition in *Manual of Painting and Calligraphy*, the first edition of which in 1977 bears the significant subtitle "ensaio de romance" with the two meanings: "an attempt at a novel" and a "novel essay." Various experiments in painting and autobiographical writing define the gradual progress of a professional portrait painter, named H, towards political consciousness. Viewing the history of the Peninsula, he perceives the eternal interweaving of authoritarian regimes and oppressive structures, from the Inquisition active in Portugal and Spain to the simultaneous dictatorships of Salazar and General Franco.[5] When he recognizes himself as a passive henchman of the dictatorial status quo, he begins to prepare his "birth" into a new life of political participation and sexuality, in spite of his age of nearly fifty—a basic plot structure that characterizes the whole (male) fiction of Saramago since *Manual of Painting and Calligraphy*. A woman always appears who "gives birth" to new life and new history, somehow ripening the still timid revolt of the man in the midst of a midlife crisis (Grossegesse, *Saramago lesen* 71, 74-77).

Precisely in the course of his comparative consideration of Spain, mingling the past with the present and the collective with his own individual situation, H recognizes himself as "the portrait-painter of the protégés and protectors of Salazar and Marcelo and their oppressive secret police" (185). In the same moment, the Machadian sentence "demos tiempo al tiempo" shows up, illustrated by the example of a Spanish painter: Francisco Goya, serving the royal court with his portrait art, mirrors—across almost two centuries and the Spanish-Portuguese border—the condition of H as a passive henchman awakened to political consciousness. H's later stage corresponds to the Goya of the *Caprichos*:

> Time only needs time. The popular rising in Madrid in 1808 only found Goya prepared in 1814. It is true that history goes faster than the men who paint and record it. (186)

This lack of synchronization between the speed of events that become history and the slow human consciousness of historical meaning or sense is the heart of the matter as it appears reflected in Machado's sentence. *Manual of Painting and Calligraphy* can be considered Saramago's basic text with autobiographic "flashes" (as the author recognizes in the interview included in Baptista-Bastos 29). This first-person narrative is rooted among social and political structures that shape the individual awareness of history as the basis for a necessary collective project. The "ensaio do romance" reveals that Saramago's *écriture* is moved by his own mortality and the search for the birth of self-consciousness, inspired not only by the reading of Marguerite Yourcenar's *Mémoires d'Hadrien* (1951), but also by the knowledge of Socratic maieutics.[6] The written book is only the product of "an identified portion of humankind" (Saramago, [No title] 174) that should take part in the making of a (more) human history, understood as a space where past and future coexist. We presume that Saramago in 1965/66 had already read the philosophical lessons of Machado's Juan de Mairena. The Portuguese writer adopts wholeheartedly Machado's/Mairena's theory of the apocryphal as a collective project to be promoted by literature:

> I advise you to make a foray into your living past, which constantly transforms itself, and which you should, in full conscience, correct, amplify, purge, and structure anew until it becomes your own true creation. I call this past apocryphal to distinguish it from the other kind, the irreparable past that is the one investigated by history… (Machado, *Obra* 2018)

A critical reader may object that Machado is too remote in time and space to gain importance for the poetics of a Portuguese writer in 1966 and 1975. Such a reader may further argue that the Latin American novel or the concepts of post-history and postmodernism are more relevant lessons for a writing that revivifies the past as a space of deliberate anachronism.[7] This opinion was voiced by the general drift of reviews concerning *Baltasar and Blimunda* and *The Year of the Death of Ricardo Reis*, especially abroad. The argument is convincing when one thinks of the literature industry as subject to fashions, which the well-informed Saramago could not have ignored. But we must also admit that obedience to fashions precisely contradicts a philosophy based on the Machadian concept of the past as "blended with the present and always affected by the future" (Machado, *Obra* 2018). I would argue that Saramago, aware of literary fashions, wanted to revitalize Antonio Machado as a poet and as a philosopher in a manner different than, yet quite complementary to, his revitalization of Fernando Pessoa via the hypothetical survival of the heteronym Ricardo Reis, exposed to the Lisbon reality of 1936.

In both cases, the making of history as a collective project depends on an individual change of mind, prefigured by Antonio Machado and an undead, more subversive Fernando Pessoa. There is no doubt that the Machadian philosophy is regarded from a Marxist angle, extensively quoted in *Manual of Painting and Calligraphy* (156-57). Immediately after drawing the aforementioned analogy between Goya and the painter H, the narrator asks himself about his possible part in the making of history: "if I were to have some role to play tomorrow, what events of today would be waiting for me?," passing this question on to both Goya and Marx (186). The idea of a coming history awaiting humankind in its process of political emancipation, or, in Marxist terms, of the revolutionary struggle, implies a notion of human history as a paradoxical, predetermined possibility of overcoming capitalism: like a religion of salvation, but without any God from above.[8] Thus, Saramago fuses Machado's notion with the historical materialism that employs theology in a sort of *materialist Messianism.*[9] Within this construct, the Portuguese writer also comes to reinterpret the native tradition of Sebastianism, especially in *Levantado do Chão* (Grossegesse "Messianismo"), approximating a Marxist version of post-history.[10] The difference is that in Saramago individual conscience—although transgressing the framework of bourgeois formation—still maintains an important role: "when I say that there is no Socialism in the Socialists, I am turning everything inside out, because I believe that Socialism is a state of mind" (Saramago, in Baptista-Bastos 45).

Obviously, critics could not ignore Saramago's firm Communist convictions, which never were concealed by the author. But his opinion of Antonio Machado, whom he considered "perhaps the greatest poet of this century"—instead of Pessoa, as the Portuguese public may have expected—was understandably ignored. This declaration, given in an interview (Saramago, Interview 26), has neither provoked protest among patriotic intellectuals (even though it was made at the high point of the "Pessoa-fever" in the mid- to late eighties), nor has it motivated critics to look for reasons in *The Stone Raft*, published at the time of the interview. The similarities with the previous *The Year of the Death of Ricardo Reis* have not yet been noticed—perhaps due to the apparently categorical difference between a novel of historical revision and an uchronic fiction.[11] To me, it seems quite obvious that both novels are based particularly on Saramago's concept of human history, developed from *Os poemas possíveis* to *Manual of Painting and Calligraphy.*

Naturally, Saramago's poetics have a more complex basis than Antonio Machado, as we have already seen. But it is significant that the saying

"Demos tiempo al tiempo" appears throughout all of his novels. Although the average reader will not perceive this as an unmarked instance of intertextuality, considering it as a rather straightforward commonplace, I am convinced of the textual memory active in the author's mind. There, the Machadian "proverbio" remains as an important reference next to the sentences of Benedetto Croce and Ortega y Gasset, which Saramago quotes over and over in essays and interviews: "all history is contemporary history" and "I am myself and my circumstance" [yo soy yo y mi circunstancia].[12]

The latter statement derives originally from Ortega's "History as a System" (1935), where the Spanish philosopher defines life as making (*faciendum*) and self-project. Saramago, who often speaks about the"human project" (Baptista-Bastos 41), certainly noticed that this definition fits in well with the ideas about the revitalization of the past that Antonio Machado significantly dedicated to Ortega y Gasset. Another Spanish writer and philosopher illustrates the central problem of the lack of synchronization between the events that become history and the slowness of human consciousness: Miguel de Unamuno appears in *Manual of Painting and Calligraphy* and *The Year of the Death of Ricardo Reis* in quite a similar way.

In the first novel, Unamuno makes an appearance after another Spanish painter who knew how to combine art with a call to political consciousness and solidarity: Picasso, with his famous picture about the air raid on Guernica in 1936. Like the case of Goya and the popular uprising in Madrid of 1808,[13] the narrator points out the possible memory and even the possible prefiguration of this example across time and space, as it arrives in the mind of H under the difficult conditions of the Portuguese Estado Novo. Inspired by the Renaissance art of Vitale di Bologna, he begins to paint a new Saint Anthony without a halo or a book, thinking at the same time about the horse of Saint George. He imagines himself able to duplicate life thanks to a time in slow motion, or even to make time turn backwards, not in order to repeat everything but to make choices and sometimes to halt, as if following literally the advice of the Machadian "proverbio" to fill time. At the same time, H is searching in his "apocryphal past" for the birth of his political consciousness:

> To take St George's horse as painted by Vitale da Bologna and lead it away, heading for Lisbon or coming from Bologna, through Spain and France, through France and Spain, to Paris, to the Latin Quarter, to the rue des Grands-Augustins, and to say to Picasso: "I say, old man, here's your model." At that time in Lisbon,

> a child who knew nothing about Guernica and very little about Spain except for the Battle of Aljubarrota, was clutching some soggy leaflets in his hands, and unwittingly distributing the political manifesto of the Portuguese Popular Front… (128)

This unconscious collaboration of the innocent boy with Portuguese groups in favor of the Spanish Republic, followed by the traumatic experience of a severe police interrogation, could have provoked—through the feeling of injustice and curiosity—the "birth" of the self, according to Marguerite Yourcenar (*Manual* 85).

At this point, the example of Miguel de Unamuno appears, related to the theme of deficient synchrony. It is only many years later that H gets to know what the political situation of Spain under General Franco was like, and what exactly happened during the celebration of the *Día de Hispanidad* in 1936 at the University of Salamanca. It is only in the last years of his life that the ancient rector Unamuno, formerly a supporter of the Franco party, became aware of his error. On that 12th of October 1936, he delivered a brilliant speech to express in public his repudiation of the barbarous new regime, in answer to the war-crippled General Millán Astray whose ceremonial address had culminated in the abominable shout "¡Viva la muerte!" [Long live death!], to be repeated over and over in Franco's times. Remembering Unamuno's late but brave act, the painter H is aware of his own belated awakening to political consciousness, ashamed of his (too) long passive tolerance for a dictatorship engaged in colonial warfare:

> Me, Portuguese, painter, alive in the year 1973, in this Summer which is almost at an end, in this encroaching Autumn. Me, alive, and dying in Africa, where there are Portuguese men whom I sent to their deaths or consented should die, men so much younger than me, so much simpler, and with so much more to offer than me, a mere painter. (128)[14]

In the second novel, the heteronym Ricardo Reis, who miraculously survives his creator Pessoa for the period of nine months, regrets that he must finally die without hearing the brave speech the ancient Unamuno made a few months before his death. He only knows the earlier Unamuno, who hailed the Franco regime as the salvation of Western Christianity. But the already dead Pessoa yields to the insistence of Reis and reveals to him the still unmade statement of rebellion (330-31). Unamuno's late change of mind mirrors the dilemma of Ricardo Reis, who represents in Pessoa's universe the most detached among the three main heteronyms, the one who views the "spectacle of the world" from a superior position of indifferent calmness. In Saramago's fiction, however, Ricardo Reis is a man going through a midlife crisis who alienates himself more and more from his perfect poetry and passivity, and who experiences instead a sexual plenitude and a desire to participate in the making of another course of history, represented by the historical revolt of Portuguese sailors against Salazar's dictatorship. Nevertheless, Reis remains on the threshold: he only observes the uprising with tears of sympathy but without making any attempt to actively intervene, as he stands at the Alto de Santa Catarina, high above the Tagus river where the sailors have failed to join their two warships to the forces of the Spanish Republic. With the hypothetical scream of the Adamastor statue at Alto de Santa Catarina, *The Year of the Death of Ricardo Reis* ends in a way similar to most of Saramago's novels, in the sense of presenting an apocryphal past through a prism of historical materialism: the paradoxical, predetermined and open ending announces a possible "rebirth" of the individual man or humanity and invites the reader to participate actively in the making of history.

The comparative view of the Peninsula, present in *Manual of Painting and Calligraphy* and *The Year of the Death of Ricardo Reis* through imagined journeys of pictures, voices and personalities in space and time, becomes the main narrative plot of an Iberian voyage in *The Stone Raft.* In conformity with the cultural identities of Spain and Portugal, it is at the same time an ocean voyage and an overland journey, with intertextual references to the emblematic fictions of both countries, *Os Lusíadas* by Camões and *La vida de Don Quijote y Sancho Panza* by Cervantes.

Antonio Machado also applied his theory of an "apocryphal past" to the destiny of Spain. In the poetry of *Campos de Castilla* (1907-17), there appears "a utopian meaning that the apocryphal acquires, as an attempt at inverting or critically reconstructing history" (Abellán 103). The central idea that the past is as unwritten as the future can be found in the final part of the poem "El Dios ibero" (CI; English translation by Trueblood):

> ¡Qué importa un día! Está el ayer alerto
> al mañana, mañana al infinito,

hombres de España, ni el pasado ha muerto,
ni está el mañana—ni el ayer—escrito.
¿Quién há visto la faz al Dios hispano?
Mi corazón aguarda
al hombre ibero de la recia mano,
que tallará en el roble castellano
el Dios adusto de la tierra parda.

[What does one day matter! Yesterday stands poised
to face tomorrow, tomorrow faces the infinite:
men of Spain, the past has never died
nor is tomorrow—nor yesterday—yet written.
Who has looked on the face of the Spanish God?
My heart awaits
The men of Iberia with the mighty hand
who shall carve from Castilian oak
the stern God of the drab-brown land.]

These verses, which certainly impressed Saramago, may guide our way from *The Year of the Death of Ricardo Reis* to *The Stone Raft*, where the future sense of history is immediately related to the actual possibilities of the Iberian Peninsula in 1986. The latter novel could be read as a complementary, revivifying "year of the death of Antonio Machado." Contrary to Lisbon's past in 1936, *The Stone Raft* is about a hypothetical near future, which nevertheless has anachronic elements. Already the motto "Every future is fabulous" (Alejo Carpentier) indicates that this narrative is looking for the utopian possibilities of the "other side of history." The "synchronicity of intentional coincidences" and the "meaningful and concentric overlapping and interpenetration of lives and events at all levels" (Daniel 540) could be seen as those features of *The Stone Raft* that reflect the transfer of the Machadian plea to fill time onto the plot by synchronizing events and consciousness.

The death of Antonio Machado is mentioned already in the second chapter, at the moment when the miraculous gap between the Peninsula and the European continent has grown to an irreversible extent, causing the depopulation of the French border region and leaving only the dead behind. At the same time, the narrative discourse, while commenting on its own revivifying capacities, establishes a significant link with Saramago's fiction of Pessoa:

> The dead souls, having died, stayed behind, with that persistent indifference that distinguishes them from the rest of humanity, if anyone ever said otherwise, or suggested, for example, that Fernando Pessoa visited Ricardo Reis, the one being dead and the other alive, it was his foolish imagination and nothing else. But one of these dead men, in Collioure, stirred ever so slightly, as if hesitating, shall I go or not, but never into France, he alone knew where, and perhaps one day we shall know too. (22)

It is remarkable that the reflection on the indifference of the dead as opposed to the activity of the living causes a digression that pertinently questions the initial opposition: the dead begin to speak and to move. While the names Fernando Pessoa and Ricardo Reis indicate clearly the characteristic Mennipean dialogue situated on the threshold between life and death of *The Year of the Death of Ricardo Reis*, Machado remains unnamed here. He is only recognized by the reader who knows that Collioure is the border village where Machado died, on 22 February 1939, after an exhausting journey across the Pyrenees while fleeing from the troops of the Franco regime. The role of intertextuality is vital for the comprehension of the meaning and of the implied author's intentions, not only in the case of *The Year of the Death of Ricardo Reis* but also in that of *The Stone Raft*, which, at the first glance, seems much less complex. It is the latter, however, that requires a Portuguese reader interested in Spanish literature and culture.

In the fifth chapter of *The Stone Raft*, the reference to Machado continues within the narrative of the Peninsula afloat in the ocean and the collective tour of five people who have come together from Portugal, Andaluzia and Galicia. The reference appears when the two Portuguese, José Anaiço and Joaquim Sassa, are on their way to visit the Andalusian place called Venta Micena near Orce where the bones of the oldest European, nicknamed "the Orce Man," were found. They want to meet Pedro Orce, an old pharmacist, who feels the earth shake beneath his feet. Immediately before this encounter, the Portuguese travelers read the news that the bones of Antonio Machado have been stolen and brought back to Spain, and reflect on it: what would happen to the bones? José Anaiço has the following opinion:

> If, despite the ups and downs of life and the reversals of fortune, everything has its place and every place claims what belongs to it, what remains of Antonio Machado today must be buried somewhere in the fields of Soria, beneath a holm oak, the Castilian word is *encina*, without any cross or tombstone, nothing but a tiny mound of earth.... (61)

The mention of the fields of Soria and the Spanish word "encina" lead back to the poetry of *Campos de Castilla*: the praise of the oak in "Las encinas" (CIII) that brings together the soil of all Spanish regions ("El campo mismo se hizo árbol en tí, parda encina [The field itself became tree in you, drab-brown oak]") reinforces the telluric divinization in the poem "El Dios ibero," which refers to the Iberian oak in the verses that precede the abovementioned final part: "No dio la encina ibera / para el fuego de Dios la buena rama, que fue en la santa hoguera / de amor una con Dios en pura llama? [Did not the Iberian oak / furnish sound branches for the blaze of God, / limbs that were one with God in purest flame / on the sacred bonfire of love?]." José Anaiço's idea of Machado's re-burial under an oak tree somewhere in the "fields of Soria," also recalls Machado's poem in memory of Francisco Giner de los Ríos (CXXXIX), written in 1915, only three days after the death of this charismatic "master" of the Generación del 98. It ends with the following verses (English translation by Trueblood):

> Su corazón repose
> bajo una encina casta,
> en tierra de tomillos, donde juegan
> mariposas doradas...
> Allí el maestro un día
> soñaba un nuevo florecer de España.
>
> [Let his heart be at rest there
> in an oak's pure shade,
> where the wild thyme draws
> the flitting yellow butterflies ...
> Up there the master dreamed one day
> that Spain would flower again.]

Machado's similar, hypothetical re-burial in *The Stone Raft* reclaims the spiritual heritage of the Generación del 98 for the "new blossoming" of the whole Iberia.[15] The description of the grave without any cross or stone is important, because it prefigures the identical funeral of Pedro Orce at the end of the novel. Instead of a cross, Joana Carda plants her elm branch over the skull of the defunct Pedro, who is buried precisely in the place from which the bones of the Orce man once were excavated (229). Replacing the cross, Joana's stick, which at the beginning may have miraculously caused the breaking away of the Peninsula when she casually used it to scratch a line in the dirt, does not restrict itself to symbolizing the suffering of humanity:

> The sacrificial cross, the tree of life, the Biblical tree of Jesse, a symbol of fertility and renewal, it is also a stick that draws a line in the sand, the pointed stylus that invents the letter and registers the word. (Rebelo 348)

Both at the level of the narrated journey and at that of the poetic discourse, Pedro Orce has a "fertile death" that revivifies Antonio Machado as an *author* of an Iberian religion of salvation lacking a God from above. His concept of Christian Communism (Abellán 89) certainly had some influence on Saramago. In the course of the journey, Pedro Orce represents among the members of the touring group "el hombre ibero," the son of the Iberian God, of the "stern God of the drab-brown land" who comes out of the Iberian soil. It is Pedro, accompanied only by the guide dog Constante (the name refers back to the dog in *Levantado do Chão*), who has the night vision of being a "Messiah of Iberia." He imagines himself able to move a petrified boat (which really exists upon the rocky Galician coast) and with this boat the whole Peninsula: "he absurdly began to imagine that this petrified ship was indeed sailing and towing the peninsula..." (168).[16]

Such an interpretation is even more convincing when we think about the later novel *The Gospel According to Jesus Christ* (1991), which elaborates an alternative, "apocryphal" biography of Jesus already sketched out in *Manual of Painting and Calligraphy*. It is a Jesus who becomes aware (albeit too late) of being manipulated by God his Father, "solemnly enthroned in the heavens" (*Manual* 82), and who struggles in vain to prevent the subsequent centuries of Christian theocracy full of martyrdom and bloodshed from happening (122). But there persists the "other side of the history" of Jesus as the son of a God who comes from within the earth as a reincarnation or return of the oldest man, Adam. His skull beneath the Cross indicates, according to the Adam legend, the fertile death of Jesus as well.[17] Saramago's interpretation in the tradition of Orphic theology, already insinuated by the detailed description of Albrecht Dürer's *Groe Passion* in the first chapter of *The Gospel According to Jesus Christ*, blends perfectly with Marxist doctrine in a way that recalls Ernst Bloch's *Prinzip Hoffnung* and *Atheismus im Christentum*—probably familiar to the Communist atheist writer (Grossegesse "Evengelho"). The peculiar nature of Pedro Orce indicates, from this point of view, a kind of Iberian Jesus who denies his heavenly Father, but follows the Iberian God of the soil.

In order to justify this interpretation, we return to chapter six of *The Stone Raft*. It begins with a description of Venta Micena as a place, arid like the desert, where the devil had his first dwelling and might have led Jesus into temptation. At the same time, the infernal nature of this Andalusian region is linked to the memory of Federico García Lorca[18] as a martyr of the Spanish soil that also had drunk plenty of Moorish and Christian blood. But now this soil remains still unprepared for the revitalization of the past—"why speak of those who died so many years ago, if it is the land that is dead, buried within itself" (66)—prefiguring the (Messianic) expectation of a "new Iberian history" at the end of the novel through the symbol of the elm branch: "The elm branch is green. Perhaps it will flower again next year" (292).

The two Portuguese travelers meet Pedro Orce in a way that recalls Jesus gathering his apostles when sitting together under an olive tree.[19] They decide to go by car to the Andalusian coast, a trip described as the possible beginning of a larger expedition to another world, in order to verify with their own eyes that the Peninsula is drifting away from the Rock of Gibraltar: "Let's go and see the rock as it passes" (70).[20] But first Pedro Orce shows the arid soil of Venta Micena to José Anaiço and Joaquim Sassa, a place that they have already visited. There, as we may now say, the skull of the Iberian Adam was found, and there—what a remarkable coincidence—Pedro Orce was born and will be buried, thus insinuating the concept of a fertile death linked to the destiny of the Peninsula. Venta Micena, near Orce, is a kind of Iberian Golgota or Calvary, which literally means (place of) the skull, mirrored subsequently by the complementary place of Villalar, significantly located "not far from Toro, Tordesilhas, and Simancas, all of them touching closely on Portuguese history in terms of a battle, a treaty, archives" (275-76). But

Villalar means nothing to the Portuguese members of the group. It is precisely Pedro Orce who explains the battle of Villalar: in 1521, the Spanish communities revolted in vain against the Emperor Carlos V, a foreign sovereign who also was supported by the Portuguese D.Manuel. The explanation triggers reflections by the group about alternative history, imagining the loser as the winner and extending this idea to the Portuguese defeat *par excellence*, Alcácer-Kebir. The battle of Villalar seems to prefigure the basic idea of *The Stone Raft*: a desired revolt of the people against a Peninsula ruled by foreign economic powers with the consent of the Portuguese and Spanish governments. Saramago's fiction of the stone raft refuses the actual situation, reinventing Villalar as Golgota or Calvary of the Iberian man: the dog Constante, Orce's inseparable companion, dreams that he is excavating the bones. Two days later, boys playing around in the fields find a heap of skulls (246).

The composition of analogies and intertextual links within *The Stone Raft* and within Saramago's work and poetics prove the apocryphal vision of the Peninsula to be a vision of the other side of history still awaiting its future fulfilment. Pedro's burial with the elm branch over his skull denies the Crucifixion by using the opposing concept of the Great Adam, the Makantropos who is born from the earth and returns to it, thus renovating himself. Saramago emphasizes the female component, imagining a collective pregnancy of all the women of Portugal and Spain, perhaps fertilized by the "great stone falling southward," the Peninsula transformed into an island (283). The ancient Pedro Orce, gifted with an unexpected sexual capacity, presumably makes Joana Carda and Maria Guavaira pregnant, thus confirming his privileged Adamic role. The promise that the elm branch over Pedro's skull will blossom next year signifies a final call to the reader to assume his or her role as an Iberian man or woman, on a Journey to the Iberian God.

This allegorical fiction can not be imagined without the revisitation of Antonio Machado and the resurrection of his poetry and philosophy within the narrative plot of an apocryphal "trans-ibericidade" (Saramago "O [meu] iberismo"). Arriving at this provisional conclusion of our short journey through Saramago's fiction and poetics, let us return to the *Poemas possíveis* of 1966, where the final verses of the poem "Criação" already suggest the future message of his novels: "To make of the Earth a God who might deserve us, / And to present the Universe with the God it awaits."

Notes

[*] This article stems directly from a lecture on Saramago's relationship with Spanish culture delivered at the University of Gießen (Germany) in 1999 at the invitation of Ruth Tobias and Prof. Wilfried Floeck. I wish to express my gratitude, and also thank my colleague Joanne Paisana for the critical reading of the English text.

[1] In the collection of interviews conducted by the Spanish journalist Juan Arias, Saramago admits, however: "in a way it is possible to say that I inhabit an idea of Portugal that no longer coincides with the Portugal of today" (Arias 56).

[2] See Garcia, "Recelo en Portugal," for a summary of the discussion of the "protagonismo español en el Nobel de Saramago" in the Portuguese press.

[3] The reader may wonder about the Portuguese reception of Goytisolo's novel. Indeed, it is curious to observe that the Portuguese translation (published in 1972 by Dom Quixote) was based on the 1971 French edition by Gallimard, to the point of including J. M. Castellet's extensive foreword directed to the French reader.

[4] In the late 1970s, Saramago translated (from the French edition) the well-known *Historia de España* by Fernando Díaz-Plaja (*História da Espanha*, Lisboa: Círculo de Leitores, 1979).

[5] The presence of the Inquisition is illustrated in the text by a long quote from the decree by King Fernando VII reintroducing the institution (261-62). Saramago's treatment of the Inquisition as a common fault of Portugal and Spain recalls Antero de Quental's analysis in "Causes of the Decadence of the Peninsular Peoples in the Last Three Centuries" (1871), where the author already pointed out the danger that the two will become "two shadows, two ghost nations, amidst the countries that surround us!" (85).

[6] Saramago's later essay "Os três nascimentos" (1991) gives an important self-interpretation. See also Grossegesse, "O grito de São Bartolomeu."

[7] For a detailed discussion of this question see Grossegesse, *Saramago lesen* 34-37 and 79-91.

[8] In Baptista-Bastos's interview with Saramago we find a critical reflection on this subject: "The past tells me that all human projects, hopes or utopias, must not be approached (and I think I am already cured of this) in the spirit of optimistic finalism, which deep down does not differ much from religions of salvation" (Baptista-Bastos 41-42).

[9] We can only speculate as to whether Saramago read Walter Benjamin before 1977 or much later. In *Blindness*, the presence of Benjamin's "Angel of History," his famous interpretation of Paul Klee's *Angelus Novus*, seems quite obvious (see Lima, "A cegueira").

[10] In Marxism, utopian possibilities exist which belong to "the other side of history" (Steiner 413-24).

[11] As defined by Ansgar Nünning (273-74), discussing Wesseling (100-05). Nünning has a more critical attitude toward the precipitous labeling of novels as postmodern.

[12] See, for instance, Saramago "História e ficção" 20, and Saramago in Serra and Planells 6.

[13] Both Goya and Picasso reappear in Saramago's later comparative reflections on the political responsibility of the writer ([No title] 172).

[14] [Editor's note] Giovanni Pontiero's translation of this passage has been slightly modified for the sake of accuracy.

[15] See, for instance, the plural Iberian vision of Miguel de Unamuno (García Morejón; Marcos de Dios).

[16] Thus continuing the central metaphor of Saramago's poetics, the moving statue or the moving stone, within the general project to dissolve petrifications (Grossegesse, *Saramago lesen* 17-29; Grossegesse, "O grito de São Bartolomeu"). On the boat of San Andrés de Texido, see Frier, "José Saramago's Stone Boat."

[17] For a detailed reading see also the mythical interpretation of the hero in *The Gospel According to Jesus Christ* by Vera Bastazin (56-60).

[18] Evoked by quoting Rafael Alberti's famous "Balada del que nunca fue a Granada," dedicated to the memory of Lorca, which ends with the final call: "Venid por montañas, por mares y campos. Entraré en Granada" (*Baladas y Canciones del Paraná*).

[19] David Frier suggests here "the implicit equation of the Peninsula with an alternative Christ" ("Ascent and Consent" 135).

[20] Saramago makes here an ironic analogy to the historic maritime expeditions to conquer the new world: "from these same southern parts men set out to discover the New World, rugged and fierce, sweating like pigs in their armor, steel helmets on their heads, they advanced sword in hand to fight the naked Indians, clad only in feathers and war paint, an idyllic image" (70).

Works Cited

Abellán, José Luis. *El filósofo "Antonio Machado."* Valencia: Pre-Textos, 1995.

Arias, Juan. *José Saramago: El amor possible.* Barcelona: Planeta, 1998.

Baptista-Bastos. *José Saramago. Aproximação a um retrato.* Lisboa: Dom Quixote, 1996. [Contains an extensive interview with Saramago.]

Bastazin, Vera. "A construção do herói mítico em *Evangelho segundo Jesus Cristo.*" *José Saramago. Uma homenagem.* Org. Beatriz Berrini. São Paulo: EDUC, 1999. 25-61.

Daniel, Mary L. "Symbolism and Synchronicity: José Saramago's *Jangada de Pedra.*" *Hispania* 74 (1991): 536-541.

Frier, David. "Ascent and Consent: Hierarchy and Popular Emancipation in the Novels of José Saramago." *Bulletin of Hispanic Studies* LXXI (1994): 125-138.

———. "José Saramago's Stone Boat: Celtic Analogues and Popular Mythology." *Raízes, Rotas, Reflexões.* Conference of the Association of Hispanists of Great Britain and Ireland. Braga, 1998.

García, Javier. "Recelo en Portugal por el protagonismo español en el Nobel de Saramago." *El País* [Madrid] 14 Oct. 1998.

García Morejón, Julio. *Unamuno y Portugal.* Madrid: Gredos, 1971.

Grossegesse, Orlando. "O Evangelho segundo Jesus Cristo." *Portugiesische Romane der Gegenwart: Neue Interpretationen.* Ed. Rainer Hess. Frankfurt/M: TFM/Domus Editoria Europaea, 1993. 123-139.

———. "O grito de São Bartolomeu ou Ensaio sobre o auto-nascimento em Saramago." *Agália* 60 (2000): 407-417.

———. "Messianismo telúrico em *Levantado do Chão* de José Saramago." *"Sentido que a vida faz."—Estudos para Óscar Lopes.* Eds. A. M. Brito and I. Pires de Lima et al. Porto: Campo das Letras, 1997. 207-215.

———. "Die Rückforderung von Al-Usbuna." *Tranvía* 33 (1994): 7-9.

———. *Saramago lesen. Werk, Leben, Bibliographie.* Berlin: edition tranvía, 1999.

Lima, Isabel Pires de. "A cegueira do 'Anjo da História.'" *Actas do Colóquio Internacional José Saramago.* [Amherst, Univ. of Massachusetts.] Lisboa: Caminho, forthcoming.

Machado, Antonio. *Campos de Castilla.* Ed. Manuel Alvar. Madrid: Espasa Calpe, 1975.

———. *Obras Completas.* Eds. Oreste Macrí and Gaetano Chiappini. Vol. II. Madrid: Espasa-Calpe, 1988.

———. *Selected Poems*. Trans. Alan S. Trueblood. Cambridge, MA: Harvard UP, 1982.

Marcos de Dios, Ángel. *Escritos de Unamuno sobre Portugal.* Paris: Fundação Calouste Gulbenkian, 1985.

Molina, César Antonio. *Sobre el iberismo y otros escritos de literatura portuguesa.* Madrid: Akal, 1990.

Nünning, Ansgar. *Von historischer Fiktion zu historiographischer Metafiktion.* Vol. 1. Trier: WVT Wissenschaftlicher Verlag, 1995.

Quental, Antero de. "Causes of the Decadence of the Peninsular Peoples in the Last Three Centuries." 1871. *The Feeling of Immortality.* Trans Richard Zenith. Dublin: mermaid turbulence, 1998. 77-117.

Rebelo, Luís de Sousa. "*A Jangada de Pedra* ou os possíveis da História." *A Jangada de Pedra.* By José Saramago. Lisboa: Caminho, 1986. 331-349.

Saramago, José. "Descobrir o outro descobrir-se a si mesmo." *espacio / espaço escrito.* 9/10 (1993): 83-92.

———. "Europa sim, Europa não." *Jornal de Letras* IX.340 (10 Jan. 1989): 32.

———. "História e ficção." *Jornal de Letras* X.400 (6 Mar. 1990): 17-20.

———. Interview with Inês Pedrosa. "A Península ibérica nunca esteve ligada à Europa." *Jornal de Letras* VI.227 (10 Nov. 1986): 24-25.

———. *A Jangada de Pedra.* Lisboa: Caminho, 1986.

———. *Manual of Painting and Calligraphy.* Trans. Giovanni Pontiero. Manchester: Carcanet, 1993.

———. "O (meu) iberismo." *Jornal de Letras* VIII.330 (31 Oct. 1988): 32.

———. *The Stone Raft.* Trans. Giovanni Pontiero. New York: Harcourt Brace, 1995.

———. "Os três nascimentos." *Jornal de Letras* XI.453 (12 Mar. 1991): 43.

———. *The Year of the Death of Ricardo Reis.* San Diego: Harcourt Brace Jovanovich, 1991.

———. [No title]. *Urogallo* 82 (1993): 172-175.

Serra, Elias, and José Planells. "José Saramago: Un Pesimista positivo." *Boca Bilingüe* 8 (1993): 5-15.

Steiner, George. "Literature and Post-History." *Language and Silence.* London: Faber & Faber, 1965. 413-424.

Wesseling, Elisabeth. *Writing History as a Prophet. Postmodernist Innovations of the Historical Novel.* Amsterdam: John Benjamins, 1991.

'Once but no longer the prow of Europe': National Identity and Portuguese Destiny in José Saramago's *The Stone Raft*

Mark J. L. Sabine

It seems paradoxical when a self-professed Marxist produces novels evincing deep scepticism about the viability of the "scientific" Marxist project of materialist historical analysis.[1] José Saramago and his fiction have presented such a paradox since *Baltasar and Blimunda* (*Memorial do Convento*, 1982), a paradox seemingly most acute in *The Stone Raft* (*A Jangada de Pedra*, 1986). Saramago's earlier novels merely questioned the accessibility of objective truth about the past. Yet the tale of an Iberian Peninsula sailing away from Europe not only denies the reader any explanation of the bizarre occurrences that it relates, but also seems to refute the possibility even of establishing a reliable approximation of the truth about the past. Moreover, the book's publication in the year of the Portuguese and Spanish states' commitment to membership of the EEC led many critics to interpret the forces that propel the fictional Iberia away from Europe as promoting not socialist internationalism but a form of separatist Iberian nationalism. Such an interpretation, however, fails to take account of two aspects of the text: first, its championing of the praxis of socialist revolution, and second, the full range of its postmodernist questioning of the nature of knowledge and historiography. While doubt is cast on the foundations of Marxist revolutionary theory, there are also clear indications at the novel's end that abandoning Europe is not in itself a solution to Spain's and Portugal's problems. This study reads *The Stone Raft* as a text that, while conducting a postmodernist critique of the historiographical premises of Marxist revolutionary theory, simultaneously attempts to redirect the aims and values of Portuguese society away from the construction of a single European free trade zone and towards the construction of an egalitarian socialist society.

The Stone Raft is set in an immediate future bearing a close but hazy resemblance to the mid-1980s. In this imaginary temporal location, a deep crack opens up along the Pyrenees, and the Iberian Peninsula wrenches itself away from Europe and sails due west across the Atlantic, like a great stone ship or raft. After near-collision with the Azores, the Peninsula changes direction several times, following by turns a rectilinear, then a rotary trajectory before coming to an inconclusive halt between Africa and Latin America, roughly the heart of the post-colonial Hispanophone and Lusophone world. This inexplicable occurrence appears to coincide with five individuals' involvement in bizarre supernatural events. In Portugal, Joana Carda scratches an unerasable line in the earth with a stick of elm wood. José Anaiço is followed everywhere by a benign, yet otherwise Hitchcockian flock of starlings. Joaquim Sassa throws a huge rock into the sea, where it bounces over the waves until it disappears from sight. Over the border in Galicia, Maria Guavaira unravels an infinite length of blue yarn from an old sock, whilst elderly Andalusian Pedro Orce becomes a human seismometer, able to feel the earth trembling under his feet. Suspecting that their actions may have precipitated the geological aberration that has thrown their communities into turmoil, the five meet up and travel the floating landmass, seeking explanations to events in the seemingly exceptional objects and animals they encounter: the elm wand, the blue yarn, the starlings and a fearsome looking yet benign dog that leads them on a circular voyage around the Peninsula.

When the stone raft stops moving and the novel ends, the eldest of the five is dead, and the other four, now two couples and expecting parents, are left debating their futures. Their uncertainty about exactly how to continue their lives and love affairs is aggravated by the failure of their mission of discovery. Throughout the novel, a heterodiegetic narrative voice exposes the characters' conclusions about the determination of history as either implausible or unprovable, but also signals itself as the voice of an outsider who is by their own confession not only far from impartial but also wholly unreliable. This narrative voice gives conflicting evidence, points to lack of proof, or, when agreeing with the characters' suppositions, reveals its assessment of observed phenomena to be highly subjective by recounting events with absurd rhetorical overkill: hyperbole, pathetic fallacy, and speculation about the symbolic nature of an object or event. By highlighting the protagonists' ignorance of their exact circumstances and playing on the reader's desire to extrapolate clues to the Stone Raft's destiny from among the array of ambiguous symbolic referents, Saramago's text points to the abuse of rhetoric in humankind's attempts to interpret the unknowable, or at least indemonstrable truth about the past.

The belief that the full truth about the past is objectively irrecoverable suggests *The Stone Raft*'s authorial ideology to be closer to postmodernism than to Marxism. Through emphasis on the inevitable shortcomings of his/her account, the narrator demonstrates by example the inadequacy of even the purportedly most scientific accounts of history. It notes both the impossibility of collating all existing "evidence," or traces of the past—"the evidence relating to the period, the various documents, newspapers, films, video recordings, chronicles, private diaries, parchments, especially the palimpsests" (25)—and the impossibility of recovering data never committed to the record, as when it claims not to have been given all of the details of the story (203).[2] The narrative voice points to the selection of data for inclusion that anyone compiling an account of the past is obliged to make; the vast bulk of data that must be rejected by foreshortening an analysis of the geological makeup of the peninsula "because of the narrator's lack of knowledge and time" (23). By constantly interrupting itself with comments that satirise, contradict or retract data it has just asserted as, if not true, then at least worthy of the reader's attention, it indicates that the traces of the past frequently contradict one another, forcing the historian to judge which traces are more reliable and which tell more about the past. Inevitably, certain traces must be chosen over others, and some people's experience of the past must be privileged whilst that of others is ignored, as is demonstrated when the narrative voice vainly attempts to include the inhabitants of the peninsula that have been excluded from the story (91). As Keith Jenkins points out in *Re-thinking History* (1991), the traces of the past, whether written or archaeological, do not actually tell us anything; rather, they are the silent pieces of data that the historian manipulates in order to tell his/her own version of events (22 and 38). The subjectivity of the historian is inevitably brought to bear as traces are analysed, processed and codified to re-create the past. The historical account reflects the assumptions and opinions of the present day, and frequently the assumptions and opinions only of a socially privileged minority.

Postmodernist historiography questions the possibility of a single, unbiased account of the past and points out that accounts that are partial in both senses of the word are presented to us as concise and objective. As Linda Hutcheon argues in *A Poetics of Postmodernism*, postmodernist narrative fiction has made a significant contribution to this critique of the assumptions of conventional historians and histories (105-12). Hutcheon uses the term "historiographical metafiction" for fictions that revisit the past to make satirical critiques of how the processing and codifying of images permits the construction of accounts of history in accordance with the dominant or "official" ideology of the present (5-6). Hutcheon's label fits perfectly for Saramago's two previous novels: *Baltasar and Blimunda* and *The Year of the Death of Ricardo Reis* (*O Ano da Morte de Ricardo Reis*, 1984). Both texts revisit key episodes of Portugal's past, drawing on data that official histories have ignored or suppressed—e.g., the experience of the peasantry and the proletariat—to create an alternative account that, while admitting its own ideological bias, asserts itself as no less valid than existing, equally ideologically motivated accounts. *The Stone Raft*, meanwhile, scrutinises the construction of the dominant conceptions of the present—1980s Portugal—and its ideological motivation: the project of EEC membership to which Saramago has repeatedly voiced his opposition. Helena Kaufman and José Ornelas, in their 1997 study of contemporary Portuguese fiction, observe how the official discourse of mid-1980s Portugal

> was already preparing the road for a union with the EEC countries, processing and codifying images which would rationalize its objectives. Even the future of Portugal was called into question; without the union there would be no future. Thus, an impression was created that the raison d'être of Portugal, the identity of its people, depended entirely on the formalization of the union. (162)

Primarily, *The Stone Raft* seeks to dismantle ideologies of EEC integration and to create a discursive space for a consideration of alternatives to EEC membership (Kaufman and Ornelas 162). The postulation of the Iberian Peninsula's inexplicable abandonment of Europe for an uncertain ultramarine destiny forms the premise for a chain of counterfactual events, which in turn facilitate the creation of a "counterdiscourse" of Portuguese identity and destiny. Interpolating the discourses of mass media, party politics and canonical literature, Saramago explores the construction and reinvention of national identity through the privileging, suppression and manipulation of both historical data and myth. The novel rearranges the building blocks of Portuguese identity formation—e.g., the nation's relationship to the oceans, the age of the Discoveries and of imperialist expansion eulogised by Portugal's national bard, Camões, and the literature of the purportedly unique

Portuguese emotion of *saudade*—in order to suggest alternative inscriptions of a national ethos.

Although the novel does not assert a monolithic ideological program, it offers these alternative inscriptions as an argument for the viability of a political future for Portugal alternative to that of EEC membership: essentially, future action to eliminate social ills such as poverty, homelessness and sexual discrimination. It may seem hypocritical to denounce one political lobby's textual remaking of past and present as biased and deceptive whilst offering equally contrived, textual evidence to support an alternative agenda. Yet arguably any postmodern text must enter into this contradiction if it seeks to make an active intervention aimed at displacing the dominant ideology. I will argue that *The Stone Raft* effects just such an intervention through the self-consciously contradictory strategy of using counterfactual events to support a political message. It repeatedly advertises its inscription of Portuguese identity and destiny as just as much a rhetorical construction as the one it displaces, but in many instances the fiction that serves to provide justification of that inscription is based on an interpretation of genuine historical data: thinly disguised accounts of the authentic convulsion of Portugal's 1974 revolution. Saramago identifies a different national spirit at work in the social transformations of that period: an aborted project, the completion of which Saramago argues should be the national community's political priority.

The second half of this study explores how the novel treats the manifest practical problems in returning to such a project. As well as looking at what I consider to be the novel's contradictory approach to questions of nationality and identity, I aim to dispute readings by Mary L. Daniel, Piero Ceccucci and others who see *The Stone Raft*'s ending as the realisation of Utopia in an Iberia that has slipped the leash of capitalist Europe. Even in this counterfactual future, displacement to the mid-Atlantic can guarantee nothing more than a chance to rethink political options in relation to arguments inevitably based either on immaterial rhetorical devices or on subjective and selective accounts of history.

The novel charts how such subjective and selective histories fuel a debate as to whether or not Spain and Portugal *are* European. As the Pyrenean rift widens, "some member states came close to displaying a certain detachment, there is no more precise adjective, even going so far as to suggest that if the Iberian Peninsula wished to go away then let it go, the mistake was to have allowed it to come in" (31). Spain and Portugal's longstanding cultural engagement with neighbouring communities to the north and east is conveniently disregarded in order to privilege the idea of the two countries' status as newcomers, based on their only very recent entry into western Europe's dominant political and commercial forum. But opinion is sharply polarized: when the Peninsula does go its own way, a self-styled movement of solidarity picks up across the continent, provoking reaction in the assertion of an ideal European quintessence against which Spain and Portugal can be measured and found wanting:

> Although it may not be very polite to say so, for certain Europeans, to see themselves rid of baffling Western nations, now sailing adrift on the ocean, from whence they should never have come, was in itself an improvement, the promise of happier times ahead, like with like, we have finally started to know what Europe is, unless there still remain some spurious fragments which will also break away sooner or later. Let us wager that ultimately we shall be reduced to a single nation, the quintessence of the European spirit, simple and perfect sublimation, Europe, that's to say, Switzerland. (125)

The irony is that the "nation" feted as "quintessential" is the one that has most consistently declined to form alliances or join a European union.[3] The so-called "Iberianist" lobby asserts the freedom of communities to control their destiny free from outside influence when it declaims a slogan echoing J.F. Kennedy's infamous "Ich bin ein Berliner": "We are Iberians too."[4] The dream of a homogenous Europe modeled on a society inaccurately touted as a fusion of the politically and economically dominant nations of the EEC is countered by an ideology of decentralisation and cultural diversity. This ideology finds its fullest expression when the slogan is scrawled on walls across Europe in seventeen languages, listed in full in the text (126). This diversity, however, is served little better by the comfortingly simplistic conception of a patchwork quilt of sovereign nation-states than by a movement towards centralisation and homogenisation. The nation-states that the political establishment eulogises as the "intrinsic foundations" of Europe's identity are not organic entities but precarious constructs, "so laboriously created throughout hundreds of years" (124). The Iberianists' slogan and their protests convulse the continent precisely because they question the integrity not only of the patchwork quilt but also that of the component patches. The narrative voice's observation that the first appearance of the graffito slogan—the French "Nous aussi sommes ibériques"—could have been proclaimed first in Belgium or Luxembourg (126) exposes what Benedict Anderson identifies as the fabrication of national consciousness through the arbitrary imposition of "print languages": standardised versions of vernacular dialects imposed as languages-of-state (67-80). As the protest gathers momentum, the phrase appears "in every conceivable language, even in regional dialects, in various forms of slang" (127) including, no doubt, the minority languages—Breton, Flemish, Alsatian, Occitan, Catalan, Basque—and dialects that French governments sought during so many years to eradicate yet which as spoken languages still extend across political borders, often merging indivisibly into one another.[5] Thus, the ethnic and cultural homogeneity of the nation-state is exposed as a mythical concept.

When European governments respond to the movement of "solidarity" with the Iberian peninsula by staging carefully rigged televised debates (127), the fragile artifice of *identidade europeia* is presented to the reader as a construction (or rather, a panicky reconstruction) in progress. Official media dictate the parameters of debates and impose a definition of opponents of European integration as "those restless spirits who unwisely ... put Europe's identity at risk" (164). Whilst in reality granting a platform only to those who will denounce the insubordination of a wayward, backward European periphery, these "debates" pay lip service to the tradition of free expression and democracy so frequently cited as a hallmark of that (western) European culture now imperilled by separatist fanatics.

This whitewash parallels that identified by Kaufman and Ornelas in the Portuguese media (162), which warned that opposition to EEC membership put the nation's future at risk. The novel also parodies media and government discourses in Spain and Portugal. In both countries an official interpretation of events on the shifting Portuguese coast is imposed through exploitation of two well-known yet conflicting inscriptions of Portuguese character: the Camonian image of heroic maritime pioneers and missionaries, and the image of a contemplative, fatalistic race abstracted in its collective sense of *saudade*, presented by the Spaniard Miguel de Unamuno in his *Por tierras de Portugal y de España* (*Through Portugal and Spain*) of 1910.[6] An embattled Portuguese prime minister apes Camões by assuring the people that the Peninsula's navigation—emphatically not a simple drift—makes Portugal the envy of Europeans who "see in this historic adventure into which we find ourselves launched the promise of a happier future, or to put it in a nutshell, the hope of regenerating humanity" (169). Meanwhile in Spain, television newscasters report Portuguese reactions to the peninsula's movement with a paraphrase of Unamuno's anthropomorphic portrait of Portugal as

> a beautiful, gentle country girl sitting with her back to Europe at the brink of the ocean ... resting her elbows on her knees and her head between her hands, as she contemplates the sun's descent into the infinite waters. (Unamuno 10)

The Spanish TV news is restricted to a single image of the coast,

> with the waves beating on the rocks ... and lots of people watching the horizon, with the tragic expression of someone who has been prepared for centuries for the unknown.... There they are now, just as Unamuno described, your dark face cupped between both hands, eyes fixed on where the sun sleeps alone in the infinite ocean. (*Jangada* 93; translation mine)

Further derision follows in the reference to the Iberian national governments rejecting European protests "with manly pride on the part of the Spanish and feminine haughtiness on the part of the Portuguese" (129). This burlesque of Unamuno's sexist designation of Spain and Portugal as respectively male and female dismisses the implication that Portugal should behave like a good, subservient lady and agree to love and to cherish, to honour and obey (Unamuno 10).[7] Appearances and commonplaces regarding national character can, as Unamuno failed to realise, be misleading: in Saramago's novel, ironically, it is the Spaniard Pedro Orce who recognises in "the apparent melancholy of the city [of Lisbon] the faithful image of his own intimate sadness" (83).

The reality—or at least that part of it experienced by the novel's protagonists—does not match with these inscriptions. The lesson to be learned is that it is easy to boast of unique specificities of national character, but quite another thing to find proof for them: a nation's "nature of conscience," if it exists at all, is plural, more amorphous and less distinctive than many commentators would like to believe.

In addition to these parodies, the novel makes its own appropriations. The echoes of the voyages of Discovery in the Peninsula's journey are exploited in order to combat both European disdain for Portugal and native nationalism. Portugal's primary role in the exporting of European languages, religion and ideas, the importing of material riches of other continents and related projects—from which stem many of the characteristics used to define modern Europe—provides a substantial argument for the Portuguese people's right to be considered European. At the same time, jingoistic notions of Portugal's uniquely exalted status as instigator of ultramarine exploration and conquest is debunked by revision of the bombastic Camonian epithet for Portugal: the prow or head of Europe. After the stone vessel turns 270 degrees on its axis, it sails south with Cap Creus in Catalunya, and not Cabo da Rocha in Portugal, as its prow (257). Elsewhere, however, the same epithet is called up to challenge Unamuno's view of the Portuguese. Portugal has ceased to be the prow of Europe not because its people are, as Unamuno asserted, exhausted and suicidal but because the country has sailed away from the European quay, as a ship of its own:

> Look at the Portuguese, all along their golden beaches, once but no longer the prow of Europe, for we have withdrawn from the European quayside to sail once more the Atlantic waves. (71)[8]

Saramago replaces these two chauvinistic inscriptions of national character with values of fraternity and pragmatism. However, he asserts these values as authentically Portuguese not by producing spurious, fictional examples, but by interpolating into the counterfactual sequence an event that parallels documented events of the revolutionary period. Just as in 1974-76 empty housing units in Portuguese cities were occupied by collectives of shantytown dwellers, so in *The Stone Raft* impoverished Algarve residents battle with police to take over abandoned hotel complexes and establish soviet-style communities.[9] The narrator sardonically recalls the Unamunian and Camonian models of Portuguese character:

> Seriously ... there are two different types of Portuguese, those who take themselves off to the beaches and sand dunes to contemplate the horizon despondently, and others who advance intrepidly on those hotels-cum-fortresses defended by the police. (75)

The old imperialist heroism gives way to a no more altruistic, but more egalitarian struggle to provide all of humanity with the basic necessities of life. This pragmatic egalitarianism informs the Portuguese people's spontaneous (if admittedly chaotic) evacuation of the coastal regions when it appears that the Peninsula is about to collide with the Azores. Saving their own skins whilst the Government of National Salvation dithers, the Portuguese confound Unamuno's expectations that they will wallow in the salt waters of their lachrymose "resigned desperation, or ... despairing resignation" (*Jangada* 17; translation mine) until the night of oblivion closes upon them.

However, in order to present this return to the values of 1974 the novel must contradict its own critique of the artificial boundaries drawn through communities by the state frontiers and print languages that, as Benedict Anderson asserts, serve as facilitators and guarantors of capitalist markets regulated by individual sovereign states (67-80). Saramago's splitting of the Pyrenees, creating an absolute division by deep blue water in place of the topographical semi-division of mountains, effectively legitimises the drawing of the boundary between citizens of two states whose only official print languages, until comparatively recently, were French and Castilian respectively. At the same time, it bisects the catchment areas of two dialect clusters that are today strongly affirmed as print languages by local populations: *Catalá* and *Euskera.* Indeed, students of separatist political movements within the Spanish state might argue that the most implausible thing about *The Stone Raft* is not that the Peninsula sails away, but that Catalonia and the Basque country do not split off and sail back to Europe. Analysis of *The Stone Raft*'s treatment of Basque and Catalan nationalisms exposes narrative "silences" and "gaps" of the type that Marxist theorist Pierre Macherey famously identifies as pointing to the flaws and blind spots of a work's authorial ideology (85). Although *The Stone Raft* signals its consideration for the cultural concerns of Basque nationalism by, for example, calling Basque cities by their *Euskera* names—"Donostia," not "San Sebastián" (232) and "Gasteiz," not "Victoria" (224)—questions of Basque identity are effaced from the novel's first fifty pages, where the Pyrenean split is established. The split in the western Pyrenees appears in Orbaiceta, Navarra, and no Basque reactions are recorded. At the eastern, Catalan-speaking end of the range, cracks appear on both the French and the Spanish borders of Andorra before the tiny principality finally cleaves to the departing peninsula (23). No such apparent conflict of loyalties, however, is reported as the autonomous province of Catalunya breaks from Catalan-speaking

Rousillon in France, while the Balearic islands—Catalan-speaking and politically united with Catalonia since the thirteenth century—disappear from the text altogether once it is reported that "so far there is no evidence that the islands have moved, but who can tell what tomorrow may bring" (29).[10] Reference to departure from the "European quayside" (71) casts Iberia in the role of one of Álvaro de Campos's "nation-vessels" [navios-nações], but the Iberian peninsula of the 1980s was surely a ship whose crew would sooner mutiny than accept the label of a single nation.[11]

Tensions between Spain and Portugal and their former colonies are similarly silenced. As the peninsula halts roughly equidistant from Puerto Rico, Brazil and Guinea-Bissau, local reactions go unreported. The narrative seems coy about admitting that the Iberian nations, rather than physically assuming a position of privileged intermediacy between Europe and post-colonial southern America and Africa, need to initiate a mutually consensual, and thereby mutually beneficial, *rapprochement* with formerly colonised peoples as an alternative to accepting the weakening of ties dictated by EEC membership in the form of barriers on trade and immigration.[12] The reader of the novel should also note how the idea of an international movement in support of Iberia's separation from Europe can only be based on the dubious assumption of a pan-European stance of opposition to an expanded, integrated EEC. Many people who lived in, for example, Poland or Czechoslovakia during the 1980s would agree with Sławomir Mrożek and Milan Kundera that the real-life 1980s counterparts of the Polish *juventude* who write *My też jesteśmy iberyjczykami* on the walls of Warsaw had a very different relationship to the idea of European identity from that either of Saramago's Portuguese or of their real-life counterparts. Mrożek and Kundera have both examined how their compatriots considered themselves to be Westerners and Europeans oppressed and isolated from Europe by a national power, Russia, which they, unlike Saramago (*The Stone Raft*, 126), defined as non-European, or as belonging to a separate, Eastern Europe.[13]

While Saramago's Poles seem to express only the aspirations of the Portuguese, in the novel there is one voice outside Iberia that is allotted the opportunity to speak on behalf of its own interests: that of the US president. Though the narrative hints that the roving Peninsula may have surprises in store for the directors of the capitalist world order (255-58), that world order is still in control at the novel's end. Contrary to what is suggested by Daniel's and Ceccucci's emphasis on portents of positive social change in *The Stone*

Raft, at the novel's end the transformation of Portuguese society remains unguaranteed.[14] Since the occupation of the Algarve hotels, there has been no clear evidence of social change. Just as the ideals of 25 de Abril had become increasingly confounded or compromised in the Portugal of the 1980s—the occupations of empty housing blocks, for example, being ruled unlawful and evictions being forced following legislation passed in April 1975—so in *The Stone Raft* processes that intimate social change are derailed or discredited.[15] The "Iberianist" solidarity movement collapses into violence and chaos, an echo of the lack of organization and pragmatism that arguably characterized many popular movements of the late 1960s and early 1970s. Meanwhile, Portugal's incoming Government of National Salvation is exposed as simply a cynical repackaging of the incumbent governmental team, whose fecklessness is revealed when catastrophic collision with the Azores threatens. Although the collision never occurs, the Portuguese government suffers the humiliation of being overruled by its US counterpart—the supreme power of international capitalism—when it attempts to monitor the situation on its own sovereign territory (189).[16]

Changes of greater profundity are initiated more adroitly by the novel's five protagonists, whose journey around the Peninsula creates new social conditions and conventions, in particular new freedoms for the two women to control their own destinies and to engage in acts of love without surrendering their liberty. Joana Carda tells her three male companions that she went to Lisbon in search of them "because I saw you as people detached from the apparent logic of the world, and that's precisely how I feel myself to be" (*Jangada* 147; translation mine). Just as the logic of natural physics is defied by the movement of the Peninsula, so the social logic of western civilisation is challenged, as conditions on the road and under canvas dictate a new and less sexist division of labor. When, for example, the five turn to peddling clothes in Spain for a living, each individual contributes according to his/her talents and training. The two women select stock, the accounting is handled by Joaquim Sassa, and the Spanish-speaking dispensing pharmacist Pedro Orce handles the sales patter whilst Portuguese-speaking José Anaiço stays back at the wagon preparing food (205-08).

Perhaps more significantly, when Maria Guavaira and Joana Carda freely admit to having had sex with Pedro Orce, it becomes clear that their new way of living means new practices of loving. Both women are determined to reject the notion that a lover is physically and spiritually the property of his/her partner, and assert that if their partners cannot understand their position, then the journey, the friendships and love affairs are all invalid and must end. When Joana Carda invokes the elm wand to support the assertion of her and Maria Guavaira's guiltlessness, she reminds her companions that for her the wand is still the totem of her freedom, the rod with which she marked her independence in the soil at Ereira and which "can still be used to draw another line here" in order to determine "who is to remain on this side and who on the other" (229): the demarcation of a new beginning and new social rules.[17] Joana Carda's relationship to the elm wand constitutes a great temptation to conjecture that the use of the elm tree as a symbol of dignity in Western Christian iconography could have relevance here, suggesting the dignity that for millennia has been denied to women while their bodies are controlled and traded by fathers and husbands.[18]

But while the two women are both "making exception the rule" in order to create more propitious rules (240), there is no reason to believe that these changes reflect transformations in society as a whole. Joaquim Sassa makes the comparison between the five friends' lifestyle and that of gypsies (202). Like gypsies, they inhabit the social and economic margins, and their lifestyle remains different whilst the rest of society recovers from the threat of collision with the Azores ("people are returning to their normal habits and pursuits, if that is the right word to describe their former habits and pursuits" [244]). On the day after meeting her new friends, Maria Guavaira rejects the privations of widowhood by substituting her old, colorful clothes for dark mourning dress. But although the flamboyant garments that she and Joana Carda hang out to air "billow and flutter like flags," and although "one feels like shouting Long live liberty" (155), there is no confirmation that shouting or flying flags will change anything. By the end of the novel, Joana Carda's cousin is presumably still "casada e mal-maridada"—married to a bad husband—in Ereira (*Jangada* 158), and, presumably, she is also pregnant.

The impregnation, shortly before the end of the novel, of the entire population of fertile women on the Peninsula throws a very big spanner into the engines of this tentative, unfinished movement towards female liberation. Critics such as Ceccucci have interpreted the mass pregnancy as a positive symbol, as the "total redemption through love" that predicates "the ascent of a new class of humanity; of a new epoch not merely hoped for and dreamed of, but also willed and constructed" (214). For two reasons, however, one must take issue with this optimism. First, unplanned pregnancy *en masse* would not universally be deemed a blessing in 1980s Portugal, given the country's long history of criminalisation of abortion and the Estado Novo's use of a cult of large families as a means to keep women in the home and out of public life.[19] Secondly, the occurrence leaves the novel and its protagonists literally in a state of expectation. The birth of Joana Carda's and Maria Guavaira's children will be the acid test of their relationships and the new rules of partnership, division of domestic labor and now paternity that they have negotiated. Furthermore, the enigma of the two foetuses' paternity, and the uncertainty as to where and by whom the children will be raised, make it impossible to guess what cultural and national or regional loyalties they will develop, or what influence they and their 12-15 million as yet unborn contemporaries will have on social organisation on the Iberian Peninsula of the future. The allegory of the peninsula's geopolitical realignment, and the new paradigms of national and gender identity, provide tentative suggestions for the future, but cannot guarantee Utopia any more than Iberia's "rebirth" can be proven by a poet comparing the rotating peninsula to a baby turning in the womb (252).

On the last page of the novel, Pedro Orce is laid to rest, the narrative voice is silenced, and fundamental and unanswered questions resonate in the air: "who knows what future awaits ... how much time, what destiny" (263). As a rainy day dawns, prospects are not much brighter for the four remaining protagonists than for the Iberianist opponents of US and EEC intervention. Neither of the two couples is completely reconciled following discussion of the paternity of the unborn children, and there is no certainty as to what they will do with their lives now that they have no dog to guide them. Will they perpetuate their journey and the new values of communality and sexual equality, or will they dissolve their ad-hoc marriages and resume their former existences? The only intimations of social change are the wholly ambivalent symbols of renewal: the unborn children, the fanciful image of the peninsula as an unborn baby, and the green but budless elm wand that Joana Carda plants on Pedro Orce's grave. The elm branch, previously possessing ambiguous resonances of a magic wand, a symbol of a wife's declaration of independence, a lucky charm, might sprout and grow to become a Tree of Life, symbol of hope and regeneration, or a broad and spreading elm, symbolic of a woman's realized independence and recognized dignity. Then again, it might not. The parallel drawn between Pedro Orce's burial and that deemed suitable for the exiled Spanish poet Antonio Machado (56 and 260) not only reopens discussion of the problematic relationship between territory and identity, but also warns against excessive optimism by highlighting the reference, on the novel's final page, to Machado's poem "A un olmo seco" ("To a dying elm-tree") in *Campos de Castilla* (Machado 799-800).[20] Machado's poem addresses a rotting, half-dead tree whose single green branch makes the poet long for "another miracle of the Spring."[21] By association with this the elm branch stuck in the barren desert of Venta Micena comes to represent not the certainty of a future Utopia but the precarious nature of human hopes and aspirations. It may develop into a "resuscitated tree," but only "if a piece of wood stuck in the ground is capable of working miracles" (263).[22] Unamuno implied that the Portuguese have been ill-served by their faith in miracles.[23] *The Stone Raft*'s inconclusive and unpromising ending argues that, even when the reassuring certainties of materialist analysis of history prove ill-founded, life, and the struggle to make life better and fairer, must go on. The only certainty, in Portugal, Spain or elsewhere, is that the actions of the common people must be added to the rhetoric of politicians and novelists, if a better society is to be built out of a humanity fragmented by economic, ethnic and generic divisions.

Notes

[1] Interviewed, in 1986, by Clara Ferreira Alves, Francisco Bélard and Augusto M. Seabra for the *Expresso* magazine supplement in "A facilidade de ser ibérico" ("The Simplicity of Being Iberian"), Saramago reaffirmed his commitment to Marxism and to "a materialist view of the world" (Saramago 1986).

[2] All quotations from *The Stone Raft*, except where otherwise indicated, are from Giovanni Pontiero's translation. All other translations of quoted material are my own.

[3] Switzerland has been neutral since 1815. In a referendum in 1993, following the creation of a European Economic Area that the Swiss government was compelled to join, the Swiss electorate rejected ratification of an agreement to enter the European Community (*New Encyclopaedia Britannica*, XXVIII.355).

[4] Kennedy's actual words were: "All free men, wherever they may live, are citizens of Berlin, and therefore, as a free man, I take pride in the words 'Ich bin ein Berliner'" (qtd. in Schlesinger Jr. 808-09).

[5] Adrian Battye and Marie-Anne Hintze identify the Revolution of 1789 as the catalyst for "the crystallisation of a feeling that the dialects and the minority languages spoken on the French national territory constituted some kind of external threat" (41). Abbé Grégoire's *Rapport sur la nécessité d'anéantir les patois et d'universaliser l'usage de la langue française* (*Treatise on the Necessity of Annihilating Primitive Speech Forms and of Universalizing the Use of the French Language*) of 1794 formed the basis for a state primary education policy with the principal objective of imposing what, 127 years later, the *Bulletin officiel de l'instruction publique* (*Official Bulletin on Public Education*) of 1921 termed "the language of Racine or Voltaire" in place of

"the urban slang ... the village patter ... the regional dialect" (Battye and Hintze 42 and 48). The teaching of such "dialects" as Basque, Catalan, Breton and Occitan in French state schools was outlawed until 1951, that of Corsican until 1974 and that of Flemish until 1976. By the mid-1970s, Basque, Breton and Corsican separatist political parties were still outlawed in France and many of their leaders still imprisoned (Gordon 100-02).

[6] Unamuno talks of two facets of the Portuguese *ethos* as represented in Guerra Junqueiro's poems *Os Simples* (*The Unaffected*) and *Pátria* (*Fatherland*): "the bucolic Portugal, impassive and unaffected ... and ... the heroic, noble Portugal" (19). In the same book, his observations on contemporary Portugal indicate that for him the latter facet is an attitude restricted to, or lost in, the Portuguese past: Unamuno compares the Portuguese to Ulysses who "returned to domesticity and ... ensconced by the hearth, contemplating the rise and fall of the flames, which call to mind the crests and troughs of the ocean waves, would recount to his children and grandchildren tales from the thick of battle and from his far-flung expeditions"(21). It should be noted that *The Stone Raft*'s Camonian references have no truck with the connection made by the organs of the Estado Novo—in works such as José Leitão de Barros's epic film *Camões* (Lisboa Filme, 1946)—between Camões, the calumniated hero who dies awaiting the return of days of Imperial glory, and the fatalistic cult of *Sebastianismo*.

[7] In one passage Unamuno compares Portugal to the hapless Inês de Castro (91).

[8] See Unamuno on Portuguese fatalism (38-39) and suicidal tendencies: "Portugal is a nation of suicides, perhaps, indeed, a suicidal nation" (80). He also quotes Camões (*Os Lusíadas* X.145) in talking of "the sea, which was once Portugal's glory, the sea, which has granted her immortality in the history of humankind, the sea has delivered her 'into the clutches of lusting greed and into the brutishness of a harsh, gloomy and detestable sadness' ['no gosto da cobiça e na rudeza / d'huma austera apagada e vil tristeza']" (Unamuno 48-49).

[9] Two detailed contemporary accounts of the post-revolutionary housing struggles are Downs and Ponte. *The Stone Raft* also recalls the collapse of the Portuguese tourist industry that accompanied the period of unrest in 1974-75 (Maxwell 141), and the subsequent use of empty Algarve hotels to accommodate not the local homeless, but some of the 500,000 *retornados* from the former "overseas provinces" in Africa. This initiative must have provoked resentment among the indigenous population, and almost bankrupted the post-revolutionary Portuguese state. Concern for the welfare of the *retornados* did not, however, extend to allowing them to stay on in the hotels once tourists could be coaxed back (Morrison 51-52).

[10] The Balearic islands were conquered by Jaume I of Aragón by 1235. Together with Catalonia they were ruled directly by the Aragonese monarchs, apart from a period of autonomous monarchic rule on the islands from 1298-1349 ("Balearic Islands," in *New Encyclopaedia Britannica*, 15th ed. [1995], 830).

[11] Campos (Fernando Pessoa), "Ode Marítima," stanza 9, line 1: "Ah, the Great Quay from which we embark in Vessel-Nations! [Ah o Grande Cais donde partimos em Navios-Nações!]" (Pessoa 136).

[12] Saramago advances the following argument regarding Portuguese and Spanish relations with former colonial communities:

> I admit that, for the right or wrong reasons, those whom we once set out to find may want to forget who we are but, if I might be permitted the indulgence of prophecy, I foresee that we will end up finding our own cultural vitality diminished if we persist in seeking or accepting solutions and goals which, through our own erroneous conception of them as exclusive of other solutions and goals, might lead us to ourselves forget who we are. ("A Península" 11)

[13] Mrożek, interviewed by Timothy Garton Ash, identifies a belief widespread amongst educated Poles that they, "unlike the Russians, indubitably belong" to Europe and to "the West"

(Mrożek 97). Kundera (in 1980) makes a distinction between two quite separate European civilizations:

> As a concept of cultural history, Eastern Europe is Russia, with its quite specific history anchored in the Byzantine world. Bohemia, Poland, Hungary, just like Austria, have never been part of Eastern Europe. From the very beginning they have taken part in the great adventure of Western civilisation... The post-war annexation of Central Europe ... by Russian civilisation caused Western culture to lose its vital centre of gravity ... and we cannot dismiss the possibility that the end of Central Europe marked the beginning of the end for Europe as a whole. (230)

[14] Daniel writes of the "promise for a brighter future of continued life on the new continent" in a novel that expresses an "optimistic and robust vein of confidence in the future" (541), while Ceccucci refers to "a new era hoped for and dreamed of, but also willed and established" (214).

[15] According to Charles Downs, the earliest enforcement of the 17 April 1975 Anti-Occupation Decree was in January 1976 (*Comissões de moradores* 20-23). Due to considerable popular opposition, it was not until 1978 that evictions took place on a large scale.

[16] This episode can be interpreted as another reference to events following 25 April 1974, specifically the intervention of the USA in Portuguese affairs, motivated by concern about the future of its air base at Lajes in the Azores. Only two months after the coup, President Richard Nixon met General Spínola for private talks about Lajes and Portugal's membership in NATO. The US Secretary of State, Henry Kissinger, apparently favoured subjecting Portugal to total isolation in order to suffocate any attempts at revolution (Morrison 26-28).

[17] Joana Carda's gesture recalls a passage in Saramago's *Levantado do Chão*. Here, a line scratched in the earth challenges abusive husband Domingos Mau-Tempo's claim to hold authority over his wife, Sara da Conceição, who has taken refuge along with her children in the home of her kinsman José Picanço:

> With his staff, Domingos Mau-Tempo scratches the earth in front of him, to all appearances it's a challenge, the signal for a brawl, and Picanço interprets it that way, and makes himself prepared, grasping hold of a stick.... Behind him, on the other side of the door, are three terrified children and a woman who would fight to the death to protect them if she could, but the two sides are badly-matched, and so Picanço takes a chance and etches his own scratch in the earth. (48-49)

Whereas Sara da Conceição, living in the Alentejo circa 1910, must rely on male relatives to protect her from her husband, Joana Carda determines not to be dependent on any man.

[18] The association of the elm tree with dignity is discussed by Roig (69).

[19] Following legislation in 1984, abortion is legal in Portugal only in certain extenuating circumstances. Prior to 1984, abortion was expressly banned in any circumstances. However, in the period immediately prior to 25 April 1974, an estimated 200,000 illegal, and often very unprofessional, abortions were carried out annually. These resulted each year in around 2,000 *recorded* fatalities (Salgado 8). In 1936, Salazar's Estado Novo established OMEN (Obra das Mães para a Educação Nacional), aiming to "bring up the 'new woman' from infancy to be a good Catholic and patriot, and in the future a 'prolific' mother and an obedient wife"(Rosas and Brito 609 and 675). These groups organized annual "Mothers' Weeks" from 1938 until the 1960s, and "attempted, by means of hand-outs of cribs, hope chests and prizes for 'prolific' mothers, to combat restrictions on the index of population growth and ... to promote the return of women to domesticity" (Rosas and Brito 676).

[20] Significantly, Pedro Orce drops dead outside the hermitage of Turruchel, just south of Bienservida, at the border between Castilla La Mancha and his native *autonomía* of Andalucía

(259). Pedro Orce's earlier declaration that "my [native] land is Andalusia," and that other parts of the Spanish state such as Galicia mean nothing to him because "it's possible for us not to know our own state, but we all know out own land" (*Jangada* 178; translation mine), can be interpreted as an attempt to distinguish between a chauvinistic, nationalist cult of *o país* ("the state") and a more benign sentimental attachment to *a terra* ("the land").

[21] The passage in *The Stone Raft* does not quote any poem from *Campos de Castilla*, but echoes the association Machado asserts between his soul and the landscape of Soria in, for example, "Campos de Soria" IX, lines 1-8:

> Yes! You travel with me, Sorian fields....
> You have found your way into my soul,
> or perhaps you were always rooted in its depths? (772)

and in "Caminos," lines 41-46:

> There, in the highlands—
> where the Duero traces
> its crossbow curve
> around Soria, amid lead-coloured hills
> and the smudges of ragged oak groves—
> my heart is wandering in dreams (804).

[22] The planting of the elm on Pedro Orce's grave also recalls the miracle of St. Zenobio, recounted in Eça de Queirós's *Dicionário de Milagres* (174). On its way to burial, the coffin of Bishop (later Saint) Zenobio of Florence accidentally struck a dead elm tree, which burst immediately into leaf. Pedro Orce, it would appear, is no St. Zenobio.

[23] "Deep down, we Spanish have less faith in miracles.... We do not believe in the return of a King Sebastian" (Unamuno 40).

Works Cited

Anderson, Benedict. *Imagined Communities: Reflections on the origin and spread of nationalism.* 2nd ed. Revised and extended. London: Verso, 1991.

Battye, Adrian, and Marie-Anne Hintze. *The French Language Today.* London: Routledge, 1992.

Camões. Dir. José Leitão de Barros. Lisboa Filme, 1946.

Ceccucci, Piero. "L'Utopia Saramaghiana come Progetto della Storia Umana." *Il Girador: Studi di Litterature iberiche e iberoamericane offerti a Guiseppe Bellini.* Ed. G. B. De Cesare and Silvana Serafin. Rome: Bulzoni, 1993. 209-15.

Daniel, Mary L. "Symbolism and Synchronicity in José Saramago's *A Jangada de Pedra.*" *Hispania* 74.3 (Sept. 1991): 536-41.

Downs, Charles. *Commissões de Moradores and Urban Struggles in Revolutionary Portugal.* Unpublished, c.1979. No. 220, 332.34 Dow. Arquivo do Centro de Documentação do 25 de Abril, Universidade de Coimbra.

Gordon, David C. *The French Language and National Identity, 1930-1975.* The Hague: Mouton, 1978.

Hutcheon, Linda. *A Poetics of Postmodernism.* London: Routledge, 1988.

Jenkins, Keith. *Re-thinking History.* London: Routledge, 1991.

Kaufman, Helena, and José Ornelas. "Challenging the Past/Theorizing History: Postrevolutionary Portuguese Fiction." *After the Revolution: Twenty Years of Portuguese Literature 1974-1994.* Ed. Helena Kaufman and Anna Klobucka. Lewisburg: Bucknell UP, 1997. 145-67.

Kundera, Milan. *The Book of Laughter and Forgetting.* Afterword by Kundera and Philip Roth. Trans. Henry Michael Heim. London: Penguin, 1980.

Machado, Manuel and Antonio. *Obras Completas.* Ed. Heliodoro Carpintero. Madrid: Plenitud, 1967.

Macherey, Pierre. *A Theory of Literary Production.* Trans. Geoffrey Wall. London: Routledge and Kegan Paul, 1978.

Maxwell, Kenneth. *The Making of Portuguese Democracy.* Cambridge: Cambridge UP, 1995.

Morrison, Rodney. *Portugal: Revolutionary Change in an Open Economy.* Boston: Auburn House, 1981.

Mrożek, Sławomir. Interview. "Under Eastern Eyes." *Granta* 20 (Winter 1986): 89-104.

New Encyclopedia Britannica. 15th ed. Chicago: Encyclopedia Britannica, 1995.

Pessoa, Fernando. *Poesias de Álvaro de Campos.* São Paulo: FTD, 1992.

Ponte, Bruno da. *Housing Struggles in Portugal.* Unpublished, c.1975-76. No. 167, 333.32 Pon. Arquivo do Centro de Documentação do 25 de Abril, Universidade de Coimbra.

Queirós, Eça de. *Dicionário de Milagres. Obras Completas.* Lisboa: Livros do Brasil, s.d.

Roig, J. Fernando. *Simbología Cristiana.* Barcelona: Juan Flors, 1958.

Rosas, Fernando, and J.M. Brandão de Brito, eds. *Dicionário de História do Estado Novo.* 2nd vol. Venda Nova: Bertrand, 1996.

Salgado, Abílio José. *A Situação da Mulher na Sociedade Portuguesa Actual: Os preconceitos e a luta pela emancipação.* Lisboa: Iniciativas Editoriais, 1978.

Saramago, José. Entrevista. "A facilidade de ser ibérico." *Revista Expresso* 8 Nov. 1986: 36-39.

———. *Levantado do Chão.* Lisboa: Caminho, 1982.

———. "A Península Ibérica entre a Europa e a América Latina." *Vértice* 47 (Mar.-Abr. 1992): 5-11.

———. *The Stone Raft.* Trans. Giovanni Pontiero. London: Harvill, 1995. [Trans. of *A Jangada de Pedra.* Lisboa: Caminho, 1986.]

Schlesinger Jr., Arthur Meier. *A Thousand Days: John Fitzgerald Kennedy in the White House.* London: Mayflower, 1967.

Unamuno, Miguel de. *Por tierras de Portugal y de España.* Madrid: Espasa-Calpe, 1941.

The Edge of Darkness, or, Why Saramago Has Never Written about the Colonial War in Africa

Maria Alzira Seixo

That notion of being captured by the incredible which is of the very essence of dreams...
Conrad, *Heart of Darkness*

One of Western culture's major literary works to be inspired by the colonial situation is undoubtedly Joseph Conrad's *Heart of Darkness* (1902). The symbolist procedures that make Conrad's narrative discourse often ambiguous decisively contribute to preserve the sense of mystery that is the central aim of the novel's fictional construction. This sense of mystery encompasses the presentation of characters, the description of territory, and the relations established between them. In this essay, I will try to show the way in which some aspects of two of Saramago's novels (*The Stone Raft* [1986] and *Blindness* [1995]) can best be understood in the light of the cultural legacy bequeathed by Conrad's novella and how they can be interpreted from a contemporary postcolonial perspective.

Given the diversity of textual procedures used by Conrad, it appears that the absence of precise references to the African territory (very probably the territory of Congo, as is now generally accepted by critics) cannot be the result of an unlikely narrative lapse. The strangeness of the details describing the environment where Marlow's voyage takes place may in fact connect the plot to any exotic country subject to colonial exploration, and the story acquires, by way of this careful erasure of most of the African specificities, an exemplary, even transcendental, dimension that is reinforced not only by its title and by the motifs of shadow and darkness constantly present in its semantic construct, but also, and very particularly, by the enigma that the core of the narrative intriguingly builds up, elevating the primarily biological notion of "heart" to an ineffable dimension of humanism. This enigma is simultaneously that of all narrative construction, the veil of obscurity surrounding the beginning of every story that can ever be told, and of this one in particular: as Marlow says, nostalgically contemplating the sunset over the Thames: "And this also ... has been one of the dark places of the earth" (6). An enigmatic aura dominates also the main character's sense of behavior; while many answers regarding Mr. Kurtz's identity and nature are progressively given to Marlow and to the reader, they only contribute to further envelop that character in an atmosphere of mystery: "a first-class agent," "a very remarkable person" (30), "a prodigy" (42). But that enigma consists mainly of the difficulty in understanding the nature of a man acting in a position of command over other men, that is, of exploitation, which in fact is Kurtz's role, who represents moreover the occupation of a land where he, a non-native, must be viewed as a declared and accepted master; in other words, an entirely strange entity made up of people's beliefs, the force of the earth, and the assumption of power by a singular, individual human being.

That combination, experienced as simultaneously positive and negative (both "a heart of a conquering darkness" and "the horror" [130]), is viewed in the text as both inevitable and unintelligible; moreover, its culmination in a process of human behavior that can not be considered accomplished by the satisfaction of greed and by the practice of power opens a clear path for postcolonial reasoning. In fact, *Heart of Darkness* remains throughout a narrative minutely engaged with the colonial project, specifically exploration and trade, dealing both with goods (ivory) and with human feelings (a taste for adventure). In this sense, it treats particular semantic concerns, such as knowledge and otherness, voyaging and the river, earth and the emergence of races, intention and contingency, the search and the enigma, and, finally—in the return to England and the *Nellie*, the cruising yawl where the story is told—the island and the unbounded vastness of the sea. But what seems particular and enticing in this narrative, and what was rendered emblematic during the widespread decolonization process of the twentieth century, is the fact that greatness is emphasized in projects, feelings and ways of acting that are turned into forms of tragic derision, into deception and the impossibility of understanding human relations and events. What is more, the spirit of adventure and the exercise of mastery seem to be reabsorbed by an ultimate reduction to limited proportions that maintains the impulse for quest but underlines its inevitable anxiety, as in the final lines of the novel: "The offing was barred by a black bank of clouds, and the tranquil waterway leading to the uttermost ends of the earth flowed somber under an overcast sky—seemed to lead into the heart of an immense darkness."

The heart, thus understood as the core of the whole mystery, which includes a strange land, different habits, unusual ways of living, incomprehensible human relations and, most of all, the ultimate level of approach to impossible knowledge (or, as the Symbolists used to express it, the quest for the Absolute), is in that way also a territory for writing and inquiry, a territory mapped for narrative and poetry. It may also be the symbol of an experience that normally has no concrete results in an objective sense, but which dwells on an artistic level as the expression of desire and intimate deep convictions.

Reading Conrad's *Heart of Darkness* is without a doubt illuminating for any attempt to better understand certain contemporary fictional constructions; in this sense, Francis Ford Coppola's adaptation in the film *Apocalypse Now* is persuasive enough. Even Coppola's version (explicitly transferred to another continent, to an unfinished and raging contemporary war, to an explicit conversion of the Absolute into a relative assumption of power) shows that Conrad's Darkness, understood as the mystery of Africa expressed by dark skins and forests of impenetrable vegetation, may be another kind of darkness, as the final sentence of Conrad's novel already emphatically suggests; nevertheless, the meaning of its "heart" persists, as both the center of life (biologically) and the irradiation of mystery (imaginatively). Yet what is crucial in the second half of the twentieth century is that the center begins to get lost, and new poetic and imaginative concepts begin to emerge in the development of cultural thought and reasoning. Here, however, we have to take into consideration the content of artistic texts along with their focalizations, both with regard to the production and the reception of literary utterances. It is not a matter of indifference whether one considers the author's origin, nationality, language, and class (as in Conrad's case), or whether one examines the sense of the most prevalent readings of his work and the historical dimension of the narrative data as well. In this respect, I find particularly interesting the case of two novels by José Saramago, *The Stone Raft* and *Blindness.* The first narrates the voyage of the Iberian Peninsula after it breaks away from the rest of the European continent by splitting at the Pyrenees, between France and Spain. The

Peninsula begins drifting across the Atlantic Ocean towards North America, but then changes direction and begins to move southward, finally stopping between South America and Africa—with a particular though not definite suggestion that it may position itself between the coasts of Brazil and Angola. Meanwhile, a small group of Iberians from both Spain and Portugal happen to meet by chance and decide to live together, traveling on board the voyaging Peninsula and investigating the reasons and solution for this unexpected situation. The other novel, *Blindness*, presents the case of an anonymous country (with all the characteristics of everyday life in contemporary Europe) where an epidemic of "white blindness" causes a rapidly growing number of people to lose their vision and forces them to face terrible difficulties in order to stay alive. Their fate is aggravated by the fact that the government quarantines them in an old hospital where groups of criminals begin to seize food and other essential goods by force—yet where one woman, the only person who has not gone blind (of which only a few of the others are aware), leads them in their quest for survival.

José Saramago is a writer of humble origins who is almost completely self-taught, and who has always remained close to the Portuguese Communist Party. Until the age of fifty-two he lived under Salazar's dictatorship and experienced the joy of seeing the regime toppled by the Portuguese democratic revolution on April 25, 1974; some six years later he also began to experience success with his novels. These novels deal mostly with periods of the Portuguese and Western historical and cultural past; but *The Stone Raft* and *Blindness*, as well as the latest works Saramago has published, take the shape of allegorical fictions, which mix elements of the fantastic either with a utopian vision of the future (especially in *The Stone Raft*) or with the dystopia of its completely abstract conception (as in *Blindness*). It is important to point out that political liberation also has brought freedom from censorship, and that Saramago and other writers in Portugal are now allowed to write in complete liberty. Since 1974, many Portuguese novelists have plunged into fictional matters dealing with the colonial war in Africa. This war, which had a devastating impact on the African countries it affected, also had a tragic effect on Portugal, ravaging the country politically, socially and culturally. It compelled young people to fight against the African colonies struggling for political autonomy (the now-independent Angola, Mozambique, Guinea-Bissau, São Tomé and Cape Verde) and in many cases against their own beliefs and wishes. In this context, an anticolonial stance began to gain ground very early on amongst Portuguese youth and intellectuals and was directed against the war itself in the form of desertion, evasion or self-imposed exile. At the same time, African writers were becoming successful in some milieux in Europe due to the positive reception that their forms of abrogation were given by leftist groups there. Some of the most important Portuguese contemporary literature published in the last three decades manifests such concerns and the effects they produced.

The fact that José Saramago has never written about the colonial war in Africa, despite having always been engaged in Portuguese politics and having taken an active part in them during most of his career (albeit without personal experience in the military, since he was not conscripted to fight against the African pro-independence movements), is, to say the least, curious. It makes us read his narratives more attentively. Keeping in mind the analysis of Conrad's *Heart of Darkness* outlined above and the contradictions this story carries with respect to late-colonial concerns, we may reread Saramago's novels with respect to the way in which power, the practice of oppression, and the emergence of autonomy are envisaged in them. As Leela Gandhi observes:

> Few critics would dispute the understanding that all literature is symptomatic of, and responsive to, historical conditions of repression and recuperation. While postcolonial literary theory invokes these cultural materialist assumptions in its account of textual production under colonial and postcolonial conditions, it goes a step further in its claim that textuality is endemic to the colonial encounter. Texts, more than any other social and political product, it is argued, are the most significant instigators and purveyors of colonial power and its double, postcolonial resistance. (141-42)

Further, after quoting Tiffin and Lawson ("Imperial relations may have been established initially by guns, guile and disease, but they were maintained in their interpellative phase largely by textuality" [Tiffin and Lawson 3]), she adds: "Conversely, it follows that the textual offensiveness of colonial authority was met and challenged, on its own terms, by a radical and dissenting anti-colonial counter-textuality" (142). The notions of offensiveness and dissent in the textuality of the contemporary novel are precisely what interests me in this reading, as well as the way in which we may question the relations of supremacy they establish.

The Stone Raft is the story of a disruption (though a disruption of unknown causes effected on the earth) that gives rise to a voyage in which some people arbitrarily participate, constructing for themselves a space of freedom, a mode of rebuilding the world, and a way of living in it. Writing on an abstract imaginative level and following both utopian and dystopian procedures, Saramago alludes to the recent inclusion of Portugal in the European Community when he makes clear his wish, or the need, for a separation of the Iberian Peninsula from that community and in turn asks for a closer relationship not only with Spain but also with Brazil and the Portuguese-speaking African countries. While not explicitly expressed in the story, this is the concrete meaning implied in the text through the composition of a very neat allegory:

> As things stand, people are no longer surprised. Several months have passed since the peninsula separated from Europe, we have traveled thousands of kilometers over this violent open sea, the leviathan just missed colliding with the terrified islands of the Azores, or perhaps, as later emerged, it was never meant to collide with them, but the men and women did not know that as they found themselves obliged to flee from one side to the other, these were only some of the many things that happened, such as waiting for the sun to rise on the left only to see it appear on the right, not to mention the moon, as if its inconstancy ever since its breaking away from the earth were not enough, and the winds that blow on all sides and the clouds that shift from all horizons and circle above our dazzled heads, yes, dazzled, for there is a living flame overhead, as if man need not, after all, emerge from the historic sloth of his animal state and might be placed once more, lucid and entire, in a newly formed world, pure and with its beauty intact. (282-83)

"There is a living flame overhead," the story continues, and nobody is trying to separate the peninsula from the continent, nobody is fighting against anything whatsoever—only some spirit of the future, some curious and inexplicable phenomenon occurring on earth and among animals that may help humankind in a transition toward a better life. In this voyage subjectively assumed by the Iberian Peninsula, there is a sure effect of reading that implies derision being heaped on the whole enterprise of the Great Discoveries, in the sense that History may assume in fantasy what it was supposed to achieve in reality. There is also a clear allusion to the peripheral expectations (from a political point of view) regarding Africa and South

America at the time, during the 1970s and 1980s, when Eurocentric perspectives replaced lost colonial insights with some minor and dubious reconfigurations of social and cultural concerns. In his important analysis of Verdi's *Aida,* Edward Said addresses a similar kind of ideological representation with the following remark: "One must remember, too, that when one belongs to the more powerful side in the imperial and colonial encounter, it is quite possible to overlook, forget, or ignore the unpleasant aspects of what went on 'out there'" (157).

The task is to determine which location Saramago assumes for his discourse, since he is no longer under the control of strict political censorship, and since allegory implies a distancing from the described (imagined) phenomena. In other words, the autonomy of life that the characters in *The Stone Raft* finally find and enjoy is not something they have had to conquer, but something that has been offered by randomness and poetic intent. Far from Africa (and closer to Brazil, which has been an independent country for almost two centuries), Saramago chooses not to write about this Africa of which he has no knowledge; rather, in a way, he writes "on the edge" of Africa, given that the peninsula finds itself in its final destiny in closer proximity to the "dark continent." Silently, and with some hope for a bright future (for the dry elm branch that precipitated the movement of the peninsula and the narrative impetus of *The Stone Raft* is now budding and will possibly soon flower, as the final words of the novel tell us), "the peninsula has stopped" (292) and the narrator, speaking apparently to (or in the name of) the female characters Joana Carda and Maria Guavaira, exclaims:

> Dear God, how all things in this world are linked together, and here we are thinking that we have the power to separate or join them at will, how sadly mistaken we are, having been proved wrong time and time again, a line traced on the ground, a flock of starlings, a stone thrown into the sea, a blue woolen sock, *but we are showing them to the blind,* preaching to the deaf with hearts of stone (290; my emphasis).

Ashcroft, Griffith and Tiffin remind us that "a distinctive use of allegory, irony, magic realism and discontinuous narratives are characteristic of postcolonial writing" (28), while Saramago's use of allegory and magic realism is currently being emphasized by critics as well. *The Stone Raft* is a marvelous example of allegorical writing, but it seems true enough that the space it offers for living (the marginal peninsula) is not the same as the space it creates for speaking: its narrative voice stems from the distance of allegory and from the very edge of the intended and approached margins, the other continents.

According to the above quotation from the novel, we may argue that people in it do not seem to be really free, or appear rather subject to superior organized forces. Randomness may be viewed as a kind of manifestation of the forces of heaven and earth, as "a line traced on the ground, a flock of starlings, a stone thrown into the sea, a blue woolen sock" are supposed to demonstrate when they set the narrative events in motion. Furthermore, the "living flame overhead" indeed does act, be it as God, government, social forces or randomness: it depends on one's cultural perception, albeit this time in a non-postcolonial mode, since Saramago makes no choice, due to the fact that the voyage does not come to an end, as opposed to the voyages of discovery that ended in triumphant arrivals or in tragic defeats. Instead, the peninsula stays away from the African and South American continents, truly on the edge. This absence of a positive, dynamic or definitive reaction may be a wise position, but there may also be claims against the "blindness" that blocks humankind from the understanding of nature, and even (or mostly) culture. Therefore, in order to avoid the obstacle of "the blind," let us imagine all humankind in blindness, and observe how thus they begin to see: "Perhaps only in a world of the blind will things be what they truly are" is one of the statements in the more recent *Blindness*.

I do not mean to claim that *The Stone Raft* was a source for the conception of *Blindness*; however, it is interesting to discuss the relation between the two allegories, that of the voyaging peninsula and that of the sudden and general blinding of a community. In both books, the allegory manifests the textual aims of a well-organized universe of fiction, where every element depends on a central, impossible idea (one that is at the same time bizarre and inconceivable, yet that deals with common details of everyday life, steering the fictional construction towards both the fantastic and the utopic). In both cases, an ironic message also can be detected: that of Portugal and Spain leaving the European Community in order to join the countries of the Third World, and that of an entire society possessing a level of cultural understanding that does not stretch to the real aims of life and its meaning. Of course, we should emphasize once again the fact that such simplistic ideas are not fostered by Saramago himself. In fact, none of these underlying central questions is even considered in the texts, either because the characters stand for common people (who usually do not seem to question events on a philosophical level, although there are in the novel many observations that reveal that they really do), or because literature today no longer conveys a sense of absolute meaning as it used to in Conrad's time. But there is a clear difference: Conrad develops his own acute experience of being in Africa (or of having been in touch with forms of otherness), which brings him closer to uncommon manifestations of different entities. This creates the need for knowing and understanding, a need that encompasses the notions of sin and culpability:

> The conquest of the earth, which mostly means the taking it away from those who have a different complexion or slightly flatter noses than ourselves, is not a pretty thing when you look into it too much. What redeems it is the idea only. An idea of the back of it; not a sentimental pretense but an idea; and an unselfish belief in the idea… (10)

This idea is undoubtedly also central in Saramago's novels, but as a kind of negative compensation for the lack of a similar experience, thus giving rise to the configuration of allegories—a common option in the fiction of the second half of the twentieth century, particularly in postcolonial narratives—as opposed to symbolist representations. Allegory implies a distance in conception and a retreat from explicit quests. In doing so, Saramago draws a parallel between the Third World and the European and Portuguese complex vis-à-vis the recently decolonized countries, but without manifesting it directly. The "heart" of the question is the object of an implication (duty or regret), not that of a statement; discovering a new way of life (as in *The Stone Raft*) is the issue for an aleatory quest, not for a precise project. Realizing the goals of living in the society and of maintaining solidarity in difference (*Blindness*) is also the issue for an aleatory event, not for a precise quest. The interest that Saramago has always shown in condemning political and social inequities reveals itself in his literary works as more and more remote from precise referential circumstances, even from concrete implications that his allegories might have in relation to contemporary situations. This is, after all, a literary attitude resulting from the sensibility of the Symbolist movement, which helps to make our approach in some way manageable. In her examination of eighteenth-century travel literature, Mary Louise Pratt finds a very close relation between Eros and abolition; in a different way, but with similar goals, we see in *The Stone Raft* the prominence of place and sexuality in erasing differences—mostly of nationality, age and strictly defined belonging. For the voyaging peninsula, Africa (but maybe also South America) is the truly unknown and forbidden (or denied) notion; the "heart of darkness" is slightly approached in *The Stone Raft*, but, one might say, only along its edge. Some further insights can be gathered, however, in the novel *Blindness*, which addresses the predicament described by Conrad ("We penetrated deeper and deeper into the heart of darkness" [60]) as a symbol of knowledge for crucial problems.

In *Blindness*, a group of blind people stays together and tries to preserve their health and dignity in the midst of an entire community that has also been struck by the mysterious epidemic. Abject attitudes and atrocities generate an atmosphere of oppression and death. The text gives us no clues as to what Saramago has in mind as the point of reference for this negative vision of life, except for the way in which Western civilization has developed and created its patterns of behavior. In the whole process there is of course room for all forms of assault and oppression, including those of the dictatorship that the Portuguese people had to endure and of the colonialism in Africa that went hand in hand with it. On the other hand, Saramago wrote his novel against the background of the definitely postcolonial attitudes of the Portuguese democratic governments, during which time the "colonial complex" was being replaced by a mix of favors, honors, offers and donations to the Portuguese-speaking African countries. Even today, such attitudes have given way to a very specific situation, in which abrogation is curiously adopted more often by the ex-colonizer than by the ex-colonized. There is no doubt that one cannot yet see the elements of this social and political situation clearly, and I am not suggesting that Saramago himself is feeling disturbed by this lack of vision—not to mention the fact that cultural analysis of these kinds of interrelations has not yet been performed for Portuguese literature and that Saramago does not seem in the least concerned with either postmodern or postcolonial labels, at least on a superficial level or in terms of meta-theoretical implications. What I am trying to show is that it is possible to read *Blindness* in a way that asks questions about the postcolonial views that are partially integrated in the conception of the novel—even with the contradictory directions and denials that after all characterize the contemporary age—if we consider that globalization has been redefining our entire political configuration as part of a postcolonial condition that reabsorbs all the social and cultural manifestations of the industrialized world. The fact that Saramago replaces the "figurative" allegory of the Iberian Peninsula with the "abstract" allegory of an entire community of blind people means perhaps that his negative conception of globalization has progressed from an initial focus on reduced nationalisms to an abandonment of that form of communitarian thinking.

Once again, experience is a kind of schizophrenic failure in Portuguese cultural life, where people fall into three categories in relation to Africa: those who went there to fight, those who did not, and those who try to establish relations between the first and the second (these are always acting dubiously, for they belong necessarily to one of the first two categories, and they sometimes forget to distinguish between the different ways in which others may have fought in Africa: idealistically, indifferently, greedily or dramatically). It is obvious that Saramago, belonging to the second category, and being a very intelligent novelist, does not forget the tragedy of the colonial war in Africa, yet cannot write directly about it. One might say, nevertheless, that Saramago has a special skill for describing environments that he has not witnessed personally: the Portuguese eighteenth century, in *Baltasar and Blimunda*; the first half of the twentieth century, in *The Year of the Death of Ricardo Reis*; or even the Middle Ages, in *The History of the Siege of Lisbon*. But then that concerns history and time, and here we are dealing with space and experience. With *The Stone Raft* and *Blindness*, allegory replaces experience, which brings us closer, once again, to the set of symbolist devices in Conrad's *Heart of Darkness*, and to the edge of the African question.

Let us push our hypothesis just a little further: in dealing with the basic contemporary problem created by the sequels of colonialism, namely, that of the unstable and conflicting dialogue between the center and the margins (which is, moreover, the major theme of *The History of the Siege of Lisbon*, expressed on the contemporary level by a love story between a well-educated woman and a second-class administrative employee, and on the medieval level by the righteous fight of the Arabs against the wrongful hegemony of the Christians), Saramago cannot *not* be in favor of the margins, for this is the politically correct contemporary position, and consistent with his personal political opinions too. Neither, however, can he erase the question of knowledge and the fact that it gives supremacy and power (Said 157), thus diverting the direction of meaning by means of an allegory, and even literally diverting the direction of the gaze by means of imagining blindness.

In fact, blindness in Saramago's novel has very little to do with not being able to see, except for pragmatic details that make the fictional construct picturesque and "realistic." Thus, for example, the central character—the doctor's wife—is the only one who never becomes blind, and for two good reasons: first, the narrator has to adopt some perspective in telling the story, and a narrative perspective is always, and also literally, a point of view; second, one cannot have an allegory if one cannot develop a reasoning, a moralistic attitude, a final judgment, and it is the doctor's wife, set apart from the entire community of the blind, who achieves the convergence of the different meanings of blindness in the text (and outside of it as well). Besides, as the only witness to what is happening, the doctor's wife says something very similar to Kurtz's final remarks in *Heart of Darkness*, and to Marlow's ongoing intertwining of memory and nostalgia: "You do not know, you cannot know, what it means to have eyes in a world in which everyone else is blind, I am not a queen, no, I am simply the one who was born to see this horror" (276).[1]

One of the most impressive episodes in *Blindness* is that of a visit to a church, where the doctor's wife notices in the paintings hanging on the walls that the images of saints have their eyes blindfolded. The allegory is here resumed as a *mise en abîme* of the plot's meaning, and the plot's frame may be seen as a possibility of other ways of framing the reference, which possibly might be lost in the vertigo of the multiple acts of framing, for the major glory of the literary artifact. Even simple sentences, similar to aphorisms, may be taken as part of the entire allegory, or as minor allegories inside the entire framework of the novel:

> Give us an example, said the doctor, Certainly, replied the old man with the black eyepatch, I went blind when I was looking at my blind eye, What do you mean, It's very simple, I felt as if the inside of the empty orbit were inflamed and I removed the patch to satisfy my curiosity and just at that moment I went blind, It sounds like an allegory, said an unknown voice, the eye that refuses to acknowledge its own absence. (127)

This last example shows that seeing or not seeing is not the major goal in the progression of the narrative, and, especially, that the central factor of meaning in the text (being blind) is not equivalent here, as commonly accepted, to being plunged in darkness. On the contrary, let us emphasize that blindness, in the circumstances created by Saramago's narrative, is a kind of luminous whiteness that borders, in a symbolic (and physical) way, on the whole set of components of reality (for instance, colors). It is insinuated that the fact of not seeing their everyday circumstances progressively allows people to become more sensitive to other objects and other realities, which are, of course, now filtered by the mind rather than by direct visual representation. The problem is that the fictional construction gives us the idea that only some groups (such as that which holds the point of view, since we follow the point of view of the doctor's wife) have access to this specific, somehow elitist, understanding. Moreover, what about the implication that only with someone such as the doctor's wife who has kept the ability to see of vision are we able to obtain such specific understanding? This "centric" perspective once more puts the narrative on the edge of the question, finding no way of relating the center and the margins, and obliterating their conflicting consistency.

Nor in Saramago's novel are we yet in the "heart of darkness." If being in the center implies the possibility of access to (and even exercise of) power, and peripheral instances are supposed to be exposed to its hegemonic irradiation, being on the edge may be considered as the privileged position for knowledge, both objective and impartial, uncontaminated by either centripetal or centrifugal concerns. Being on the edge is obviously the convenient place for a wise witness (like the Old Man of Restelo, in *The Lusiads*, inveighing against the earliest stages of Portuguese colonialism) who is not quite "marginal" and able to ponder the issue of observation and of its exercise as a decisive contribution to a better way of seeing. This, in the final analysis, is a position that emulates power and covets supremacy, and is very likely opposed to adventure and modernity. It is a particular way of deserving reverence, brought about by a more respectable, equidistant knowledge, or by seeing inside, as is the case, once again, with Saramago's blind:

> It made no difference to them whether it was day or night, the first light of dawn or the evening twilight, the silent hours of early morning or the bustling din of noon, these blind people were for ever surrounded by a resplendent whiteness, like the sun shining through mist. For the latter, blindness did not mean being plunged into banal darkness, but living inside a luminous halo. (89-90)

Thus, "banal darkness" (into which one might be plunged by common blindness or by other causes) is not a way of living but rather a way of being close to death. This is a symbol for Western culture, from the divine manifestations of Antiquity or the Middle Ages that are normally enveloped in light, to the marvelous and contested "enlightenment" of modernity. This leads us once more to problematize Conrad's heritage and the relation he establishes between darkness and the ivory trade: ivory opens up the possibility of a replacement of darkness with whiteness, which may well mean that it is in Kurtz that the darkness lies. It leads us also to consider that in the art of the novel there are two kinds of composition: one that organizes the invention of realizing circumstances (which takes as its point of departure a vague reference, with this reference being gradually surpassed in order to build another reality, an allegory, where reality seems more real); and another that assembles problems (where interrogations of the reference may dismantle reality in order to reconsider and remake, not only by symbol but also by open-endedness, the given reality). Here is the way the Russian and Marlow describe Kurtz:

> "He made me see things—things"… He had, as he informed me proudly, managed to nurse Kurtz through two illnesses (he alluded to it as you would to some risky feat), but as a rule Kurtz wandered alone, far in the depths of the forest… "What was he doing? Exploring or what?" I asked. "Oh, yes, of course"; he had discovered lots of villages, a lake, too—he did not know exactly in what direction; it was dangerous to inquire too much—but mostly his expeditions had been for ivory. "But he had no goods to trade with by that time." (98)

Being "on the threshold of great things" (116), Kurtz tried to capture the dream of possessing the distant and the incredible, made concrete by Marlow's narrative perspective—this was then the way to the heart of darkness. At the end of *Blindness*, looking at the sky and seeing "everything white," the doctor's wife thinks, "It is my turn," and we learn that "Fear made her quickly lower her eyes"; as the novel ends, she immediately feels that "the city was still there" (326). Thus the narrative is brought again to its normal place, to brightness in an urban mode, to proximity, in a word, to the centers of this world, although it was built aside from it. That is the center from which Saramago writes in any case, perhaps inevitably so, given the Europeanness of his gaze and condition. For his being on the edge (more of an aesthetic position, with inquisitive and decisive yet distant implications) is apparently different in this context from being on the margins (a political and ethical confinement implying the eventual beginning of a process of struggle or conciliation), and Kurtz's threshold is finally the crossroad containing both the sources of imprisonment and the dream of accomplishment.

Notes

[1] In the Portuguese original these last words read "sou simplesmente a que nasceu para ver o horror," that is, literally, "I am simply the one who was born to see *the* horror" (276; my emphasis).

Works Cited

Ashcroft, Bill, Gareth Griffith, and Helen Tiffin. *The Empire Writes Back*. London: Routledge, 1989.

Conrad, Joseph. *Heart of Darkness*. 1902. New York: Barnes & Noble, 1994.

Gandhi, Leela. *Postcolonial Theory. A Critical Introduction*. Singapore: Allen & Unwin, 1998.

Pratt, Mary Louise. *Imperial Eyes. Travel Writing and Transculturation*. London: Routledge, 1992.

Saramago, José. *Blindness*. Trans. Giovanni Pontiero. NewYork: Harcourt Brace, 1997.

———. *The Stone Raft*. Trans. Giovanni Pontiero. New York: Harcourt Brace, 1995.

Said, Edward. *Culture and Imperialism*. London: Vintage, 1994.

Seixo, Maria-Alzira, John Noyes, Graça Abreu, and Isabel Moutinho. *The Paths of Multiculturalism. Travel Writing and Postcolonialism*. Lisboa: Cosmos, 2000.

Tiffin, Chris, and Alan Lawson. *De-scribing Empire. Postcolonialism and textuality*. London: Routledge, 1994.

Cruising Gender in the Eighties: From *Levantado do Chão* to *The History of the Siege of Lisbon*

Ana Paula Ferreira

> ...for no journey is but one journey, each journey comprises a number of journeys, and if one of them seems so meaningless that we have no hesitation in saying it was not worthwhile, our common sense, were it not so often clouded by prejudice and idleness, would tell us that we should verify whether the journeys within that journey were not of sufficient value to have justified all the trials and tribulations. (Saramago, *The Stone Raft* 222)

One of the most textually productive aspects of Saramago's self-avowed essayistic penchant—"probably I am an essayist who needs to write novels because he does not know how to write essays"[1]—is the revision of certain foundational myths of Western culture, first and foremost that of woman as subordinate and, hence, subservient to "Man." In line with the historians of the *Annales* and the "nouvelle histoire" of Georges Duby and Jacques Le Goff, that revision entails calling attention to the particulars of everyday life of the anonymous lot traditionally left out of official history.[2] It is thus not incidental that, as the most obscured in that group, female characters assume decisive roles in the development of Saramago's fictional plots.[3] The latter tend to privilege the instinctual, intuitive, relational and contingent character of the "feminine" acts and words characteristic of the so-called private sphere. Such a domain of experience implicitly questions masculine pretensions of reason, presence, autonomy and transcendence informing public exploits that go on record as part of a narrative of historical progress. Leading to an aporia of gender predicates, this argumentative confrontation is evinced in the five novels published between *Levantado do Chão* (1980) and *The History of the Siege of Lisbon* (1989). They outline a fictional-essayistic inquiry responding not only to feminist appeals and debates in the wake of 1975, the first year of the UN-declared International Women's Decade, but, more specifically, responding to post-April 1974 revolutionary discourses of popular emancipation not necessarily open to women's voices or demands. In view of a historical and more broadly discursive context where the "question of woman" cannot be disassociated from the question of revolution or, better, the Revolution in question, Saramago's textual journey posits an imaginative term of struggle against the ever normative and oppressive effects of structurally persistent patterns of gender domination in socio-economic and symbolic orders.

I. Avoiding the Question

That the term thus pursued cannot be confused with simulacra of real women nor, much less, with some notion of the "eternal feminine" is perhaps the biggest theoretical-ideological challenge presented by Saramago's investment in figurations of gender difference. It is a challenge that perhaps can only begin to be met in the light of the decontextualized and isolated descriptions of feminine images promulgated by those intent on defining a model of Saramago's female characters. Thus, Maria da Conceição Madruga, for instance, ascribes paradigmatic status to characters whose design is strictly confined to the semantic economy of the fantastic functioning in two specific texts, *Baltasar and Blimunda* and *The Stone Raft*. Without even acknowledging this literary-generic fact as a condition for the characterization of either Blimunda or Joana Carda, Madruga presents both as exemplary figures on account of their simultaneously exceptional and realist attributes (85, 97). Although Beatriz Berrini detaches this model from the figures of Blimunda, Joana Carda and, eventually, the doctor's wife (from Saramago's novel *Blindness*)—the trio of "seers" into the commonality of women's experience such as it is epitomized in *Levantado do Chão*—she does not fare better by submitting all of Saramago's female characters to patriarchal ideals of womanhood.[4] (Nevertheless, her assertion that they point to man's lack of understanding of "woman's interior face" [141] may be well founded.) Elsewhere the same critic in fact ends up extrapolating from one famous line in *The Year of the Death of Ricardo Reis* the inference that, in all of Saramago's texts, woman is nothing but "an enigma, a labyrinth, a charade" (*Year* 312).[5] Here is yet one more atemporal cliché inherited from an essentially misogynist tradition that even leads one to question the critical validity of defining an abstract model of femininity or of womanhood in Saramago's fiction.

As "fine and penetrating [an] understanding and respect for the feminine" as his novels may suggest,[6] it is important to note that Saramago rejects any potential mystifications of the subject founded on unexamined critical assumptions. In an interview appended to Berrini's 1998 study, Saramago rejects the view that he "venerates" women, going on to denounce "certain commonplaces as 'the eternal feminine' or 'inspiring dreams'" redundant in "'Marianist'" claims (240). He asserts, on the other hand, that his "respect" for women does not translate into any pretension of knowledge, but is part of his awareness that woman, even more so than man, is always "*an other being*" whose distance is insurmountable (for "she is always on the other side of the sea..." [240; emphasis in original]). Hence his insistence, appearing for example in Carlos Reis's *Diálogos com José Saramago*, that his female characters are totally "imaginary"; they are neither projections of himself nor "copies of any woman" (135). Leaving aside for now possible counter-readings, such statements are useful to pull the matter of Saramago's female characters away from an idealist/idealizing and dangerously cooptative representational register, pushing it closer to the experimental material(ism) of language in the open, multi-layered and movable space of textuality.[7]

Such a turn to the text as a performative space of "imagination" is suggested by Teresa Cristina Cerdeira da Silva in a study centered on how Saramago's feminine figures question the basic misogynous postulates of traditional Portuguese "marialva" culture. Contrary to other critics who fetishize such figures in reductive and decontextualized attempts to "chercher la femme," da Silva points out the need to keep in mind the post-April 1974 revolutionary context that informs the author's work and, consequently, his imaginings of women. It is in the liberating, emancipatory space afforded by Saramago's texts that women become full-blown actors of a revolutionary process that threatens to discount them, steeped as it is, both at the level of social relations and of partisan politics, in patriarchal (if not male chauvinist) beliefs (215). From *Manual of Painting and Calligraphy* (1977) to *All the Names* (1997)—the latest novel published at the time of the study under review—this textual space would be inscribed therefore with the more radical implications of an otherwise imperfect revolutionary process by means of figurations of women and the feminine not limited to representations of female characters.

In view of the above, one should avoid neutralizing what appears to be a subversive, inherently dialogic textuality by relapsing into a linear, homogenous model of femininity or of textuality. As historically relevant and as seductive as either of these may be, revolutionary processes, textual and otherwise, are known to occur in leaps and bounds and to occur vis-à-vis the many differences—and deferrals—that haunt them.[8] By critically appropriating Saramago's notion quoted above of woman as a totally foreign, "*other being*," a notion that echoes the second-wave feminist discourses departing from, if indebted to, Simone de Beauvoir's *The Second Sex* (1949), the rhetorical-argumentative movement of the figure (and of the textual space) can be brought to light. Rather than simply woman or the feminine, what is at stake in various ways throughout the several texts is the historically dynamic and ever contingent term of gender difference. The author's creative-essayistic investment in women may be said, in fact, to probe the changing status of gender difference within a historical-materialist ontology of struggle and conflict that is played out textually. This probing locates itself discursively at a specific time and place, when the crisis of Enlightenment ideals encounters the crisis of the so-called Revolution of Carnations, opening the traditional Marxist "question of woman." What the series of five novels published throughout the decade of the eighties presents (at least to those interested in the issues of women, men and revolutions—all in the plural) is a textual journey illustrating the consequent search for an axiology of difference moving from the critique of the classic revolutionary model of woman, to the complex discursive webs of gender and, finally, to the deconstructive, "feminine operation" of language.[9] The following will focus principally on the first of these experimental stages or debates in Saramago's fiction, attending to the premises and argumentative figurations that are at the basis of further textual incursions into the question of gender difference.

II. On the Horizon of Women's Struggle

> We will continue to speak about men, but also more about women.
> (*Levantado do Chão* 138)[10]

One of the most nagging issues confronting traditional, and not-so-traditional, Marxist thinkers has been the place and role assigned to women in revolutionary struggle. The unequal and hierarchical relation of the sexes was recognized early on not only as the cause of women's oppression but also as the index of all forms of oppression in a stratified socio-economic order founded on the institution of private property. Following Engels's systematization of Marx's ideas in *The Origins of the Family, Private Property and the State* (1857), the discussion of women's inequality became attached to the family as a basic structure of, and pre-condition for, relations of domination based on the possession of private property. From this perspective, emancipation would depend first of all on woman overcoming her (biological) limitation to reproductive labor in the family and becoming an active producer alongside man in the public work force. Yet only with the liberation of the working class from the bonds of private property and economic exploitation would woman finally be able to rise from her subordinate position in the family.[11] The subsumption of women's struggle for complete subjectivity and independence, including sexual independence, to the struggle of the working class naturally would be the most contentious aspect of Marxist and socialist feminist agendas, even in recent times.[12] The *New Portuguese Letters* (1973), both as text and political event, would bring the conflict home in a dramatic form with well-known repercussions.

Although it could be argued that Saramago drew inspiration from this controversial theoretical context in several of his novels published in the eighties, the fictional exploration and the critique of revolutionary thought concerning woman and the family is put forward directly in *Levantado do Chão* and, in a more complex way, in *The Year of the Death of Ricardo Reis.* These two texts complement each other in their respective temporal frames, with the diachronic panorama of the first and the synchronic focus of the second shedding light on interconnected histories of oppression and revolutionary resistance in 20th century Portugal. They also complement each other in their diverse social, cultural and regional locations, following the genealogical line of a family of landless wage laborers in a southern plantation in one case, and in the other presenting a cross-section of urban, very diverse working-class experiences centered on the life of a humble hotel servant. In either case, female figures are cast in typical conditions of subservience to male privilege in the private sphere, this being determined by the prevailing economic system. Their function in male-centered movements of popular emancipation is, as might be expected, an extension of their roles in that sphere. Within this frame, women's struggles for liberation emerge as metonymies for the concrete historical experience of a collectivity that transcends them.

In *Levantado do Chão*, the omnipotent economic law of the Alentejo "latifúndio" transpires in the deeply ambiguous but structurally indispensable hierarchical relation between men and women through four generations of family life, from the years just before the proclamation of the First Republic in 1910 to shortly after the 1974 democratic revolution. Even if one allows for the possibility of encountering a desirable sexual partner,[13] women are traditionally passed on from father to husband as commodities necessary for the realization of their manhood as wage-earning providers for their families. The uncertain availability of paid work ultimately determines women's dependant status both at home and, consequently, in socio-economic relations outside the home.[14] Even if they move into the role of producers, working for wages on the plantation, the law of patriarchy, which is also the law of property, does not accord men and women equal pay (215). Women therefore seem fated to carry the ancestral burden of their biological sex as men's obscure and silent, but fertile helpmates in face of a common, basic need for survival.

It is that need that prompts men to rebel against their own victimization at the hands of plantation owners, a male rebellion that depends upon as much as it perpetuates women's being limited to "passing shadows or sometimes indispensable interlocutors, feminine chorus, normally quiet due to the weight of their work burden or of their bellies, or else suffering mothers for various reasons..." (183).[15] Gracinda Mau-Tempo is, indeed, an example of a partly emancipated wife-mother taught how to read and write by the revolutionary Manuel Espada even before their marriage in 1948. But like other women of both her own and previous generations, she never assumes a direct, "productive" role in the underground workers' movement.[16] It is not until after the April Revolution that women born to her enlightened kind—namely, her daughter Maria Adelaide—are invited by their fathers, husbands and brothers to join them in what was to become the (albeit short-lived) historical event of Alentejo land reform. One wonders if Saramago's choice for the masculine singular case in the title of the novel, *Levantado do Chão*, does not bespeak his critical awareness of the overriding economy of male-sameness to which the historical, finally victorious struggle of the Alentejo plantation workers here memorialized reverts. For beyond the supposed universal equality achieved by those implied in the passive verb form, "levantado," remain "others" still lacking the social, economic and, above all, cultural space in which to raise/emancipate themselves on their own, by their own means, and not merely as men's helpmates. Is woman irrevocably collapsed on the patriarchal ground of her reproductive physiology? Or, in becoming a revolutionary subject like Adelaide Espada for example will she be able or necessarily want to give up maternity? In what circumstances can maternity become a deliberate step in women's struggle?

Going back within the frame of male-centered historical time to *The Year of the Death of Ricardo Reis* (1984), set in the ever sinister year of 1936 in the Lisbon of Salazar's Portugal, one can determine the centrality of such (not merely rhetorical) questions in Saramago's textual journey. Their pertinence in expounding traditional Marxist thought on woman's condition as subsumed under that of the family under capitalism is all the more instructive inasmuch as this particular text directly engages the fascist ideology of family and motherhood. The picture is complex: what is at stake in those two radically different perspectives of collective redemption or national salvation, as any improbable "unity" before "two things opposed, divergent" (*Year* 51), is woman's difference as a sexually marked body relegated to the private sphere. Her status as economically dependent theoretically makes her available to being coopted for the moral support and sexual reproduction of the family-nation—as may be Marcenda's case—or, conversely, to find herself fulfilling an extension of the same functions in the horizon of the (all-male) movement of resistance against fascism and capitalist oppression—Lídia's case. It is at this juncture that Saramago's text leads one to intuit the potentially subversive historical-materialist meaning of Fernando Pessoa/Ricardo Reis's dictum, "woman continues to be more Eve than man Adam, [...], I say this because for all of us it should be so" (204).

Considering that Salazar's New State holds the family as the basic nucleus and moral guarantee of the corporative system, in this text family economics is shown to be the determining law of all identities and relations of social exchange. According to the New State's Constitution, in effect since April 1933, "the differences resulting from [woman's] nature and the good of the family" justify the exclusion of women from the supposed rights of citizenship, along with all those falling under the category of others due to "the diversity of circumstances and the nature of things" (*Constituição* 4-5). This exclusion in principle would require that women not work outside the home and that they become servants of the nation by being, first and foremost, servants of the proprietors of the family-home. It is thus not incidental that the text focuses on a moving, deconstructive simulacrum of the desirable fascist family—not the privately owned family home (known as "casal de família"), but a sequence of two temporarily rented spaces, not a decorous marriage, but an illicit sexual relation that is the extension of a (licit) economic relation of female rented labor.[17] In addition, it is not incidental that the class difference founding this relation spectrally figures a bygone monarchic/imperialist past, upon the image of which the economic and moral order of the family-nation is refracted. In other words, Ricardo Reis's surplus material and symbolic capital vis-à-vis the destitute hotel servant, Lídia, summons the seemingly eternal, yet always historically contingent, relation between man as king—his name is, indeed, "Reis"—and woman as his dependent people-vassals.

Every fascist corporative ensemble mirrors this pervasive patriarchal structure of class/gender relations. The distance between the private and the public, home economics and state economics, between man as king-master of his property at home and the dictator as paternal(ist) emperor of it all is, therefore, collapsed under the aegis of the primary moral order here in question.[18] Everything, everyone, everywhere is exposed to scrutiny and vigilance in a "politics of the visible" (Pickering-Iazzi) hypothetically mobilizing all eyes to ensure that not a single gesture escapes that endless mirroring order.[19]

It is because the reproductive functioning of the corporative system makes itself so present in peoples' lives that Lídia can judge matter-of-factly, "[t]he people are like me, a hotel chambermaid who has a revolutionary brother and sleeps with a doctor who is against revolutions" (324). The birthing analogy she uses to explain her (Engels-inspired) historical-materialist comprehension of the class relation of dependency and, simultaneously, struggle between her and Reis is not to be taken lightly.[20] It is suggestive of the revolutionary appropriation of the supposed "natural" role that maternity plays within the seemingly endless reproductive, oppressive corporative system of the family-nation. Even if the nation's feminized servants are compelled, out of sheer economic necessity—the paupers that Reis sees all over the city are a telling sign—to offer themselves as instruments of the family-based economy sustaining the nation, in a sense those servants have the power to subvert the politically desirable ends to which the products of their labor may be put.

Lídia's spring cleaning spree, following her decision to keep a pregnancy that Reis condemns, is a good example of how people-serfs can overturn not only the expectations of the fascist/paternalist reign but, along with it, the historical and cultural tradition feeding its myths. Lídia not only foregoes the fiction of paternity upholding the family property system—"If you don't want to acknowledge the child, I don't mind, the child can be illegitimate, like me" (307)—more subversively, she performs mimically the quintessential act of ideal homebound femininity by cleaning and shining Reis's "abode."[21] If, in recognition of the product of her labor, the master would exclaim "blessed be Lídia among women," comparing her favorably with the bourgeois, left-handedly crippled Marcenda (308), the servant is no asexual Virgin Mary or fascist woman "saint."[22] In fact, she exploits the master's desire for her own physical, now compelling sexual fulfillment (309). It can be argued that her gratification is of paramount importance in leading her to recognize the revolutionary need to stop abetting her own class/gender domination: "Is she the doctor's maid, his cleaner, she is certainly not his lover, because the word implies equality, no matter whether male or female, and they are not equal" (338). Reis, from then on, is positioned as the class enemy, or "stranger," whom the proletarian, mutiny-identified, Lídia will refuse to sleep with and, someday hopefully, serve—even as she continues to work for paid wages as a hotel servant (349).

In view of the slow but sure change of fortune laying ahead for the class of men-kings left wanting continually abnegated, reproductive feminine or feminized serfs, it makes *historical* sense for them to see woman as "an enigma, a labyrinth, a charade" (312).[23] More pointedly, it makes sense that the "reis" of 1936 should feel threatened by women like Lídia, fraternally aligned with the (possibly communist) left, and who merely would use them to produce (not reproduce) a new kind of men and women free from their bondage. In the context of the Estado Novo, unsurprisingly breeding a new generation of women who resist its particular mandate for feminine "difference," men like Reis have reason to be more afraid of women than were the "pessoas" of the First Republic afraid before women of the kind perhaps represented by Marcenda's dead mother:[24] "You are as frightened of women as I was, Perhaps even more" (313).

The text leaves no doubt as to the familial relationship that enables Lídia's consciousness of political class (and ensuing class struggle). It is through her brother serving in the navy that the hotel/Reis servant learns both about his group's subversive activities as well as the resulting tragedies, the text ending after Reis finds out in the newspaper about Daniel's death in the failed insurrection (356). Lídia's relationship with her brother represents an interesting foreclosure of paternal lineage—as if Lídia, along with him and his revolutionary friends, were all illegitimate children made kin through a commonly exploited, abandoned and now, symptomatically, invalid mother. This suggests a possible horizontal brotherhood different from the more hierarchical, father- and husband-dominated scene of the rural working class in *Levantado do Chão*. Yet it does not make for Lídia's active, direct participation in that brotherhood: she remains physically very distant from it—the revolutionaries are a group of marines. Further, she ends up, like Gracinda Mau-Tempo, performing a merely supportive, suffering, maternal role vis-à-vis her brother's ultimately tragic activities.

However, Lídia's insurgency against Reis's class/gender privilege, and the much broader historical context that it entails, is nothing less than an exemplary woman's struggle. It culminates in her leaving the emblematic figure of men-kings without a servant and, what is more, without an "other" in whose face he can recognize his self-sameness.[25] If Lídia's "mutiny" is parallel to and related in class and kin to that being carefully prepared by her brother and his comrades, it is also very different, because gender-specific. Her apparently silent, resigned, giving gestures of domesticity in the end mine the very basis of the economic-as-gender/class relation that sustains the family-nation. Before and beyond the overthrow of a whole patriarchal economic system inherited from a seemingly ancestral tradition, before and beyond the eradication of any one dictator or a few capitalists can be eradicated, there are—and probably will continue to be—many anonymous (or not-so-anonymous) "reis" to be dethroned. And these are likely to include men in the brotherhood of resistance, as may be the case of that other Ricardo Reis, in *Levantado do Chão*, who gives shelter and food to the ex-Caxias prisoner, João Mau-Tempo, in the humble home he shares with the maternal figure of Ermelinda (264).

Lídia's coming to revolutionary consciousness of *and* action upon her own condition is firmly rooted in her courageous (thought to be so matter-of-fact, so "natural") experience as a sexually embodied female human being. After all, she is the one who literally and not just figuratively makes the bed on which she sleeps with the doctor at the Hotel Bragança and beyond. Nor is her sexual decisiveness or arguably continued "availability" prosaic. It can be interpreted as an affirmation of feminine selfhood against a whole Christian-Judaic patriarchal tradition of thought that proscribes sexual pleasure as women's worst sin. Like her, the female wage-laborers in *Levantado do Chão* welcome men's desire in response to their own, "maybe because the world is indeed going to be better" after their sexual fulfillment (105). Similarly, even a woman such as Manuel Espada's mother, apparently made of "granite stone," "sweetly overflows at night in her bed" (*Levantado* 218). Such a valorization of women's sexual enjoyment obviously confronts the fascist law against the moral "corruption of customs,"[26] with woman-as-asexual-mother being the "saintly" cornerstone of that law. More than that, Lídia's and, by extension, other female characters' uninhibited sexual expressions also offer an important corrective to the normative Marxist tradition regarding women's sexual liberation that perpetrates patriarchal control of women's sexualities.[27] This corrective does not aim to erase sexual difference in the interests of a hypothetical gender equality attainable only on condition that women become transcendental subjects through the sacrifice of the immanence of their bodies, as Simone de Beauvoir would propose following Engels. The privileging of sexual difference is, on the contrary, mobilized in the interests of a revolutionary struggle that should (ideally) take off from the forever historically and ideologically sedimented platform of oppressed feminine sexuality, including maternity as an essential part of that sexuality, against all types of oppression ensuing from the law of patriarchy, which first of all implies a law that, regardless of class, brands women as part of men's estates.[28]

To understand that "the father"—as Ricardo Reis would have it—"is an accident [...], dispensable once the necessity has been provided" (313) is perhaps all that women would need in order to prompt a gender/class struggle with their quotidian gestures. This struggle is shown to be played out in temporally and spatially heterogeneous ways, according to a "woman's time" that intersects with but is not to be collapsed into the linear time of a class struggle enacted within a male-centered community or "brotherhood."[29] From submitting to their ancestral "fate" as "birthing canals and work animals" (*Levantado* 125) belonging to family property to expressing a choice for motherhood independently of the paternal seal or of family ties—"I am going to have the baby" (*Year* 307)—Saramago's figurations give reason for women to be increasingly discussed as regards the ancestral means and emergent ways of their common sexually embodied difference. In regard to this potentially empowering, not victimizing, difference, the two texts add to each other in presenting a complex panorama of the underground, anonymous and ever-conflicting quests for revolutionary change occurring throughout the greater part of the 20th century in "a country of men" in constant strife, strife that is economic through and through, to prove to one another that they are indeed men (*Levantado* 75).

The Stone Raft (1986) picks up on that textual journey exploring gender difference, extending the historical frame to a time already far from any one short-lived revolutionary victory. This text may be said to illustrate graphically a rebellion against the patriarchy/private property dyad that is ultimately played out at the level of poetic language. Like women who walk out on or find themselves free from any master, language can escape the bondage of the Father's privileged reason and, thereby, privileged possession, to engender itself freely and thus recapture a long withheld impulsive fertility analogous to a "resurgence of the maternal spirit" (*Stone* 281).[30] This resurgence would eradicate, or at least subvert, the imposition of any one official account of public life that excludes the productive, and not simply reproductive, role of women's labor in the ups and downs and the many circular detours of human (or still man's?) history.

III. By Way of Conclusion: The Aporia of Difference

> [T]he kingdom on earth belongs to those who have the wit to put a 'no' at the service of a 'yes,' having been the perpetrators of a 'no,' they rapidly erase it to restore a 'yes.' (*Siege* 296)

Precisely by virtue of the ideological and, yes, deconstructive/poetic, importance that the "question of woman" assumes in Saramago's contentious fictions, the issue of gender difference is batted around (cruised, if you will) in and out of the meanderings of class struggle in order to explode a discursive, cultural constructedness that pits women and men against each other as class enemies forever destined to be in a mutual state of siege. The story featuring the dialogue between a hermit and a queen in *Baltasar and Blimunda* (1982) is significant for the extent to which the question of difference is not positively, biologically determined but, rather, is the product of socio-economic locations and corresponding discursive conventions. The webs of identity take possession of each one's being in a necessary, though despotic way, inasmuch as they endow that being with human-social intelligibility. Hence, the hermit's reply to the rebellious queen, who is not happy being a queen and who would like to find out how she can be a woman without being also a queen: "No one can be without being, men and women do not exist, all that exists is what they are and their rebellion against what they are" (232).

Since, however, "what they are"—man and woman, rich and poor and any other ensuing dichotomous, always relationally hierarchical, identity construction—is a story that seems to be always already written, the question again emerges as to what language has to do with it. More precisely, what does a cultural tradition inscribed in and handed down through books of supposed historical truth have to do with the various, interconnected relations of domination that give social meaning to those identities? In postulating a hypothetical case of an accidentally induced creative project of re-writing history, *The History of the Siege of Lisbon* (1989) attempts to prove that words are not immoveable stones, but rather discursive constructions that can be made malleable, interchangeable and provisional. If only those who use words could forego a patriarchal, phallogocentric or "macho" position of authority over their many possible pairings and meanings.

Saramago does not, to be certain, signal the female character as the one who carries out such a revolutionary task: Maria Sara, like Joana Carda of *The Stone Raft*, is much too steeped in the humanist/rationalist/enlightened system of thought that awarded her a university degree in the first place. She cannot do it, yet she can recognize a rebellious (feminine-intuitive) insurgence in the logic of linguistic truth when she sees it, as she does with respect to the mistake of her vassal proofreader, Raimundo Silva. Not only does she encourage the "mistake's" further unfolding/engenderment in creative practice but she also pushes for its conceptual underpinnings: "Your idea would never have occurred to me, to negate an incontrovertible historical fact. I myself no longer know what made me do it, Frankly I'm convinced that the great divide between people is between those who say yes and those who say no..." (296). Echoing in part the hermit's philosophy of negation ("men and women do not exist, all that exists is what they are and their rebellion against what they are") the proofreader's theoretical estimate goes right to the point of a post-structuralist Marxist "negative dialectic," according to which any revolutionary critique of culture or society can only take place within its oppressive structures—even while risking complicity with it (Adorno).

Such a theoretical perspective might explain Saramago's insistent experimentation with sanctioned scripts of gender and class divisions that go all the way back to the story of Adam and Eve in order to subvert and, even, revert their pervasively tyrannical meanings. In the utopian space of artistic creation the operation may bear some revolutionary textual fruit, envisioning the "yes" of individual and collective lives without any masters' chains. One might want to debate, however, the implications of a textual model of affirmative negativity that suspends in bliss the continued siege, the violence, and what lies beyond the "woman's question" in the question of what love has to do with it. Or, perhaps not; perhaps the last three lines of this last text from the decade of the eighties summon it all up: "Forget it, we're staying. Maria Sara's head is resting on Raimundo's shoulder, with his left hand he strokes her hair and cheek. They did not fall asleep at once. Beneath the verandah roof a shadow sighed" (*Siege* 312).

Notes

[1] In an interview with Carlos Reis, Saramago quotes himself as often stating: "'Provavelmente não sou um romancista; provavelmente sou um ensaísta que precisa de escrever romances porque não sabe escrever ensaios'" (Reis 46). Unless otherwise noted, all translations in this article are mine.

[2] In the interview with Reis, Saramago associates his attempt to represent a temporal "whole," in order to understand the interconnection between what History reports and what it excludes, with the work of "uns quanto autores (os homens dos *Annales*, os da Nouvelle Histoire, como Georges Duby ou o Jacques Le Goff), cujo olhar histórico ia por esse mesmo caminho" (80-1).

[3] In a very brief article, titled "Figuras de mujer: presencias femeninas en la narrativa de José Saramago," Basilio Losada suggests that Saramago's feminine figures corporealize the pain as well as the virtues of the common people, or those vanquished by history (36).

[4] After pointing out how, in *Levantado do Chão*, woman is always shown to be morally superior to man, Berrini synthesizes Saramago's representations of woman in the following terms: "Humilde, oculta, silenciosa, é contudo a força, a coragem, a paciência, a sagacidade, a intuição, tudo posto ao serviço dos outros, em especial do marido e dos filhos" (*Ler Saramago* 139). Noting, in addition, the beginnings of woman's emancipation in the figure of Gracinda Mau-Tempo, the critic concludes: "As figuras femininas das ficções de Saramago podem quase todas espelhar-se nas personagens de LC [*Levantado do Chão*]" (140).

[5] "Não é possível, também, esquecer que o ser feminino, nos textos de Saramago, nesse e nos demais romances, é qualificado por sua vez de enigma, quebra-cabeças, charada" (Berrini "*O ano*": 81).

[6] I borrow the phrase from Berrini (*Ler Saramago* 150).

[7] This understanding of language and textuality, inspired by Mikhail Bakhtin and, more generally, by post-structuralist Marxist thought, appears to be more in tune with Saramago's

creative practice, rooted in a historical-materialist worldview (see, for example, Voloshinov and Kristeva).

[8] Twenty years of textual production, which is also twenty years of lived experience witnessing (among other things) the very different cultural and political contexts of the Portuguese eighties and nineties, would also likely have an impact on how the author figures the subject at hand.

[9] This notion was coined by Jacques Derrida as part of his critique of the metaphysics of presence. It had a decisive impact on post-structuralist (French) feminist conceptions of language, difference and the "feminine." See, for example, Derrida's *Spurs* and "Choreographies."

[10] This and all subsequent translations of the text are my own.

[11] For the now classic feminist account of the well-known narrative here briefly summarized, see Juliet Mitchell, esp. 19-24.

[12] Besides Mitchell, see, for example, Millet, Hartman, McKinnon and Barrett.

[13] A good example is found in the scene where, embracing her father who has just been released from prison, Gracinda Mau-Tempo sizes up Manuel Espada, who had also been suspected of subversive activities, and—with the matter-of-fact interpellation, "So, Manuel"—initiates what is going to be their life together: "[W]hoever thinks that much more than that is needed, is wrong" (162).

[14] While the man is expected to go outside the home to get paid work, the wife is expected to account for and excuse the family provider from the debts incurred in buying food items. The anonymity of the couple discussing this situation in bed is telling: after the wife asks the husband how much he is going to earn, the dialogue evolves in the following manner: "I don't know, don't bother me, woman, and she would say, It's not because of me, it was the baker who asked me due to the outstanding debt, oh those miserable dialogues" (196).

[15] This is well illustrated by the narrative of underground subversive activity that takes off decisively when men find themselves without work. From women waking their husbands to go to meet their comrades (203-06), to the drama of looking for their whereabouts in the local prison (237-38) and, subsequently, to their emotional visits with the political prisoners in Caxias (257-58), wives and daughters are positioned in the indispensable but victimizing role of mothers of the revolutionaries.

[16] See Barrada for an illuminating study of the "supportive" role to which women were limited in the underground activities of the Portuguese Communist Party in the forties.

[17] That the hotel servant, Lídia, refuses to accept payment for her continued services once Ricardo Reis moves into the furnished apartment is symptomatic of how it figures somewhat more closely, and more cynically, to what would be a family home. Would-be wives do not charge for domestic tasks, including sex.

[18] One should perhaps remember that Article 14 of the New State's Constitution leaves no doubt as to the extent to which the home ("casal de família") is compelled by "State and local autarchies" to engender and mantain this order. Line 5 of the article reads thus: "Tomar todas as providências no sentido de evitar a corrupção dos costumes" (*Constituição* 10).

[19] This is dramatized throughout the novel, not only by the PIDE agent popping up here and there to investigate Reis or, better, the latter's relationship with the sister of a revolutionary, but, most importantly, by the hotel servants and, subsequently, the women in Reis's apartment building, who keep constant watch of his movements, his relations, the "private" space he occupies.

[20] "Well perhaps in my case it is like having a baby, which grows without our noticing it and is born when the time comes" (324).

[21] This point is indebted to Luce Irigaray's argument about the transgressive potential of feminine mimeticism.

[22] The women pictured as "saints" by the cultural apparatus of national propaganda are those who would deter men from resistance activities, leading them to follow the fascist path into the so-called holy Portuguese family: "We Portuguese have also our share of holy women, two examples will suffice, Marília, the shining heroine of *Conspiracy*, and the innocent saint of *The May Revolution*" (326); "Only the other day we heard a simple Portuguese film producer say that on this side of the Pyrenees all women are saints" (327). Those "saints" would likely form the hosts of OMEM, the fascist organization of "Mothers for National Education" that Marcenda is thought to eventually join (314).

[23] See earlier in this essay my critique of the current decontextualized, atemporal reading of this statement.

[24] Marcenda's losing the movement of her *left* hand after her mother's death, three years before (1933), is suggestive of the crippling effect that Salazar's New State had on the (bourgeois) Republican Feminist women's movements.

[25] Ricardo Reis's losing his job is not as important as his feeling of losing Lídia, since he has the means to maintain himself without work. "This face covered with lather is a mask that could fit any man's face, and when the razor little by little reveals what is underneath, Ricardo Reis is intrigued by what he sees, and disturbed, as if afraid some evil might emerge. He examines himself carefully in the mirror, comparing his face with the different, unknown face he once had" (299).

[26] See note 18.

[27] Lenin, for example, repudiates women's complete sexual liberation as being contrary to the interests of communism, since it poses a threat to the future of the Soviet family (Fauré 382; 388). Even Trotsky, an apparent sympathizer with women's liberation, does not broach the question of sexuality aside and apart from that of maternity.

[28] As the "three Marias" would put it, "Woman: man's wealth, his image, his land, his inherited estate" (*New Portuguese Letters* 105; my translation).

[29] I partly evoke here Julia Kristeva's argument in "Women's Time" (esp. 188-94)

[30] For a detailed study of this process using a Kristevean notion of poetic language, see my manuscript "As Mulheres de Saramago na 'Jangada' da Significação."

Works Cited

Adorno, Theodor. *Prisms: Cultural Criticism and Society*. London: Neville Spearman, 1967.

Barradas, Ana. "Anos 40: As Clandestinas." *História* XVIII [Nova Série].17 (Fev. 1996): 40-9.

Barreno, Isabel, Maria Teresa Horta, and Maria Velho da Costa. *Novas Cartas Portuguesas.* 3rd ed. Lisboa: Moraes, 1979.

Barrett, Michelle. *Women's Oppression Today: Problems in Marxist Feminist Analysis.* London: New Left Books, 1980.

Beauvoir, Simone de. *The Second Sex.* Trans. and ed. H. M. Parshley. New York: Vintage, 1989.

Berrini, Beatriz. "*O ano da morte de Ricardo Reis*: sugestões do texto." *José Saramago: Uma Homenagem.* São Paulo: EDUC, 1999. 63-83.

———. *Ler Saramago: O Romance.* Lisboa: Caminho, 1998.

Constituição Política da República Portuguesa e Acto Colonial. 2nd ed. Lisboa: Moraes, 1936.

Derrida, Jacques. "Choreographies: An Interview with Jacques Derrida." Ed. and trans. Christie V. McDonald. *Diacritics* 12.2 (1982): 66-76.

———. *Spurs: Nietzsche's Styles.* Trans. Barbara Harlow. Chicago: U Chicago P, 1979.

Fauré, Christine. "The Utopia of the New Woman in the Work of Alexandra Kollontai and its Impact on the French Feminist and Communist Presses." *Women in Culture and Politics: A Century of Change.* Ed. Judith Friedlander et al. Bloomington: Indiana UP, 1986. 376-89.

Ferreira, Ana Paula. "As Mulheres de Saramago na 'Jangada' da Significação." *José Saramago. Actas do I Colóquio Internacional. University of Massachusetts-Amherst. Sept. 19-20, 1996.* Eds. Paulo de Medeiros and José Ornelas. Lisboa: Caminho. Submitted Ms.

Hartmann, Heidi. "The Unhappy Marriage of Marxism and Feminism: Towards a More Progressive Union." *Capital and Class* 23 (1979): 1-33.

Irigaray, Luce. *This Sex Which Is Not One.* Trans. Catherine Porter. Ithaca: Cornell UP, 1985. 23-33.

Kristeva, Julia. "Women's Time." Trans. Alice Jardine and Harry Blake. *The Kristeva Reader.* Ed. Toril Moi. New York: Columbia UP. 1986. 187-213.

———. "Word, Dialogue, and Novel" (1969). *Desire in Language.* Trans. Thomas Gora, Alice Jardine and Leon Roudiez. New York: Columbia UP, 1980. 64-93.

Losada, Basilio. "Figuras de mujer: Presencias femeninas en la narrativa de José Saramago." *Quimera* 150 (Sept. 1996): 36-7.

Madruga, Maria da Conceição. *A Paixão Segundo José Saramago: A Paixão do Verbo e o Verbo da Paixão.* Porto: Campo das Letras, 1998.

McKinnon, Catherine. "Feminism, Marxism, Method and the State: An Agenda for Theory." *Signs* 7.3 (Spring 1982): 514-44.

Millet, Kate. *Sexual Politics.* London: Virago, 1977.

Mitchell, Juliet. *Women: The Longest Revolution. Essays on Feminism, Literature and Psychoanalysis.* London: Virago, 1986.

Pickering-Iazzi. *Politics of the Visible: Writing Women, Culture, and Fascism.* Minneapolis: U Minnesota P, 1997.

Reis, Carlos. *Diálogos com José Saramago.* Lisbon: Caminho, 1998.

Saramago, José. *Baltasar and Blimunda.* Trans. Giovanni Pontiero. San Diego: Harcourt Brace Jovanovich, 1987

———. *The History of the Siege of Lisbon.* Trans. Giovanni Pontiero. London: Harvill, 1996.

———. *Levantado do Chão.* 7th ed. Lisboa: Caminho, 1986.

———. *The Stone Raft.* Trans. Giovanni Pontiero. San Diego: Harcourt Brace Jovanovich, 1995.

———. *The Year of the Death of Ricardo Reis.* Trans. Giovanni Pontiero. San Diego: Harcourt Brace Jovanovich, 1990.

Silva, Teresa Cristina Cerdeira da. "Mulheres e revolução: a cultura marialva posta em questão." *O Avesso do Bordado.* Lisboa: Caminho, 2000. 213-24.

Trotsky, Leon. *Women and the Family.* Ed. Caroline Lund. New York: Pathfinder, 1970.

Voloshinov, V. N. *Marxism and the Philosophy of Language.* Trans. L. Matejka and I. R. Titunik. New York: Seminar Press, 1973.

The Bureaucratic Tale of the Harbor Master and the Collector of Customs

José Saramago
Translated by
George Monteiro

When the Harbor Master entered his office and saw the sheet of blue paper on the table, he nodded slowly and grimaced so that no observer, even one ignorant of all that had gone before and the reasons behind the matter, would have had any doubt that the gesture was ironic, as if by its simple presence that paper had confirmed certain pleasurable and, by anticipation, tasty expectations. He sat down at the desk, and his first gesture, after having stretched smooth the coat-sleeves of his uniform and brushed away invisible dust from his gleaming stripes, was to push this piece of paper aside. Then, methodically, he examined and signed documents, made some telephone calls, answered some, gave out orders and instructions to the workers on his staff, received and talked with captains of two ships at anchor in the harbor, and, when it was time, went home to lunch, as always. After lunch, as she poured the coffee, his wife asked him if he had already taken care of the request, to which he replied that he would do it that afternoon. Indeed, on his return to his office, the Harbor Master, after having sat down and repeated the gesture of straightening his sleeves and brushing off his stripes, took up the paper that in the morning he had rejected without so much as reading it, settled on calligraphy, round and airy, that seemed appropriate to a seaman but contrasted with the miniscule, crawling handwriting of the petition, and he wrote, Taking into consideration its manifest ill-timing and that it seems deliberately to ignore that a reduced staff makes uncertain the provision of service, this petition is denied. He rang his bell and told the sailor who was acting as messenger, Go to the Customhouse and place this on the director's desk. When, hours later, at the end of his workday, the

Harbor Master returned home, his wife once again questioned him, Did you take care of it? and he responded, I took care of it. He didn't say how, because, as he understood the matter, confirmed through long observation, the separation of functions implies that in no instance does the knowledge of facts anticipate the moment of occurrence, for if it were otherwise there would be a dangerous alteration in the harmony of the world, which, given as it is to lack of reflection and caprice, would not survive for long.

On the following day the Collector of Customs entered his office and, spotting the petition, felt a pounding at his heart. He knew that the news in the dispatch was not good. As a candle in the wind bends and stiffens, the Harbor Master's handwriting scrawled across the paper and, dominating the petitioner's low, flat writing, evoked an image of the victorious fleet, hovering proudly in sight of the floating wrecks of its enemy. The Collector of Customs did not have to look to the reasoning of the dispatch; he looked only at the ominous word Denied. In an angry outburst he dashed the paper to the floor, only to retrieve it, soon afterwards, in humiliation. Then, keeping himself from thinking about the lot that compelled him, as the Head, to be a subordinate as well, he plunged into the work that had accumulated since the day before. He looked up rules and regulations, worked out percentages, calculated duties, issued instructions and gave out orders, received two dissatisfied exporters and one grateful importer, sent word to a freight agent to come back in a couple of days, and, when it was time for lunch, went home to eat, as usual. He was hardly in the door when his wife asked him, Well, and he answered, Denied. You mean to say that we are not going on vacation? Exactly, we are not going on vacation. And why not? Because we are short of help in Customs and in the Harbor. You are not part of the Harbor staff, you are Collector of Customs. So I am, but in the administrative hierarchy, Harbor Master outranks Collector of Customs. And now what? We shall have to wait until things improve. And in the meantime there will be no vacation? That's right, there'll be no vacation. And does that seem right to you? It doesn't seem to be right or wrong; I'd have done the same thing in his shoes. Why don't you write him a conciliatory letter, appealing to his feelings, telling him that you are very tired, that your wife has been dreaming about this vacation, things like that. I don't think it will work, but I can try it. And that's what he did. Returning to the Customhouse, he told the clerk that for the next hour he wasn't in for anyone. Then he locked himself in his director's office and set about writing his letter. Not a single letter, but various letters, because he did not like the first drafts; to him they seemed feckless, spineless, unpersuasive, and if they were unconvincing even to him, the one writing them, they would be even less capable of bringing about a change of mind in the Harbor Master. Finally he satisfied himself when, trembling out of pure compassion for himself, he found his eyes welling up as the words issued forth from his wounded psyche. Only if the Harbor Master's heart were made of stone would he be able to keep himself from giving in. He folded his letter, inserted it into an envelope, and called out to the messenger. Go to the Harbor Master's and place this on the Master's desk. Afterwards, alone, he leaned back in his chair and let himself go imaginatively to the place he had chosen for his longed-for vacation, for he wanted to believe that, before a letter steeped with humility, pungent, even straying off course, the Harbor Master, out of pure compassion, would annul his first dispatch and grant the request. At home, his wife, even without having read the letter, was of the same opinion and shared the same hope. To get a jump on things, she began to pack.

The Collector of Customs was right, but only up to a point. Indeed, on the next day the Harbor Master could not keep from shedding a tear or two while reading the letter—of course it was only a couple of tears, but, since we are dealing with the military, this effect is worth noting. If this commotion lasted any longer than the exact time it took him to dry his tears, there's no way of knowing, but his hand did not tremble when, in turn, he wrote the word that would shrivel and dry up the Collector's blossom of hope. It was No, that he was very sorry, that no one understood the situation better than he, but that the duties of his charge and the responsibilities that went with each of the two jobs did not permit him to decide unjustly by ignoring the letter and spirit of the law and the regulations pertaining to the case, which, under these circumstances, as in all other instances, call from those in public service a dignified example representing the sacrifice of particular interests in favor of the common good. For these reasons, and despite his regret at having to disappoint him, he stood by his dispatch and maintained his denial. He ordered the letter taken to the office of the Collector of Customs and—in sorrow—went home early. His wife thought it strange, grew worried, Don't say you're sick, now that the Collector of Customs has gone on vacation, and he responded, Neither am I sick nor will the Collector of Customs go on vacation. But then, what about the letter? It hurt me but regulations are there to be followed, I am merely the hand through which the law enacts its sentences. Do you think he'll come to accept that? He'll have no choice, countered the Harbor Master. He paused, then said, I'm going to lie down for a bit, maybe I'll get some sleep, and while I sleep, I'll forget. Wait a moment, let me unpack first.

The next day the Collector of Customs responded with a fiery letter in which he began with the accusation that the Harbor Master lacked a sense of institutional solidarity, and ended, feigning irony and eschewing all distance, by asking himself if he, the Harbor Master, did not constitute an acute case of clinical megalomania. Had his braid gone to his head, did he think he was an admiral, he remonstrated. The Harbor Master, his authority under attack, did not respond well to this impertinence. Again he wrote, threatening the Collector of Customs with disciplinary action, punishment, and suspension, but his threats went for naught, because the Collector of Customs came back insolently, Suspension, suspension, that's the way I'll take my vacation. There was, therefore, no disciplinary action, and the bitter exchange of correspondence continued. At some point all reference to the central reason for their discord ceased altogether—no longer was there any mention of vacations—the letters, on both sides, were now taken up with accusations, denunciations of ancient and recent mistakes, of slights, a complicated history of bureaucratic indolence and sloppiness, and, the worst thing of all, by insinuation at first, then with open displays of proof, of acts of active and passive corruption committed on both sides in the course of their jobs. Where did he get the money to buy a car? Where did he get the money to build his house? The Harbor Master no less than the Collector of Customs was going around with his head cut off, feverishly writing letters in which the very handwriting had undergone change, the Harbor Master's now level and small, the Collector's challenging, contentious. At home, each of the belligerents would get things off his chest by talking with his wife—The Harbor Master belongs in jail, The Collector of Customs should be in a madhouse—but her replies, while proffered with different intentions or inflected differently, were, word for word, the same. It was all over a vacation, to which the Harbor Master would reply, No, it was all the blame of an insubordinate, and the Collector of Customs, No, blame it all on an authoritarian. In an attempt that would turn out to be his last, the Collector of Customs changed his tune. Too late, as it turned out, if there ever had been a time when the Harbor Master's obstinate resistance could have been removed. To the imploring tone of the Collector of Customs, the Harbor Master came back with the words, dry and definitive, Stow it.

With this, the Collector of Customs committed suicide. On the way to the cemetery, the funeral procession paused before the Harbor Master's building and the Customhouse. In both places flags were flying at half-mast, and from the windows of each building the sailors and the civilians whose duties kept them from joining the cortege said their goodbyes to their chief. Crushed by this unexpected mourning, his wife was advised to stay behind, at home. After her friends had left, leaving behind their many recommendations that she must be patient and resign herself, she returned to her husband's goodbye note and reread it. This is what it said, Now you can go on vacation; never again will the Harbor Master deny requests. Then, thinking about dresses that might be suitable for dyeing black, the widow opened the chifferobe. There it was, with its shining braid, the uniform of the Harbor Master.

Reviews

José Saramago: O Ano de 1998. Colóquio-Letras 151/152 (Janeiro-Junho 1999)

Onésimo Teotónio Almeida

Colóquio-Letras, which in recent years has published a number of monographic issues on individual authors, has dedicated its most recent double-numbered edition (151/152) to the Nobel Prize winner José Saramago. Carried out under the direction of Maria Alzira Seixo, from the outset the issue's size and extravagant aspect make it quite impressive. To say that it is an edition of 500 pages about Saramago and his work is insufficient to describe the colorful and diverse profusion of essays interspersed with memorabilia, reproductions, and facsimiles of every kind. In reality, it is a luxurious and jubilant volume. Its title—*José Saramago: O Ano de 1998* (*José Saramago: The Year 1998*)—adeptly captures the celebratory tone that characterizes this collection.

In her presentation of and justification for this collective work, Maria Alzira Seixo notes that Portugal's first Nobel Prize winner stands in need of an essential critical bibliography, as there is only a limited number of published volumes dealing with his work. (It should be noted here, and with reason, that, curiously enough, the only existing bibliography of Saramago was published in German by Orlando Grossegesse.) The editor continues by saying that one aspect of this lack of critical work is that it has given rise to areas of Saramago's writings concerning which nothing, or at least no systematic research, has been done—"from his poetry to his short stories, from his chronicles to his novels, from his plays to his journals, from his writings of uncertain genre to his dramatic compositions written as opera libretti" (12). For various reasons, the editor's objective for this volume was to fill these important gaps and, even if not totally successful, the result has clearly validated the attempt, since all of us know very well how difficult such collective projects are in our literary and critical environment, just as we know that each of us is, in some way, a participant in them.

The essays nearly cover the whole of Saramago's work. "Saramago: uma elaboração em torno da metáfora da pedra" ("Saramago: an elaboration of the metaphor of the stone") by Luciana Stegagno-Picchio; an attempt at a framework for Saramago's poetry (Fernando J. B. Martinho); two studies concerning *Os Poemas Possíveis* (*Possible Poems*) (Maria de Lourdes Cidraes and Cristina Serôdio); two other studies about his chronicles (Isabel Moutinho and Adriana Alves de Paula Martins); two on his theatrical works (Luiz Francisco Rebello, Christine Zurbach and Graziella Seminara); and two on the nature of the voyage, voyages and the voyager (Tânia Franco Carvalhal and Maria Luísa Leal). After these, there are a variety of studies concerning his fiction, whether relative to specific works or to themes—e.g., "writing as the site of memory" (Teresa Cristina Cerdeira da Silva) and "the poetics of speech and writing" (Maria de Lourdes Câncio Martins)—some of which pay particular attention to history (Ana Paula Arnaut, Ettore Finazzi-Agrò, Isaura de Oliveira and Agripina Carriço Vieira), but also others that strike at the construction of fictional characters (Horácio Costa), "the two Saramagos" (Vítor Viçoso) and "the construction of the multitude" (Vibha Maurya). Still others are dedicated to the intersection between writing and life, the purpose of *The Year of the Death of Ricardo Reis* (Jean-Marc Moura), and also annotations for a reading of the notebook about the writing of *The Stone Raft* (by the editor of this volume), as well as essays dedicated to other minor writings (by Américo António Lindeza Diogo, who writes about *O Ano de 1993* [*The Year 1993*], and Margarida Braga Neves, who deals with Saramago's short fiction).

The most recent works by Saramago deserve particular individual attention: *The Gospel According to Jesus Christ* (Douwe Fokkema and Wladimir Krysinski), *Blindness* and *All the Names* (Isabel Pires de Lima, Leyla Perrone-Moisés, Ana Monner Sans, Adrián Huici and Jean Bessière). Finally, we have his journal, *Cadernos de Lanzarote* (*Lanzarote Notebooks*), about which the collection has two studies (Juan M. Ribera Llopis and Fernando Venâncio).

The collection's tone is serene and restrained, yet reverent and admiring. The occasion is celebratory: there is neither room for dissidence nor for problematic critical analyses. Even Fernando Venâncio, who habitually produces praises plaited with thorns, has in this volume a bridled and tame essay.

Intermingled with this richness of reflections and commentaries we find an unpublished short story and a notebook for *The Stone Raft* reproduced in facsimile, an "intimate" illustrated journal of Saramago's wife Pilar del Río from the days of the glorious celebration in Stockholm, many photographs and, last but not least, drawings by Bartolomeu Santos and photographs by Bário Piçarra. The list continues, beginning with a *Memorandum on the*

Nobel Week, original in its every aspect, and ending with reproductions of pages from various manuscripts.

It is rather difficult, if not practically impossible, to comment on all of the papers within this volume. To comment on some of them at the expense of others would be unfair. Taken as a whole, however, the essays present an overall unity in Saramago's writings, in particular those that address Saramago's so-called lesser works. It becomes apparent that the idea of the "two Saramagos," mentioned by others, but here specifically addressed by Vítor Viçoso, simply does not survive close scrutiny. Saramago clearly and ardently expresses his worldview, with its concomitant ethical dimension, through his writing. If he cannot be interpreted theoretically to be a strict, fundamentalist Marxist, this worldview spans his entire opus, as his writings are traversed by a line of thought and a string of ethical concerns included even in the speech he wrote for his Nobel Prize ceremony in Stockholm.

Saramago himself has disavowed all attempts to identify cleavages, ruptures, or breaks in his works, and has openly supported the critics who privilege readings of his writing where unity prevails: a unity of mind and heart, a unity of worldview and its ethical dimension, and a unity not to be belayed at the aesthetic level even when substantive stylistic changes in his writing can be identified. Saramago too makes note of his change of style in reference to *Levantado do Chão*, where he has pointed out that some twenty pages into the novel his writing developed new level of expression, the literary language that so much distinguishes him from all of his contemporaries. But stylistic evolution aside, Saramago yet supports criticism that favors analyses of the unity within his writings.

Hence, the inappropriateness of the postmodernist label that has frequently been attributed to Saramago. Though touched upon in some regard, overall within this volume of papers there is nothing that seriously supports a reading that would place such a label on him. Of course, the authors of these essays were concerned with other issues than an attempt to provide an overall assessment of Saramago's complete opus; nonetheless, the papers reinforce the impression that a unity exists beyond the aesthetic dimension where substantial narrative changes can be detected in his writings. Supported here is Saramago's often repeated claim that there is no split between the author and the narrator, a claim that implies a deeper concern on his part, namely, that there is no split between Saramago the citizen and Saramago the artist, nor between Saramago the journalist and

Saramago the novelist, nor even between Saramago the poet, Saramago the diarist and Saramago the columnist. This volume, having privileged the less studied areas of an impressive opus, has provided a great body of criticism in support of Saramago's contentions in this regard. As such, this collection becomes an important set of tools to help scholars of Saramago and the interested reader to reconstruct the author's heart and mind.

In sum, a volume of this kind is, in fact, a collector's item (and the author of this critique is pleased by the fact that for writing these few lines he will have the right to a copy of it). Its almost coffee-table book appearance should not, however, lead one to assume that it is merely a decorative work. In all actuality, it contains essays that everyone should read. If some of its collaborators had already relegated to other publications the most interesting commentaries that they possessed concerning Saramago's work, it should leave no doubt that the wave of new contributors to this collective discourse pertaining to Saramago's writings constitutes a more than sufficient reason for this special number of *Colóquio-Letras* to remain, both in the short and in the long term, *the* text for obligatory reference.

Carlos Reis. *Diálogos com José Saramago.* Lisboa: Caminho, 1998.

Mark J. Sabine

The etymology of the word *interview/entrever* permits an alternative definition to that of a two-way verbal exchange. To interview (from Latin, INTER- + *videre*, via Old French *entrevue*) could also be considered as the act of *viewing between* things: scrutinising the spaces amongst the obvious, the superficial, the familiar in order to perceive what remains undiscovered. When José Saramago describes the experience of being interviewed as one of being besieged in the "Encerramento" that he contributes to *Diálogos com José Saramago*, he appears to entertain such a definition: "[a]s perguntas, ou batem no muro que todo o entrevistado é, e ressaltam trazendo mecanicamente a resposta, ou abrem nele uma brecha" (161). An interviewer's key skill, Saramago indicates, is the ability to look between those parts of the wall already tested, to single out the less stable areas and to dispatch address questions which that the besieged interviewee cannot deflect. Where a wall is breached, "o entrevistado terá de olhar devagar para o interior da ferida, não porque não tenha apreendido a pergunta, mas porque necessitará apreender-se a si mesmo" (161): effectively, the interviewee must inter-view himself/herself. When Carlos Reis's interrogatory skills extend to leaving his "defesas ... em campo raso," Saramago finds himself "a perder-se tanto mais quanto mais supusesse ter-se achado" (162), and forced to contemplate formerly unrecognized aspects of himself and comment thereupon.

Casting Reis's volume as a blow-by-blow History of the Siege of José Saramago, Saramago evokes Raimundo Silva's discovery (in *The History of the Siege of Lisbon*) that each successive seizure of the citadel of History must be challenged in order for the true complexity of past events to be illuminated. The reader is encouraged to view Reis as a besieger of the accepted account of Portugal's Nobel laureate. Reis himself claims that the "refutação da existência de uma realidade singular ou de uma História irreversivelmente fixada" (23) is the rationale of all Saramago's fiction. The corollary conviction that a biographical profile of an author can be as much a "veículo de subversão de imagens estabelecidas" (26) as that the author's work itself is the *raison d'être* of this elegant, incisive and hugely significant contribution to the burgeoning stock of Saramago interviews.

Saramago is adamant that the vast and varied range of interviews he has given since publishing *Levantado do Chão* in 1980 does not invalidate attempts to uncover new perspectives. The meticulous investigations of Juan Arias in *El amor posible*, or of Baptista-Bastos in *Aproximação a um Retrato*, do not alter the fact that "todas as respostas são e hão-de ser sempre incompletas, que por muito que o entrevistado possa chegar a entrever-se, outro muro ao fundo estará a levantar-se por trás daquele que as perguntas fizeram mais ou menos cair" (162). Each successive appraisal of the author must yield to reappraisals that will draw out distinct, but equally authentic, answers to questions of the nature of the author and the signification of his/her work.

Even so, one might reasonably ask whether another full-length volume of conversations could make a substantial addition to the existing body of work. The answer, in the case of *Diálogos com José Saramago*, is a resoundingly positive one. The eight discussions, framed by individual contributions from interviewer and subject, make optimal use both of Reis's expertise as analyst and historian of literature and ideology in twentieth-century Portugal, and of his clearly abundant sympathy with Saramago's output and opinions. These qualities equip Reis to lift his interviews to the level of spirited, erudite dialogues. Not only is he at least as thorough as his predecessors, he also succeeds in eliciting from his subject answers that combine Saramago's customary discursive grace with a particular degree of precision. The result is as illuminating as it is entertaining. It is a study that will stimulate all categories of reader whom Reis seeks to address, "do leitor corrente dos romances de Saramago ao estudioso da sua obra, passando pelo professor que trabalha com os seus textos e o estudante que (supostamente) os lê" (9). In addition, this volume vindicates Saramago's claim that each new interview produces a new perspective on its subject, by inviting the reader to contextualize Saramago's *oeuvre* within the Portuguese literary canon while eliciting Saramago's own re-visiting and re-viewing of that canon.

Saramago himself pays tribute to Reis's literary knowledge and intellectual sympathy in equal measure. Reis, he claims, eyes him throughout the interviews "com uma doce e irónica curiosidade, porque conhece quase sempre a resposta antes que lhe seja dada, ou é capaz de adivinhar o mais interessante dela quando a não conheça toda" (161). Indeed, Reis has evidently done his homework. He arrives in Lanzarote armed not merely "de gravador, bloco-notas e benevolência" (31) but with a clutch of well-chosen quotes from Saramago's previous interviews and an impressive familiarity with the full gamut of the author's output over a fifty-year time span. He applies this knowledge shrewdly, readily proposing textual examples that elucidate the more opaque of Saramago's epigrammatic dicta. When he suggests that Saramago's contention that "a História é parcial e parcelar" (83) "[p]oderia ser uma epígrafe para o *Memorial do Convento*," the author enthusiastically concurs. It is easy to agree that Saramago's most widely read novel provides the most helpful and appropriate illustration of his desire to highlight the gaps in the historical record, and restore some of the data that previous historians rejected as irrelevant. The same discussion demonstrates Reis's sensitivity to the two seemingly contradictory impulses within Saramago's historiographical novels: an "eventual correcção ou compensação da História" and "uma reinvenção da História ou ... uma sua reinterpretação" (86). Although Reis understands how these impulses are harmonized, he nonetheless holds Saramago to an explanation.

Here and throughout the discussions, Reis scores not so much through his commendable persistence, but through knowing the answers he seeks, and formulating questions that will secure those answers promptly yet fully. Frequently, Reis marshals his inquiries into a sequence that allows Saramago to take the discussion first one way, then another, before being pinned down on a key point. The discussion of whether a text can ignore, defy or slavishly promote a given ideology is exemplary (72-75). Saramago's response ranges widely, from relating his belief that literature "não pode ... viver fora da ideologia" to a consideration of the phenomena of censorship, party policy and authors' political allegiances. While Reis welcomes these meanderings, he is not diverted from his ultimate goal: an explanation of how Saramago the author of texts that reject unstinting allegiance to a party line coexists with Saramago the Communist Party activist. Saramago's response is unequivocal: "mesmo que eu não esteja a dizer naquilo que escrevo 'Viva o Partido!,' é facílimo ao leitor atento entender que o autor que ele está a ler pensa de uma maneira determinada" (75).

Reis also manages to satisfy the demands of a heterodox readership through deft variations of his interviewing style, and by addressing key issues through an approach that permits one answer to be expressed in more than one manner. He tackles Saramago's representation of time in narrative fiction by quoting in full the author's description of "tempo poético" (from "Do canto ao romance, do romance ao canto," *Bulletin of Hispanic Studies* 71.1 [Jan. 1994]: 119-23) as "simultaneamente linear e labiríntico," and by then requesting an explanation of this oxymoron. His reward is a considerably more technical account of how "a escrita do romance permite ... dar [uma] sensação de linearidade, mas ao mesmo tempo encontrar nela [uma] espécie de turbilhão interno que é, pela sua própria definição, labiríntico" (135-36).

The epithet "labyrinthine" is not, however, applicable to *Diálogos com José Saramago*. The sequence of interviews progresses neatly from discussion of themes and ideologemes to consideration of the architecture of Saramago's writing and back again, but not before Reis's lucid prefatory essay, "O autor em construção," and the semi-biographical material of *Diálogo* 1 have provided a thorough induction into Saramago's world. The weightier topics of ideology and historiography are broached in *Diálogo* 2 and *Diálogo* 3. Here Reis—for the sake of the "harmonia global desta indagação" (79)—covers some well-trodden ground yet succeeds in opening up new avenues to an understanding of Saramago's conception of History. Quoting lines from the essay "História e Ficção" back at their author, Reis is rewarded with the beautiful image of time as a canvas upon which "tudo está ao lado de tudo, numa espécie de caos, como se o tempo fosse comprimido e além de comprimido espalmado ... como se os acontecimentos, os factos, as pessoas, tudo isso aparecesse ali não diacronicamente arrumado, mas numa outra arrumação caótica, na qual depois seria preciso encontrar um sentido" (80). With this conception of an obviously unrealizable representation of the totality of the past, Saramago presents another novel demonstration of how "a História é parcial e é parcelar."

The "questões ... mais técnicas" (91) of *Diálogo* 4 allow Saramago to assess the mechanics of novelistic production, including his attempts to "traduzir uma simultaneidade ... dizer tudo ao mesmo tempo" in order to present his view of history in a narrative format, and his strategy, in *Levantado do Chão*, of writing "como se eu estivesse a contar às pessoas que me contaram as suas histórias essas mesmas histórias" in order to expose how our perceptions of past events are conditioned by the subjectivity of their participants and witnesses. *Diálogo* 5 investigates his output in other genres in roughly chronological order, and leads into *Diálogo* 6's consideration of the inevitable generic overlap between the novel and, in particular, the philosophical or historical essay. Together, these discussions test Reis's thesis that Saramago is less a jack of all literary trades and more a novelist who "irrompeu (o termo não é excessivo) para a escrita do romance" only after a thirty-year apprenticeship of writing journalism and poetry. This assessment—and Reis's identification of the "ensaio de romance" *Manual of Painting and Calligraphy* as the last of the formative works—are only half endorsed by Saramago. As he prefers to put it, "[p]rovavelmente não sou um romancista; provavelmente eu sou um ensaísta que precisa de escrever romances porque não sabe escrever ensaios" (46).

Frequently, Reis concludes a discussion by asking Saramago to comment on current discursive commonplaces: the End of History, the Death of the Novel, the Death of God, the Death of Ideology. It is as refreshing to read Saramago's droll confession that "eu tenho notado que nós temos uma tendência para dizer que as coisas morrem" as it is to be told, half a page later, that to talk of the death of ideology "é o discurso mais ideológico que há" (76). *Diálogo* 7's review of matters religious, political and moral adds intellectual meat to these bones, before Reis uses the concluding *Diálogo virtual* to put Saramago in dialogue with his literary ancestors. Replacing questions with quotations from Garrett, Antero, Eça, Pessoa and Carlos de Oliveira among others, Reis provides a lighthearted culmination to the serious scholarly undertaking of gauging Saramago's position within the Portuguese literary canon. From his opening essay onwards, Reis has remarked similarities between Saramago's works and those of Eça (9) and Garrett (117). His chosen quotations now serve to reinforce a notion of Saramago as heir to a specifically Portuguese tradition of literary radicalism: not simply a writer who rejects the "idiotice do Ricardo Reis" that claims that "[s]ábio é o que se contenta com o espectáculo do mundo" (160), but also a man passionate in defence of his country's cultural individuality, yet dismayed by its prevailing "mesquinhez," which, he believes, still justifies Garrett's observation that "a terra é pequena, e a gente que nela vive não é grande" (145-46).

Yet the breadth of Reis's inquiries, and the detailed responses they provoke, prevent such an appraisal of Saramago from becoming reductive. On page 70 Saramago warns that writers whose work is not continuously re-examined and debated "vão a caminho da invisibilidade. O Camões transformou-se numa coroa de louros e num olho fechado, e o Fernando Pessoa é um chapéu, uns óculos e um bigode." No doubt he recognizes that he is himself in peril of being reduced to a Nobel medal, horn-rimmed specs and a Lanzarote suntan. By acquiescing to besiegement by an expert interviewer who leaves no stone unturned, Saramago grants his readers and admirers greatly enhanced opportunities for a more sophisticated reformulation of his self and his work.

Maria Alzira Seixo. *Lugares da ficção em José Saramago.* Col. Temas Portugueses. Lisboa: Imprensa Nacional-Casa da Moeda, 1999.

Ana Sofia Ganho

Maria Alzira Seixo is without a doubt one of the foremost critics of the works of José Saramago in Portugal and abroad, as well as his most assiduous reader since the times when the name "Saramago" did not command the praise it does today. *Lugares da ficção* confirms this, as it includes essays both on texts by Saramago, the publication dates of which go as far back as 1966, and on others as recent—as of January 1999—as his then-latest novel *All the Names.*

This volume consists of a collection of short to medium length texts previously presented to the public in the form of chapters of books, papers given at conferences, and articles published in academic journals and in the weekly periodical *Jornal de letras.* The exception is the last essay, written with this book in mind. Thus, *Lugares* does not constitute a whole, nor were the texts re-edited with a unified context in mind. The main consequence is the frequent reiteration of information on the writer and the chronology of his books, which could perhaps have been avoided by including this information only in the introduction instead.

Lugares opens with a chronological summary illustrating tensions and preoccupations in Saramago's writings, which Seixo links to questions of genre, by pointing out the writer's shift from the chronicle and poetry to the novel. In this process, the idea of progression or qualitative evolution is implied; Seixo, contrary to a general and unnamed number of other critics, does not dismiss Saramago's poetry as unworthy literary attempts, considering them instead as representing points of departure for a reflection on the literary experience developed further in the writers's works: from the genre of the chronicle, the fundamental characteristic Seixo retains is that it is a form of "journey," something that later will be said about the novel as well. While analyzing the four main novels that had been published by the time of her essay's original publication in 1987 (*Levantado do Chão, Baltasar and Blimunda, The Year of the Death of Ricardo Reis* and *The Stone Raft*), Seixo draws two important conclusions, one regarding the constitutive nature of the category of time in Saramago's "novelistic form," insofar as it is through the writer's particular conception of the conjunction between time and human agency that alterity becomes a platform for dialogue; the second conclusion points to fiction as the best way to access "truth," making the novel "the most adequate genre to the expression of the world and of mankind" (39).

The following essay, on *The History of the Siege of Lisbon*, opens a series tackling the issues of historical representation and history writing, while a few other essays later in the volume turn to questions of structural organization. Ultimately, as becomes more visible towards the end of *Lugares*, the critic aims at placing her analysis and Saramago's literary production within the broader, international context of contemporary fiction, which signals her background in comparative literature, but also serves to "legitimize" Saramago's work. With regard to the novels included in the first category, Seixo does not consider them "historical novels," as she makes sure to state as clearly as possible; interestingly, it is on the basis of the effect of reading, as a type of uncanniness, that she discusses, instead, similarities with the fantastic in the representation of that "other" time (54). In the essay that follows, however, the critic does not develop the analysis of temporality hinted at earlier. Towards the end, a few remarks, stylistic in nature, are made, pointing out some implications of the punctuation and parataxis in the text.

Thus, the attempt to theorize an approach does not quite follow through and will only be resumed, albeit all too briefly, in the essay "José Saramago e o tempo da ficção." Nevertheless, history is examined as a subject of writing: with regard to the ambiguity between the "written" and "writing," and therefore also with regard to the potential for alteration and failure, such as in the case of the insertion of the "not" in *The History of the Siege of Lisbon*; as a sum of other, smaller, collective, and individual writings/stories; from the perspective of the "orality of writing," and the link between prosody ("ritmo") and the collective, a context where the proverb is seen as a "voice of the times." A bit of wisdom that surely deserves more of an elaboration, and which is inadequate as an ending, is that History touches closely upon literature (82). As a result, history is reduced to literature, if not even eclipsed altogether in the process.

"Factualidade da ficção: Ricardo Reis e Pessoa em Saramago" proceeds in a seemingly opposite way insofar as it assumes writing as fiction and searches for the factual reality in it. Things are not quite as simple as that, however. The critic's focus is on a certain notion of "fact" as the basis for the fictional process of the novel *The Year of the Death of Ricardo Reis*, and the relation of such facts to the mechanisms at work in a historical novel. Seixo further uses Lubomir Doležel's notion of "literary transduction," and Alan Bailin's "semantic deviation" to illuminate the model of historical reading at stake here. Nevertheless, it would have been helpful to use other terms to break the circularity of words like "fiction" and "fictional fact," and to investigate further the (non)existence of Herbert Quain as an example of the play around "fact," especially given Borges's legacy in this matter. This constitutes the main problem of the essay, detracting from the validity and interest of what the critic is arguing.

Seixo returns briefly to the role of history with "Saramago e o tempo da ficção," placed towards the end of the book. The criteria behind the organization of *Lugares* are clearly more chronological than thematic, or the piece would have been grouped with the earlier essays devoted to the same subject in *The History of the Siege of Lisbon*, *Baltasar and Blimunda*, and *The Year of the Death of Ricardo Reis*. This constitutes after all the bulk of Seixo's reflection.

"Crónica sobre um livro anunciado," and "Os espelhos virados para dentro," both on *Blindness*, are part of the second, distinct group of essays that are not focused on historical representation. The latter provides the depth of analysis of the narrative and constitutive process of this novel that the first one, probably for reasons of readership, does not include.

Seixo first focuses on a few "clusters of meaning." These are, namely, the allegorical level of meaning, the way characters are developed, the symbolism of colors, and the role of women, in this order. All these aspects are explained in a straightforward manner except that of the allegorical meaning, which in the end might be read as a sign of Seixo's difficulty in interpreting Saramago's style and allegorical language in *Blindness*, a complex and intriguing novel.

The preoccupation with the meta-fictional dimension is revealed in the analysis of the narrator's presence and function, its "enunciative presence," which is unrelated to its role of *telling* the story, but rather sets the stage for the distinction structuring the narrative: the textual vs. the narrative beginning, or "incipit." The critic insists on the importance of symbolic elements such as color to link "textual" elements unrelated to the plot to those elements directly related to the story line of the text. One might say that, for all the emphasis placed on their significance, colors end up not signifying much in the end, but that is precisely Seixo's point. The fact that reality is not described in different terms in the beginning and at the end of the book leads her to conclude that the writer can only warn the reader about the results and consequences of the given situation, but is powerless to fix anything just because his characters have recovered their sight. Such seem to be the limitations of fiction and the true "allegorical" significance of this book. However, the fact that the main characters keep a certain degree of spiritual awareness gained from their blindness certainly does not leave matters "the same" as at the beginning.

Another issue of great importance mentioned is the relation of Saramago's narrator to the narrators of both Romantic and postmodernist novels. Unfortunately, Seixo does not return to this topic, and thus one is left with an important question, and no answer in sight as to how she would relate Saramago's "narrational superiority" both to Romanticism ("ironic modality") and to postmodernism.

Instead, the critic recalls the distinction between the textual and narrative "incipit," stressing the gap between the two (rendered as the odd-sounding "descoincidência," a nonexistent word in Portuguese), which she sees as producing a multiplicity of discourses that is responsible for the originality of the book, insofar as it questions the very category of the novel (109). It is as if, by insisting on the clear separation of narrative and "digression," the critic momentarily forgot, against her better judgment, that the history of the novel indeed incorporates a reflection on the genre just as much as frequent interruptions of the act of telling. At another level, when discussing the episode of the characters' bathing in the rain, Seixo observes that in this passage the narration has more than one mode, even though she has stated earlier that the narrator is "omniscient and testimonial" (109), without ever tracing the varying degrees of his "knowledge" and lack thereof.

Another analytical focus is the pause in the narrated action, and the functional role it plays, equated literally with those moments when the characters' movements are limited to increasingly more confined spaces. Seixo's analysis is valuable and meticulous, and is complemented by the two sections following it, which concentrate on the characters' movements as organizing the narrative action, and, conversely, on scenes of immobility. In this context, the ekphrastic mode and the meta-commentary on writing become more visible, as the critic demonstrates through an intelligent choice of scenes upon which to comment. Unfortunately, for the most part only general conclusions are drawn, when the reading could have been enhanced by a review of theoretical texts on ekphrasis (e.g., the relationship between writing, description and movement on the one hand, and the traditional immobility of painting vs. resistance to linguistic apprehension and temporality on the other).

Between the conclusion, and a brief return to the role of history in Saramago's fiction, Seixo includes a reflection on *All the Names*, "O caso da mulher desconhecida." She starts by pointing out Saramago's use of Baroque techniques and traits. These aesthetic presuppositions have their natural continuation in the reflection on Symbolism, a rather narrow but usual one, as in previous moments in *Lugares*, which indicates a clear and exclusionary opposition between the Baroque and Symbolism. The brief analysis of the spaces visited in the novel is subordinated to the principle that the main character follows a journey ("percurso") which is that of the quest for knowledge, the meaning behind a name, and existence. At the narrative level, Seixo remarks on its greater distance from the characters' world, due in part to the fact that the narrator has both a more descriptive function as well as a solitary existence, generating a more intense inner monologue and a less fluid sentence.

Conveying a particular and specific message of redeeming social value to the readers is always part of Saramago's overarching purpose, Seixo argues, even if the "daily life" is absent from his novels and the tendency to use "allegorical" and "abstract" language can make such a transparent reading difficult. This is compensated, in the critic's eyes, by Saramago's use of "concrete," or easily identifiable, settings (128), as well as of powerful human feelings and emotions. Instead of seeing this "ambiguity" between the "lesson" to be drawn and the fact of its encryption as a problem, Seixo considers it as a sign of the careful architecture of the novels, best seen in the meta-fictional reflection Saramago carries out on writing, representation, and time. The conclusion lies in the peculiar, instantly recognizable pattern of "Saramago's sentence," which seizes the author's preoccupations, establishing a clear causal link between form and content (130-31).

The last essay, "Lugar e deslocação em José Saramago," was written in 1999 as a conclusion to *Lugares da ficção*. It reevaluates Saramago's work, once again from the poetry to the chronicles, the short stories, and the novels. This time, however, the novels are seen through the prism of a poetics of "place." The shift from a poetics of time to one of place is further justified by invoking Paul Ricoeur's work. Gradually it becomes clear that the multiple meanings of "lugar" are better understood in relation to dislocation, process, and even journey through the "ideas and the poetic motifs" and "the gesture of knowing" (167), all signs that Seixo's reading has turned more hermeneutic over time.

Upon reaching the end of *Lugares*, one has to wonder what the overall goals of the author were, and for whom the book was originally destined. Seixo is a well-known academic in Portuguese and Comparative Literature in Portugal who, very clearly, also enjoys reading José Saramago. From the academic or scholarly point of view, the book pursues questions fundamental to the original work of this contemporary Portuguese writer through a patient close reading. It would have been desirable, nevertheless, for Seixo to sustain a more thorough discussion of the concepts, implications, and theoretical contexts of the critics she invokes, specifically regarding Doležel's and Ricoeur's hypotheses on history and fiction; the same applies to Compagnon's and De Certeau's. Finally, the seamless transition from chronicle to novel begs further investigation, since the subjects of enunciation in the two genres are not equivalent. Acknowledgment of the "polemic" around the status and figure of the narrator (regarding this polemic, see Abel Barros Baptista's article in *Ler* 43 [1998]) would also have added to a constructive discussion of an important topic in Seixo's writings.

Some of the book's formatting might have been presented better had the work been revised thoroughly: small mistakes (a mysterious digit occasionally appearing at the bottom of the page), quotations not followed by a page number, bibliographies not thorough and uniform, book titles given in distinct styles. These problems, however, do not take away from the importance of *Lugares*. It goes without saying that it deserves a place of its own in the critical literature about Saramago (which is, surprisingly, not so abundant after all, particularly if we consider longer studies), as it draws both the untrained eye, as well as the more critical one, to fundamental issues raised by this unsettling body of work.

Moreover, *Lugares* incorporates an undeniable component of pleasure. The long, dense, at times beautiful, though not always intelligible, passages are to some extent a result of the desire not to exclude from the reading the pleasurable impression the book caused on the particular reader that Seixo is. And to have some of those intricate sentences and ideas developed further, perhaps avoiding the long parentheses, would have worked to the critic's advantage, as well as to the reader's. Helas, to convey the "joy of reading" has become an increasingly difficult task. Therefore, if a larger public begins to read a few books by Saramago, *Lugares da ficção* will have been worth while.

Beatriz Berrini. *Ler Saramago: O Romance*. Lisboa: Caminho, 1998.

José N. Ornelas

Even before José Saramago was awarded the Nobel Prize for literature in 1998, many critical works on the author had already appeared, providing invaluable insights into one of the most fascinating and acclaimed Portuguese writers of the twentieth century. Among these, Beatriz Berrini's *Ler Saramago: O Romance* (1998) must be singled out. Berrini, a well-respected Eça de Queirós scholar, published her collection of critical essays in the same year that Saramago was honored by the Swedish Academy with the world's highest literary prize. Her text is constituted by seven long chapters analyzing the author's work, followed by a short epilogue, an interview with José Saramago, and a series of photographs interposed between the critical section of her book and the interview. Although the majority of the photographs are in color, a few are in black and white, especially some where the author is the object of the photograph. There is a two-fold purpose for the inclusion of the photographs in Berrini's text: firstly, to show Saramago in his natural environment, starting with his humble beginnings in rural Ribatejo and ending up with photographs that reveal his growing literary prestige prior to his being distinguished with the Nobel Prize; and, secondly, to link some of the author's novels to the spaces that happen to be the focus of the stories told in those narratives. The later group of photographs depicts life in the Alentejo of *Levantado do Chão*, the opulence associated with the nobility in eighteenth-century Portugal, as it is referenced in *Baltasar and Blimunda*, the many different images of Portugal in the middle 1930s that relate to the oppressive climate of fascism in *The Year of the Death of Ricardo Reis*, and, finally, a certain Lisbon ambience that reminds the reader of the city's Muslim past. Medieval Lisbon is one of the privileged cultural, social and political sites of Saramago's *The History of the Siege of Lisbon*.

Berrini's choice of photographs, which imbue specific spaces, geography and also the Portuguese nation with a set of traits, images and values, is intimately related to her selection of Saramago's novels for analysis. Each of the three novels mentioned above, *Levantado do Chão*, *Baltasar and Blimunda* and *The Year of the Death of Ricardo Reis*, is the object of study of a particular chapter. In these three chapters, Berrini offers various critical perspectives on Saramago's novels through an exploration of their ideological, historical and cultural frameworks. She argues convincingly that her critical reading or, as she puts it, her "voyage" through Saramago's works, is also a voyage through Portugal's past and present. Indeed, her main critical interest is in those novels that offer fascinating and provocative insights into the complex relationships that have shaped and are the foundation for the construction of Portuguese national and individual identity. Although she is of the opinion that *The Gospel According to Jesus Christ* marks a turning point in Saramago's evolution from a novelist grounded in his roots to one that veers into more universal avenues, exemplified by such novels as *Blindness* and *All the Names*, she nevertheless concentrates most of her critical energy on those novels where Saramago tries to define, articulate and highlight the rich complexities of those roots and, in the process, challenge and question the figures of authority who insist on denying that heritage is subject to a constant interplay of continuity and transformation.

The book also includes four other chapters that do not focus on just one of Saramago's novels: the introductory chapter and three other essays. One of the latter concentrates on the crucial and powerful role that women play in the Portuguese writer's novels; it is entitled, unsurprisingly, "Mulher, Mulheres" ("Woman, Women"). Another is an in-depth examination of the relationship between the titles of the novels and the themes and topics that are developed in them, which is coupled with a comparison of the title with the novel's close in order to shed further light on the choice of title and to suggest further readings and interpretations of the work. Still another interprets critically the magical and fantastic qualities of many of the author's narratives and relates them to an allegorical bent present in several of them.

Berrini does attempt to give the reader a broad picture of Saramago's novels by exploring not only the many complex relationships between the narrator and the narrative itself, and but also between the narrator, reader and characters. She also delves into the many dialogical connections between Saramago's narratives and other literary and non-literary works, especially the Bible and classical texts of Portuguese literature. However, it is still quite obvious that her central focus is on the representation of history in the author's narratives and on the manner by which transformations in history continuously redefine the configuration both of the Portuguese space and its cultural practices and, consequently, of the Portuguese identity. Many critics before Berrini, including Teresa Cristina Cerdeira da Silva in her pioneering book, *José Saramago entre a história e a ficção: uma saga de portugueses* (1989), had already analyzed the link between fiction and history in the author's novels and his interest in revising Portuguese history through a process of recuperation of the political and cultural significance of historical memory on behalf of those who had never occupied a place in the official record. In a sense, Berrini, like many other scholars of Saramago's vast literary production, seems attracted to particular aspects of the author's works: his reading of history from the perspective of those without history, his mapping of the historical attempts of the voiceless to take into their own hands the transformation of their own circumstances, his undermining and subversion of the ideological fictions by which the dominant classes can and do script and trope the identities, values and cultures of the oppressed, as well as dismiss their cultural productions as inconsequential. Even Berrini's choice of novels for critical examination shows exactly where her interest lies. She barely touches upon *Blindness* or *All the Names*, two novels that she considers to have greater universal and global appeal than the others, because they are more abstract and more concerned with seeking solutions for the problems that affect the world through a discussion of ideas. Her preference for those among Saramago's novels that (re)imagine Portugal as a configuration of political, ideological, social and cultural intersections in need of continuous historical reappraisal is more than evident in *Ler Saramago.*

In *Ler Saramago: O Romance*, Berrini reveals not only her in-depth knowledge of biblical narrative through the many connections that she establishes between Saramago's novels and the Bible, but also shows her familiarity with classical, as well as contemporary literary texts. Moreover, she is conversant with both Portuguese and Brazilian literatures. Her many literary references make for an entertaining and fascinating commentary, although at times her ability to converse intelligently with other texts forces her into digressions that frequently obfuscate the task at hand, that is, the analysis of Saramago's narratives. Her reflections on the limits and/or the relationship between fiction and history that appear throughout *Ler Saramago* are a case in point. For example, on pages 12-26 she reflects on this particular topic by citing the views of several important Portuguese writers, including Eça de Queirós, Oliveira Martins, Alexandre Herculano, and Fernão Lopes. Reading about these writers' views of the borderlines between fiction and history is indeed enriching and enthralling, but ultimately her digressions shortchange Saramago's views on the same matter. She is able to inscribe the author within a very old Portuguese tradition in which history and fiction vie with each other for the representation of Portuguese reality, but she would have accomplished much more by reflecting comparatively on the subject, that is, by showing the similarities and the differences between Saramago and the authors mentioned previously. Such an approach would contextualize more effectively the relationship between Saramago and other Portuguese writers, and it certainly would give a greater meaning to those links, while also showing how the Nobel laureate has challenged established views on the limits between history and fiction.

In Berrini's provocative and incisive book on Saramago, there is what I would consider a very glaring omission. Although already by 1998 a remarkable number of articles and books had appeared analyzing and theorizing about the vast literary production of the Portuguese writer, none of these articles or books is really incorporated in *Ler Saramago.* Berrini's very short bibliography includes only two of these many reference works; both are cited in her text, but neither one can be considered a major contribution to the understanding of Saramago's literary production. I do not have a plausible explanation for this omission, except for the possible fact that Berrini did not want to be influenced by others in her very personal reading of Saramago's novels. However, I am also fully aware that my explanation is probably without any substance, since *Ler Saramago,* in many ways, has definite affinities with other critical works that had appeared prior to 1998, which clearly indicates that Berrini was very much conscious of this body of critical work. Whatever the reason for the omission, it undoubtedly detracts from the value of her critical text. Many of Berrini's arguments would have been strengthened and reinforced if she had dialogued with other critics of Saramago's work, especially those that have dealt with the limits between fiction and history, the relationship between fiction and the real world, the many complex links in the triad narrator/text/reader, or, as Saramago would prefer, *author/text/reader*, the dialogical connections with other texts, and finally the incorporation of magical and fantastic elements in the writer's works. The lack of an inter-critical dialogue or other critical referents in

Berrini's text weakens some of her arguments; some of her positions and many of the enigmas present in the writer's novels would have been clarified through a dialogue with other critics.

As I have mentioned before, Berrini's *Ler Saramago* traces a voyage through Saramago's novels with special emphasis on those that privilege incursions into the construction of Portugal and Portuguese identity. She is very eclectic in her approach to the author's works, given that she incorporates many critical perspectives into her discussion. Her book, notwithstanding its apparent lack of integration with the voices and ideas of others who have written on Saramago, offers an invaluable venue for the understanding of Saramago as a novelist. Berrini's text, written in a very clear and accessible language, is a significant contribution to the already substantial body of critical work on the Portuguese Nobel laureate. The book engages intelligently with Saramago's novels at the level of the literary and, at the level of the extra-literary, it dialogues with and explores the conceptual concerns that crosscut the articulation and the (re)imagining of Portuguese history and identity in Saramago's novels.

Bibliography of José Saramago

Anna Klobucka

I. Works by José Saramago

Only original Portuguese editions of Saramago's works are listed in this bibliography, and therefore no mention is made of their multiple reprintings (except where the new edition was significantly revised or augmented, for instance by adding a foreword); Saramago's Brazilian editions are likewise omitted. English translations that were published both in the United Kingdom and the United States are represented here by their first US editions.

For a comprehensive list of Saramago's miscellaneous publications, including essays (those uncollected in volumes), interviews, and translations, see the bibliography in Orlando Grossegesse, *Saramago Lesen. Werk, Leben, Bibliographie* (Berlin: tranvía/Walter Frey, 1999).

Novels

Terra do Pecado. Lisboa: Minerva, 1947. Second edition (with a foreword by the author): Lisboa: Caminho, 1997.

Manual de Pintura e Caligrafia. Lisboa: Moraes, 1976. Second edition (with a foreword by Luís de Sousa Rebelo): Lisboa: Caminho, 1983. English translation by Giovanni Pontiero, *Manual of Painting and Calligraphy.* Manchester: Carcanet, 1993.

Levantado do Chão. Lisboa: Caminho, 1980.

Memorial do Convento. Lisboa: Caminho, 1982. English translation by Giovanni Pontiero, *Baltasar and Blimunda.* San Diego: Harcourt Brace Jovanovich, 1987.

O Ano da Morte de Ricardo Reis. Lisbon: Caminho, 1984. English translation by Giovanni Pontiero, *The Year of the Death of Ricardo Reis.* San Diego: Harcourt Brace Jovanovich, 1991.

A Jangada de Pedra. Lisboa: Caminho, 1986. English translation by Giovanni Pontiero, *The Stone Raft.* New York: Harcourt Brace, 1995.

História do Cerco de Lisboa. Lisboa: Caminho, 1989. English translation by Giovanni Pontiero, *The History of the Siege of Lisbon.* New York: Harcourt Brace, 1996.

O Evangelho Segundo Jesus Cristo. Lisboa: Caminho, 1991. English translation by Giovanni Pontiero, *The Gospel According to Jesus Christ.* New York: Harcourt Brace, 1994.

Ensaio sobre a Cegueira. Lisboa: Caminho, 1995. English translation by Giovanni Pontiero, *Blindness.* New York: Harcourt Brace, 1998.

Todos os Nomes. Lisboa: Caminho, 1997. English translation by Margaret Jull Costa, *All the Names.* New York: Harcourt Brace, 1999.

A Caverna. Lisboa: Caminho, 2000.

Short Stories and Narratives

Objecto Quase [short stories]. Lisboa: Moraes, 1978.

All stories from *Objecto Quase* were translated into English by Giovanni Pontiero and published independently in the following venues:

"Centaur" ["Centauro"]. *Passport to Portugal.* Huntingdon, Cambridgeshire: Passport, 1994. 5-19. Reprinted in *The Literary Review* 38.4 (Summer 1995): 543-556.

"The Chair" ["Cadeira"]. *Passport to Portugal.* Huntingdon, Cambridgeshire: Passport, 1994. 136-151.

"Embargo." *Cimarron Review* 110 (Jan. 1995): 10-18.

"Reflux" ["Refluxo"] and "Revenge" ["Desforra"]. *Frontiers (Leopard III).* London: Harvill, 1994. 293-304 and 305-307.

"Things" ["Coisas"]. *The Translator's Dialogue: Giovanni Pontiero.* Eds. Pilar Orero and Juan C. Sager. Amsterdam and Philadelphia: John Benjamins, 1997. 187-243.

"O Ouvido" [short story]. *Poética dos Cinco Sentidos.* Lisboa: Bertrand, 1979.

Viagem a Portugal [travel narratives]. Lisboa: Círculo de Leitores, 1981. English translation by Amanda Hopkinson and Nick Caistor, *Journey to Portugal: In Pursuit of Portugal's History and Culture.* New York: Harcourt, 2000.

"O conto burocrático do capitão do porto e do director da alfândega" [short story]. *O escritor* 7 (1996): 81-84. English translation by George Monteiro, "The Bureaucratic Tale of the Harbor Master and the Collector of Customs." *Portuguese Literary and Cultural Studies* 6 (Spring 2001).

O conto da ilha desconhecida [novella]. Lisboa: Assírio & Alvim, 1997. English translation by Margaret Jull Costa, *The Tale of the Unknown Island.* New York: Harcourt Brace, 1999.

Crónicas, Columns, and Diaries

Deste Mundo e do Outro [contributions to *A Capital*]. Lisboa: Arcádia, 1971.
A Bagagem do Viajante [contributions to *A Capital* and *Jornal do Fundão*]. Lisboa: Futura, 1973.
As Opiniões que o DL teve [contributions to *Diário de Lisboa*]. Lisboa: Seara Nova-Futura, 1974.
Os Apontamentos [contributions to *Diário de Notícias*]. Lisboa: Seara Nova, 1976.
Cadernos de Lanzarote. Diário-I. Lisboa: Caminho, 1994.
Cadernos de Lanzarote. Diário-II. Lisboa: Caminho, 1995.
Cadernos de Lanzarote. Diário-III. Lisboa: Caminho, 1996.
Cadernos de Lanzarote. Diário-IV. Lisboa: Caminho, 1997.
Cadernos de Lanzarote. Diário-V. Lisboa: Caminho, 1998.

Poetry

Os Poemas Possíveis. Lisboa: Portugália, 1966. Second edition (revised and with a foreword by the author): Lisboa: Caminho, 1981.
Provavelmente Alegria. Lisboa: Livros Horizonte, 1970.
O Ano de 1993. Lisboa: Futura, 1975 .

Plays

A Noite. Lisboa: Caminho, 1979.
Que Farei Com Este Livro?. Lisboa: Caminho, 1980.
A Segunda Vida de Francisco de Assis. Lisboa: Caminho, 1987.
In Nomine Dei. Lisboa: Caminho, 1993.

II. Selected Critical Studies of José Saramago's Work

In the last two decades, and particularly since the mid-1980s, a great many critical essays on the work of José Saramago have been published in Portuguese (as well as in Spanish, German, Italian, French, and English). Two recently published bibliographies catalogue this immense output: in addition to the abovementioned volume by Grossegesse, the interested reader will do well to consult the issue of the journal *Vértice* 91 (Jun.-Set. 1999), which contains a very extensive (although qualified as "fatally incomplete") "Bibliografia sobre José Saramago" by Teresa Liparulo (69-95). I gratefully acknowledge my indebtedness to both authors in preparing the following selected bibliography. The first section lists books and unpublished dissertations, in any language, dedicated exclusively to Saramago's work; the second, in keeping with the general orientation of this issue, is limited to critical studies in English published in journals and collected volumes.

Books and Theses

Allemand, Maria Lúcia de Oliveira. "Tempo e voz: o percurso trágico-ideológico na narrativa de José Saramago." Diss. Univ. de São Paulo, 1996.

Arias, Juan. *José Saramago: el amor posible.* Barcelona: Planeta, 1998.

Arnaut, Ana Paula. Memorial do Convento*: história, ficção e ideologia.* Coimbra: Fora do Texto, 1996.

Azinheira, Teresa, and Maria da Conceição Coelho. *Uma leitura de* Memorial do Convento. Venda Nova: Bertrand, 1995.

Baptista-Bastos. *José Saramago: a aproximação a um retrato.* Lisboa: Dom Quixote, 1996.

Basto, José Moura de. *Deus é grande e José Saramago o Seu evangelista.* Lisboa: J. Basto, 1993.

Berrini, Beatriz, ed. *José Saramago: uma homenagem.* São Paulo: EDUC, 1999.

———. *Ler Saramago: o romance.* Lisboa: Caminho, 1998.

Calbucci, Eduardo. *Saramago: um roteiro para os romances.* Cotia, São Paulo: Ateliê, 1999.

Ceccucci, Piero, ed. *Viaggio intorno al Convento di Mafra: dal* Memoriale del convento *di José Saramago alla* Blimunda *di Azio Corghi: atti del seminario italo-portoghese.* Milano: Guerini, 1991.

Coelho, Maria da Conceição, and Teresa Azinheira. Memorial do convento *de José Saramago.* Mem Martins: Europa-América, 1997.

Costa, Dias da. *O evangelista ateu: resposta ao Evangelho de Saramago.* Rio de Mouro: Argon, 1993.

Costa, Horácio. *José Saramago. O período formativo.* Lisboa: Caminho, 1998.

Fernandes, Ceres Costa. *O narrador plural na obra de José Saramago.* São Luís: Univ. Federal do Maranhão, 1990.

Grossegesse, Orlando. *Saramago lesen: Werk, Leben, Bibliographie.* Berlin: tranvía/Walter Frey, 1999.

Jones, Haydn Tiago. "*Memorial do Convento*: A Textual Construction of Myth and History." M.A. thesis. Univ. of North Carolina at Chapel Hill, 1990.

Júlio, Maria Joaquina Nobre. Memorial do Convento *de José Saramago: subsídios para uma leitura.* Lisboa: Replicação, 1999.

Lanciani, Giulia, ed. *José Saramago. Il bagaglio dello scrittore.* Roma: Bulzoni, 1996.

Lopondo, Lilian, ed. *Saramago: segundo terceiros.* São Paulo: Humanitas, 1998.

Lucas, Ana Maria, and Fátima Vieira Correia. Memorial do Convento *de José Saramago: uma proposta de abordagem.* Mem Martins: Sebenta, 1998.

Madruga, Conceição. *A paixão segundo José Saramago.* Porto: Campo das Letras, 1998.

Margato, Izabel. "Ler (com) Saramago." Diss. Univ. Federal do Rio de Janeiro, 1992.

Martins, Adriana Alves de Paula. *História e ficção–um diálogo.* Lisboa: Fim de Século, 1994.

Mesquita, Maria Luísa Raimundo. "Do estatuto polifónico do narrador em *História do Cerco de Lisboa* de José Saramago." M.A. thesis. Univ. Nova de Lisboa, 1993.

Moniz, António. *Para uma leitura de* Memorial do Convento *de José Saramago: uma proposta de leitura crítico-didáctica.* Lisboa: Presença, 1995.

Oliveira Filho, Odil José de. *Carnaval no Convento: intertextualidade e paródia em José Saramago.* São Paulo: UNESP, 1993.

Real, Miguel. *Narração, maravilhoso, trágico e sagrado em* Memorial do Convento *de José Saramago.* Lisboa: Caminho, 1996.

Reis, Carlos. *Diálogos com José Saramago.* Lisboa: Caminho, 1998.

Reis, Manuel. *Crítica necessária a José Saramago: a falsa questão ateismo-teismo.* Aveiro: Estante, 1992.

Sabine, Mark J. L. "Form and Ideology in the Novels of José Saramago, 1980-1989." Diss. University of Manchester, 2001.

Schor, Andreas. *Schreiben gegen Mythen: Die Romane von José Saramago.* Bern: Peter Lang, 1997.

Seixo, Maria Alzira. *O Essencial sobre José Saramago.* Lisboa: Imprensa Nacional-Casa da Moeda, 1987.

———. *Lugares da ficção em José Saramago: o essencial e outros ensaios.* Lisboa: Imprensa Nacional-Casa da Moeda, 1999.

Silva, Teresa Cristina Cerdeira da. *José Saramago. Entre a Historia e a Ficção: Uma Saga de Portugueses.* Lisboa: Dom Quixote, 1989.

Soares, Maria Almira. Memorial do Convento *de José Saramago: um modo de narrar.* Lisboa: Presença, 1999.

Stegagno Picchio, Luciana. *José Saramago: instantanee per un ritratto.* Firenze: Passigli, 2000.

Tomás, Maria Manuela Rodrigues. "O *Ensaio sobre a Cegueira* na construção de um Anti-Édipo." M.A. thesis. Univ. Nova de Lisboa, 1998.

Valença, Ana Maria. "O amor é o fim do cerco: o erotismo em *História do Cerco de Lisboa*, de José Saramago." M.A. thesis. Pontifícia Univ. Católica do Rio Grande do Sul, 1993.

Viegas, Francisco José, ed. *José Saramago, uma voz contra o silêncio.* Lisboa: Caminho, 1998.

Wittmann, Helena Luzia. "*Levantado do chão*: um romance de fé." M.A. thesis. Univ. Nova de Lisboa, 1991.

Articles

Costa, Horácio. "The Fundamental Re-Writing: Religious Texts and Contemporary Narrative (Gore Vidal's *Live from Golgotha*; Salman Rushdie's *The Satanic Verses*; José Saramago's *O Evangelho Segundo Jesus Cristo*)." *Dedalus: Revista Portuguesa de Literatura Comparada* 6 (1996): 245-53.

Daniel, Mary L. "Ebb and Flow. Place as Pretext in the Novels of José Saramago." *Luso-Brazilian Review* 27.2 (Winter 1990): 25-39.

———. "Symbolism and Synchronicity: José Saramago's *Jangada de Pedra*." *Hispania* 74.3 (Sept. 1991): 536-41.

Fokkema, Douwe. "The Art of Rewriting the Gospel." *Colóquio/Letras* 151/152 (Jan.-Jun. 1999): 395-402.

———. "How to Decide Whether *Memorial do Convento* by José Saramago Is or Is Not a Postmodernist Novel?" *Dedalus: Revista Portuguesa de Literatura Comparada* 1 (Dez. 1991): 293-302.

Forrest, Gene Steven. "The Dialectics of History in Two Dramas of José Saramago." *Hispanófila* 1.106 (Sept. 1992): 59-68.

Frier, David. "Ascent and Consent: Hierarchy and Popular Emancipation in the Novels of José Saramago." *Bulletin of Hispanic Studies* 71.1 (Jan. 1994): 125-38.

———. "In the Beginning Was the Word: Text and Meaning in Two Dramas by José Saramago. *Portuguese Studies* 14 (1998): 215-26.

———. "José Saramago's Stone Boat: Celtic Analogues and Popular Culture." *Portuguese Studies* 15 (1999): 194-206.

———. "'Tan largo me lo fiáis': Saramago's Ricardo Reis as a Don Juan manqué." *Selected Interdisciplinary Essays on the Representation of the Don*

Juan Archetype in Myth and Culture. Eds. Andrew Ginger, John Hobbs and Huw Lewis. Lewiston, NY: Edwin Mellen, 2000. 245-64.

Kaufman, Helena. "Evangelical Truths: José Saramago on the Life of Christ." *Revista Hispánica Moderna* 47.2 (Dec. 1994): 449-58.

Lough, Francis. "Narrator Versus Plot in Saramago's *Jangada de Pedra*." *Raízes, Rotas, Reflexões 1498-1998*. Eds. Bruce Babington, Bernard McGuirk, Marina Heck. São Paulo: Fundação Memorial da América Latina, 1998.

Maurya, Vibha. "Construction of Crowd in Saramago's Texts." *Colóquio/Letras* 151/152 (Jan.-Jun. 1999): 267-78.

McCarthy, Thomas. "José Saramago: Portuguese Iconoclast." *Cimarron Review* 110 (Jan. 1995): 7-9.

Pontiero, Giovanni. "The Apotheosis of Blimunda: An Opera by Azio Corghi Based on Saramago's *Memorial do Convento*." *Hispanic Studies in Honour of Geoffrey Ribbans*. Eds. Ann L. Mackenzie and Dorothy S. Severin. Liverpool: Liverpool UP, 1992. 335-343.

———. "José Saramago and *O Ano da Morte de Ricardo Reis*: the Making of a Masterpiece." *Bulletin of Hispanic Studies* 71.1 (Jan. 1994): 139-48.

Preto-Rodas, Richard. "José Saramago: Art for Reason's Sake." *World Literature Today* 73.1 (Winter 1999): 11-18.

———. "A View of Eighteenth-Century Portugal: José Saramago's *Memorial do Convento*." *World Literature Today* 61.1 (Winter 1987): 27-31.

Tesser, Carmen Chaves, coord. "A Tribute to José Saramago." *Hispania* 82.1 (Mar. 1999): 1-28.

Other Reviews and Articles

Antero de Quental. *A Poesia na Actualidade*. Intro. Joaquim-Francisco Coelho. Vila do Conde: Centro de Estudos Anterianos, 1999

George Monteiro

This book—a handsome production—reproduces in transcription and facsimile the holograph copy of Antero de Quental's 1881 essay "A Poesia na Actualidade" from the papers of Joaquim de Araújo now in the Biblioteca Marciana in Venice. It includes as well Joaquim-Francisco Coelho's graceful and informative introduction.

Asked to review Joaquim de Araujo's *Líra Intima*, Antero responded with an essay on the state and fortunes of modern Western poetry. Locating its beginnings among the shepherds of ancient Israel, he traces its development to its apogee in the Renaissance, and laments its becoming a diminished thing ever since. It is the rise of analytical science in the nineteenth century that has brought poetry down, reducing it to an ever more unsatisfactory expression in the small voices of individuals, of the ever-secluded self. This has been the story of poetry from the pre-Romantics and Romantics, including that proto-Decadent, Edgar Allan Poe (whose story, "The Assignation," Antero translated in 1864) and his first European translator, Charles Baudelaire, to the Decadents of Antero's own day. Diminished to throbbing subjectivity, poetry faces extinction.

> E àquela voz sarcasticamente desesperada [Heine's] respondiam outras: Baudelaire, em França, prostituindo a poesia, a antiga inspiradora da virtude e do heroísimo, e obrigando-a respirar as pestíferas *flores do mal* e a cantar o vício incurável, a maldade impenitente—e, além dos mares, na América democrática e cientificamente brutal, Poe assentava o Desespero no sólio sagrado, a repetir num sonambulismo de tédio incurável, de tédio infinite, o sue estribilho de morte: "Never, oh, nevermore!"

As Antero probably knew, Poe had also complained, in the face of what he took to be historical fact, that the smothering triumph of rational, analytical, scientific thought had dis-empowered those poets who had hitherto enjoyed a substantial purchase on the expression of religious-mythic truths. In "Sonnet to Science," published in 1829, he cried out:

> Science! True daughter of Old Time thou art!
> Who alterest all things with thy peering eyes.
> Why preyest thou thus upon the poet's heart,
> Vulture, whose wings are dull realities?
> How should he love thee? Or how deem thee wise,
> Who wouldst not leave him in his wandering
> To seek for treasure in the jewelled skies,
> Albeit he soared with an undaunted wing?
> Hast thou not dragged Diana from her car?
> And driven the Hamadryad from the wood
> To seek a shelter in some happier star?
> Hast thou not torn the Naiad from her flood,
> The Elfin from the green grass, and from me
> The summer dream beneath the tamarind tree?

Himself anticipated by the Poe who complains that the poet's privileged mythicizing faculty has been severely superseded by the successful rise of rational and analytical science—though not by the Poe who reveled in the ratiocinative tale as well as the analytical criticism of the poetic process—Antero singles out those who, like Poe, responded to the powerful changes resulting from the rise of scientific thought, without allying himself to them. In his recognition that the "irrational, decadent" voices that have responded to the triumph of scientific thinking are morally reprehensible, however, Antero anticipates the attacks of those like Max Nordau, whose attack in *Degeneration* (1893) is based on esthetic and moral dictates rather than the principles of reason and science. Championing the production of traditionally rational art—especially in poetry, drama, and fiction, but even in music—Nordau wages war on all those irrational, decadent, and "insane" artists, suggesting that their very existence poses a deathly threat to the continuation of Western art.

Strangely, neither Nordau nor Antero was much taken with Walt Whitman. Nordau attacks him directly, calling him a "mad," "morally insane, and incapable of distinguishing between good and evil, virtue and crime." Always insisting that art be moral, Nordau affirms that "it does not occur to any reasonable man of the present day to demand of poetry the teaching of scientific truths, and for generations no serious poet has thought of treating astronomy or physics in a didactic poem." He has no use, apparently, for Whitman's grand poetry celebrating the large universal virtues and truths of democracy and the common man.

Antero, on the other hand, whether disdainfully or simply out of ignorance, makes no mention of Whitman. Still, the American poet aside, Antero seems to have been largely right about the future of that Western poetry that has continued to matter. Confronting what are essentially the same determinant conditions that faced Antero, twentieth-century poets have found it increasingly difficult to consider poetry to be a creditable medium for voicing humankind's large truths.

To say that poetry's "great" voice has over the last century or so grown completely silent, as Antero predicted, may be an exaggeration. Still, it may not be misleading to say that poetry has probably not, during that period, managed to regain its once privileged position in human affairs with its concomitant power to address humankind's large general truths. Twentieth-century attempts to regain that power, especially in the efforts of poets whose first work established them as Modernists, have been especially instructive. To what extent they have succeeded in restoring to poetry the privileged voice seems to depend largely on any given reader's ideology or predilections. T. S. Eliot, for example, having produced in 1915 the decadent complaints of "The Love Song of J. Alfred Prufrock," put together the fragmented prophecies of *The Wasteland* in 1922 as preparation, it now seems, for "Ash Wednesday" and *Four Quartets*, personal poems of affirmative religious-mythic thought and feeling; Hart Crane, reacting against the nay-saying voice of Eliot's *Wasteland*, produced *The Bridge*, an arrangement of otherwise free-standing pieces intended to be the epitomizing expression of a nation's ethos.

When we turn to Antero's Portuguese successors, we find the story to be much the same. Similarly, there have been notably ambitious efforts to recuperate the lost "great" voice of poetry. As the all but self-identified "supra-Camões," Fernando Pessoa produced *Mensagem*, a collection of lyrics and elegies that look back generically and historically to Portugal's role in the Renaissance. Miguel Torga's *Poemas Ibéricos* attempts to recover the great historical past and its virtues, the waning and virtual disappearance of which is already registered in Camões.

The publication under review presents itself as the most local and modest of tributes to Antero. Nevertheless, it also serves to remind us that Antero's thinking was always passional, never more so, in fact, than when he was dissecting the literary and spiritual currents of his and, as it has turned out, our age as well.

Shit, Shrimps, and Shifting Sobriquets: *Iracema* and the Lesson in Lost Authority

Phillip Rothwell

Any reader approaching José de Alencar's novel *Iracema* predisposed to maritime references could scarcely be disappointed. From its famous opening lines, "Verdes mares bravios de minha terra natal" (20), to its final chapter in which the sad figure of Poti gets up every morning and looks out to the ocean in anticipation of the return of his friend and master, references to the sea saturate the novel. The thalassic allusion, however, that marks the text most is the one which Alencar, the meddling author, attempts to foreclose: the name of the "jovem guerreiro" (20). This preclusion, which may be seen to fail, is the first of three such restrictions imposed on the text by the Brazilian author. Along with the other two, the name of the eponymous heroine and the fluctuating name applied to the Pitiguara Indian, the warrior's name demonstrates the iconoclastic power that intertextuality exercises over any tale that seeks to establish a single voice.

As Luis Filipe Ribeiro has pointed out, through the tactical deployment of footnotes, letters, and prologues, Alencar "interfere antes, durante e depois do texto, participando exaustivamente na produção do sentido" (219). But this exhaustive interference never achieves its ultimate goal of semantically closing the text. The first time that the white warrior is named, we are told by both the character, and lest we doubt him, the author, what his name means: "Meu nome é Martim, que na tua língua quer dizer filho de guerreiro" (23). The accompanying author's note seeks to validate the veracity of the character's assertion, grounding it diachronically: "Martim—Da origem latina de seu nome, procedente de Marte, deduz o estrangeiro a significação que lhe dá" (68). However, this example of authorial intrusion does not prevent the sea from being seen in Martim's name. Alencar's act of restriction falls short in its objective of connotative limitation and renders the reader suitably suspicious of further interventions from the author. As far as names go, a synchronic reading of the text sullies Alencar's authority, reducing him to the status of a voice that "can make itself heard only by blending into the complex choir of other voices already in place" (Todorov ix).

If we accept Todorov's reading of Bakhtin's theory of dialogism, then the word "Martim" enters into a discussion with utterances both past and future. Indeed, Todorov asserts the following:

> After Adam, there are no nameless objects nor any unused words. Intentionally or not, all discourse is in dialogue with prior discourses on the same subject, as well as with discourses yet to come, whose reactions it foresees and anticipates. (ix)

Not only is Martim affected by the discourse of the sea, he also affects it, becoming another voice in the intertextual dialogue that permeates the Lusophone representations of the deep. He changes and is constantly changed by that maritime discourse.

From Camões onwards, the primordial mass has been a central feature of the Lusophone cultural unconscious.[1] Furthermore, its representations have often been tainted by the polar ambiguity of glory and disaster, or by the blocked dialectic of discovery and return. The repeated references in *Os Lusíadas,* for example, to the cutting open of the sea[2]—symbolic of the opening up of a frontier—are read alongside the Velho do Restelo's warning:

> Oh! Maldito o primeiro que, no mundo,
> Nas ondas vela pôs em seco lenho!
> Digno da eterna pena do Profundo,
> Se é justa a justa Lei que sigo e tenho! (IV.102)

For the Velho, the sea serves as a boundary, part of the natural separation of the world. In seeking to cross that boundary, to cut open the sea and change its nature from separator to link, the Portuguese are, in his opinion, making a date with Nemesis. The sea may thus be read, just within the epic poem, as containing the ambiguous duality of threat and prospect, of reward and retribution.

Ambivalence is a characteristic that the deep retains in many of its manifestations in Lusophone literature. As a synecdochic representation of the act whereby the Portuguese set out to discover the globe, the sea also bears within itself the symbolism of a desired return to Portugal. In the words of Luís Forjaz Trigueiros, "Portugal é terra de Mar" (91). Oliveira Martins, amongst others, made a similar observation. The geography of the nation made the "enigma absorvente de um mar desenrolado diante da vista" an overpowering force that led to a glorious history (I.6). But at the same time, the cost to the nation of the maritime venture was high. The sea behaved like an enticing mermaid, leading the Portuguese astray. The true cost became apparent at the disaster of Alcácer Quibir (Oliveira Martins I.7).

Ambivalence also affects representations of the sea in the post-independence literatures of the Lusophone world. From the perspective of the formerly colonised, one would expect the oceans to bear within themselves the notion of the cursed medium over which the coloniser arrived. One can see examples in the work of the Mozambican author, Mia Couto, of the sea literally being tainted by the blood on the hands of the oppressor. But even as the sea turns red in Couto's novel *Vinte e Zinco*, it also transmits the idea of a cleansing of the past, of the possibility of a rebirth and redefinition of the role of the deep (92).

The Angolan author Pepetela portrays the sea in an equally ambiguous way in *A Geração da Utopia*. As the character of Vítor contemplates the ocean, he finds it hostile because of its associations with the slave trade—a trade that, for many years, linked Angola and Brazil. The vicious activities of the Portuguese colonisers link the sea to death and oppression. However, as Vítor continues to observe the ocean, the binary of oppressor-oppressed/master-slave begins to crumble. Vítor realises that the slave trade was far more complex than he would like to imagine, involving as it possibly did members of his own family (85). The sea is thus not only contaminated by African blood but also by the blood on African as well as Portuguese hands.

Slavery dominated Brazilian political life for much of the nineteenth century, only finally being abolished in 1888. Bradford Burns suggests that its abolition was a key factor leading to the military coup that ended the reign of the Emperor Pedro II (Burns, *History of Brazil* 228). The sea, in Brazilian national identity, serves as both the bringer of the Portuguese and the medium over which African slaves were introduced to Brazilian society.

In the foundation novel *Iracema*, the descriptions applied to Martim include "guerreiro branco" (24), "guerreiro cristão" (48) and "guerreiro do mar" (46), all three of which point back to a rather bellicose Portugal. The sea operates as the medium over which the cross of Christ will be brought to bear by the white man on the indigenous population of what would become Brazil. Any doubt that this is what is going to happen is squashed at the end of the novel, as Poti is wholly assimilated into the religion, culture, and language of the coloniser. The negative consequences of the colonising process in the Brazilian context—both its propensity towards the erasure of the colonised and its glottophagic imperialism—ought to be borne in mind when reading the text. The reason why they are often neglected and "o genocídio real transforma-se no casamento ideal" (Ribeiro 223) may be traced, as Ria Lemaire intimates, to *Iracema*'s status as an aesthetic masterpiece (69). This poetry in prose, as Machado de Assis designated it, rhetorically deploys language in a way that may be read to conceal the horror of the process of colonisation, portraying betrayal and destruction as true love and constructive sacrifice.

There are clearly dangers in any reading of the text that seeks to re-instate some agency to those who were colonised, as this reading, in part, attempts to do. The reading may unintentionally imply the possession of a spuriously overwhelming power by those who historically have been reduced to a position of subalternity, and, in the context of Brazil, literally to non-existence. A balance, therefore, must be struck. An attempt to show the ways in which language may be read to escape authorial control does not imply that the voice of the colonised destroys colonial power, but rather that colonial authority is slightly undermined by the whispering trace that remains on the names it sought to make its own.

In the case of *Iracema*, there is the additional complexity of its traditional reading as a novel that sought to establish Brazilian cultural independence from Portugal (Coutinho III.241; Filho 134-36). The Indian, as Bradford Burns points out, became a useful if paradoxical tool in the climate in which Alencar wrote:

> Although the Indian as an individual was scorned, as a symbol he was cherished. He came to represent the original Brazil before the coming of the detested Portuguese. (*Nationalism* 44)

The coloniser had split into two groups, the Brazilian elite and their Portuguese counterparts. Both relied on the Portuguese language as the medium for their expression.

Alencar was well aware of the power of language in the creation of a national identity, famously asserting that "a língua é a nacionalidade do pensamento como a pátria é a nacionalidade do povo" (qtd. in Jobim 107). As various commentators have pointed out, Alencar believed that Brazilian national identity, as it would come to be manifested in a culturally specific literature, required of its exponents a knowledge of the indigenous languages of Brazil (*Nationalism* 45; Filho 134). His project may thus be read as the attempted consumption of the pre-Portuguese languages of what would become Brazil, in an effort to brazilianise Portuguese. Indeed, the author himself claimed in his "Carta ao Dr Jaguaribe," published as an appendix to *Iracema,* the following:

> Verá nele [neste livro] minhas idéias a respeito da literatura nacional; e achará aí poesia inteiramente brasileira, haurida na língua dos selvagens. (78)

But the languages on which the novelist dines leave him with a bad case of indigestion, for like the sea in Martim, they introduce a network of possible meanings beyond authorial control, despite Alencar's attempt to force the languages to submit to his own intentions. As Bakhtin points out, all discourse in any novel is "overpopulated with the intentions of others" (294). This is ever more the case when a novelist attempts to appropriate the language of another and in the process to restrict its possible meanings. The more Alencar attempts to preclude semantic networks, the more he dares the reader to go beyond the limit he sets. Each morpheme that he borrows from Tupi and Guarani arrives burdened with the linguistic baggage of another language system, not to mention the dialogical agitation that the word brings with and on itself. Thus the *mar* of Martim may be seen to echo the Sumerian for both uterus and sea (Croutier 14). Freud explained the equation in dreams of water with birth, in terms of the evolution of humankind from the deep (194). Our emergence from the womb mirrors life's emergence from the sea. Ferenczi would later develop Freud's ideas, arguing that our entire existence as humans is premised on a desired return to the sea from whence we came. Martim can be seen to embody all of these ideas. He is both the symbol of death and destruction and of the birth of a nation. He is both warrior and womb, Mars and *mar.* Increasingly, he looks out to the sea, which forms a link to the *pátria* from where he originated. He thus marks the deep with "saudades" (47) in a manner analogous to Herculano's strategy in *Eurico, o Presbítero.*[3]

The sea, in Lusophone tradition, has always served two purposes, to link and to separate. The sea *for* Martim serves to remind him of his "berço natal" (47), and to remind him of his absence from it. The sea *in* Martim will serve as the link between the new world and the old world. At a diegetical level, he will bring the value system of Europe to bear on America. But at the same time, the novel in which he is cast will form part of the armoury distinguishing Brazil from Portugal.

Much has been made of Iracema's name, particularly that it is an anagram of America.[4] In fact, the status of Iracema's appellation has been one of the most contested aspects of the novel since it was written. Sânzio de Azevedo claims that Afrânio Peixoto was the first person to notice the anagram in 1929. Azevedo describes a polemic that ensued, in which the intentions of Alencar, as author, were hotly debated (274). Did he mean Iracema to be read as America or not? Leaving aside the fact that Barthes's ideas had not filtered through to Fortaleza when Azevedo wrote his article, his definitive proof that Alencar did not mean Iracema to be read as America fails in its own terms. For Azevedo asserts that true authorial intention can be extracted from Oscar Mendes's discovery of an unpublished early manuscript of the novel in which "o primeiro nome criado pelo autor para a sua heroína era *Aracema* que, anagramado, não daria 'América'" (275). This proves nothing beyond the fact that Alencar chose to change his heroine's name. Indeed, contrary to what Azevedo concludes, it is possible that Alencar noticed that by changing the "A" to an "I," "Aracema" could be converted to an anagram of "America."

More interestingly, Mendes's discovery can be used to call into question Alencar's fluency in indigenous languages. The author explains Iracema's name as the contraction of the Guarani words for honey and lips. It is one of many etymological explanations that Alencar gives in the notes: "*Iracema—Em guarani significa lábios de mel—de* ira, *mel e* tembe—*lábios.* Tembe *na composição altera-se em* ceme" (67). If "Iracema" was always meant to be "lips of honey," was "Aracema" a mistake? In any case, the extent to which "Iracema" means in Guarani what Alencar claims it does is questionable. According to the *Diccionario Guaraní-Español*, published by Editorial Tupã in 1952, "honey" is spelt "eíra" in Guarani, and retains the "e" in most of its renderings (340). M. Cavalcanti Proença's notes on Alencar's notes cast further doubt on the author's prowess in indigenous languages: "Para Alencar, *tembe* se torna *ceme,* fonética não muito explicável, pois o natural seria tornar-se *reme* (com r franco)" (Alencar 80). Once again, in trying to restrict the meaning of the name, Alencar challenges the reader to challenge him. By citing the authority of an external language system, the author invites the reader to leave the text and check his facts. In one crucial case, such an investigation reveals a semantic multiplicity in both Guarani and Tupi that underlines both the author's desire to sanitise the savage and the author's loss of authority, since Poti is not so far removed from the English homophone that enters the Anglophone reader's head as he or she reads the Brazilian text. But before considering the problematic role that Martim's Pitiguara friend and his name play in the novel, we turn our attention to the ways in which Martim comes to over-write, or more appropriately over-speak, Iracema's name and voice.

The role of the spoken word is given primacy by Alencar, in a way that mirrors Rousseau and prefigures Lévi-Strauss. In all three cases, orality runs parallel to a vision of the noble savage. In Alencar's case, a discussion of Poti's provenance in the author's notes is rendered conclusive by the assertion that "a tradição oral é uma fonte importante da História, e às vezes a mais pura e verdadeira" (66). The noble Poti is legitimised by an oral source. The spoken word rules supreme. If this is the case, license is granted by Alencar to consider precisely what the spoken voice does in his text. The first duty that it performs is to introduce Iracema, in the anachronic first chapter:

> A lufada intermitente traz da praia um eco vibrante, que ressoa entre o marulho das vagas:
>
> —Iracema! (20)

The sea metonymically interferes with Iracema, through the "marulho das vagas." The enunciation of her name is thus always already marked by Martim. Before the story unfolds analeptically, the sea has permeated her. Ria Lemaire points out that as the narrative develops, Iracema loses power at various levels to Martim (63-68). This is paralleled by her absorption into the sea. The first time that she lays eyes on her future lover, he is described as having "nas faces o branco das areias que bordam o mar; nos olhos o azul triste das águas profundas" (21). Not only, therefore, is Martim linked to the deep appellatively and in terms of provenance, but also descriptively. Iracema's increasing association with the sea mirrors his attempted erasure of her name. Before she leaves and betrays her tribe, she has never seen the sea. She is "a virgem da serra, que nunca desceu às alvas praias onde arrebentam as vagas" (34). The voices associated with the sea, such as that of the "gaivota," are alien to her. But almost immediately after her flight, they begin to enter her head: "O grito da gaivota terceira vez ressoa a seu ouvido" (35). The reader learns that the sea becomes an intrinsic part of her new existence. It is a symbol of what links her to her lover and separates her from her past: "Iracema achara ali nas praias do mar um ninho do amor, nova pátria para seu coração" (50-51).

After a very short period of conjugal bliss, Iracema realises that the sea also acts as a block between her and Martim. A distance develops between the two that she associates with the voices that the sea carries over from Martim's homeland (58). The sea thus becomes a barrier between her and her lover, representing the immense distance between their two cultures as well as the means over which her culture will be consumed by his.

In Alencar's romantic vision of Iracema, she is allied to the purity of nature. His descriptions of her form a link to various aspects of flora and fauna. The nature of her voice is that it is the voice of nature. Her name is articulated by the "jandaia." But, by the final chapter, her erasure appears to be total: even the faithful bird is no longer able to speak "o mavioso nome de Iracema" (65). The only voice left appears to be that of Martim. Iracema's dying request is to be buried where she can hear the sea, and thus the voice of her lover:

> Enterra o corpo de tua esposa ao pé do coqueiro que tu amavas. Quando o vento do mar soprar nas folhas, Iracema pensará que é tua voz que fala entre seus cabelos. (63)

The power of her own voice is transformed in the novel, from its halcyon ephemerality as the echo that inhabits the heart of her lover—"As falas da virgem ressoaram docemente no coração de Martim" (34)—to the point where even her thoughts require linguistic mediation through the warrior's tongue—"A voz do cristão transmitiu a Poti o pensamento de Iracema" (39). Is there any trace, therefore, left of her by the end of the novel, other than a dialogic resonance of what once was but is no more?

One answer could be that she has the power to name the future and to have her own name conflated with it. Her suffering is imprinted on the name of her son, a name that the "jandaia" mixes with that of his mother (60). Iracema tells him "Tu és Moacir, o nascido de meu sofrimento" (60). One interesting feature of this declaration is the use of the first person possessive pronoun, which she almost immediately reiterates in her subsequent designation of her son as "filho de minha angústia" (60). As Maria Manuel Lisboa has pointed out, Iracema "invariably refers to herself in the alienated third person" (101), something that she reads as part of the erasure of Iracema associated with the European presence of Martim. But Lisboa also asserts that the "act of naming is... an act of affirmation of primacy and mastery" (101), a claim that can be read to support the apparently permanent restitution of Iracema to a position of eternal power, since she has named the future: Moacir. In the act of naming, she regains, even if in a refracted way—through the genitive and the generative—some of her subjectivity.

Yet it is a peculiarly absent future to which Iracema stakes her possessive claim. Moacir, like the epitaph of the novel, becomes "um filho ausente" (17), strangely missing at the end of the tale, since "[o] primeiro cearense, ainda no berço, emigrava da terra da pátria" (65). The little power granted to Iracema by the text is slight and distanced, in contrast to the seemingly total control asserted by Martim as the novel draws to a close and Poti is linguistically recodified before the Christian/Portuguese cross. But that is precisely the point at which the text becomes unstuck, because attention is drawn to the meaning of the Pitiguara's name, as Alencar seeks to foreclose it once and for all.

The reader's suspicions should have been raised by Alencar's repetitive assertions throughout the novel with regard to the meaning of Poti. The Pitiguara are insultingly referred to as "potiguara, comedor de camarão" (24). The author's notes once again seek to validate the etymological assertions of the body of the text: "*Potiguara—Comedor de camarão; de* poty *e* uara. *Nome que por desprezo davam os inimigos aos pitiguaras*" (69). A little later in the novel, the narrator reiterates the assertion:

> Os guerreiros da grande nação que habitava as bordas do mar, se chamavam a si mesmos pitiguaras, senhores dos vales; mas os tabajaras, seus inimigos, por escárnio os apelidavam potiguaras, comedores de camarão. (34)

Poti himself has his nature determined by his name:

> O valente Poti, resvalando pela relva, como o ligeiro camarão, de que ele tomara o nome e a viveza, desapareceu no lago fundo. (36)

With his conversion to Christianity, Poti is reborn as "Camarão."

One thing that is peculiar about Alencar's assertions is the thought that being called a "shrimp-eater" is a term of abuse, particularly given the positive status bestowed on the shrimp when it is associated with the character of Poti. Something that is "ligeiro" and full of "viveza" is difficult to envisage as denigrating. The entries in the *Pequeno Vocabulário Tupi-Português* of Pe A. Lemos Barbosa are somewhat illuminating in this respect and speak for themselves:

> poti—defecar; excremento
> poti—camarão (130)

The Guarani-Spanish dictionary previously cited confirms these possible connotations (119). As Poti becomes Camarão, Alencar attempts to clean him up, to expunge this other meaning and to turn him into a successful European man. This attempt, particularly in the context in which Alencar situates the novel as an example of literature "haurida na língua dos selvagens," may be read to fail. That "língua dos selvagens" haunts the text and undermines the authority of its author, the very same author who introduced it into the text. The nobility bestowed on the first and most complete convert to the new Brazilian order that Alencar was seeking to reflect culturally, drawn primarily as it was from an oral source, is dirtied by the dialogue of the spoken word that crosses the text and destroys Alencar's dream of a completely closed and coherent network of meaning. Like Martim, who intertextually resonates with the sea, or Iracema, the explanation of whose name—both through its labial and linguistic associations—draws the reader's attention towards the pre-existing oral cultures of Brazil in a way not quite envisaged by Alencar, Poti's name reflects the fact that the author's control is never total.

Notes

[1] "Cultural unconscious" is used here in the post-Jungian sense of the aspects within the psyche that link the individual to the group with which he or she culturally identifies (see Anne Singer Harris 31). The literature written in a particular language may at some levels be read as a conscious manifestation of the preoccupations of the cultural unconscious of that language group. Interpreted in this way, the cultural unconscious is different from national identity since one language can operate across various nations.

[2] See, for example, Camões I.19; I.42; I.45; II.8; IV.76; V.24; V.37; V.73; VII.70; IX.51; X.144.

[3] In the sixth chapter of *Eurico, o Presbítero,* set in Ilha Verde, the narrator asserts that "uma saudade indizível atraía-me para o mar" (Herculano 54).

[4] See for instance Ribeiro 220; Lisboa 98; Azevedo 274-78.

Works Cited

Alencar, José de. *Iracema: Lenda do Ceará.* Ed. M. Cavalcanti Proença. 31st ed. Rio de Janeiro: Ediouro Publicações, 1995.

Azevedo, Sânzio de. "Releitura de *Iracema.*" *Alencar: 100 anos depois.* Ed. Cláudio Martins. Fortaleza: Academia Cearense de Letras, 1977. 261-289.

Bakhtin, M. M. *The Dialogic Imagination: Four Essays.* Trans. Caryl Emerson & Michael Holquist. Austin: U of Texas P, 1981.

Barbosa, Pe A. Lemos. *Pequeno Vocabulário Tupi-Português.* Rio de Janeiro: São José, 1951.

Burns, E. Bradford. *Nationalism in Brazil: A Historical Survey.* New York: Frederick A. Praeger, 1968.

———. *A History of Brazil.* 3rd ed. New York: Columbia UP, 1993.

Camões, Luís de. *Os Lusíadas.* Ed. António Leitão. 3rd ed. Lisboa: Ulisseia, 1994.

Coutinho, Afrânio, ed. *A Literatura no Brasil.* 3rd ed. 6 vols. Rio de Janeiro: José Olympio, 1986.

Couto, Mia. *Vinte e Zinco.* Lisboa: Caminho, 1999.

Croutier, Alev Lytle. *Taking the Waters: Art, Spirit, Sensuality.* New York: Abbeville, 1992.

Diccionario Guaraní-Español y Español-Guaraní. [n. ed.] Buenos Aires: Editorial Tupã, 1952.

Ferenczi, Sandor. *Thalassa: A Theory of Genitality.* Trans. Henry Alden Bunker. London: H Karnac, 1989.

Filho, Luís Viana. *A vida de José de Alencar.* Rio de Janeiro: José Olympio, 1979.

Freud, Sigmund. *Introductory Lectures on Psychoanalysis.* Trans. James Strachey. Harmondsworth: Penguin, 1987.

Herculano, Alexandre. *Eurico, o Presbítero.* 5th ed. Mem Martins: Europa-América, 1994.

Jobim, José Luís, & Roberto Aúzelo de Souza. *Iniciação à Literatura Brasileira.* Rio de Janeiro: AO Livro Técnico, 1987.

Lemaire, Ria. "Re-reading *Iracema:* The Problem of the Representation of Women in the Construction of a National Brazilian Identity." *Luso-Brazilian Review* 26 (1989): 59-73.

Lisboa, Maria Manuel. "A Mother is a Boy's Best Friend: Birth and Kinslaying in the Brazilian Foundation Novel." *Portuguese Studies* 13 (1997): 95-107.

Oliveira Martins. *Portugal nos Mares.* 2 vols. Lisboa: Guimarães, 1954.

Pepetela. *A Geração da Utopia.* Lisboa: Dom Quixote, 1992.

Ribeiro, Luis Filipe. *Mulheres de Papel: Um Estudo do Imaginário em José de Alencar e Machado de Assis.* Niterói: EDUFF, 1996.

Singer Harris, Anne. *Living with Paradox: An Introduction to Jungian Psychology.* Pacific Grove: Cole, 1996.

Todorov, Tzetan. *Mikhail Bakhtin: The Dialogic Principle.* Trans. Wlad Godzich. Manchester: Manchester UP, 1984.

Trigueiros, Luís Forjaz. "Ao acaso da memória." *Onde o Mar Acaba: Antologia de Poesia e Prosa sobre as Descobertas.* Ed. Ana Hatherly. Lisboa: Dom Quixote, 1991.

Violent Games: Towards an Historical Understanding of the Portuguese Bullfight*

Rita Costa Gomes

In June of 1999, a curious debate was taking place on the floor of the Portuguese Parliament. At its center was the question: should the law that forbids the killing of bulls in the country's arenas be modified? Following a series of events that have had as their principal protagonists a small border town (Barrancos), animal rights groups, the courts, and, last to arrive, political parties and opinion groups, the discussion has raged on. This debate poses a number of problems to the historian, whose attention is naturally aroused by the constant use of such words as "tradition," "civilization," "community," and "history" in the speeches that proliferate and intersect in the newspapers and other media. The study that follows tries to formulate and resolve some of these problems, notably those connected with justifications or condemnations of the bullfights based on "Portuguese tradition" and its supposed "medieval origin."

By examining, *à la* Hobsbawn, the different steps involved in processes such as "inventing tradition," and by looking specifically at the role of games in medieval and early modern Iberian societies, I hope to contribute to the discussion of the historical relationship of violence and Portuguese society. Using contemporary examples, my investigation will look objectively at the historical depth and complexity of the processes of symbolic re-elaboration and claims of identity currently taking place, while also observing their fabrication by the various mechanisms of communication, political negotiation of normative models, and shared or contradictory discourses on violence.

Barrancos, A Fetish of Identity?

First, a brief summary of recent events: in 1998, animal rights groups persuaded the courts to enforce a 1928 Portuguese law in the town of Barrancos, a decree that specifically forbids bullfights resulting in the killing of the bull in arenas. Barrancos, located on the southern border of Portugal, is a small village with approximately 2000 inhabitants. As a part of its annual festival, a rather modest bullfight takes place in which a bull is killed in a delimited space of the town square, which serves as an arena. In 1998, following an order of the Lisbon Tribunal, authorities summoned police to supervise the festival. The police attended without intervening in the festival's events, which included a bull being killed in the village's improvised arena. This episode quickly became a political affair when numerous voices were heard protesting the people of Barrancos' defiance of the "State's authority" and of the legal order. The course of the "case of Barrancos" thus began in the public sphere, spurring debate in Parliament as to the relative legality of bullfights.

An exhaustive analysis of the many arguments that have proliferated since August 1998 in both political and judicial settings is outside the general scope of this study. Suffice it to say that, with predictable banality, these arguments develop under the pressure of subsequent events. They focus on the problem of the legal framing of so-called "local traditions," and they pragmatically skirt the problems in the interpretation of symbolic conflicts that bullfighting raises. Animal rights groups and associations have linked the Barrancos case to a more general discussion of the validity of the bullfight—a spectacle they would prefer to see banned. One will note that, in a generalized fashion, the identity argument obviously taints the discussion. For example, the Lisbon Tribunal's decision states, "it may well be a question of simply imitating the Spanish tradition, and not establishing a Portuguese tradition or one specific to Barrancos" (Tribunal da Relação de Lisboa, Autos de Agravo, Proc. 7689/98). Indeed, in opposition to the Spanish custom of killing the bull within the public space of the "corrida," it is common knowledge that the same practice is not part of "Portuguese tradition." This is merely one among an entire constellation of stereotyped images that have contributed to the definition of a national identity. In an effort to have specificity legally recognized, defenders of the position of Barrancos appropriate this very stereotype and use it in another line of argument.

Situated on the border, Barrancos belongs to the "Raia." The "Raia" acts as an operative notion for a scholarly tradition that claims the border region is distinct from the rest of the country, and in particular, distinct from urban and coastal parts of the country represented by the capital (the systematic formulation of this notion may be found in a text contemporary with the legal norm in question, viz., Basto, "A fronteira hispano-portuguesa"). This is a first attempt to situate the debate on grounds of territorialization and definitions of identity. It is also a first attempt to question what it means to be Portuguese, taking into consideration a diversity that is defined by the mediation of ethnology and history. By noting the specificity of people from the border ("raia"), the reality that this concept evokes appears once again as a place of definition *par excellence*, a place for the fabrication of national identity itself (Sahlins). Recognizing the legitimacy of the bullfights of Barrancos does not merely emerge as a form of negotiation with "borders," that is, with these territorial zones where difference with the "other" (in this case the Spanish as a stereotyped entity) becomes blurred and diluted. It also allows the people of Barrancos themselves to appropriate their own practices. Thus, the bullfight that culminates in the killing of the bull becomes a sign of differentiation, and as such it presents the entire repertoire of attitudes inherent to a supposed autonomy that would permit the people of Barrancos to negotiate their belonging to one or another of the affective national communities. One curious behavior serves as an example of this: since the 1970s, as a gesture of defiance, people from the small towns that make up the "raia" have ritually jeered the Spanish flag on occasions of crisis. The media have duly promoted this gesture, intended to incite the country's emotions.

On this slightly anecdotal ground, a rather simplistic set of oppositions becomes apparent. In the different areas where it succeeds in mobilizing differentiated positions, these oppositions contaminate nearly every aspect of the debate. An opposition, linked to the spilling of the bull's blood, is established between the civilized (us, the Portuguese) and the uncivilized (the "other," the Spaniard with whom the "barranquenho" identifies), or between the repulsion felt by the civilized person when confronted by the spectacle of the suffering animal and the enjoyment derived from the same scene by the uncivilized. In regards to the last opposition, one should note the efforts of ecologists, inspired by discussions taking place in Spain and Latin America about the interdiction of bullfighting. Brazil in particular, where bullfighting has been banned, has been used to exemplify a symbolic extension of the "mild customs" of the Portuguese national character. In the proliferation of discourses in the media, other oppositions have been made, notably the opposition between community ("us," i.e. Barrancos) and society ("the other," i.e. Lisbon, associated with the State and authority). These are two antinomic social orders that allow various antagonists engaged in the public debate a permutation of positions—in particular, from those of political agents. Of equal significance is the opposition between the "popular" and "folkloric" bullfight that underlies a possible integration of Barrancos' practices, viewed as rustic and justifiable according to "local traditions," and the urban leisure-time activities in which all violence directed against animals must be prohibited.

At this point, some facts drawn from the available studies conducted on the sociology of the leisure-time activities of the Portuguese and on the specific social field of bullfighting should be mentioned (Capucha). In 1994 a maximum of 500,000 people attended various bull-related spectacles, a figure obtained from a direct enquiry made by a state department (*Direcção Geral dos Espectáculos*) and probably closer to the facts than published national statistics. This figure represents one of the smallest numbers of spectators for this sphere of activity. The public attending these events is concentrated primarily in Lisbon and in the southern cities (in particular, those in the Setúbal and Santarém regions), with the highest concentration being in the extreme southern region of Algarve. This fact is obviously connected to the enormous impact of the tourist industry in this region. This, in turn, has led to recent construction of an arena for bullfights in the small city of Albufeira. Construction of an arena in such a town demonstrates signs of occupancy and frequentation that are not negligible in relation to the significant under-attendance in other regions of the country. Out of a total of 61 set and 34 traveling venues where bullfights took place in Portugal that same year of 1994, few of these places reached its maximum capacity, according to the available statistics. Most were often partially empty. Within this context, approximately a mere 300 professionals organize some 250 shows each year (and it should be mentioned that this number is obviously underestimated, given the unknown number of unauthorized shows that take place).

Within this framework one must include the annual bullfight of Barrancos, which hardly corresponds to the folkloric image that has been evoked by the media. In fact, this bullfight conforms to the same framing and uses the common mechanisms of this type of public spectacle. The law, for instance, requires a specialized agent, the "director of the bullfight," whose job is to preside over what happens in the arena much like a soccer referee. Control is further reinforced by engaging the services of professional bullfighters such as the "matador" or "toureiro," as well as the mechanisms necessary for providing the indispensable element of this activity—which represents an increasing portion of expenditures required in organizing these events—the bull itself. These facts can help us avoid the trap of a radical contrast, postulated but not problematized, between the "modern" or current world and the "traditional societies" for which Barrancos seems to have become today's symbol in the Portuguese media.

In its hybrid nature, as a living spectacle in which people participate, the bullfight of Barrancos is also a product of processes that fashion and transform Portuguese society as a whole. Moreover, the bullfight creates the possibility of discourses and actions that belong to a historically situated repertoire. While refusing an atemporal conception of this local dimension (Schulte), it remains to be proven that today's inhabitants of Barrancos constitute a "sub-culture" identifiable *en-soi*, or even a marginalized minority, in spite of the apparent autonomy of their discourse, which has been constructed from the illusionary effect allowed by an ethnographical register that owes almost uniquely to historical contexts that date back to the 1910s or 20s. Certainly the people of Barrancos are speaking out, intervening in the public space, and spreading out before our eyes the attitudinal differences, silences and fractures that are expressed throughout this debate—a debate, however, which tends to be organized in a growing way more around the bull than around the men themselves. Only an investigation that probes more deeply into the very terrain could clarify the mechanisms that allow Barrancos its position as an actor of speech, and discover who is its protagonist and from what local dynamics this speech is produced.

The "specificity" of Barrancos, in its practice of acts perceived as violent, in fact offers a contrast to a stable public composed of those used to the bullfights happening elsewhere with their curious mélange of "aficionados" ("enlightened" admirers of this game) and tourists fond of such "typical" commodities. This adept public is precisely characterized by the total absence of externalized violence, while Barrancos is laying claim to a specificity that finds a place in the common perception of bullfighting as an archaic, ludic activity with violent characteristics. It exists at the opposite extreme from the postmodern "corrida," evoked by the figure of the female "torero" or by a demi-monde of socialites for whom the bullfight affirms a social distinction that brings them closer to a phantasmatic and bygone era of aristocrats. Inside this same field, agents connected to this activity and to its reproduction are outlining a multitude of strategies that disparage both the most recent public, the tourists (who nonetheless contribute decisively to the survival of this type of activity), and the spectacles that take place on lower levels of social and professional sophistication. Simultaneously, they do not disdain to show their support of the Barrancos cause, which in itself guarantees that the "traditions of bullfighting" will continue.

Where does this specificity of Barrancos come from? How does it become a rallying cry, attached to a debate on violent games and their role in Portugal today? If we move beyond the obvious fetishism of the identity debate, an answer is not readily available. Taking into consideration this complexity, let us look at some problems from an historian's point of view, following the course of the two major themes that can be isolated in this debate: tradition and civilization. We will do this before returning to a discussion of an important aspect of our common enterprise: the representations and the experience of violence as socially, culturally, and historically constructed.

Hide, Flesh, and Bone: On the Invention of "Bullfights"

The history of bullfighting is a domain where it is possible to follow these lines of questioning, focusing on the construction of the idea of a "Portuguese tradition." It is often a history written by and for "aficionados." And in this respect it is singular because it rarely addresses the problems of the signification and the context of ritual and ludic practices from past societies so as to inscribe within them the place of the combat or the "game" with the bull. As often happens with other objects of Portuguese historiography, bullfighting is viewed as self-evident, that is to say, as an object that is readable simply by systematically peeling back the surface of the sources, epoch after epoch. In the texts of the past, bullfight is simply described, remaining for most historians a given object (Claramunt; Rodrigues). To a great extent, because of the scarcity of analysis a great variety of medieval practices are held to be possible antecedents of modern bullfighting, provided that there exists a sacrificial rapport between the bull and man, and assuming that there is a ludic signification in all of the identified cases.

For reasons of clarity, and given the variety of facts mentioned by historians of bullfighting, we should offer a definition of the idea of "game."

A game is an activity of an organized group, made up of a loose network of individuals, whose behavior is structured according to a set of fixed rules that establish a ludic space-time relationship, providing a final resolution (Huizinga; Elias and Dunning). Consequently, games may have in medieval and modern societies diverse functions for the participants, the spectators (if there are any), and for the society as an ordered entity. In the case of games in which it is a question of combat with, or the ritual/ludic utilization of, a bull, one can detect for instance a large set of problems related to a series of processes of incorporation of social rules that remain to be studied in Portugal, as well as in other Iberian kingdoms of the Middle Ages.

An obvious case is the incorporation of social hierarchies. There was a bullfighting specific to the aristocracy, tied to the equestrian arts and the hunt, and the contrasting "lower" version of the game (*corrida*) with the employment of other animals (notably dogs). In this latter case, the group attacks the animal, with or without the preliminary goal of the combats of the first type. But the medieval game seems also to be related to the incorporation of rules concerning violence that are correctly characterized by a total inversion of contemporary, post-Enlightenment values. The violence in question is in fact that of the animal on man, since the main problem of the combat was one of containing the violence of the bull through the implementation of repressive strategies of the game itself. Underlying these strategies was the value attributed by Christian religion to human life (Sorabji 195-207). This problem is linked to the probable origin of "techniques" for the manipulation of animals, similar to those of modern bullfighting. These techniques, which in the Iberian case can be dated back to the thirteenth century, were used in games taking place in closed or delimited spaces. It also explains the relatively well-known facts concerning the radical interdiction of bullfights established by ecclesiastical authorities—in particular, the papacy—in the final epoch of the Middle Ages and at the beginning of the Modern age.

But there was also in the medieval games using bulls and men the incorporation of notions related to the natural world by the killing of the animal. The killing of the bull precedes its distribution and consumption either by participants in the game or by the community in general. This process is recognizable in a variety of practices mentioned by medieval texts. All have in common a participation in the mytho-ritual complex of the monarchy, in which this relationship between human societies and the natural order is necessarily interwoven (Benveniste; Hocart). We can cite the following examples: commemorating events on the "royal calendar" (weddings, births, etc.) with bullfights; the ritual meal of a bull (which had often been "fought" just prior) for inaugurations, notably for the feasting of the coronation of royalty; and the sacrificial ritual of killing a bull (preceded by a fight) to demarcate territories, which has been studied within the context of fifteenth-century Andalusia (Delpech). The importance of this mythic complex was not lost by the Papacy, which, during the sixteenth century, pondered the idea of creating an exception by removing the ban on bullfights conducted on the authority or in the presence of kings.

The strangeness of these practices is also evident in the various inscriptions and uses of the bull's corpse. For example, in the royal banquets of the fifteenth century, the bull's hide was used in the creation of a rather strange dish. The hide, once removed, was stuffed with a number of other animals symbolizing the monarchy, for instance cocks and other foul. Sewn back together and cooked, this culinary monument would then be served to the public during meals called royal "convites" in Portuguese and Castilian ("convit," in Catalan) (Bertelli; Gomes). The hide also served as a physical support for the royal emblems: bulls, grazing in fields near city walls, would "wear" the royal coat of arms for the entry of the monarchy into the city (Andrés Diaz 328-29). Or the bulls, ornamented in heraldic signs by the inhabitants of the different parishes of the city, would be displayed and later used for games during the coronation of the king.

The bull's flesh is an essential element in these various practices known from medieval and early modern times. As we have noted, sharing of the flesh is symbolically linked both to the sharing of land in territorial demarcation and to sharing of the royal body during royal banquets. However, the flesh of the bull, utilized in these ways, can only be obtained by the game. Thus, it is difficult to see which is, in fact, at the origin of the other. The bull is killed so as to be eaten; the bull is eaten so as to allow for the existence of the game. The complicated schema of such medieval "bullfights" is also seen in the variety of human roles and activities they involve—be it in cases where whole communities participate in the game before the collective meal, or in cases where agents specifically linked to the killing of the bull are involved. These latter, the "matatoros," mentioned for example in the thirteenth-century code of the "Partidas" of Alfonso X, are distinguished from other participants in the game because they are paid and because, within medieval juridical discourse, they occupy roughly the same social space as the butchers, prostitutes, and minstrels, that is, the so-called "impure" professions (Rodrigues 352-53; see also Bennassar).

All of this evidence indicates a cultural framework in which violent games involving men and animals functioned very differently from those of contemporary society. In a cultural and symbolic interpretation of today's bullfighting, this cannot be overstated (Pitt-Rivers; see also Déveaux and Saumade). Some observations, pertinent to our discussion, are necessary: the nonexistence of observable differences regarding the practice of killing bulls in various Iberian contexts (the "Portuguese tradition" was obviously created sometime after the eighteenth century), but especially its distinction from the so-called "art of bullfighting" in the nineteenth and twentieth centuries. Regarding medieval games and "bullfights," one has to keep in mind the following aspects of this question: the very limited role and the specific nature of the participation by professional, remunerated agents in them; the ambivalence of the observable interweaving of certain types of collective rituals and the games with animals; the strangeness of perceptions and representations of violence in these societies. These practices, without contextualization and with only a fragmented knowledge on the part of the historian, are often incomprehensible to our contemporary minds (Farge).

All of this leads us to realize, following a few of the classical studies on bullfighting "traditions" by insightful observers such as Cossío and Ortega y Gasset, that contemporary bullfighting is a phenomenon that is not easily comparable to the practices of the medieval and early-modern eras. This fact has also been underscored in a recent excellent monography on Spanish bullfighting by the historian Adrian Schubert (1999). Cossío had already established the three essential components to an archaeology of bullfighting in the eighteenth century:

> 1) The bull must be viewed as an animal that requires special breeding. The animal is in fact a genetic "fossil," modeled by the practices of bullfighting, and consequently, indissociable from them. These practices cannot be traced prior to the late period of the "Ancien Régime."
> 2) The agents come to represent new types of professionals, such as the "matador" and the "cavaleiro" which become a part of the fabric of bullfighting. This is a condition necessary for the establishment of a unique language, which targets the malleable reformulation of "spectacular" components of this game.

> These components could, moreover, become periodically renewable inside the frame of modern professionalised leisure activities, experimenting with several forms of spectacle aiming at commercial profit.
> 3) And finally, there is a necessary separation of the spectators and the action of the game. This becomes homologous to an entire series of practices of "popular" leisure and their insertion into a complex of festivities distinctive to the final period of the "Ancien Régime." During the nineteenth century, for example, one observes in Portugal the occasional association of the world of bullfighting with that of the circus. The latter was responsible for creating variants of the spectacle that were later to be banned from the arenas. These spectacles involved, for instance, combats between the bull and other animals (lions, elephants, etc.) (Noronha). It is the separation between the spectators and the game that is at the origin of a spatial and material condition necessary to the modern bullfight: the arena. The first examples of arenas in Portugal, within urban settings, date back to the end of the eighteenth century (Romero de Solis; Abreu).

In endowing itself with more ancient origins, contemporary bullfighting constructed a narrative that sought to legitimize itself according to a few essential elements: the prestige of monarchial traditions, association with the "noble" and "privileged" art of the hunt and combat on horseback, nostalgia for the dominating and instrumental rapport with "wild" animals. And, last but not least, it has created the aura of an activity that hearkens back to an hierarchical social order. This social order is fixed and organized according to microcosmic grounds; even the "reality" upon which it is based is best characterized as a form of fiction. That is to say, as with all games, it is more immediately readable, more condensed, and more intentional than the historical reality it wants to evoke ever could be.

Violent Games and the Process of Civilization

Born in an era of change in Portuguese society in the final period of the "Ancien Régime" (late eighteenth and early nineteenth centuries), bullfighting carried, in its many forms during the nineteenth century, the marks of a lively and mobilizing debate. This debate is focused on establishing a definition of "civilization" and the place of Iberian people in it. At the same time, bullfighting, like so many cultural objects and practices, was taking part in the formation of a political discourse regarding the identity and destiny of nations. In Iberian cultures, the relationship of civilization—

a fundamental myth of the Enlightenment—to the perception of violent practices that had been institutionalized in the public space took on particular forms. A debate developed about certain rituals or spectacles that would henceforth be viewed as too controversial, such as the "Auto-da-fé." A formidable tool used in the social debasement of an individual, leading eventually to the execution of the person, the "Auto-da-fé" has a multi-secular history that is in absolute contradiction to the increasingly important value of "Tolerance." Because of this disparity, in the eighteenth century the "Auto-da-fé" was withdrawn from important public spaces in urban settings such as main squares, or places associated with secular power such as the royal palaces, and was relocated inside, mainly within churches or cloisters. It was an act of violence condemned to disappear with the extinction of the courts of the Inquisition in the nineteenth century (Bethencourt).

Since the Enlightenment, bullfighting has become a similar object of reflection for intellectuals. This reflection has been focused primarily on two problems: the definition of supposedly universal values and the game as a sign of Iberian particularity. In relation to this latter problem, scholars have sought an object that would help formulate the reasons for the Iberian peninsula's unique historical trajectory, an object that would explain the "obscurity" and the "barbarism" seen in a panoply of its social practices. The history of this debate is in itself fascinating, providing a thematic center for the passionate evaluation and claiming of national stereotypes, these same discourses being manipulated to launch traditionalist "trends" ("neocastizismo") from the interior of the field of bullfighting itself (Cambria).

In the constant renegotiation of the terms in which the violent game of bullfighting has survived and has been integrated into "popular" leisure-time activities, one can follow the definitions of socially accepted limits for the use of violence in public in the nineteenth century. Following more and more pressing attention on the part of royal authority itself during the final decades of the eighteenth century, the first systematic regulation of the game appeared in 1776, followed by modalities of repressive discourse that led to interdictions in 1790. By 1820, bullfighting had become an affair of the State and was the object of formal and reiterated interdictions in Portugal. In a contradictory way, it would come to be a practice that was both repressed and tolerated throughout the nineteenth century. The reasons for this intermittent repression can be found in a dispassionate reading of the sources of the epoch (Crespo). The game is repeatedly considered to be *en soi* "beneath civilized nations." We find this expression, in those exact words, in all the Portuguese legal rulings. It becomes a veritable "topos" for argumentation, notably in the Prologue to the law of 1928 that is still in use. Already during the great political upheaval that accompanied the end of absolutism in 1820, the crux of this debate resided in transforming the violence of the animal and of the man who kills it into a recreational spectacle, that is, to insert the violence into a new public space that was then in gestation, that of leisure.

Nevertheless, bullfighting found a place, more or less stable, within the festivities of the epoch. Its violent drives "domesticated," it became a complementary activity to masses and religious feasts, to dances, to festivals, and to other collective "celebrations." As Jorge Crespo has proven, the initiative to introduce bullfighting into civic holidays—which also distinguishes, in their often commemorative function, bullfights of the nineteenth century from those of today—is in great part the result of the uncertain relationship between the local, peripheral dimension and the central authority of the State. The principle of interdiction, acknowledged by "enlightened," "modern" sovereigns and recognized by the law, was based on the idea of the inadmissible nature of this game. However, it has survived this struggle because of the pragmatism of local state controls that were more open to religious and political arguments for the existence of the game. As reports from the local authorities and the police attest, bullfights took place on numerous occasions with varied characteristics. They were often promoted by local powers, such as municipalities and powerful religious organizations like the confraternities, perhaps involved in the non-negligible economic aspects of the activity, as was then the case in Spain (Schubert 17-29). The geography of bullfighting in Portugal showed a clear predominance in the central region and in the south of the kingdom. These were areas of large agricultural estates that were previously owned by ecclesiastical institutions and the royal family and later sold to private families and is where the breeding of bulls, necessary to bullfighting, was introduced.

The modes of the game that were later compiled and studied by ethnologists at the turn of the twentieth century also took place in the frontier regions (Beira, Alentejo) or in the Azores. These were similar in that a collective meal, symbolizing the closure of the game, took place within a cycle of religious festivities (Dias; Ribeiro; Leal). This diversity suggested the establishment of a division, more theoretical than verifiable in all cases, between professional bullfighting and modalities of the game that were not systematically framed by the autonomous logic of that form of commercialized leisure. In the first type of bullfighting, the separation of the public from the action of the game is complete. A space proper to the game, an arena, is required. This, in turn, played a crucial role in the equipping and the urban landscape of cities of the south of Portugal. In the second case, the "bullfight" proper does not exist since the game takes place outside this physical framework and outside regulated practices, and most of all, because its declared purpose is not commercial profit. According to the information available, however, the practices of the 19th and early 20th century show signs of an unequal expansion of the "bullfighting culture" in all of its aspects—prescriptive, economic, and cultural. Since the classification of "popular" games was made taking into consideration the products of this cultural industry, it can be said that these contributed in a decisive way to define what was a "true corrida," and what was not (Guillaume-Alonso).

Some recent bibliography reproduces this division by making a distinction between two types of "fiesta," the "rural-ethnographic" and the "urban." This division, treated as an *a priori* fact, should also be historically situated. With the first type, that of the "rural fiesta," one author declares the practices "unchanged since the earliest times of the Middle Ages" (Gil Calvo 40). This declaration is made even though testimony from those who observe and describe aspects of these games mention the use of certain protective measures (the use of ropes and certain collective techniques of control, such as wooden stalls) used to weaken and tame the animal, measures that have direct links to the historical process of the repression of violent games: they focus on the protection of men and they laud evasive combat techniques, inculcating the value of human life.

On both sides of this theoretical divide between "genuinely popular" and "commodified" games, the ban on killing the bull in public is a constant, put into place by the State in the nineteenth century. This issue can be spotted in the debates taking place in the "Cortes" of 1821 in Portugal, as well as in Spain, where, in 1807, a law of royal initiative repressing the killing of the bull was decreed. The bans had unequal results because of differences in bullfighting practices and structures between the two countries, and because of the diversity within each country's own social realities. The arguments used in the nineteenth century to justify this ban on the killing of the animal stressed the dangerous nature of fostering familiarity with killing. The killing of the bull was seen as a habit that could create a disposition towards murderous violence on the part of the "dangerous classes." After having been "fought," the bulls would be killed in the wings of the spectacle, outside of the view and outside the experience of the public. This was done as a means of preventing the bull's carcass from undermining the culture of "tolerance" and anti-cruelty advocated by legislators and institutions (for a comparison with the situation in England, see Thomas). Consequently, we can say that the limitations placed on the experience of violence were centered on the social and collective dimension of the spectators. Not killing the animal in public was intended to promote an idea of bullfighting compatible with the pacification of the crowd through leisure activities.

The constitution and "domestication" of the public in the nineteenth century is essential to the "process of civilization" described by Norbert Elias (Defrance). The history of bullfighting is another strong case for detecting this same "process of civilization" in Iberian countries. One finds during this era the representation that underlies the contemporary game, but one can also see that the devices of control were concentrated mainly on the spectators and on molding their behaviour and emotional lives, aiming at the "calming down" of possible "cycles of violence" (Elias and Dunning). Through regulation of the professionals' activities, it is clear that the threat to order posed by the game was what was in question. Becoming a spectacle, bullfighting is inscribed in the logic of the leisure-activity market, powerful ally of social discipline and the normative mechanisms put into place by the State. These mechanisms were focused almost exclusively on the conduct, the "appetites," "instincts," and the violent drives of the masses. Moreover, these aspects would be collectively transferred by the crowd onto the bullfighter, the "toureiro." Now, it is time for us to go back to Barrancos and to the debate on human-animal relations.

Hidden Violence, or the Art of Being Portuguese

Underlying the alternation between two forms of combat in the so-called Portuguese bullfights—combat on horse, combat on foot—there is a curious presentation, almost a sort of re-enactment, based on a perception of social hierarchies of the "Ancien Régime." In the first form, the cavaliers wear stylized clothes, which recall those worn in the eighteenth century (like the wigs worn by judges in English tribunals); in the second, groups of men dressed in livery immobilize the animal by attacking it without any weapons. Remuneration is *de rigueur* in the first case, purely symbolic in the second, since the "forcado" (the combatant on foot) generally receives no money for his participation in the spectacle. This mimetic relationship between "aristocracy" and "people" is nonetheless, as we have seen, a product of the structuring of a domain of a specialized activity subjected to the logic of professional competence and of the leisure-activity market in search of its public since the 19th century. Concurrently, this relationship reproduces a legend of the imaginary autonomy of the game, "frozen" in time and carrying the signs of its own history, by associating it with the end of the "killing of bulls" in public in the eighteenth century. However, this is a universe the valences and meanings of which are becoming more opaque in relation to contemporary mass culture and less susceptible to various appropriations, beyond the sphere of the obvious common denominator of the "national" motif. Bullfighting of the "Portuguese sort" is a product the current definition of which is the fruit of recent history, being particularly cultivated and successfully marketed in Portugal's "golden decades" of bullfighting, that is, the post-war period until the sixties. The so-called "Portuguese tradition" is a product that strives to sell within a market that fears a total absorption into nearby countries' bullfighting networks. Its defenders hold fast to it by stressing its uniqueness and making it appear "traditionalistic." In this small world of Portuguese bullfighting, dominated by the cavalier who propagates a sense of "caste" and social distinction and whose activity depends, to a much greater extent than his "forcado" counterpart, on the economic resources generated by the spectacle, the bullfight represents the continuity of a certain "order of things" (Capucha). As a cultural object in Portugal, bullfighting occupies a space that distinguishes itself from other signs of modernity by playing more and more upon the notion of a "national" logic of identity. This idea is promoted despite the fact that the public of "aficionados" often venture outside Portugal's borders for the same sort of cultural product. Spain, in particular, where bullfighting includes killing the bull in the arena, holds a specific allure. The world of professionalized bullfighting also relegates "popular" occurrences of the game, which often are nothing more than makeshift versions operating according to the same codes of this ludic universe, to the minor status of "rustic" activities. Of course, the professionalized world also uses the "popular" game in its arguments for the survival of this menaced activity (bullfighting is still loved by "the people").

None of these conflicts, however, occupies the center of the debate of Barrancos. The debate currently being held in Portugal organizes itself around violence directed at the bull, while also adopting the universalistic discourse of the values of civilization in which the animal is conceived as a moral subject with its own rights. The anthropocentric and instrumental relations of humans and animals that were characteristic of modern culture are being transformed, in contemporary societies, in a variety of ways (Franklin). Obviously, ordering the debate in this way demonstrates an increasing lack of understanding, if not a total rejection of the internal codes of bullfighting as a specific cultural field. The use of violence, if we understand the term in its etymological meaning of "the projection of physical force against someone or something," implies lower levels of tolerance in Portuguese society today, but these do not have a general, indiscriminate value; they function in the specific case of the projection of aggressive drives towards the animal. There lies the perception of the violence, invisible elsewhere. One should also realize that the local publics that were so arduously created in the past by older forms of "popular" pastime have given way to the masses avid for the excitement lived and reproduced by visual media, notably, by television. The practices and "traditions" of bullfighting have attempted in vain to adapt to the new media, the characteristics of which seem to impose a stricter respect for specific timings and rhythms of action than the living realities of the arenas allow.

Has bullfighting become a thing of the past? Although the interest in bullfighting is primarily limited to a minority of the Portuguese population, we must not underestimate the capacity for change of a cultural object that still wields the symbols of a number of passionate and mobilizing discourses. The role of the bull has been introduced into this dense network, a move that has modified the perception of the game, and it has forced changes of position and new compromises on the issues at stake. Taking refuge behind the reassuring image of a "Portuguese tradition," the prevailing discourse of the "fiesta" in Portugal has recently been challenged by Barrancos. The debate invites us to contemplate what it reveals about us all as agents and objects of contemporary violence.

Notes

* This paper was originally given at the conference "Minoranze, Marginalità et Violenza nelle società mediterranee," held in Naples in June 1999 and organized by the Centre d'Études Méditerranéennes. I would like to thank all of the participants for their insightful comments and critiques, in particular Anthony Molho, Rada Ivekovic and Francesca Trivellato. In Lisbon, I am indebted to Carlos Fontes, Nélia Dias and Eurico Figueiredo, for their useful advice and for providing access to important data.

Works Cited

Abreu, Carlos. "A Praça de Touros do Salitre." *Feira da Ladra,* II (1930): 15-27.

Diaz, Rosana Andrés. "Fiestas y Espectáculos en las Relaciones Góticas del siglo XVI." *En la España Medieval* 14 (1991): 306-336.

Basto, Artur de Magalhães. "A fronteira hispano-portuguesa." *O Instituto* 70 (1923): 103-117.

Bennassar, Bartolomé. *Histoire de la Tauromachie.* Paris: Desjonqueres, 1993.

Benveniste, Émile. *Le Vocabulaire des Institutions Indo-européennes,* II – *Pouvoir, Droit, Religion.* Paris: Minuit, 1969.

Bertelli, Sergio. *Il corpo del Re. Sacralità del potere nell'Europa medievale e moderna.* Florence: Ponte alle Grazie, 1995.

Bethencourt, Francisco. *História das Inquisições. Portugal, Espanha e Itália.* Lisbon: Círculo de Leitores, 1994.

Cambria, Rosario. *Los Toros: tema polémico en el ensayo español del Siglo XX.* Madrid: Gredos, 1974.

Capucha, Luis. "O campo da tauromaquia" *Sociologia.Problemas e práticas* 5 (1986): 147-165.

Claramunt, Fernando. *Historia Ilustrada de la Tauromaquia.* Madrid: Espasa-Calpe, 1989. [2 vols]

Cossío, José Maria de. *Los Toros.* Madrid: Espasa-Calpe, 1986.

Crespo, Jorge. *A História do Corpo.* Lisbon: Difel, 1990.

Defrance, Jacques. "Le goût de la violence." *Norbert Elias. La politique et l'histoire.* Eds. Alain Garrigou and Bernard Lacroix. Paris: La Découverte, 1997. 290-301.

Delpech, François. "Symbolique territoriale et système sacrificiel dans un ancien rituel de 'terminatio' andalou: notes pour une anthropologie des confines." *La Fiesta, la Ceremonia, el Rito.* Granada/Madrid: Universidad de Granada/Casa de Velázquez, 1990. 147-164.

Désveaux, Emmanuel and Frédéric Saumade. "Relativiser le sacrifice ou le quadrant tauromachique." *Gradhiva* 16 (1994): 79-84.

Dias, Jaime Lopes. *Etnografia da Beira.* Lisbon: Livraria Morais, 1929. Vol. III.

Elias, Norbert and Eric Dunning. *The Quest for Excitement: Sport and Leisure in the Civilizing Process.* Oxford: Blackwell, 1986.

Farge, Arlette. "De la violence." *Des Lieux pour l'Histoire.* Paris: Seuil, 1997. 28-45.

Franklin, Adrian. *Animals and Modern Cultures. A Sociology of Human-Animal Relations in Modernity.* London: Sage, 1999.

Gil Calvo, Enrique. *Función de Toros: una interpretación funcionalista de las corridas.* Madrid: Espasa-Calpe, 1989.

Gomes, Rita Costa. "Sobre a festa e o rito, na corte medieval." *A Festa numa perspectiva transdisciplinar – Cadernos do Noroeste,* 9 (1996): 9-22.

Guillaume-Alonso, Araceli. *Naissance de la Corrida. Rites, jeux et spectacles taurins en Espagne, au XVIe et XVIIe siècles.* Bilbao: Ed. Laga, 1994.

Leal, João. "Festa e construção de identidade. O nível regional e nacional." Paper presented at the Seminar "Problemas da Sociedade Portuguesa" of the Gabinete de Sociologia Histórica da Universidade Nova de Lisboa, 1993.

Hocart, Arthur M. Kings and Councillors. *An essay in the Anatomy of Human Society.* Chicago: U of Chicago P, 1970.

Huizinga, Joan. *Homo Ludens. Essai sur la fonction sociale du jeu.* Paris: Gallimard, 1951.

Muntaner, Ramon. *Cronica.* Madrid: Alianza, 1970.

Noronha, Eduardo de. *Historia das Toiradas.* Lisbon: Companhia Nacional de Edições, 1900.

Ortega y Gasset, José. *Sobre a Caça e os Touros.* Lisbon: Cotovia, 1986.

Pitt-Rivers, Julian. "El sacrificio del toro." *Revista de Occidente* (1984): 27-47.

Ribeiro, Luis da Silva. *As Touradas da Ilha Terceira (Açores).* Lisboa XIII Congresso Luso-Espanhol para o Progresso das Ciências (Separata), 1951.

Rodrigues, Ana Maria. "Festas de touros no Portugal medievo." *Cadernos do Noroeste* 4 (1991): 343-358.

Romero de Solis, Pedro. "L'invention du 'ruedo'. La plaza de toros de Sevilla et les ruines de Pompéi." *Gradhiva* 16 (1994): 67-77.

Sahlins, Peter. *Boundaries: the making of France and Spain in the Pyrenees.* Berkeley: University of California Press, 1991.

Saumade, Fédéric. *Les Tauromachies européennes: la forme et l'histoire, une approche anthropologique.* Paris: Ed. C.T.H.S., 1998.

Schubert , Adrian. *Death and Money in the Afternoon. A History of the Spanish Bullfight.* Oxford/New York: Oxford UP, 1999.

Schulte, R. "Village Life in Europe." *Comparative Studies in Society and History* 27 (1985): 195-206.

Sorabji, Richard. *Animal Minds and Human Morals. The origins of the western debate.* London: Duckworth, 1993.

Thomas, Keith. *Man and the natural world: changing attitudes in England, 1500-1800.* London: Allen Lane, 1983.

Abstracts

Saramago's Construction of Fictional Characters: From *Terra do Pecado* to *Baltasar and Blimunda*

Horácio Costa

This essay tracks the evolution of José Saramago's fictional characters. Beginning with Saramago's first novel, *Terra do Pecado* (1947), Costa outlines a dynamic of anachronism, where Saramago's characters and plot bear a stronger resemblance to nineteenth-century works of naturalism than to the twentieth-century modern novel. It is this initial asynchronism, Costa argues, that paves the way for Saramago's later originality. Following a nineteen-year hiatus from literary writing, Saramago published two books of poetry and two volumes of *crónicas*, wherein Costa identifies the revival of the creative impulse. In two subsequent texts, *O Ano de 1993* (1975) and "O Ouvido" (1979), Saramago creates narration without constructing fictional characters marked by "subjectifying" characteristics. In the novel *Manual of Painting and Calligraphy* (1976), Saramago returns to constructing complete fictional characters, inaugurating a series of middle-aged male heroes and female characters who come to populate his later novels. The tension between a character's anonymity and individuation, between sociological collectivity and psychological singularity constitutes an important vector in Saramago's work. In addition to the relapsing of Saramago's characters along the axes of these two poles, the multiplication of dystopic-futurist plots points to an important dynamic of auto-intertextuality. The internal cohesion of Saramago's work affirms the importance of comparing the texts of Saramago's formative period to his later works in an evolutionary trajectory.

José Saramago's Historical Fiction

Adriana Alves de Paula Martins

Starting from the assumption that one of the major trends in postmodern literature is the historical fiction that aims to reassess and revise the ambiguities and contradictions of historical discourse, the author focuses her attention on José Saramago's novels whose main subject is the historical and symbolic representation of Portuguese past events. Being particularly interested in the analysis of the ways Saramago's literary texts examine the epistemological and the ideological heritage of the Portuguese nation from a historical, human, linguistic, literary, ethical and political viewpoint, the author proposes a typology comprising the main trends of postmodern historical fiction. The objective of this proposal is to study the meanings projected onto Saramago's novels by the explicit transformation of History into narrative subject matter, defining an important aspect of the writer's politics of symbolic representation of the empirical world.

On the Labyrinth of Text, or, Writing as the Site of Memory
Teresa Cristina Cerdeira da Silva

One of the distinguishing characteristics of Saramago's fictional discourse is that it functions as a site where cultural memory is activated through a complex web of intertextual references, as the author engages in a comprehensive re-reading of the Portuguese, Iberian, and generally Western cultural tradition. This essay considers the novels of Saramago's first major narrative cycle, from *Levantado do Chão* (1980) to *The Gospel According to Jesus Christ* (1991), as labyrinthine agglomerations of discourses belonging to different times, places and genres, whose fragmentary irruptions break up the apparently smooth continuity of the text. Its main focus is on Saramago's engagement with the poetry of Luís de Camões, particularly *The Lusíads*, with the Bible, and with the historical intertext, the latter comprising both primary source materials and historiographic narratives.

Righting Wrongs, Re-Writing Meaning and Reclaiming the City in Saramago's *Blindness* and *All the Names*
David Frier

In both *Blindness* and *All the Names* Saramago exploits the archetypal narrative of the descent into the underworld in order to portray characters engaged in a search for renewed meaning in modern life, with a subsequent turn to creativity as the novels' protagonists emerge from what is either a nightmarish reality (in *Blindness*) or one devoid of all emotion and individuality (in *All the Names*). In both works the focus of the narrative gradually moves away from the public sphere to the private, thus emphasising the developing relationships amongst individual characters and leading to a more appropriate balance between fulfilling personal needs and respecting those of others. This in turn leads to a recognition that a society worth living in must be based on the preservation of human values and on the active participation of all of its citizens in its affairs. The recognition that it is these values that turn human society into a civilisation is a necessary prerequisite for the construction of a better society.

Saramago, Cognitive Estrangement, and Original Sin?

Kenneth Krabbenhoft

The events portrayed in José Saramago's 1975 prose poem *O Ano de 1993* and his 1995 novel *Blindness* take place in a near future in which the normal protections of society and government have broken down. The purpose of this essay is to show how, by stressing the closeness of these dystopias to the readers' present-day experiences, Saramago creates the effect of cognitive estrangement first fully explored by Darko Suvin, and how this in turn provides him with a kind of fictional laboratory for exploring the positive and negative aspects of human nature. By allying Saramago with a number of science fiction writers, in particular Anthony Burgess in his 1962 novel *The Wanting Seed*, the essay expands our understanding of the Portuguese writer's inquiry into a range of concerns and how certain of his novels reflect the historical antagonism between the Augustinian and the Pelagian views of human morality.

"The One With the Beard Is God, the Other Is the Devil"

Harold Bloom

The essay analyzes, in turn, the three major personages of *The Gospel According to Jesus Christ*; God, Pastor or the devil, and Jesus Christ. God is seen by Saramago as a great humorist, but profoundly unloving towards everyone, including his son Jesus Christ. Saramago's God is interested only in extending his domain, so that he will become the God of the Catholics as well as of the Jews. Pastor is portrayed by Saramago with a certain enigmatic reserve, yet essentially is seen as being more sympathetic than not, and certainly preferable to Saramago's God. Jesus Christ, as new-created by Saramago, is a superb and loving personality, but sadly perplexed by God's murderous scheme against him. Nevertheless, Saramago eloquently allows Jesus Christ and Mary Magdalene an authentic and loving erotic fulfillment. The epilogue of my essay concerns Saramago's charming "The Tale of the Unknown Island," which I read as a lighthearted allegory that reverses the tragedy of *The Gospel According to Jesus Christ.*

Journey to the Iberian God: Antonio Machado Revisited by Saramago

Orlando Grossegesse

Besides being a stubborn Communist and atheist, José Saramago maintains an Iberian vision that injures patriotic feelings and the traditional discourse of Portuguese identity set against Spain. The study shows how the author's interest in Spanish history, culture and literature throughout his entire work is closely related to poetics and ideology, even before the overt reclamation of Iberian identity in *The Stone Raft* (1986). The poetry and the philosophy of Antonio Machado, especially his theory of the apocryphal, play an important role in Saramago's writing, which enlivens the past as a paradoxical space of anachronic future. Machado also applied his theory to the destiny of Spain: the final verses of the poem "El Dios ibero" can be understood as a basis for *The Stone Raft*, read as a narrative complementary to *The Year of the Death of Ricardo Reis.* In both cases, the making of history as a collective project depends on the individual's change-of-mind, prefigured by the disinterred Antonio Machado and an undead, more subversive Fernando Pessoa. In the course of the journey depicted in *The Stone Raft*, Pedro Orce represents among the members of the touring group "el hombre ibero," the son of the Iberian God. At both levels, that of the narrated journey and that of poetic discourse, Pedro Orce has a "fertile death" that revivifies Antonio Machado as an *author* of an Iberian religion of salvation without a God from above, following the Machadian concept of Christian Communism, and announcing the Orphic and Marxist interpretation of Jesus in *The Gospel According to Jesus Christ.*

"Once But No Longer the Prow of Europe": National Identity and Portuguese Destiny in José Saramago's *The Stone Raft*

Mark J. Sabine

This article examines Saramago's construction of a "counter-factual" scenario in *The Stone Raft*, and assesses what destiny the novel proposes for Portugal as an alternative to integration into an EEC committed to market freedom at the expense of cultural diversity and of member nations' links with extra-European former colonies and neighbours. It argues that interpretations of the Peninsula's displacement as a utopian vision of a united Hispanophone and Lusophone community ignore both the narrative's dismantling of myths of national character—effected in part through Saramago's dialogue with Unamuno—and the novel's effacement of inter-regional tensions current in both Iberia and the post-colonial Hispanophone and Lusophone world. In place of an ideology of integrated Iberian separatism, the article identifies an appeal for greater interaction between European countries, as opposed to the integration of a subordinate "periphery" into what is perceived as a richer, stronger European "heartland." The article also investigates the novel's allusions to Portugal's partially abortive April revolution in the protagonists' tentative establishment of new economic, social and sexual values and customs. It argues that the inconclusive ending of the Peninsula's story represents a crisis of identity and destiny, challenging the novel's protagonists and readers to somehow move beyond a stereotypically Portuguese faith in messianism and miracles.

The Edge of Darkness, or Why Saramago Never Wrote about the Colonial War in Africa

Maria Alzira Seixo

One of Western culture's major literary works to be inspired by the colonial situation is undoubtedly Joseph Conrad's *Heart of Darkness* (1902). This essay is an attempt to sketch out a way in which some aspects of two of Saramago's novels, *The Stone Raft* (1986) and *Blindness* (1995), can best be understood in light of the cultural legacy bequeathed by Conrad's novella and how they can be interpreted from a contemporary postcolonial perspective.

In the final analysis, Saramago is shown to be writing neither from the center nor from the margin, but rather "from the edge" (of Africa). While being in the center implies the possibility of access to (and even exercise of) power, and peripheral situations suffer from exposure to its hegemonic irradiation, being on the edge may be considered as the privileged position for knowledge, both objective and impartial, uncontaminated by either centripetal or centrifugal concerns. It is the convenient place for a wise witness, making him able to ponder the issue of observation and of its exercise as a decisive contribution to a better way of seeing.

Cruising Gender in the Eighties (from *Levantado do Chão* to *The History of the Siege of Lisbon*)

Ana Paula Ferreira

In the ongoing process of revision to which Saramago's fiction submits certain foundational myths of Western culture, the notion of woman as inferior and therefore subservient to Man is contested with particular emphasis, as female characters assume decisive roles in the development of Saramago's fictional plots. In the five novels published in the 1980s, from *Levantado do Chão* (1980) to *The History of the Siege of Lisbon* (1989), the writer's textual journey posits an imaginative term of struggle against the oppressive effects of normative and structurally persistent patterns of gender domination in socio-economic and symbolic orders. Although some critics have attempted to define an abstract model of femininity in Saramago's fiction, this essay insists on pulling the discussion of his women characters away from both an idealist/idealizing and a dangerously cooptative representational register, while pushing it closer to the experimental material(ism) of language in the open, multi-layered and movable space of Saramago's subversive, inherently dialogic textuality.

Shit, Shrimps, and Shifting Sobriquets: *Iracema* and the Lesson in Lost Authority

Phillip Rothwell

This article considers the way in which the text of José de Alencar's *Iracema* defies the semantic preclusions that the author seeks to impose upon it. Crucial to this defiance is the resonance implicit in the names chosen by the author for the protagonists. These names escape closure by a variety of means. One is the Lusophonic echo inscribed in the warrior's name. Another is the recourse to an etymological survey legitimised by the author's own actions. In both cases, the text becomes partially liberated from Alencar's authority.

Violent Games: Towards a Historical Understanding of the Portuguese Bullfight

Rita Costa Gomes

The aim of this study is to provide a critical examination of the contemporary debate about the "affair of Barrancos," and in turn the history of bullfighting in Portugal. After establishing the role played today by the killing of the bull in the arena as a fetish for local and national identities, the essay proceeds with an analysis of some medieval examples of games using bulls in order to compare these with the modern "invention" of the bullfight as as a traditional activity unchanged since the Middle Ages. I argue, on the contrary, that bullfights are a form of modern leisure, a game that indicates changing perceptions of violence, and that bullfights played a role in inculcating social discipline in the 19th century. In spite of its being contested in the name of "civilization" and of being the object of anti-cruelty legislation, the Portuguese bullfight, as a vehicle of collective excitement and the quest for profit, is perhaps facing its ultimate challenge—the extension of the moral debate about violence to a non-human actor of history, the bull itself.

Contributors

Onésimo T. Almeida is Chair and Professor in the Department of Portuguese and Brazilian Studies, Brown University. Among his most recent writings are essays on Saramago, Antero de Quental, Vergílio Ferreira, José Rodrigues Miguéis, Fernando Pessoa, and Francisco Sanches, all forthcoming in various journals or collective volumes. His present research continues to revolve around themes related to Portuguese cultural history, with more essays on the debate over national identity, Portugal and the dawn of modern science, and Portuguese-American Literature, also forthcoming in academic journals in Portugal and Brazil. On the creative side, his *Viagens na Minha Era*, consisting of "dia-crónicas," was just published (Temas & Debates and Círculo de Leitores), as was a second edition of his short stories *(Sapa)teia Americana* (Salamandra).
E-mail: Onesimo_Almeida@Brown.edu

Harold Bloom is Sterling Professor of the Humanities at Yale University and Berg Professor of English at New York University Graduate School. He holds honorary degrees from the universities of Rome and of Bologna, and was awarded the Gold Medal for Criticism by the American Academy of Arts and Letters in 1999. He is the author of twenty-four books, including *The Anxiety of Influence, The Book of J, The Western Canon, Shakespeare: The Invention of the Human*, and the recent *How to Read and Why*.
E-mail: harold.bloom@yale.edu

José Horácio de Almeida Nascimento Costa was born in São Paulo in 1954. Architect and urban planner (USP, 1978); MA (NYU, 1983); PhD

(Yale, 1994). He teaches both at the UNAM (Mexico City) and the USP (São Paulo). Critical books are: *José Saramago: O Período Formativo* (Lisboa: Caminho, 1997) and *Mar Abierto-ensayos de literatura brasileña, portuguesa e hispanoamericana* (Mexico: Fondo de Cultura Económica, 1998). He has six books of poetry published in Brazil (including *Quadragésimo* [1999] and *O Menino e o travesseiro* [1994]), four in Mexico (including *El libro de los fracta* [1990] and *The Very Short Stories* [1995]), one in the United States (*O menino e o travesseiro*) and one in Venezuela (*Los jardines y los poetas* [1993]). His work has been translated into Spanish, English and French. He has translated Mexican and American poets into Portuguese, has organized two poetry conferences in São Paulo (1990 and 1998) and has been awarded academic and cultural prizes in Mexico and in Brazil.
E-mail: horaciocosta23@hotmail.com

Ana Paula Ferreira is an Associate Professor of Portuguese, Critical Theory and Women's Studies in the Department of Spanish and Portuguese at the University of California, Irvine. She has published widely in the areas of Neo-Realism and Portuguese women writers; her book *A Urgência de Contar: Histórias de Mulheres, Anos 40* is forthcoming from Caminho, Lisbon. She is currently finishing a manuscript titled *Homebound: Femininity, Women Writers and the Nationalist Order.*
E-mail: apferrei@uci.edu

David Frier is Senior Lecturer in Portuguese at the University of Leeds, England. He is author of the monograph *Visions of the Self in the Novels of Camilo Castelo Branco (1850-1870)* (Edwin Mellen Press, 1996) and is currently preparing a Portuguese version of the same work. He has also published a number of articles on Camilo and on Saramago in journals in Britain, Portugal and the United States, as well as one article on Miguel Torga (*Portuguese Literary & Cultural Studies* 1). He is currently preparing a book on José Saramago.
E-mail: david_frier@hotmail.com

Elena Zagar Galvão has an MA in English from the University of Tennessee at Knoxville, where she was a Fulbright student and teaching assistant. She also has a degree in translation from the School of Modern Languages for Translators and Interpreters at the University of Trieste, Italy, with a thesis on Bobbie Ann Mason's short stories and their translation into Italian. She is

currently teaching English as a foreign language and translation from Portuguese into English in the Department of Anglo-American Studies at the University of Porto, Portugal. She is also a freelance translator and interpreter working for various agencies and public institutions both in Portugal and abroad. Her articles on translation have been published in *Máthesis* and in *Jornal da APT*, the journal of the Portuguese Translators Association.
E-mail: jp.egalvao@mail.telepac.pt

Ana Sofia Ganho is Assistant Profesor of Portuguese at Emory University where she teaches Portuguese, Brazilian and Lusophone African literatures and cultures. She has two books forthcoming, one on applied linguistics with Cambridge University Press, and another on the poetics of modernity in Europe and Latin America. She has also written on contemporary Portuguese poetry, the relationship between image and literature (painting, ekphrasis, cinema), and women writers, her next project being Lusophone women writers of the nineteenth century.
E-mail: aganho@emory.edu

Rita Costa Gomes is an historian of Late Medieval Portugal. She does research on medieval kingship, court society in Iberia, the history of nobility, and medieval landscapes. A member of the Faculty of the Universidade Nova de Lisboa, she has been Visiting Professor at Brown University (1996), Johns Hopkins University (1997 and 2000-2001), and the École des Hautes Études en Sciences Sociales, Paris (1999). She is writing the series *Castelos da Raia* (one volume published, one in print), and preparing the English edition of her study on the Portuguese royal court (Cambridge University Press, forthcoming).
E-mail: ritagomes@excite.com

Orlando Grossegesse holds a PhD in Romance Philology and Social Communication. His doctoral dissertation dealt with the relationship between literary writing and conversation in the works of Eça de Queirós (1988/89, University of Munich; published in book form as *Konversation und Roman*, Stuttgart: Franz Steiner, 1991, 343 pp.). Since 1990 he has taught German literature at the University of Minho in Braga, where he also served (in 1991-93) as the Director of the German Studies Program. He has published many articles on Saramago, as well as a book, *Saramago lesen* (Berlin: Edition Tranvía, 1999), of which a revised second edition will be published in Fall 2001. He is currently writing a new book on Saramago,

designed to complement his earlier study; it will have the form of a "manual" in ten chapters, each dedicated to a single novel, from *Manual of Painting and Calligraphy* to *A Caverna.*
E-mail: ogro@ilch.uminho.pt

Kimberly DaCosta Holton is Assistant Professor of Portuguese and Program Coordinator of Portuguese and Lusophone World Studies at Rutgers University-Newark. Her articles on twentieth-century Portuguese culture have appeared in journals such as *The Journal of American Folklore* and *Text and Performance Quarterly*, with two chapters forthcoming in *Vozes do Povo: Folclorização em Portugal no Século XX*, edited by Jorge Freitas Branco and Salwa Castelo Branco. Holton is completing a book entitled *Staging the Nation in Flux: Revivalist Folklore Performance in Twentieth-Century Portugal.*
E-mail: kholton@andromeda.rutgers.edu

Anna Klobucka is Associate Professor of Portuguese at the University of Georgia. She received an MA in Iberian Studies from the University of Warsaw, Poland, and a PhD in Romance Languages and Literatures from Harvard. She is the co-editor of *After the Revolution: Twenty Years of Portuguese Literature 1974-1994* (Bucknell UP, 1997) and the author of *The Portuguese Nun: Formation of a National Myth* (Bucknell UP, 2000). She has also published on twentieth-century Portuguese and Brazilian women writers, the theory and practice of feminist criticism in the context of Luso-Brazilian literature and culture, and the construction of collective identities in national cultures of the European periphery. Her articles have appeared in the *Luso-Brazilian Review, Colóquio/Letras, SubStance, Estudos Portugueses e Africanos,* and *symplokē*, among other journals.
E-mail: klobucka@arches.uga.edu

Kenneth Krabbenhoft is Associate Professor of Spanish and Portuguese at New York University. He has written about Portuguese and Brazilian literature, the Spanish Golden Age, Christian and Jewish mysticism, and science fiction. His books are *Abraham Cohen de Herrera: Puerta del cielo* (Madrid, 1987), *El precio de la cortesía* (Salamanca, 1994), and *Neoestoicismo y género popular* (Salamanca, 2000). He is currently working on an English edition of Cohen de Herrera to be published by Brill in 2002.
E-mail: ForMer111@aol.com

Adriana Alves de Paula Martins has an MA in Portuguese Literature from the University of Coimbra with a thesis on José Saramago's novel *The History of the Siege of Lisbon.* Her thesis, entitled *História e Ficção: Um Diálogo*, was published in Lisbon in 1994. In the same year, she started working as Assistant Professor at the Portuguese Catholic University in Viseu, where she has been teaching English Literature and supervising the teacher training program. At present, she is writing her PhD dissertation on Comparative Literature. Her research focuses on José Saramago's and Gore Vidal's historical fiction. She has presented several papers on Saramago's literary production at international meetings in Portugal, Holland, Brazil, and the US, and has published various articles in journals, such as *Colóquio/Letras* (the special issue on José Saramago), *Máthesis, Cadernos de Literatura Portuguesa e Brasileira*, and *Veredas.*
E-mail: adrimartins@mail.telepac.pt

George Monteiro's most recent books are *The Presence of Camões* (1996), *The Presence of Pessoa* (1998), *Stephen Crane's Blue Badge of Courage* (2000), and *Fernando Pessoa and Nineteenth-Century Anglo-American Literature* (2000). Forthcoming in 2001 are bilingual editions of Miguel Torga's *Poemas Ibéricos* and *Selected Poems* by Jorge de Sena.
E-mail: GEORGEMONTEIRO@prodigy.net

Robert H. Moser is a PhD student in Portuguese and Brazilian Studies at Brown University. His publications include articles in *Revista Leituras, Brasil/Brazil*, and "The Carnivalesque Defunto: Death and the Dead in Modern Brazilian Literature" in the forthcoming volume *Representations of the Dead.* His current research addresses the figure of the dead, and related expressions of haunting and mourning in modern Brazilian literature.
E-mail: Robert_Moser@brown.edu

José N. Ornelas is Professor and Chair of the Department of Spanish and Portuguese at the University of Massachusetts Amherst. He has published widely on Portuguese contemporary fiction as well as on nineteenth-century and Lusophone African narrative. He is currently doing research on areas related to Cultural Studies: constructions of gender, class and national identities, questions of representation, colonial and post-colonial issues, and subject-formation in its political, historical, cultural, and sexual dimensions.
E-mail: ornelas@spanport.umass.edu

Phillip Rothwell is an Assistant Professor of Portuguese at Rutgers University, New Brunswick. He recently completed a PhD on the Mozambican author, Mia Couto. His current research interests include the representations of power discourses in Lusophone African literature, and portrayals of the sea.
E-mail: philroth@rci.rutgers.edu

Mark J. L. Sabine has recently completed his doctoral thesis, *Form and Ideology in the Novels of José Saramago, 1980-1989*, at the University of Manchester, England, where he was formerly a student of Saramago's English translator, Giovanni Pontiero. In addition to his research and lecturing on Saramago, he has conducted research on the work of Eça de Queirós, Leopoldo Alas, Fernando Pessoa and Clarice Lispector, and has a particular interest in representations of gender and sexuality in modern Iberian writing.
E-mail: mark.j.sabine@stud.man.ac.uk

Maria Alzira Seixo is Professor of French and Comparative Literature at the University of Lisbon. She was President of the International Comparative Literature Association (1991-94) and is currently serving as President of the International Federation for Modern Languages and Literatures. She is the author or editor of fourteen books, including *A Palavra do Romance* (Lisboa: Horizonte, 1986), which won the Pen Club Essay Prize, and *Lugares da Ficção em José Saramago* (Lisboa: IN-CM, 1999), distinguished with the Jacinto do Prado Coelho prize for criticism. Among her latest edited volumes are *The Paths of Multiculturalism: Travel Writing and Postcolonialism* (Lisbon: Cosmos, 2000) and *Travel Writing and Cultural Memory* (Amsterdam: Rodopi, 2000), as well as the special issue of the journal *Colóquio/Letras* dedicated to Saramago. She has a new collection of essays, *Outros Erros: Ensaios de Literatura*, forthcoming in 2001.
E-mail: abrilmas@mail.telepac.pt

Teresa Cristina Cerdeira da Silva teaches at the Universidade Federal do Rio de Janeiro where she earned her PhD in Portuguese Literature in 1987. Her doctoral dissertation, published two years later as *José Saramago: Entre a história e a ficção, uma saga de portugueses* (Lisboa: Dom Quixote, 1989), was the first book of criticism dedicated to Saramago's work. Over the past twenty years she has authored many articles and book chapters on nineteenth- and twentieth-century Portuguese writers, which have appeared in journals and collections of essays published in Brazil, Portugal, France, Italy, and England. Her latest book, *O avesso do bordado,* was recently published in Lisbon (Caminho, 2000).

E-mail: cerdeira@nitnet.com.br

Issues of *Portuguese Literary & Cultural Studies*

Portuguese Literary & Cultural Studies 1. Fall 1998.
Fronteiras/Borders.

Portuguese Literary & Cultural Studies 2. Spring 1999.
Lídia Jorge in other words / por outras palavras.
Guest Editor: Cláudia Pazos Alonso, Oxford University

Portuguese Literary & Cultural Studies 3. Fall 1999.
Pessoa's Alberto Caeiro.

Portuguese Literary & Cultural Studies 4/5. Spring/Fall 2000.
Brazil 2001. A Revisionary History of Brazilian Literature and Culture.
Guest Editor: João Cezar de Castro Rocha, Universidade do Estado do Rio de Janeiro

Portuguese Literary & Cultural Studies 6. Spring 2001.
On Saramago.
Guest Editor: Anna Klobucka, University of Georgia

Forthcoming
Portuguese Literary & Cultural Studies 7. Fall 2001.
Portuguese Poetry Since 1961.

Portuguese Literary & Cultural Studies 8. Spring 2002.
On Cape Verdean Literature and Culture.
Guest Editor: Ana Mafalda Leite, Universidade de Lisboa

Portuguese Literary & Cultural Studies 9. Fall 2002.
Post-Imperial Camões.

Volumes of *Portuguese Literary & Cultural Studies Book Series*

Forthcoming

Eduardo Lourenço. *Selected Essays.*
Edited by Carlos Veloso, New York University

Transdisciplinary Readings of Garrett's Travels in My Homeland.
Edited by Victor J. Mendes

The Later Eça Revisited.
Edited by Frank F. Sousa

Eça de Queirós. *The Relic.* Trans. Aubrey Bell.
Preface by Harold Bloom

Portuguese Language Textbooks Series

Francisco Cota Fagundes. *Mais Um Passo No Português Moderno: Gramática Avançada, Leituras, Composição e Vocabulário.*

The Portuguese in the Americas Series

Who are the Portuguese? The New Evidence—Five Studies on the Portuguese-American Community of Southeastern Massachusetts
Coordination by Clyde Barrow, Center for Policy Analysis, University of Massachusetts Dartmouth

Jerry R. Williams. *And Yet They Come. Portuguese Immigration from the Azores to the United States.* 2nd edition.

University of Massachusetts Dartmouth

Center for Portuguese Studies and Culture

Founded in 1996, the University of Massachusetts Dartmouth Center for Portuguese Studies and Culture is designed as a forum for the interdisciplinary study of the language, literatures, and cultures of the Portuguese-speaking world. The Center aims to serve as a liaison between the University of Massachusetts Dartmouth and other institutions involved in Portuguese Studies in the United States and abroad.

The Center proposes to develop pedagogical materials to aid in the teaching and learning of the Portuguese language at all levels of instruction through its Portuguese Language Textbook Series. The Center will publish an advanced grammar textbook in 2001 written by Prof. Francisco C. Fagundes, entitled *Um Passo Mais no Português Moderno: Leituras, Gramática Avançada e Composição.* In addition, a first-year textbook (*Encontros*), for the teaching of both Brazilian and European Portuguese at the college level, is currently in preparation.

The Center fosters the development and dissemination of knowledge about the Portuguese-speaking communities of the United States through the Portuguese in the Americas Series. The first volume, *Who Are the Portuguese? The New Evidence – Five Studies on the Portuguese-American Community of Southeastern Massachusetts,* will be published this year. This initial publication is undertaken collaboratively with the University of Massachusetts Dartmouth Center for Policy Analysis.

The agreement between the University of Masschusetts Dartmouth and RádioTelevisãoPortuguesa (RTP) in 1999 established RTPi's North American television studio on the UMD campus. Locally produced programming will be transmitted internationally to more than 20 million homes, including 1.1 million in the United States. In turn, the University has received a complete RTP Video Collection that will soon be available at the University Library.

Accentuating its commitment to the intellectual preparation of students at all levels of higher education, the University of Massachusetts Dartmouth recently created the Department of Portuguese, with support from the Luso-American Foundation. The new Department is in the process of creating an Endowed Chair in Portuguese Studies and a graduate program in Portuguese. In this context, the semiannual publication of the scholarly journal, *Portuguese Literary & Cultural Studies,* underscores both the Center's and the Department's research goals in the field of Portuguese Studies. Further, the Summer Program in Portuguese, founded in 1994, will hold its 8th annual program this year (June 25-July 27), offering seven different courses, from beginning language to a seminar on Portuguese Women's Literature in Translation and a production of a classic Gil Vicente play. The Center will once again organize the Summer Program in Portuguese for Children to run concurrently with the regular Summer Program in Portuguese.

The Center also promotes exchanges of students and faculty with universities in the Portuguese-speaking world, as exemplified by the University's agreement with the University of the Azores, signed in 1998. In addition, the Center is developing a Study Abroad Program that will make UMD a conduit for any American student who wishes to study in Portugal.

The Center also promotes international colloquia on topics and authors related to the Portuguese-speaking world. Conferences include "25 Years of Portuguese Democracy" (October 2, 1999), "Garrett's *Travels* and Its Descendants" (October 22-23, 1999), "The Later Eça Revisited" (November 3-4, 2000), and "Race, Culture, Nation: Arguments across the Portuguese-speaking World" (April 6-8, 2001). On April 30, 2001, the Center cosponsored a colloquium at the Library of Congress entitled "Brazil 2001: A Revisionary History of Brazilian Literature and Culture."

Other activities, such as lecture, concert, and dance series and art exhibitions, emphasize the Center's commitment to the University community and local region. In Fall 1999 the University Art Gallery hosted an exhibition on the drawings and etchings by Paula Rego. Another exhibition is being planned for 2002. The Center also supports a Visiting Distinguished Scholar program, and in Fall 2000 Prof. John Russell-Wood of Johns Hopkins University taught a course on the Portuguese Discoveries. In addition, the Center takes active part in recommending candidates for honorary degrees. Largely through the efforts of the Center for Portuguese Studies and Culture, in October 1999 the University of Massachusetts Dartmouth awarded a Doctorate *Honoris Causa* in Humane Letters to the Nobel Laureate for Literature, José Saramago. And acting on the Center's recommendation, the University will award an honorary doctorate to world-renowned literary scholar Harold Bloom, on September 14, 2001, with participation by José Saramago. In connection with this occasion, the Department of Portuguese and the New York Public Library will cosponsor an evening with Saramago and Bloom in New York City, on September 17, 2001. Both will also participate in the launching of this volume at the Luso-American Foundation, on May 22, 2001.

The Center's objectives and endeavors are made possible by the generous support of the following individuals and institutions: Chancellor Jean F. MacCormack and Provost Thomas J. Curry, University of Massachusetts Dartmouth; the Luso-American Foundation, the Foreign Ministry of the Government of Portugal, the Embassy of Portugal in the United States, the Camões Institute, and the Calouste Gulbenkian Foundation. In addition, the Center gratefully acknowledges the financial support of individuals and institutions in Massachusetts and Rhode Island, such as Lawrence Fish, President of Citizens Financial Group; Anthony Andrade, former President of Universal Press; Manuel Fernando Neto, President of Neto Insurance Group; and Frank B. Sousa, President of Colonial Wholesale Beverage Corp. In particular, the Center wishes to thank Representative Robert Correia and the other Portuguese-American members of the State House and Senate of the Commonwealth of Massachusetts, for their tireless efforts in the development and funding of the Center for Portuguese Studies and Culture.

Portuguese Literary & Cultural Studies Subscription
Center for Portuguese Studies and Culture
University of Massachusetts Dartmouth
North Darthmout, MA 02747 USA
Tel. (508) 999 9270 Fax (508) 999 9272 E-Mail greis@umassd.edu

Name

Address

City **State** **Zip**

Country

☐ **Annual Individual Subscription $ 40 (2 issues)**
☐ **Annual Institutional Subscription $80 (2 issues)**
☐ **Single Issue $25 (Issue Number __)**
Outside of the USA add $12.00 for shipping and handling

Payment enclosed
☐ **Check** ☐ **Visa** ☐ **Mastercard**

Credit Card Number **Expiration Date**

Signature **Date**